Instrument of the State

AMERICAN MUSICSPHERES

Series Editor Mark Slobin

Fiddler on the Move Exploring the Klezmer World
Mark Slobin

The Lord's Song in a Strange Land Music and Identity in Contemporary Jewish Worship
Jeffrey A. Summit

Lydia Mendoza's Life in Music
Yolanda Broyles-González

Four Parts, No Waiting
A Social History of American Barbershop Harmony
Gage Averill

Louisiana Hayride
Radio and Roots Music Along the Red River
Tracey E. W. Laird

Balkan Fascination
Creating an Alternative Music Culture in America
Mirjana Laušević

Polkabilly
How the Goose Island Ramblers Redefined American Folk Music
James P. Leary

Cajun Breakdown
The Emergence of an American-Made Music
Ryan André Brasseaux

Claiming Diaspora
Music, Transnationalism, and Cultural Politics in Asian/Chinese America
Su Zheng

Bright Star of the West Joe Heaney, Irish Song-Man
Sean Williams and Lillis Ó Laire

Romani Routes
Cultural Politics and Balkan Music in Diaspora
Carol Silverman

Voices from the Canefields Folksongs from Japanese Immigrant Workers in Hawai'i
Franklin Odo

Greeted with Smiles Bukharian Jewish Music and Musicians in New York
Evan Rapport

Resounding Afro Asia Interracial Music and the Politics of Collaboration
Tamara Roberts

Singing God's Words
The Performance of Biblical Chant in Contemporary Judaism
Jeffrey Summit

Cajun Breakdown
The Emergence of an American-Made Music
Ryan Andre Brasseaux

Jump Up!
Caribbean Carnival Music in New York
Ray Allen

Capital Bluegrass
Hillbilly Music Meets Washington, DC
Kip Lornell

Sound Relations
Native Ways of Doing Music History in Alaska
Jessica Bissett Perea

Instrument of the State
A Century of Music in Louisiana's Angola Prison
Benjamin J. Harbert

Instrument of the State

A Century of Music in Louisiana's Angola Prison

BENJAMIN J. HARBERT

Oxford University Press is a department of the University of Oxford. It furthers
the University's objective of excellence in research, scholarship, and education
by publishing worldwide. Oxford is a registered trade mark of Oxford University
Press in the UK and certain other countries.

Published in the United States of America by Oxford University Press
198 Madison Avenue, New York, NY 10016, United States of America.

© Oxford University Press 2023

All rights reserved. No part of this publication may be reproduced, stored in
a retrieval system, or transmitted, in any form or by any means, without the
prior permission in writing of Oxford University Press, or as expressly permitted
by law, by license, or under terms agreed with the appropriate reproduction
rights organization. Inquiries concerning reproduction outside the scope of the
above should be sent to the Rights Department, Oxford University Press, at the
address above.

You must not circulate this work in any other form
and you must impose this same condition on any acquirer.

Library of Congress Cataloging-in-Publication Data
Names: Harbert, Benjamin J., author.
Title: Instrument of the state : a century of music in Louisiana's Angola prison / Benjamin J. Harbert.
Description: [1.] | New York : Oxford University Press, 2023. | Series: American musicspheres series |
Includes bibliographical references and index.
Identifiers: LCCN 2022060595 (print) | LCCN 2022060596 (ebook) | ISBN 9780197517512 (paperback) |
ISBN 9780197517505 (hardback) | ISBN 9780197517536 (epub) | ISBN 9780197517543
Subjects: LCSH: Music in prisons—Louisiana—Angola. |
Prisoners—Louisiana—Angola—Social conditions. | Louisiana State Penitentiary—History.
Classification: LCC ML3920 .H33 2023 (print) | LCC ML3920 (ebook) |
DDC 365/.668—dc23/eng/20221219
LC record available at https://lccn.loc.gov/2022060595
LC ebook record available at https://lccn.loc.gov/2022060596

DOI: 10.1093/oso/9780197517505.001.0001

Paperback printed by Marquis Book Printing, Canada
Hardback printed by Bridgeport National Bindery, Inc., United States of America

Contents

List of Figures	ix
Forewords by Calvin Lewis, Myron Hodges, and Wayne Kramer	xi
Acknowledgments	xv
Note to the Reader	xix
About the Companion Website	xxi

Introduction	1
The Book as a Multimovement Musical Piece	4
Uncovering Histories	6
The Musicality of Prison	9
A Brief Overview of Louisiana Behind Bars	12
1. Astonishment	15
Models: Angola's Preprison Polyphony	17
Outlawry | Out-of-Law	18
Penance | Penitentiary	19
Slavery | Plantation	21
Imagining Folklore in the Convict-Lease System	24
The Astonishing Polyphony of State Control	27
Enter Lomax and Lead Belly	37
Curating "Prison Music"	43
Conclusion	51
2. Association	53
Thinking Beyond the Individual	54
Carceral Associationalism	57
Songs of the Gunmen	59
Finding Swing in a Prison Newsmagazine	65
A Sudden Call for Attention	67
Hillbilly to Jazz in Camp E	69
The Rhythm Makers of Camp A	74
The All-Stars Start in Camp H-2	78
Minstrelsy to Jazz with the Nic Nacs in Camp A	82
The Nic Nacs Occupy the New Prison	87
The Warden's Band	93
Listening to Jazz in Prison	99

3. Politics ... 103
  Singing Out-of-Law ... 106
    Outlawry of the Field ... 108
    Music of Outlawry ... 110
  Associations/Cliques and By-Laws/Muscle ... 114
  The New Feel ... 118
  Freedom in a New Unity ... 121
  Transforming the Listenership ... 125
  Adding Rhythm to the Concept ... 128
  The Long Arm of the Band Room ... 131
  The New Nic Nacs ... 135
  Coda ... 140

4. Surfaces ... 143
  War Zone ... 145
  The Rodeo Surface Redraws Boundaries ... 146
  The Westernaires 1.0 ... 149
  The Westernaires 2.0 ... 153
  Silencing the Black Panthers ... 157
  Free-World Surfacework ... 157
  The Demise of the Westernaires ... 163
  Banquets ... 166
  Sublime Surfaces ... 173
  Lingering Surfaces ... 181

5. Inflection ... 187
  The Promise of Otis Neal ... 189
  Uneven Reforms of the Field ... 194
  Time Factor ... 201
  Def Posse ... 208
  Megasound ... 211
  Big River Band ... 215
  Gospel Melodies ... 221
  Conclusion ... 231

6. Recapitulation ... 233
  Inflection by Statute ... 238
  Strapped Rodeo Surfaces ... 243
    Transposed Secular Banquet Surface ... 247
    Hostile Takeover ... 251
    Banjo Scars ... 253
  Playing Politics ... 257

Association for Rights	262
Property	266
Assembly	268
Mobility	271
Astonishing Call of the Canaries	272
Lead Belly Remembered	273
A Radical Revision of an Old Metaphor	275
Notes	279
References	317
Index	331

Figures

1.1. Angola landing on the Mississippi River, ca. 1900–1910   29
1.2. Picking cotton, Angola State Farm, 1901   30
1.3. Map of Angola Camps (illustration by William Livingston)   31
1.4. Quarters A, Angola State Farm, 1901   32
1.5. "Fun in levee camp, Atchafalaya River"   35
1.6. Stills from "Leadbelly," in *March of Time*   49
2.1. Men singing for Harry Oster   60
2.2. A trusty guard on duty, 1955   63
2.3. White jazz orchestra rehearsing in Camp E   72
2.4. Outdoor festival performance   76
2.5. 1940s Camp A Minstrel Troupe   84
2.6. The new main prison, 1955   88
2.7. Voting for Inmate Council in the main prison, 1955   92
3.1. Transcription of "Rumor Enough," sung by Charles Neville   113
3.2. Transcription of "Tone the Bell," sung by Charles Neville   113
3.3. Horizontal and vertical illustrations of music   122
3.4. The major (Ionian) and the Lydian scales   123
4.1. The Westernaires at the 1968 rodeo   150
4.2. Westernaires playing an outside show   155
4.3. The Scientists of Soul perform in front of the Big Stripe Band Room, 1976   180
5.1. Otis Neal, left, 1978   193
5.2. Fieldworkers after the decommissioning of the sugar mill, ca. 1989   196
5.3. Photos from a 1983 banquet   206
6.1. Filming *Follow Me Down* with the Pure Heart Messengers, 2009   236
6.2. Larry Wilkerson and Myron Hodges perform outside the Ranch House, 2013   240

6.3. Guts and Glory Band performing in the crow's nest, 2013   245
6.4. Dancing to the Jazzmen at the music stage outside the rodeo ring, 2013   249
6.5. William Hall in his woodshop in the recreation building, 2013   254
6.6. John Henry Taylor singing on the perimeter of the main prison, 2009   259
6.7. Mickey Lanerie and Laird Veillon in the band room at the main prison, 2008   263

Forewords

People on the outside say we are "scums of the earth." Others treat us like we are just a number. And yet, we are human beings, musicians with gifts that will never be confined. When I was first introduced to Benjamin J. Harbert, I thought he was just another free person that would come in, take pictures, and tell us what he wanted—and that we would never hear from him again. But he continued his communication with the musicians and continued to come back. Harbert is not just an author/filmmaker or music scholar/educator. In our eyes, he's a person that incarcerated musicians in Louisiana prisons can call a friend. Harbert allowed the men and women to share their musical experiences without dictating our words, as other authors and film directors have done. He was genuine and down-to-earth.

Harbert not only interviewed those of us in the music fraternity, but he also researched books, magazines, and newspapers and spoke with historic legends who had been incarcerated. He did this to fully understand what it means to be a musician while incarcerated. He cared about our stories. *Instrument of the State* covers present musicians and the legends that paved the way for today's musicians. Harbert researched all the different entities that made Angola what it is today, from administration, government, wardens, floods, legislations, movies, documentaries, and the legendary musicians incarcerated at Angola. The author covered it all, and I am amazed by his research.

As a musician, I know that this is a community where the past means so much. At Angola, someone will always speak of earlier bands and musicians and ask to hear the music from the bands that made an impact in the past. You need to know the history of the past musicians because you want to continue that legacy.

By educating me about the history of music here at Angola, this book allows me to better pave the way for up-and-coming musicians and bands at the prison. Hopefully, new arrivals will be inspired to become part of a legendary music scene during their incarceration. Reading *Instrument of the*

State has inspired me to work harder to keep the musical legacy alive here. This is why we care about legacy—we are caring human beings.

Calvin Lewis, drummer for the Angola Jazzmen Band
Angola, LA
April 2022

I want to say how deeply honored I am to be a part of *Instrument of the State*. Words cannot express the debt of my appreciation to the author for being so intrigued with Angola's music culture and investing so much of himself through years of research and hard work. The book highlights a prison music culture that exists in no other prison in the nation.

For prisoners in other parts of the country, I imagine that the notion of a convicted felon, especially a lifer, privileged with so much liberty to play music would be inconceivable. Nonetheless, this level of performance is managed and produced by the inmates themselves. Here, an inmate band can be commissioned to play for events ranging from interinstitutional banquets to festival fairs throughout Louisiana. *Instrument of the State* details how musicians of Angola at times seem to possess an uncanny ability to take even the most unlikely mixture of people, and unify them with music.

Having been incarcerated for over thirty-eight years, I've spent much of my time playing music for various events inside and outside of Angola. Some people (or fans) whom I've met along the way travel long distances to hear me play or see a particular Angola band, purchase a band T-shirt, have it autographed by certain band members, and appreciate a rare personal encounter with those of us behind the music.

Instrument of the State is like no other book I've read about Angola because it doesn't stereotype its subjects. Instead, it focuses on the musical history and the endeavors of men serving time, those of us who seek to achieve a sense of purpose, meaning, peace, and normalcy in our lives, using our musical abilities to captivate the hearts and minds of our audiences and our keepers. In this way, we transcend the social boundaries of prison itself. This book is a true testament to the ability of the human spirit to thrive, even under the worst circumstances.

Myron Hodges, guitarist for Angola Big River Band
Angola, LA
April 2022

The Framers started out with a truly revolutionary idea: democracy, "with liberty and justice for all." A grand reach, no doubt about it. To date, though, the in-real-life application of this aspirational principle has fallen woefully short. As it stands, "all" turns out to mean white, male, middle class (or above), and decidedly heterosexual. You're not "all" if you're anything other than white and are of limited economic means. Nowhere is this reality more apparent in America's jails and prisons.

Today, over two million of our fellows—men, women, and children—are incarcerated. Let that sink in. The United States of America has more American citizens locked up *today* than any country *in the history of the world*, most of whom are part of the aforementioned *not all* group. That we had outlawed slavery via the Thirteenth Amendment to the US Constitution "except for the punishment of crime" explicitly represents a degree of deliberate human suffering and cruelty that is as vicious as is possible to imagine.

Instrument of the State chronicles this derangement using stories of people going as far back as 1699 when Louisiana was still a French colony. Harbert documents stories of prison sentences served in the American South, namely Louisiana State Penitentiary, Angola. This history is not only rich and complex, it is often incredibly cruel yet tempered with life-affirming music made by people who were forced to endure disproportionately heavy sentencing inside profoundly corrupt institutions. It's a mouthful, I know, but this is not a simple account of one man's struggle. These are centuries of inequity.

Instrument of the State is a deeply and accurately researched work. Harbert reconstructs the events and abuses that grew out of the "convict leasing" system in American corrections. From the founding of the penal system through the decades, up to and including today, this book is a journey worth taking. You will experience it through the lens of musicians who lived and expressed it. From the early deprivations up through the time of Alan Lomax and Lead Belly to today, music serves as a salve and a rejuvenator for us all—and even more poignantly for those who were locked up.

Prisoners found release and hope in the music they could create and share in prison. This may be the most revolutionary, life-affirming act ever to grace humanity. A tradition born in pain and cruelty that has been forged into a powerful transformative force is an exceptional American undertaking. Here, you will feel that walk to freedom. It reads like fiction, but it's not. This is the real deal and more inspiring than you could have dreamed.

Author Benjamin J. Harbert has done this country a great service. *Instrument of the State* is a major work of social, cultural, and academic accomplishment. It's a story that should be required reading for every student in America and every musician as well. It shows us who we are at our worst and what we're capable of at our best, reminding us that America's prisons are an abomination of justice and that the people who have populated them over history have discovered, through the art form of music, a path to unadulterated transcendence.

Wayne Kramer, cofounder of Jail Guitar Doors USA
and guitarist for the MC5
Los Angeles, CA
July 2022

Acknowledgments

The musicians at Angola who informed this book include Jerry Allison, Russell Joe Beyer, Darryl Bowman, Clint Bracken, Leotha Brown, Curtis Carmac, Sidney DeLoach, Michael Dyer, A. J. Freeman, Darren Green, Jason Hacker, William Hall, Clifford Hampton, Warren Harris, Lionel Jackson, Gary Jameson, Jimmy Johnson, Frederick Jones, Johnny Jones, Ray Jones, John Kennedy, Gary Landry, Mickey Lanerie, Emmanuel Lee, Jesse Lee, Stanley Lindsay, Kernis "Big Lou" Louviere, Donald Lumbel, James Marsh, Emmitt Messick, Thomas Oliver, Albert Patterson, Robin Polk, Walter Quinn, Brian Russel, Art Silvertone, Jewell Spotville, Samuel Stark, Herman Tausing, John Henry Taylor Jr., Donald Thomas, Merrit Thomas Jr., John Tonabee, Matthew Trent, Laird Veillon, Charles Venardo, Daniel Washington, Bud Wilkerson, Larry Wilkerson, Andre Williams, and Herbert Williams. Assistance from the staff at *The Angolite* came from Kerry Meyers and Jeffrey Hilburn. Thanks to Wayne Kramer for years of support and for writing a foreword. Special thanks to musicians Calvin Lewis and Myron Hodges, who read a draft of the book, gathered and delivered feedback, and took the time to write forewords, all while still incarcerated at Angola.

Staff and administration who provided coordination and additional conversations include Secretary James LeBlanc, Communications Secretary Pam Laborde, Assistant Warden Cathy Fontenot, Public Information Officer Gary Young, Executive Management Officer Angie Norwood, Major Wilfred Cazelot, Major Joli Darbonne, and Recreation Director Gary Frank. Sheryl Ranatza and Stephanie Perrault with the Angola Museum also helped with research and during visits.

Student research assistants were Rose Hayden, Bethany Hou, Susanna Jivotovski, James Khoury, Sophia Kloncz, Viktoriya Kuz, Nadia Mahmassani, Samantha Pasciullo Boychuck, Allie Prescott, Dominique Rouge, and Jin-Ah Yang. They contributed hundreds of hours of interview transcription, media logging, reading, editing, historical research, and critical listening.

Many experts at various institutions assisted me in finding traces of Angola's music in the historical record. These include Todd Harvey at the American Folklife Center of the Library of Congress, Jeff Place at

Smithsonian Folkways, Anna Lomax Wood at the Association for Cultural Equity, John Leonard and Adam Machado at the Arhoolie Foundation, Germain Bienvenu at the Louisiana State University Libraries, and Charlene Bonnette at the State Library of Louisiana. Ian MacKaye helped repair and digitize old audio cassettes I brought back from the prison. The most expert and sustained assistance and camaraderie came from Marianne Fisher-Giorlando. She has given her boundless energy to this book and countless other histories of Louisiana's prisons.

Several organizations offered me a public forum to present components of this book and walk away with critical feedback, including Smithsonian Folkways, the Radcliffe Institute for Advanced Study, the Society for Ethnomusicology, the International Council for Traditional Music, Georgetown University's America's Initiative, the Academy of Criminal Justice Sciences, the American Society of Criminology, Georgetown University's Prisons and Justice Initiative, the Council of State Governments Justice Center, Resurrection After Exoneration, the Society for American Music, the International Association for the Study of Popular Music, the West Baton Rouge Museum, and the University of Oslo.

Many colleagues helped read through chapter drafts, strengthening the scholarship from many disciplinary perspectives. Readers were Mike Amezcua, Katie Benton-Cohen, Denise Brennan, Matthew Carnes, Anna Celenza, Kate Chandler, Louis Chude-Sokei, Nicole Brittingham Furlonge, Jenny Guardado, Brian Hochman, Birgitta Johnson, Erick Langer, Mireya Loza, Chandra Manning, Brian McCabe, Ingrid Monson, Ricardo Ortiz, Douglas Reed, Adam Rothman, Milena Santoro, Carole Sargent, John Tutino, and the peer reviewers through Oxford who gave invaluable feedback for the proposal and the first draft.

Writing for Oxford University Press made this a better book. Series Editor Mark Slobin encouraged the work, eventually reading multiple drafts quickly and carefully. Oxford editors Suzanne Ryan and Lauralee Yeary both gave encouragement and expertise through the complexities of publishing.

Many others helped in various ways, from engaging in sustained discussion, offering perspectives, listening, supporting, to joining me somehow in the project. These people include Marié Abe, Jack Bowers, Laurie Brooks, Charlotte Brown, Gwynne Brown, Katherine Brucher, Brendan Canty, Bill Cleveland, Mary Cohen, Bernie Cook, Andrew Raffo Dewar, Mark DeWitt, Consuela Gaines, Jesse Gilbert, Chauncy Godwin, Christoph Green, Mark Howard, Wendy Jason, Wayne Kramer, Ashley Lucas, Bill Macomber, Áine

Mangaoang, Bryan McCann, Andy McGraw, Maria Mendonça, David Novak, Marina Peterson, Ali Jihad Racy, Matt Sakakeeny, Roger Savage, Huib Schippers, Anthony Seeger, Aram Sinnreich, John Slattery, Maria Sonevytsky, Nick Spitzer, Chris Waterman, Peter Yates, and also my departmental colleagues in music at Georgetown, current and former, Anna Celenza, Anthony DelDonna, Jay Hammond, Rufus Jones, Carlos Simon, and Robynn Stilwell.

My family has been a part of this, willing and occasionally unwilling. Thanks to my wife, Alison, my parents, Dick and Janet, and my children, Eli and Bea.

And a very special thank you to the late Charles Neville.

Note to the Reader

A few comments about this book before you begin.

Reactions

If the stories of musicians in this book move you, and if the perspective on incarceration and the criminal justice system shocks you, I encourage you to do something with those feelings. Consider supporting the following organizations. Ones that support incarcerated musicians and prison art programs include:

Justice Arts Coalition, www.thejusticeartscoalition.org
Jail Guitar Doors, USA, www.jailguitardoors.org
William James Association, www.williamjamesassociation.org
Beyond the Bars, www.beyondthebarsmusic.org
Give a Beat, www.giveabeat.org
Music on the Inside, www.musicontheinside.org
Songs in the Key of Free, www.songsinthekeyoffree.com
Musicambia, www.musicambia.org

Organizations that address mass incarceration in the United States through research, information presentation, lobbying, and direct involvement with prisoners and returning citizens include:

ACLU of Louisiana, www.laaclu.org
Louisianans for Prison Alternatives, www.prisonreformla.com
VOTE | Voice of the Experienced, www.vote-nola.org
Southern Poverty Law Center, www.splcenter.org
Justice and Accountability Center of Louisiana, www.jaclouisiana.org
Power Coalition for Equality and Justice, www.powercoalition.org
The Sentencing Project, www.sentencingproject.org
The Marshall Project, www.themarshallproject.org

Conventions

For this book, I capitalize "Black" and "White." With my capitalization of the word "Black," I follow the growing standard convention to convey a sense of shared experience in a racialized country, signify that race is a historical and social construction and not a natural trait, and encourage respect. Throughout the book, I also capitalize "White," which is not a widely used convention. My reasoning is different than for capitalizing "Black." By no means are Whiteness and Blackness balanced racial equivalents. I am aware that many white supremacist groups capitalize "White" and also understand how "white" signifies a neutral racial category (a signal that most Americans of European descent benefit from not having to think about "Whiteness" every day), but I believe that "White" is a useful convention for a book that engages race at Angola Prison.

In a historically and majority-Black prison, Whiteness is a complex, evolving, and everyday experience with its own history. Whiteness at Angola comes with its own set of privileges and challenges. Capitalizing the term signals that race is a social convention at play in macro- and microlevels in the lives of prisoners, guards, administrators, and visitors. This conventional binary of "Black/White," however, ought not to simplify the gray areas, the complications, and the changing definitions of racial logics.

About the Companion Website

http://www.oup.com/us/InstrumentoftheState
Username: Music1
Password: Book5983

This book features a companion website that provides material that cannot be made available in a book, namely audio recordings and video clips that supplement the discussion and specific musical examples. The reader is encouraged to consult this resource while reading through the book.

Introduction

Guitarist Russel Joe Beyer finished tuning his Telecaster and glanced at the other men assembled on stage. Each band member was engaged in a discrete task in preparation for their performance. It was intensely foggy, a day when most prisoners slept in if their jobs allowed it. Beyer and his bandmates wore T-shirts decorated with musical notes and their band logo emblazoned on the front: THE JAZZMEN. Despite the name, the band played just about every style of popular music. Their versatility and repertoire kept them in demand for events within the prison. Beyer was one of several top-notch musicians in the band that defined Angola's secular music scene at that time. Influenced heavily by R&B, they adapted popular songs but were always ready to launch into a distinctive second-line groove if they saw anyone from New Orleans in the crowd.

As I talked to Beyer, another prisoner jokingly asked him for an autograph. We both smiled. Riffing off the joke, Beyer told me that his real motivation for playing wasn't fame. It was to engage in a rare creative experience behind bars. "If you're a musician," he said, "you know the feeling. You kind of live for that, just to be able to improvise and get a group going. . . . It gets you out of here for a while. You're no longer at Angola." In other words, music was a limited experience of freedom for those who had mostly lost theirs. Adding up the time served by the seven members of the band, they had been in Angola for exactly 100 years.

I found myself talking to Beyer during one of several research trips to Angola, investigating music at the Louisiana State Penitentiary. A guitarist myself, I noticed his instrument and asked him about it. He handed it over, and I played a few chords, testing the neck's action and balance. Most musicians who played in the church groups at Angola had recent models of affordable Yamaha guitars, bought by evangelical organizations whose sponsorship had an outsized influence on Angola's music scene. In contrast, Beyer's instrument seemed like it had seen better days. "The tuning keys were on a pedal steel guitar, and the neck was a Fender copy guitar," he explained.

"It's got a Fender Tele pickup and a Gibson humbucker pickup, so it's got everything on it. Nothing original except the body."[1]

It was hard not to read that last statement as a powerful metaphor: "Nothing original except the body." It seemed to mimic the dehumanizing way prison wipes away individual identity, leaving behind only the physical form. I imagined the original Telecaster's transformation as a symbol of mortification. Or perhaps Beyer's guitar was a metaphor of transformation, closer to something heard from prisoners: that they have changed, that they are new people now, bearing little resemblance to who they were when convicted. But wandering into the realm of metaphors took me away from the moment. I risked missing the more intriguing stories that Beyer's guitar held. Who had played those instruments that contributed the various parts to the Telecaster? Under what circumstances were those instruments decommissioned? How did prisoners learn to modify and repair their instruments? What allowances did the prison give to use tools and salvage instrument parts? Did Beyer have to keep it safe, guarding against scavengers who might envision other uses for guitar parts? These questions about materials promised to get me closer to the musician's everyday experiences than metaphor would. I kept this in mind when attempting to describe how prisoners have managed to be musicians while incarcerated at the Louisiana State Penitentiary, also known as Angola.

Metaphor is a strong temptation in representations of incarceration, as, from afar, prison seems to encapsulate fundamental aspects of the human condition. A book about prison music risks conjuring poetic images. "Prison" and "music" seem perfectly opposed, the former representing a limitation and the latter, ultimate freedom of expression.

And it is true that punishment can silence the voice. In Lars von Trier's *Dancer in the Dark* (2000), Selma, played by Björk, begins singing on the gallows. As her executioners watch, they can't help but listen. The trap beneath her feet opens. Her death stops the song, the rope against her now still throat. Music can also subvert oppression. Momentary freedom of song can reveal a fundamental unfreedom. Countless protest songs capitalize on this. Prison and music can also exist in tension, such as in the songs that incarcerated musicians sang to folklorists in the early half of the twentieth century. Listening in context, we can hear injustice, the humanity calling to us in song through the gates or from shackled prisoners. But as I said earlier, poetry can get in the way of understanding the everyday. Prisoners come to prison with an urgent set of more practical concerns.

Early in my visits, saxophonist Leotha Brown shifted me away from my poetic notions of "prison music." As he explained, the prison was not what he expected upon arrival in 1964. "I wasn't used to a penitentiary culture," he said. "It was like going into another country. There were things that I was not accustomed to—things I didn't even know existed. The only thing I knew about prison was what I had seen in movies. I thought everybody would have chains around their legs."[2] In time, Brown learned to navigate prison and adapt to the changes over the years, and his experience is both tragic and illuminating.

Having played music while incarcerated in Angola for forty-five years, Leotha Brown was the de-facto music historian. Over the decades, he participated in and witnessed multiple changes in the music scene. Brown had firsthand experience singing while working in the fields, learning to play avant-garde jazz at yard shows, running a radio show for the prisoner-run radio station, and supporting gospel musicians in the prison chapel. His broader perspective as a practicing musician at Angola revealed the complexity of musical life. Brown and dozens of other musicians helped me understand how to separate poetry from realities, tying musical activities to social conventions at Angola.

In the Camp F band room, where we often met, the mere presence of musical instruments transformed a drab cinderblock room into a space filled with possibilities. Perched on stools, we moved from decade to decade as I took notes. We usually discussed how important music was to his life and the lives of his collaborators. Wrapping up our discussion one day, I asked: "Where did all these instruments come from?" Leotha answered, matter-of-fact:

> Some are personal instruments, and some belong to the state. The Inmate Welfare Fund has supplied instruments for them. But some of the guys have taken the initiative to form what you call a music club. They raise money. They sell food for concessions and buy instruments. The traveling band itself, I think they have T-shirts, and then they have a CD that has been made here, too. All of that goes towards the purchasing of instruments for the musicians.[3]

The rush of practical concerns immediately seemed more interesting than any "prison music" poetics. How do you form a club? Who manages club finances? Were the Jazzmen T-shirts and the po-boy sandwich I had ordered from the concession stand all part of a music economy? How might a self-produced CD differ from the folkloric recordings we have at the Library of Congress? These practical questions led me to conversations about everyday experiences that seemed unique to Angola, understanding a musical history of a prison built from the sheer effort of prisoners who had a million reasons to play music.

Leotha Brown was one of a few people I talked to who understood what it was to be a musician based mainly on his experience playing music in prison. While I will always remain interested in musical style and untangling aesthetic experiences of music, learning about the practical aspects of being a musician in prison helped me pull "music" and "prison" together in meaningful ways. For prisoners, I would discover, prison affects music, limiting opportunities to perform certain styles, in certain places, or with particular other musicians. Or the prison administration might request certain kinds of performances for free world audiences. These performances might cater to audiences curious about the welfare of prisoners or doubtful of the administration's competence. Music also affects prison. Many prisoners told me that music was a way to escape. Indeed, music can distract from harsh and intolerable conditions, but music can also be a pretext for prisoner negotiation with officers and administration. Musical needs can trump custody needs, for instance, securing rehearsal space, acquiring proper equipment, and moving band personnel through ordinary security. In this way, prisoners can use musical activity to negotiate the terms of their confinement, even if only in small ways.

It quickly became clear that for incarcerated musicians, prison and music constantly intertwine. As one veteran officer told me early in my visits there, "Music is entangled in everything we do."[4] Music and imprisonment are both social phenomena initiated, maintained, and negotiated by all members of the institution. For my purposes, understanding "prison music" means attending to dynamic relations between these two words. Prison music is the organized sound of laws, policies, missions, and social consequences.

The Book as a Multimovement Musical Piece

As you will read chapter by chapter, from the nineteenth-century preprison slave plantation to the late twentieth-century prison, political, economic, and racial issues are inseparable from music. Policy changes, legal decisions, demographic shifts, reform, and economic realities all change the sound of music. I am interested in that change. Various styles of music will wax and wane. Listening to change will help us hear the connections between prison rules and music. In contrast with folklorists who preceded me, I am not collecting two-and-a-half-minute-long songs. I am trying to listen longer. What if we think of Angola's music as a song cycle, a musical sound that has continued for over a hundred years?

Ethnomusicologists gain from thinking of music in larger chunks. Kai Fikentscher suggests that we understand electronic dance music better when listening to the whole evening: the transitions, peaks, and a DJ's gauge of audience energy on the dance floor.[5] Tony Seeger describes how the Suyá in the rainforests of Brazil produce year-long suites of music, following cycles of ritual affirmations of community ties.[6] But how might we listen if Angola's music has continued throughout the twentieth century? How do we listen to shifting prison philosophies, management, and operations? These nonmusical changes become audible when they create and collapse new opportunities for prisoner collaboration.

The chapters will trace an overall stylistic arc that includes an active jazz scene in the 1950s and a shrinking secular music scene in the 2000s that finds room in the institutional support for gospel music. Each chapter develops a specific theme, often related to developments during that era. The stories of collaboration create a series of perspectives that I have found useful for thinking about music in prison.

Chapter 1 accounts for the *astonishment* that music often adds to social encounters. Resurrecting an older definition of "astonishment" to mean a shock to the senses, I consider how music can refine experiences, stereotype or redefine performers, shock people out of prejudices, or distinguish a moment from ordinary life. In the early years, music at Angola develops into a symbol of oppression, control, promise, horror, and folk tradition. Crucially, this chapter identifies the three main strands of Angola's mission: outlawry, plantation, and penitentiary.

Chapter 2 develops the idea of *association*, a collaborative music-making that relies on the institution's support and is therefore tied to the multiple missions of incarceration. Association, the act of coming together for a common purpose, is inherent to music anywhere. But the folkloric notions of prison music as an individual endeavor obscured the prolific jazz practices that dominated Angola's musical activity in the 1950s. This chapter reveals how jazz depended on and supported the prisoner associations that flourished during a decade of progressive reform. The focus on jazz, prisoner-run media, and the shift to a modern prison building show how collective activity can secure small individual freedoms.

Chapter 3's focus on *politics* follows a group of musicians who develop avant-garde jazz to think beyond the status quo. Despite the institution's oppressive formal and informal rules in the 1960s, musicians helped define and articulate higher principles of music and radical politics.

Chapter 4 examines the many ways prisoners engage *surfaces* of the prison—boundaries where they interact with outsiders. These meeting places develop out of negotiations with an administration under fire for mismanagement and facing underfunding. The alliances that form help fund music programs and offer slim chances for release as the concept of prisoners' rights develop.

Chapter 5 traces the years following prisoners' rights gains. A wake of musical change followed dramatic changes of the mid-1970s when court decisions resulted in federal receivership. Accounting for the *inflection* of post–prisoners' rights reveals how music maintained incremental gains and expressed the unevenness and failure to deliver reform.

Chapter 6 picks up on my visits to the prison from 2008 to 2016, offering a *recapitulation* of all five themes. I argue that music is still astonishing, associative, political, part of prison surfaces, and inflected toward disparate goals and promises. In this final chapter, I aim to show how these five historical perspectives of the prison illuminate current practices.

Ultimately, I hope to show that music reveals less about the nature of the prisoner than it does to make audible the many social interactions that prisoners negotiate. As you imagine the sounds described in each chapter, I urge that you listen for the roots of prison music: changing laws and policies, economic and moral exchanges, claims for rights, and legacies. This approach to prison music is listening to its resonance, how sound butts up against structures and makes legacies audible. The musicians themselves are the ones who initiate the sounds, find the means for achieving a new level of musicianship, encourage others to do the same, make unlikely bargains with administrators, study their audiences, and reveal their fundamental sociality and undeniable humanity.

Uncovering Histories

The research for this book comes from four interrelated efforts: a dissertation, a feature-length documentary film, archival research, and an oral history collection. The first two were part of my first phase of documenting the lives of musicians in Louisiana prisons (from 2008 to 2012). The second two parts were part of a follow-up phase (from 2012 to 2016) to add historical research and more in-depth personal accounts from a wider range of people at Angola. As a more minor yet crucial follow-up effort, I mailed a draft of this book to incarcerated musicians I had interviewed for their feedback.

In the first phase, I received permission from the Department of Corrections to make a film about music in Louisiana prisons. I made several research trips and assembled a crew (sound recordist Chauncy Godwin and cinematographer John Slattery) to film musicians over a year of their lives while incarcerated. We worked within the constraints and the imaginations of prisoners and administrators to identify what to document on film. We wanted to show how music functions in prisons. Angola was one of three sites that we used to present the diversity of musical activity, style, and purpose in Louisiana. As I show in my film and discuss in my dissertation, Elayn Hunt Correctional Center's more transient population and its designation for prisoners with mental and physical health issues made for an emotionally charged music scene.[7] The Louisiana Correctional Institute for Women, the state's only facility for women, offered a comparative perspective on how gender and incarceration intersect musically. Mental health, a lack of support for musical instruments, more robust family connections and responsibilities, and emotional labor made their choir a place where varied interpersonal dynamics unfolded.[8]

Angola's musical history, by contrast, was longer and more plentiful. The state's most notorious prison had a musical legacy that lives in the archives of the Library of Congress and the record grooves of well-known folkloric recordings. What's more, the musicians I spoke with at Angola had been there for an incredibly long amount of time. Some began their sentences in the 1960s and remained there when I visited last in 2016. Somehow, they managed to preserve sanity, find unlikely collaboration, and navigate violence at least in part through their engagement with music.

Having screened my film at Angola, I continued working with the musicians who participated in *Follow Me Down* and the administration as I moved into the second research phase. Angola has a museum and cultivates a public-facing image, complete with what is essentially a public relations staff, making music research potentially valuable in the administration's eyes. I struck up an arrangement with Assistant Warden Cathy Fontenot to continue my work by collecting oral histories of musicians there. The deal was that I could use the interviews to research this book, and the museum could have the interview recordings and transcripts for their archives. By then, I had established more trust with both prisoners and administrators. I also had demonstrated to them my commitment and follow through, having completed major projects and initiated a related new project with a clear mission for all: to document the musical histories of the prison.

Another possible reason for my access is that music seems innocuous. Often, it is thought of as a light diversion from more serious topics, a "good news" story to counter unsavory attention. Criminologist Leonidas Cheliotis has warned against the arts filling the role of "decorative justice," a distraction that turns the public away from the urgent problems of mass incarceration.[9] Regardless, I knew that the arts were part of daily life in some prisons, that prisoners, administrators, guards, and volunteer outsiders used art to reimagine prisons, find sanctuary, and negotiate small details of their incarceration. I had written my master's thesis on the Prison Arts Project in California prisons and later created an archive at UCLA of the program's decades-long history.[10] Art can transform experiences and relationships. In prison, that can be powerful. Prison arts programs have provided critical spaces for people to discover possibilities.

In many cases, art that emerges from prisons can offer critiques of the structural problems that lead many to prisons in the first place—primarily economic and racial inequalities. Nonetheless, artistic practice is vital outside of its political promise. Practicing art for the sake of art, as much as incarcerated artists can manage to do that, can offer lessons in how and why we create, collaborate, and step onto the performance stage.[11] The stories of that attempt can also reveal incarceration's brutality, austerity, and ineffectiveness.

I chose to highlight stories of collaboration rather than those of individual struggle. As an ethnomusicologist, I have learned how music does more than transform individuals. It affects groups of people, the way people relate to groups, and the ways that groups relate to other groups. That perspective has helped me develop questions for incarcerated musicians. Changing my perspective was difficult. It was tempting to focus on individuals because prison's coercive power significantly pressures individuals—ideally to reform but more often to destroy prospects, family roles, and emotional stability. Music does transform individuals, but it also transforms communities, economies, politics, and interpersonal relationships. My studies led me to broader studies of change at the intersection of the transformative powers of prison and music, accounting for empowering and destructive community transformation.

This book is a story of music in the service of and in the defiance of prisons, by those who are incarcerated there and supported by various prison stakeholders. I never became an insider, and that was never my goal. As a fellow musician, however, I learned through extended discussion, intent on drawing connections and distinctions. I retooled questions before each visit to the prison and before each time I looked over historical documents. When appropriate, I related my knowledge of global musical practices and my experiences as a musician, a method at the heart of ethnomusicology. My experience participating in musical traditions around the world helped me be nimble with how we discussed music and understood facets of musical practice in prison. It gave me perspective on familiar and often naive understandings of music in the United States. For instance, Americans often assume that music is primarily expressive, that music is a straightforward authentic text, that talent dictates who has the right to sing, and that music is a leisure activity.

I approached interviews with people who have spent decades in prison ethically and reflexively. I was keenly aware that this was a project predicated on the suffering of others. Was I at risk of collecting "material" from (mostly Black) wards of the state to write a book that would advance my academic career? Is that an act of transforming the violence inflicted on others into capital for me? Was I re-presenting salacious stories of violence produced by people desperate for release to capitalize on the spectacle of racial suffering or consequences of poverty? Was I presenting myself as a compassionate free person while delivering nothing to help the people who participated in the project? These questions guided me, informed by my study of reflexive ethnographies in the 1980s and suspended through the current concern over decolonizing academia. Being a musician helped me wrestle with these issues.

The Musicality of Prison

A unique research tool in ethnomusicology (among the social sciences) is the concept of "bi-musicality." In the early 1960s, scholars interested in cultural studies of music asserted that being a student of a musical practice was an essential tool for understanding a particular musical culture.[12] As researchers, ethnomusicologists became students of traditional masters of musical performance. As educators, they established world music performance ensembles—Indonesian gamelan and Ghanaian drumming, for instance—to provide students with a musical and social perspective. I was part of the second generation of these students, developing as a scholar while playing in ensembles as an undergraduate at Wesleyan University and later studying with master musicians in many countries.

On the surface, this method seems irrelevant to studying music in prison. Would I need to join a prison band to learn how to play like a prisoner? Not necessarily. The fundamental legacy of bi-musicality is the notion that musical perspectives give insight into social elements that you cannot get through studying music from a distance. My conversations with prisoners were musical. They sometimes began with discussions of music theory or arrangement, or stories of performances gone wrong or surprisingly right. Occasionally, in the band room, we would pick up instruments to examine an idea through sound rather than words. I adapted the classic concept of bi-musicality from being a student of a non-native musical practice to activating a shared interest in music. Moreover, our acceptance of difference gave power to a joint project of exploring the *musicality* of human experiences, a way of thinking together from sharing musical worlds, yet occupying different positions.

Starting with a common interest in music, our work of understanding music moved out to stories of musical capacity I had never imagined. Through this process, I learned that being a musician behind bars can be similar to being a musician in the so-called free world (struggling for resources and space, dealing with noise complaints, negotiating interpersonal dynamics of a band). At other times, it was markedly different (the rampant distrust, the ultimate yet unpredictable authority of officers you depend upon, the lack of privacy, the complications of getting out). Other differences grew from this fundamental difference—experiences of racism, geographies, personal histories, occupation, poverty, family, and religiosity. Some of these factors were part of the complex fabric that makes a diverse and unequal American society. So for this project, I tried to keep music at the center and looked for connections to nonmusical aspects.

Approaching prison through musicality gave me a way of thinking about what I was doing from the perspective of musical principles. I saw myself writing this book more as an arranger or a bandleader, rather than using writing to speak for, give voice, or command authority. As an arranger, I sought to amplify unheard voices, use some to harmonize with others, put melodies in counterpoint, assign soloists, and think of textures of backgrounds. As an arranger, I assume responsibility for the accuracy, legibility, and the work in its entirety.

My research methods included various approaches. I interviewed musicians, attended rehearsals, and saw various performances. I also did archival research at the American Folklife Center in the Library of Congress—primarily reviewing the recordings and papers of folklorists who visited Angola. But I was particularly drawn to the prison newsmagazine, *The Angolite*, and regional newspaper stories about music.[13] I will discuss the limitations of gleaning data from a prison newsmagazine in chapter 2, but what I discovered in these accounts of musical life confirmed what prisoners had been telling me—that musical styles were diverse and that musicians were incorporated into daily prison operations and were constantly under threat of being shut down.

As I bounced between archival research and collecting oral histories, stories emerged. As older prisoners told me about the personalities of key players, I read newsmagazine reports of concerts, festivals, and justifications for having access to musical resources. Eras of extraordinary musical accomplishment became clear. I pieced together histories of remarkable individuals who organized and innovated only to have those efforts buried in the cold anonymity of prison. As I put together clues about the dynamic musical history of Angola prison, I became an unlikely music historian of the prison, not a prisoner, not an administrator, but a musician and ethnomusicologist.

While writing, I was active with musical projects in other prisons. Since the release of *Follow Me Down*, I have screened the film internationally. Typically, when invited to a university, I also used the opportunity to screen the film in a nearby prison. The screening would often support the hosting university's prison outreach programs, like the Bard Prison Initiative or the Saint Louis University Prison Education Program. Showing the film to prisoners at other prisons helped me understand aspects of incarceration unique to Angola. I also taught classes in Maryland prisons and the Washington DC Central Detention Facility. Classes gave me a weekly forum to discuss incarceration and music more broadly—even to discuss draft chapters of this book with prisoners. Thus, this book is a culmination of these varied musical approaches to prison. The stories of musicians that fill these pages engage the many modes of research. Each method of investigation has its insight and limitations.

The stories of these men as prison musicians help show the tremendous efforts, contributions, and ingenuity of individuals joining together in collaboration. I attempt to let their musicality rise above their conviction. Aside from Charles Neville, James Booker, and James Black, the musicians in this book are absent from music histories. Here, their names loom large— the musicians who kept creative activity alive for seventy years against all odds: Les Winslow, Lester Thompson, Louis Surgent, Russell Sweet, Leotha Brown, Bud Wilkerson, John Henry Taylor Jr., Otis Neal, Robin Polk, Myron Hodges, Larry Wilkerson, Jewell Spotville, Albert Patterson, Calvin Lewis, and Laird Veillon, to name but a few musical legends. Their stories will lend us a particular human account of incarceration, often absent in prison studies. Research restrictions often limit the testimony we get from the people experiencing incarceration. Prisoners' voices get buried in statistics, legal histories, historical contextualization, and brief or limited visits that turn impressions into policy positions. I am hoping to let a musical focus offer granular and messy humanity to a consideration of incarceration.

My relationship with Angola and the people there was—and still is— conditional, partial, incomplete, and inherently bound to my background. But it has changed over twenty years. I began studying music in prison in 2003, while incarceration rates were still rising and before Americans who were distanced from the carceral system understood prisons to be a social justice issue. This sentiment is old in the communities more targeted by policing and more afflicted by incarceration. The recent political discussions of prison and the criminal justice system on the right and left sides of our political debate do inform my interest in the role of music in prison, but they don't overwhelm it. I try to present music *in a context of* political disenfranchisement, the structural violence of the state, and the prison-industrial complex, instead of using music to make political arguments.

A Brief Overview of Louisiana Behind Bars

Music programs have a long history in US prisons. Many of these were initiated and maintained in the name of education, rehabilitation, and religious programs. What sets Angola apart is that musical activities have by and large been created and maintained by prisoners. Coordinating players, space, learning, and equipment requires dialogue with the administration, which, given a prison's focus on custody, creates a conversation that would not otherwise occur. Through these voluntary though conditional activities, organized music at Angola takes place. This book focuses on the history of association and negotiation at the intersection of prison and music.

The backdrop to this book is mass incarceration. Statistics in Louisiana and at Angola in particular plainly show trends toward mass incarceration and racial disparities in the United States. In 1901, when Louisiana took responsibility for its prisoners by ending its practice of convict leasing, it held 1,142 prisoners. At that time, the state's incarceration rate was eighty-one per 100,000 residents. Eighty-six percent were Black, 3.5 percent were women, and one was a White woman.[14] Incarceration swelled over the following 120 years. Even when crime rates decreased, prisons grew. They multiplied beyond Angola to newer facilities throughout the state in the 1970s. Declining budget allocations from the state simply forced the prisons to deal with austerity.

As of 2022, Louisiana had 26,377 people behind bars.[15] At a rate of 680 adults per 100,000 compared to a national average of 419, it is the highest in the country.[16] In the state facilities, 65.92 percent are Black, 33.64 percent White. Compare this to the general breakdown of the state of Louisiana, where African Americans constitute 32.8 percent of the population and Whites 62.8 percent.[17] Put differently, African Americans in Louisiana are four times more likely to end up in prison than their White counterparts. Twelve of the facilities hold the male population (95.38 percent of the total), and one, the Louisiana Correctional Institute for Women, holds the female population (4.62 percent).[18] About half of those under the charge of the state remain in local jails due to space shortages.

Louisiana has the stiffest sentencing in the nation, leads the world in the rate of incarceration, and maintains stark racial disparities. At a 143 percent increase from 1970, nearly 6,000 people (19 percent of the prison population) are serving life with parole, life without parole, or virtual life sentences.[19] Disproportionate by race again, 74 percent are Black. Louisiana is one of the few states that does not grant parole options for life sentences. As the population rises, the average age also increases due to the high proportion of prisoners sentenced to natural life. As of this writing, the average age of prisoners in Louisiana is forty-one years old and rising.[20] At some point, the death rate may stabilize the average, in a bleak computation of human life. And the harsh approach to punishment extends beyond the prison walls. Louisiana ranks thirteenth in the number of people barred from voting due to a felony conviction. Felony voting disenfranchisement is 4.41 percent for Louisiana's African American population compared to 2.23 percent for Whites.

The demographic makeup of the prison, of course, impacts the music scene there: much of the music-making and musical taste is African American. But music does more than audibly represent demographics. It also reveals prisoner aspirations. It is dependent on the types of music supported by the administration and outside organizations. The state maintains many of its older prison farm practices and prides itself on a system distinct from other correctional systems. Angola's distinctive musical practices create as much public noise as the music itself. The controversy surrounding the Angola rodeo with its prisoner "volunteer" exploitation or the heavy-handed Christian programming remains a point of pride for many corrections workers and an easy target for activist groups and journalists.

Music has occurred and does occur in many prisons. Nonetheless, Angola's relatively well-documented history of musicality reveals the many ways music interacts with imprisonment. Reports of music go as far back as 1901, when the state of Louisiana bought the former plantations to establish the penitentiary. Angola's musicality is perhaps best known from twentieth-century folkloric recordings, primarily of the famed musician Lead Belly, but also of Robert Pete Williams and others heard on many folkloric albums. Since then, music produced by prisoners at Angola has been part of regular media coverage, state festivals, and public events throughout Louisiana. Many of these musicians brought practices from New Orleans—professional skills and attitudes as well as specific traditions that gave focus and direction to Angola's music scene.

Indeed, musicians at Angola have used music in similar ways to those in other prisons—as work song, entertainment, protest, diversion, collaboration, expression, intellectual activity, and relief, for instance. But prolific music-making and shifting management practices of Angola over 120 years allow us to see all these musical functions wax and wane. And as the first chapter shows, importantly, the history of music at Angola also reveals the prison's unstable and ill-defined mission.

1
Astonishment

Sitting in the back of the chapel with a dozen of the most active musicians incarcerated at the Louisiana State Penitentiary in Angola, I prepared the last question of our two-hour interview. I had been listening to stories, trying to understand music's role in the twenty-first-century prison. By their account, music connected to both ordinary and extraordinary elements of their lives. To me, everything about prison life seemed extraordinary. My last question was an open one. I had been trying to envision a film about music at Angola and was fishing for general directions: "What do you think are important things to show about music or your lives as musicians here?"

Answers flowed in: the importance of documenting the older musicians and how music improves character. Laird Veillon waited his turn, considering how my film might most productively strike an outside audience—no small task. Veillon had been incarcerated at Angola for twenty-five years, serving a life sentence without possibility for parole on a murder conviction. He now played in several Angola bands after learning electric bass three years into his sentence. With an understated Louisiana drawl, he offered, "The amazement of it. You got a bunch of murderers and rapists and robbers and all, and they're all making harmony and making music and making people stomp their feet and smile. These a bunch of hardcore dudes, and you really wouldn't expect that."[1] I would learn through historical research how deep the history of musical amazement at Angola is, stretching back to the prehistory of the prison.

Sugar Lake is about a forty-minute walk through the fields from the main prison chapel where I first interviewed the musicians—if you don't count the time it takes to get through security. The long and narrow lake has had many names despite being the same body of water. For a time, it was Lake Angola. Before that, it was briefly called Lake of the Cross. In 1699, Pierre Le Moyne d'Iberville, the founder of the French colony of Louisiana in what was then New France, erected a cross when he and his party discovered the lake. One of d'Iberville's lieutenants, André Pénicaut, himself indentured as a carpenter to d'Iberville, described an encounter with a group of indigenous

Instrument of the State. Benjamin J. Harbert, Oxford University Press. © Oxford University Press 2023.
DOI: 10.1093/oso/9780197517505.003.0002

people, likely from the Tunica Indian nation. It is the first written record of music at the site of what is now a state prison.

> We sang there a Véxilla Regis on our knees, which seemed to astonish these Savages very much. We made them understand that His cross was an object greatly esteemed in our religion, and that they must take care that no harm befell it. Nearby, on the bluffs above the river, was the Houma village, where in the Spring of 1700 Father Du Ru, the Jesuit missionary with d'Iberville, made a model of a church which he instructed the savages to build in his absence.[2]

The use of music to amaze and astonish, the coercion, the identification of savagery, and the missionary instruction to build are all themes I can't help but trace from this early encounter of difference and music.

Astonishment, which we typically understand as the sudden cause of wonder, also has an archaic meaning: losing sensation, becoming numb, and losing the presence of mind. I'd like to recover this older sense of the word and add it to how we use it today, giving "astonishment" laudatory and cautionary meanings as we investigate how music operates. What does music do to amaze and astonish? What does astonishment do to numb our apprehension of prisons? How do incarcerated musicians use astonishment to their advantage? How is astonishment woven into the history of Angola Prison? These two understandings of astonishment account for how music can stun audiences in both productive and unproductive ways.

Angola has forever operated with absence as a fundamental feature. The power of absence distinguishes Angola from other prisons in the United States.[3] At times it has functioned with only a handful of free staff members, relying on prisoners to be guards, clerks, secretaries, and musicians. Angola suffers and simultaneously draws its power from the absence of law, the lack of budgets, and the absence of family, community, and hope. As I reread the above account of this astonishing hymn, the last part, the seemingly separate part of the quotation, lingers in my mind: a colonial mandate to build an institution in their absence. Oddly, it presages the way prisoners at Angola would have the task of associating with one another within their own confines—for instance, serving as prisoner guards, constructing their own living quarters, and filling quasi-administrative jobs to maintain custody and the business of the prison farm. In that absence, prisoners at Angola form surprising musical associations.

Again in that last part of the quote from Sugar Lake, the instruction is to build from a model. Angola is fundamentally a set of models, birthed as an institution serving capitalism, jurisprudence, and religiosity. Sociologists Georg Rusche and Otto Kirchheimer long ago argued that modes of production drive types of incarceration. They posit that "[p]unishment as such does not exist; only concrete systems of punishment and specific criminal practices exist. The object of our investigation, therefore, is punishment in its specific manifestations."[4] The prison farm is a hybrid institution created as a reform effort after Reconstruction.[5] Laws, state and national economic changes, politics, and technologies all play a part in changing models. Yet immutable factors underpin these models: capitalism, racism, local authority, and religiosity. Let's start with models, move to astonishment, and then get to association within the shadow of state power. We will see how musical possibilities develop within these dynamic changes as we progress.

Models: Angola's Preprison Polyphony

"Prison" is a suitcase term. It means many things—control, custody, punishment, rehabilitation, and public safety primarily. Thinking of prison, therefore, requires some unpacking. In the early nineteenth century, local parishes administered their punishment. Jails, the one in New Orleans being the most infamous, were places where people were sent if they went through a court process. On plantations, the punishment was at the discretion of the landowner. Local vigilantism also played a role. Two nineteenth-century innovations marked Louisiana's modern initiative: the state penitentiary in Baton Rouge (before the Civil War) and convict leasing (after the Civil War).

The many practices combined in Angola developed differently. These historical developments are part of larger global projects—colonialism, Christianity, and capitalism. This section of the chapter then traces the growth of three general practices: *outlawry*, *penance*, and *slavery*. Understanding these three practices will help us discern different aspects of the prison as we pick up the chronology in 1901, when the state of Louisiana took ownership of multiple properties that surround Sugar Lake.[6]

Angola has sustained many missions, sometimes conflicting, sometimes overlapping, sometimes official, and sometimes unofficial. The practices of outlawry, penance, and slavery intermingle historically. They linger as the invisible threads that continue to drive Angola's tangled mission. These missions—or, for the prisoners, conditions—also become the context for musical activity and themes that I will address throughout the rest of this book.

Outlawry | Out-of-Law

The outlaw has persisted in American mythology, often representing rugged individualism and American exceptionalism. Plenty of American stories offer an authentic foil to civilization, adapting a romanticist fascination with the social outcast. A diverse cast of outlaws loom large in American folk culture, for example, Lead Belly (discussed below), Billy the Kid and Butch Cassidy, narcocorrido singers, and the badman archetype that has moved into gangsta rap.[7] But as an instrument of punishment and control, outlawry is at least two thousand years old.

Outlawry is the practice of legally placing someone outside the protections and entitlements of the law. It is also the condition of not being protected by laws. As a legal practice with deep history, outlawry strips an individual of their humanity and creates categories of legal nonsubjects. The history of outlawry is long and its application broad, dating back at least to Roman and early Germanic practices.[8] It was a widespread and notoriously harsh punishment in medieval Europe.[9] Banishment, exile, infamy, excommunication, and civil death are variations of a mode of punishment that has denied rights in the name of legal retribution. Existing outside of the law, the outlaw is subject to the whims of specially empowered public officials and private citizens. Outlawry entitled those "in-law" with free rein to hunt and kill outlaws.

Outlawry is an instrument of power. Employed as a tool of colonization, it affected entire populations. Across the globe, British colonists dismantled local government systems to destabilize communities, rendering them unable to coordinate resistance. Outlawry was a strategic form of legalized lawlessness enacted through declared states of emergency and martial law.[10]

In eighteenth-century American towns, outlawry persisted as a severe punishment option brought on individuals. The official practice remained a legal procedure in early nineteenth-century America, gradually losing favor to incarceration.[11] Northern states developed penitentiaries, using architecture as a means to encourage penance or correct community members, thus ending outlawry as a widely used method of punishment.[12]

Southern systems, however, developed differently. Many of the states supporting the institution of slavery maintained outlawry as a legal instrument amid a blurry landscape of judicial and extrajudicial practices.[13] For example, there were some Black people—enslaved or free—in Louisiana's antebellum prisons, but a significant degree of punishment occurred in the margins of the law.[14] Required by law, private White citizens enforced the strict Black code regulations, a set of protections that included state guidelines from French law that regulated plantation treatment of enslaved people.[15] Despite the codes, antebellum practices mainly dealt with criminal accusations of enslaved people extrajudicially through hanging, mutilation, and flogging. A crime committed by a free Black man or woman in the South that did not result in an extrajudicial hanging could be a pretext for selling the person into slavery.[16]

After the Civil War, more Black people in the South accused of criminal behavior fell under the law. At the same time, parish jails lacked state funding. With no training and little procedure, subordinate officers at jails often abused prisoners. Building conditions varied but were generally substandard.[17] Revisions to Louisiana's civil codes abolished the use of outlawry as a legal instrument in 1917. Still, outlawry's influence persisted within the criminal justice system and during Jim Crow. The state granted prisons the authority to lock people up and turn their backs on the consequences after the official practice of outlawry ended.

The consequences of outlawry in the US continues in many spaces. They are observable when weakened rules and procedures on all sides of power create a culture of disregard.[18] When combined with unreliable and conditional legal entitlements, outlawry contributes to a condition of "legal liminality" for individuals or groups of people who live in between law and lawlessness.[19] State use of selective denial of certain rights and benefits of citizenship continues in many forms (for instance, today in suspending voting rights or withdrawing access to welfare and public housing, as well as denying parental rights or due process for extradition).[20] In prison, the legacy of outlawry persists as one of many missions of American incarceration. It continues in the notion of "lock them up and throw away the key" and strict life sentencing policies. Prison's power is often not in its ability to see all through constant surveillance, as some have suggested, but in the state's ability *not to look* over its prisoners.[21]

Penance | Penitentiary

As outlawry waned in the United States, a new instrument developed centered on an audacious concept—that a person could return as a productive member of society. (Of course, the person in question must necessarily qualify as a citizen in the first place.) Penitentiaries evolved from jails. These massive buildings were designed and built in the early- to mid-nineteenth century to address White criminality. Penitentiary design built on the notion that a soul could be mortified, given a temporary civil death, and then be reborn into society.[22] Idealistic as that may seem, people sent to penitentiaries often faced brutal treatment, mental illness, and filthy conditions. From a nineteenth-century perspective, however, the imposing buildings were architectural marvels and represented a humanitarian turn from outlawry, public spectacle, execution, corporal punishment, and decrepit local jails.[23]

In 1835, when Angola was a functioning plantation, Louisiana's first state penitentiary opened fifty miles south. The new Baton Rouge Penitentiary was reserved for those sentenced to hard labor. It provided an alternative to the dilapidated, rat-infested New Orleans parish prison eighty miles farther south.[24] On first encountering the New Orleans facility and its prisoners in 1831, French chronicler Alexis de Tocqueville wrote, "We saw there men thrown in pell-mell with swine, in the midst of excrement and filth. In locking up criminals, no thought is given to making them better but simply taming their wickedness; they are chained like wild beasts; they are not refined but brutalized."[25] Tocqueville was particularly appalled because he had crossed the Atlantic to see the marvel of new American penitentiaries.

New York and Pennsylvania penitentiaries had gained an international reputation for having humane techniques. Reportedly, they changed individuals. Isolation was not for punishment but an opportunity to give penance to God or to force labor and thereby create productive citizens. Though they ultimately failed, early-nineteenth-century penitentiaries promised removal from harmful environments and guaranteed convicts backbone, skills, and a reclamation of the self.[26] Baton Rouge was to fulfill those promises on the heels of Tocqueville's visit.

The principles of the modern penitentiary were stirring as jurist and statesman Edward Livingston hammered out *A System of Penal Law for the State of Louisiana* in 1833. Although the General Assembly did not pass his penal codes (and wouldn't codify criminal law until 1942), his ideas influenced jurisprudence. Livingston held that the purpose of prisons was, in his words, "to ameliorate punishment and not to avenge society; to reform the criminal and to prevent crime."[27]

In 1835, fewer than 100 state prisoners sentenced to hard labor took residence at the new state penitentiary.[28] Governor André B. Roman's goal, like those of others who developed Southern penitentiaries, was to alleviate jail overcrowding and save costs—if not turn a profit. Pragmatics aside, the model for Louisiana's Baton Rouge Penitentiary was Wethersfield State

Prison in Connecticut, one that followed early experiments with architecture and whose regime alternated nighttime solitary confinement (ostensibly for forced reflection or "penitence") with hard group work under the rule of silence.[29] Under what was known as the Auburn model or the "silent system," the cost-saving pragmatics overlapped with rehabilitative goals. Factory work, during which prisoners were not allowed to talk or even glance at each other, was instituted to combat idleness, instill obedience, and transform criminals into law-abiding citizens.[30] At the Baton Rouge Penitentiary, they marched lockstep in chains between their jobs and their isolated cells. Men made crafts and learned to operate machinery. Women washed and sewed.[31]

By 1844, the costs of the facility were too much for the legislature and public to accept. The South had suffered severe economic depression, and the penitentiary seemed an expensive luxury. The state followed the example of Kentucky, leasing the convicts to McHatton, Pratt, and Company, a private firm.[32] Hard labor for redemption became hard labor for profit. By 1873, the facility had emptied. Subcontractors had prisoners working throughout the state.[33] Over the decades, the building in Baton Rouge was relieved of its penitentiary mission. It became a place to stage convict laborers for building levees and railroads and working in fields around the state.

For those incarcerated in Baton Rouge, there were opportunities for music in moments stolen in between punishment, penitence, and increasingly grueling labor. In 1893, in the final years of the penitentiary—long after officials abandoned the regime of silence—Theo Hester was serving three years for check forgery. Hester wrote to his parents about life there: "While I am writing a Negro is playing a guitar and an Italian singing. . . . Sundays in the dining they have a great time [line?] dance and sing. . . . All boys dance to themselves. But there are no girls to dance. Only two women are here. A good many negro women are at Angola on Major James Farm."[34] This account of interracial entertainment, relegated to off-time, also points to the fact that Louisiana had shifted most of its wards from the penitentiary to the site of a recently active slave plantation.

Slavery | Plantation

Louisiana abandoned the idea of the state penitentiary out of financial necessity. In doing so, they ditched a model that at least gave promise to humanitarian principles articulated by Edward Livingston and the Auburn penitentiary model. Outlawry and penitentiary practices ceded to convict leasing as the shifting Reconstruction economy of the late nineteenth century created a desperate need for labor. While it is hard to disentangle outlawry and convict leasing from slavery, it helps to identify the centrality of Angola's agribusiness and the governance structure of the plantation. The plantation offered the idea that people could be controlled by binding them to land. The plantation model was ready-made, an existing model of self-sufficiency that the penitentiary never managed to achieve. Angola as a major plantation had developed in the mid-nineteenth century.

The plantation was part of a cultural and economic ethic that championed self-sufficiency and private investment. The plantation owner was an idealized individualist given freedom from the state. As historian Richard Follett explains:

> Louisiana cane planters were doubtlessly capitalist in their economic vision and invested in highly developed plantations, but they simultaneously embraced a social ethic based on mastery, individualism, and independence. As a generation of scholarship has now shown, the culture of American slave-holding ultimately bred jealous independence, myopic focus on the individual, one's own authority, and upon personal liberty.[35]

Symbolism aside, plantations were part of significant expansions of capital and slavery in the mid-nineteenth century.

Franklin & Armfield was the largest slave-trading firm of the 1830s. Isaac Franklin had bought massive amounts of land in West Feliciana Parish. When New Orleans banks rose to prominence through a series of mergers in the 1840s, they offered planters powerful financial instruments for real estate and capital investment.[36] Angola was one of the plantations and the first on which Franklin began improvements. He brought 104 enslaved workers there to clear cypress trees and open a steam-powered woodyard. White squatters proved to be a nuisance, and managing the land proved challenging. Workers resisted the work, died, and ran away.[37]

Eventually, profits came in. Livestock, crops, and raw goods swept into Nashville, New Orleans, and Cincinnati markets. When Franklin died in 1846, the West Feliciana plantations were part of assets that would now be worth $435 million. Adelicia and Joseph Acklen eventually inherited the land, built an impressive residence, and maintained the plantation.[38] By 1860, it was a massive agricultural project that produced 3,100 bales of cotton a year. Forced labor migration, disease, hunger, and death accompanied the profits.[39]

White observers cast Black music as simultaneously dangerous and fascinating. In 1839, Louisiana passed an act restricting the use of drums. The legislature knew enough about African music to understand that drum sounds could carry coded information. Other European and Euro-American accounts marveled at Black musical accompaniments to work.[40] But the songs that set the tempo for cane-cutting may have lost favor when machines began to set the pace of labor in the 1840s and 1850s. The advent of steam-powered sugar mills increased the speed of harvest, turning already difficult work into brutal labor.[41]

The dominant sound on the plantation was not a musical one. Isaac Franklin purchased a plantation bell, an expensive tool primarily for signaling work routines.[42] European traditions had used bells as what R. Murray Schaffer called "soundmarks." Church bells established acoustic communities and defined the center of a village or town through a community's sense of sound.[43] Similarly, the acoustic footprint of a plantation bell ties loudness to authority, but in this case, the sound signals the inescapable disciplining of the enslaved population. The constant ringing of the bell measured a listener's distance from the plantation's center. By listening, everyone knew where they were. Simultaneously, they knew when they were on the schedule of any given day. The last bell ring of the day meant that no one was to move about the plantation freely.[44]

The only musical object found on site from the nineteenth century is a Jew's harp from an excavation of the old slave quarters.[45] The rhythmic instrument, familiar to many global traditions, offered moments of diversion and perhaps even coerced performances. Likely, it was a way of tuning the ear to something other than the bell.

There is surprisingly little documentation of the sounds of Angola before the state purchased it in 1901. Beyond this scant legal and physical evidence of sound, we can only imagine that work songs accompanied the agricultural use of this land. Part of the soundscape of forced labor, any singing would have mixed with sounds of agony, protest, brutality, and occasional revolt.

Collections of slave songs, beginning in 1867 with *Slave Songs of the United States*, systematically describe the disappearing repertoire of songs seen to reflect the institution of slavery.[46] None transcribed the entire soundscape. For some of the White readership, the astonishing song collections drew attention away from the brutality of the institution.

Angola may now be the focal point of Louisiana's prison system, but understanding the prison's evolution reveals it as more of a constellation of models. Angola has inherited disparate parts of nineteenth-century punishment and profiteering. The plantations at Angola became principal parts of the state's criminal justice apparatus, which then included the Hope Plantation and other agricultural lands, the New Orleans Parish Prison, several levee camps, and the Baton Rouge Penitentiary. These plantations were also part of the state's commercial exports. Louisiana provided a quarter of the world's sugar.

At this point, we can return to Angola's chronology through a convict-leasing system that leads to Angola becoming a state prison—one that eventually bundles the legacies of outlawry, penance, and slavery. Along the way, Americans began associating the sounds of convict labor with folkloric tradition.

Imagining Folklore in the Convict-Lease System

During Reconstruction, a new category of unskilled and semiskilled work with inherent danger and low wages replaced rural sharecropping and tenant farming practices. Generally, White Louisianans were unwilling to take these jobs. What ended up being called "negro jobs" resulted from many unsuccessful attempts to bring foreign labor to the state. An 1871 experiment with Chinese laborers failed. An effort to lure Swedish laborers ended when prospective laborers learned of the horrific work and low wages from fellow passengers en route and jumped off the boat at Memphis before getting to Louisiana.[47] Had either of those attempts succeeded, American field songs may have had roots in melodically interlinked Chinese *tian'ge* brought from Yangtze River rice fields or high-pitched Swedish *lålning* brought from high mountain Scandinavian pastures.

Various types of music accompany labor all over the world. The songs that developed in the South during Reconstruction were stylistically African American because Louisiana's unappealing jobs fell to workers emancipated from slavery. Women took live-in domestic work while men went to slaughterhouses, flour mills, fertilizer plants, lumber mills, and iron foundries. Day laborers cut cane, picked cotton, and harvested vegetables. Many used music to ease the labor conditions.

Labor had become racialized. So the general conceptions of who was suited for specific jobs became a model for prisoner classification in the late nineteenth century. Officials did not classify prisoners by the crime they had committed but by what work they would have to do and how long they would do it. White prisoners went to the factory. Black prisoners went to the field. A narrower official classification distinguished between long-timers and short-timers.[48] Specific work details were at the discretion of private contractors. Following the Civil War, many Southern states developed convict-leasing arrangements with private contractors who put state prisoners, primarily Black, to work on railways, roads, levees, and former plantations.[49] Unlike other states, Louisiana contracted with only one person.

In 1870, former Confederate Major Samuel L. James won the contract for leasing prisoners in Louisiana. Ten years later, he bought the West Feliciana plantations from Adelicia Cheatham (once Acklen), who, as described earlier, had inherited the Angola property from Isaac Franklin. James's lease of state prisoners is notorious for being the most brutal period of Louisiana's prison history.[50] While slavery had given African bodies a market value, the convict-lease system made them replaceable.[51] James oversaw plantations that produced cotton, corn, sugar cane, and rice. He also subcontracted prisoners for building back Southern infrastructure, stationing them in remote work camps throughout the state.[52] They labored in plain public view and within earshot, generating a fair amount of public debate. Singing was often cited as evidence that Black people did not mind the terms of their incarceration, that they simply carried on their "ordinary" ways of life: singing, playing games, and eating.[53] But not everyone was convinced.

In 1884, the editor of the *Daily Picayune* wrote that immediate death sentences would be more humane since the average convict survived no more than six years at work.[54] The brutality of forced labor had brought additional danger to the already grueling nature of prisoner work. The human toll of the lease system was severe. As convict labor moved closer to towns, the poor treatment caught the attention of the local public, tourists, and potential Northern investors. Another newspaper reported:

> Men on the [Samuel L. James] works are brutally treated and everybody knows it. They are worked, mostly in the swamps and plantations, from daylight to dark. Corporal punishment is inflicted on the slightest provocation.... Anyone who has travelled along the lines of railroads that run through Louisiana's swamps... in which the levees are built, has seen these poor devils almost to their waists, delving in the black and noxious mud....

Theirs is a grievous lot a thousand times more grievous than the law ever contemplated they should endure in expiation of their sins.[55]

Without the constant noise that marks a twenty-first-century soundscape—produced by cars, air conditioners, and airplanes—the sounds of convict labor would have been more audible to passersby. To them, it was the noise of Reconstruction and criminal justice, a mix of brutality and racial difference, until folklorists picked up on the distinctive singing.[56]

Work songs astonished Americans. Even if only partially, they drew attention away from the horrors of convict leasing. When the American Folklore Society began in 1888, early music collectors began to incorporate the sounds of Black labor into an aural portrait of American heritage.[57] They found evidence of tradition buried in conditions of brutality and represented it in musical notation. Songbooks (and later, audio recordings) captured how conscripted laborers used solo and group singing to cut down trees, pick cotton, swing hammers, weed with hoes, cut sugar cane, and other racialized stoop labor. As presented, the songs were vestiges of lost musical culture.

Louisiana's reformists, however, heard the pain in convict leasing, sounds that did not astonish from a broken criminal justice system. In Saidiya Hartman's words, applied to slavery but relevant here, "the fixation on the slave's 'good times' conceals the affiliations of white enjoyment and black subjection and the affective dimensions of mastery and servitude."[58] The prisoner's "bad times" became uncomfortable for those who saw the violence.

In 1886, a committee of the Louisiana General Assembly visited the work camps as public criticism grew. At one site, they found Theophile Chevalier, a Black prisoner missing both of his feet. Chevalier explained that while working outdoors without shoes during the winter of 1884–1885, one foot was frostbitten, leading to gangrene and eventual amputation with a penknife. The other foot rotted off soon afterward. Chevalier was serving a five-year sentence for stealing $5.[59]

After a long political battle, an 1898 constitutional amendment ended convict leasing in Louisiana. Samuel L. James's contract with the state was allowed to finish through 1901 as a concession.[60] James had died in 1894, but his family held the contract and carried on control of the area. While convict leasing drew to a close, convict labor continued. The shades of differences between convict "leasing" and "labor" were in the procedure (the elimination of private contracts in favor of using state administration) and its visibility (the labor was less conspicuous behind prison fences).

With the end of the convict lease system, vestiges of slavery and outlawry moved into the prison. Throughout late nineteenth-century America, corporal punishment lost favor. It represented an attack on republicanism.[61] But that didn't mean it ended. Whipping, for instance, relocated to where republicanism did not exist—behind prison walls and within the legal allowances for slavery. As specified by the Thirteenth Amendment in 1865, the prison remained partially out-of-law. "Neither slavery nor involuntary servitude, *except as a punishment for crime whereof the party shall have been duly convicted* [emphasis added], shall exist within the United States, or any place subject to their jurisdiction."[62]

During the nineteenth-century preprison era of Angola, a racialized set of labor, punishment, and musical practices moved from a plantation system to convict leasing. Knowing this history reveals how music operates within outlawry, penance, and slavery. After the state stopped leasing prisoners and established a new penitentiary at Angola, prison music became the testimony of the outlaw in songs, the righteous cry for redemption in spirituals, and the sound of anachronistic labor in its recorded work songs and field hollers. In this way, prison music practiced at the Louisiana State Penitentiary at Angola is polyphonic, in dialogue with multiple legacies of punishment and control.

The Astonishing Polyphony of State Control

As the James lease ran out, the state had to figure out what to do with its prisoners. Legislators were still not comfortable assuming the full responsibility of managing and funding a burgeoning inmate population.[63] Convict leasing was illegal and unpopular. Politicians occasionally advocated for their free constituents who had trouble competing for prisoner-contracted farming work or rail and levee construction.[64] Newspaper editorials expressed sympathy and outrage at the lease system. The general public, however, was in favor of convict labor as punishment or at least indifferent.[65] A majority of new Black convicts had skills conveniently fit for agricultural work, and legislators were comfortable with purchasing former plantations.[66] Louisiana's profit motive stayed alive in the desire for institutional self-sufficiency amidst rising racial tensions.

On March 27, 1901, the Board of the Central Louisiana State Penitentiary purchased four plantations on which Samuel L. James had worked his leased prisoners.[67] The collective property became the Louisiana State Penitentiary.

Though it was nominally a penitentiary, it combined a penitentiary with a plantation and outlawry. The Prison Reform Administration revived goals of creating an actual rehabilitative system in the wake of the lease system. But the governor and other state officials conceived of using prison labor as a state income source. The legislature refused to budget for operations, forcing a mission of self-sustenance on the rich soil cornered by a bend in the Mississippi River.[68] Since then, there has been a perennial issue of not having funds to implement reforms and improvements.[69] Austerity and legacy contributed to a convoluted mission.

Designated as a "penitentiary," the new prison held at least a promise of Edward Livingston's design for redemptive criminal justice. Nonetheless, its continued moniker "Angola," the name of one of the four plantations, is a living reminder of the prison's roots in slavery. Continuities with the nineteenth century remained. The physician who had worked for James became chief warden.[70] The state designated James's son to be the plantation manager. James's estate executor became chairman of the penitentiary board.[71] Despite the continuity with the James era, the new prison was a shift—a major state purchase toward a modern institution. The institution of slavery is indeed a tributary, but Angola is not simply an extension of slavery. The Southern penitentiary was understood to be a less brutal alternative to the convict-lease system—a project of reform.[72] And at the cost of $300,000 in taxpayer dollars, the modern project drew broad public interest.

In the summer of 1901, seven months after the purchase, the Board of Control boarded a steamboat to travel up the Mississippi River and survey the new prison. Guests and members of the press accompanied them up a busy trade waterway. They passed Baton Rouge, where White prisoners would have disembarked. As they later put in their report, "being accustomed to work in the fields," Black prisoners came to Angola while White prisoners went to the still active penitentiary in Baton Rouge to perform "skilled" production of clothing and shoes.[73] Raw materials from Angola flowed back down the Mississippi River to be part of developing global trade. Wood sent down to New Orleans, for instance, was exported to Germany to make toys and champagne boxes (see figure 1.1).[74] Upon arrival at the new prison, the Board of Control and guests spent two days investigating operations and conditions.

With a mix of matter-of-fact reportage, quantitative data, and nostalgic accounts of music produced by the prisoners, the Board of Control concluded that "Louisiana can be said to lead every state in the Union in the scientific and humane treatment of her penal labor."[75] Mortality had dropped from

Figure 1.1. Angola landing on the Mississippi River, ca. 1900–1910. Detroit Publishing Company photograph collection, Library of Congress Prints and Photographs Division, Washington DC. LC-D4-34337.

9.6 percent to 2.6 percent. The Board reported that prisoners received thirty to sixty minutes of time off for accomplishing a certain amount of work: "For this time off the average negro will work with a will and get through twice as much work as he would if he were made to complete the 'day.'"

The changes in labor routine have the mark of the nationally emerging "scientific management" later codified by Pennsylvania mechanical engineer Frederick Winslow Taylor with his *The Principles of Scientific Management* in 1911.[76] At Angola, a new method of extracting labor from a workforce sprang from analyzing workflows and asserting greater managerial control. Field bosses didn't need music to coordinate labor (see figure 1.2). The whip and the stopwatch were more effective. Decades later, folklorists arriving at Angola failed to find the kinds of work songs that they had heard in Mississippi and Texas prison farms.[77] It's possible that the modern practice of what would later become "scientific management" silenced work songs to make way for systematic workflows of prisoner labor—regulating routines of work under threat of corporal punishment.

30 INSTRUMENT OF THE STATE

Figure 1.2. Picking cotton, Angola State Farm, 1901. Henry L. Fuqua Jr., Lytle Photograph Collection and Papers, Mss. 1898, Louisiana and Lower Mississippi Valley Collections, LSU Libraries, Baton Rouge, LA. 1898_016.

As the Board described in their report, Angola was a constellation of work camps.[78] Administrators classified newcomers by their labor potential, assigned them suitable jobs, and sent them to a corresponding camp at Angola (see figure 1.3).[79] The camps organized work and created opportunities for stoking competition among groups. The Board praised humane reform. Living conditions seemed favorable to convict-lease arrangements (see figure 1.4). With a paternalistic tone, they mused that the prisoners were not accustomed to such good treatment, citing state-provided nightshirts, clean facilities, and regular food. Music was part of their evidence.

As with earlier plantation accounts of music indicating well-being, the board described a typical end of the day:

> After work hours they have plenty of liberty, and after night fall[,] the plunk of banjos, the twang of guitars and the mellow notes of negro voices come floating over the fields from the Quarters, musical and sweet. The singing ceases the dancing begins and the thump of feet and patting of hands denote that the dancers are pounding out the double shuffle, "railroadin," "gwyne ter N'aw'leens," cutting the "pidgin wing," "pass-a-ma-la," "Mobile,"

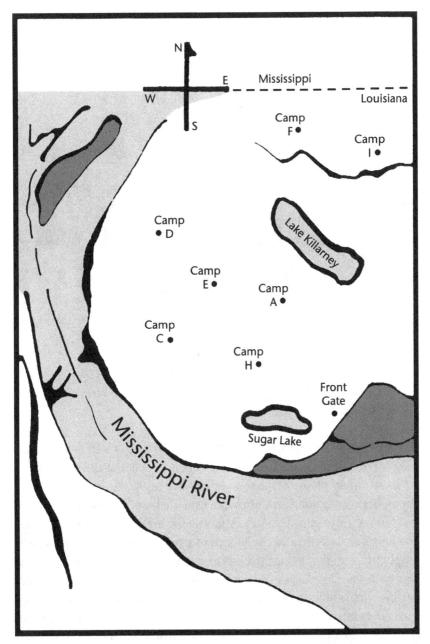

Figure 1.3. Map of Angola Camps (illustration by William Livingston).

Figure 1.4. Quarters A, Angola State Farm, 1901, from Andrew D. Lytle's Baton Rouge Photograph Collection (LSU Special Collections).

and a hundred and one fancy steps known only to the gentleman of color when he gets in a weaving way.[80]

It's important to note that the ear-witnessed evidence of well-being is from afar, that the commentators are hearing not only music but also distance.

The "floating" nature of the sound described in the report is likely due to atmospheric inversion, a shift in air density that creates channels of sound that carry at surprising distances. Atmospheric inversion occurs twice a day. You may have experienced the sounds of a train or a bell from afar in evening hours, sounds making their way to you from a remarkable distance. You hear both sound and space. As ethnomusicologist Martin Daughtry argues, nearby sounds differ from distant sounds. Nearby sounds entangle the listener. They often prompt a reaction and, if they are human sounds, prompt empathy. Distant sounds present an ethical distance.[81] Distant sounds, in what Daughtry calls the "narrative zone," bring ethical deafness, a psychoacoustic erasure.[82] The Board's description of songs floating over the fields presents a sound portrait at an ethical distance. Up close, the same music may have helped prisoners connect to home, provided a temporary escape, and committed stories and feelings to memorable lyrics. At a distance, music astonished the Board and those who read their report, fitting into a narrative that prison innovations were working and Black prisoners were in their natural state.

On the final evening, members of the Board of Control and their guests gathered for the new prison's distinctive hospitality. As described in the report:

> The night before the party left[,] the negroes on the place came up front to the big house and entertained the guests with a serenade, singing and dancing. Three guitarists made music that is not known in the classical folios, but the exquisite touch and perfect time told stor[i]es that Paderewski, Gilmore, Brooke and Sousa and a few other effete masters were not masters of. The melody of the rich toned voices of the sextette which stood just outside the front stoop rose and fell in old plantation songs and in the quicker and inexplicable negro chants—not ragtime, but something akin and far more musical. The dancing negroes were best, however, and then one, tall, lanky, long-necked awkward darkey, who was black as the Hat of Hades and "nigger" all over, jumped out into the middle of the piazza and did the "buzzard dance," he held his spectators in convulsions of mirth while he went through his unctions and absurd contortions.[83]

Musical accounts of prison forged lasting representations of prisoners. I quote extensively above and will quote more below to give a sense of the wording and tone. It is remarkable that in the original ten-page report on the new prison, two whole pages focus on music.

The description of the dance is as if it were from colonial-era travel literature, laden with authority and measured cultural distance describing the significance of a relatively contemporary American dance. The Buzzard Lope was not considered folkloric or even that old at the time. It was trendy entertainment, a routine that an emerging professional class of musicians might present. In 1901, the very distinction between professional "minstrel" and amateur "folkloric" forms of music was only beginning to emerge, the latter form marked by its purity and authenticity.[84] The Buzzard Dance was as contemporary as TikTok dance challenges are as of the writing of this book, having swept through American concert stages in the 1890s and inspiring clubs dedicated to teaching the dance.[85] It was a national minstrel hit usually performed by local musicians—typical of American musical life at the turn of the century. As described in the report:

34 INSTRUMENT OF THE STATE

> The "buzzard dance" be it know [sic], is a true delineation of the actions of a turkey buzzard when he cites carrion in the field. The buzzard is an errant coward and is extremely charry about approaching a carcass lying in a field until he knows it is dead. He will step up cautiously and, with his head to one side, star[e] at the carcass and then hop back in fright at his own temerity. This, he will keep up for a while and if the wind but ruffles the hair of the carcass he will go away for a while. After so long a time, the carcass not moving, he will step nearer and nearer and take a peak [sic], then hop back. Eventually he will get to work on the carcass.[86]

The need for such a detailed description in the Board of Control report is baffling. Together with the photograph "Fun in levee camp, Atchafalaya River" (see figure 1.5) that accompanied the *Biennial Report*, documentation of prison music helped astonish people who reviewed the state's investment in incarceration.

The photograph was part of a larger documentary project on Louisiana's prison system, contracted by the state to offer more evidence of supposedly content prisoners. The staged photo is not of the Buzzard Dance. Neither is it a candid representation of off-hours prisoner life. Nonetheless, its inclusion in the report uses music as evidence of successful prison management. By state accounts, the Louisiana State Penitentiary was a Janus-faced institution that resembled both a nostalgic plantation order and modern approaches to agricultural labor. These depictions are not folklore but rather astonishing "good fun," gleaned from an ethical distance.

The end of the report gets to what, to me, is the key to understanding music at Angola, evidence of something else, probably unintended: musical labor embedded in a capitalist and moral economy of prison. The report describes the delivery of what seems to be a practiced musician leveraging racial difference and convict status.

> The long-necked negro who did the buzzard dance for the party knew his business; placing his slouchy hat on the floor to represent the carrion, he held his hands up, with his elbows to his sides to indicate wings and commenced dancing. He danced around the hat, to it, from it, over it and each time he would get nearer and would hop back with a look of grotesque fright on his face. Another negro would move the hat in time with the music every now and then. The dance was highly amusing and as the dancers were dancing "over coin," they and the musicians and singers picked up several

Figure 1.5. "Fun in levee camp, Atchafalaya River," from Andrew D. Lytle's Baton Rouge Photograph Collection (LSU Special Collections).

dollars in small change. The life of a convict may be a hard one, but there was little evidence of it at Angola.[87]

What strikes me about this account is how musicians incarcerated at Angola have continued to use their professional skills to gain attention and forge connections with outsiders. The 1901 report reveals how the state and its prisoners engaged a curious public with music.

That December, the first cotton harvest at the new penitentiary at Angola was the best since 1896. The news made the papers.[88] Angola held a holiday for prisoners with games and music, marking the ginning of 1,895 500-pound bales of cotton. The Board of Control sent apples, oranges, and candy.

The first decades of the Louisiana State Penitentiary kept violence and austerity out of sight and earshot. Newspaper articles gave periodic financial reports, citing profits and providing accompanying data on harvest yields as well as assuring humane treatment of an increasing prison population.[89] Intercamp end-of-harvest festivals, what Dennis Childs aptly calls "plantation holidays," developed into regular seasonal music events at the prison for decades to come.[90]

Religious practice was another place for music. At the outset, Chaplain John L. Sutton took up residence and immediately took donations of secondhand organs and other instruments for services.[91] Not all the church music, however, was directed by the chaplain. Stella Johns heard singing entirely unfamiliar to her in the services her husband, the Reverend Henry Johns, led at Angola from 1908 to 1928. She recalls services at a female prisoner's funeral when a Black prisoner stepped in as preacher.

> Singing in any of the camps is ever interesting because everyone sings. The women have a very unique way of having a leader who chants the words, then they all sing a refrain. As their emotions rise, they clap their hands and pat their feet. Then here and there someone says, "De Lawd done lay his hand on Sis Jenny." "Sis Jenny done gone to meet de Lawd!" As the preacher raised his hand, to indicate that he was ready to begin his talk [he] was a bit more subdued but it never subsided. They continued to sway and moan and answer back almost every sentence he uttered. He told how we're born to die, how the good Lawd done die for us; how he's goin come some day and call us. With that, he walked up to the coffin, tapped on it and said, "The Lawd going to say 'Sister Jenny, come forth!'" Two of the women rose to their feet, their arms outstretched and fists tightly clenched. "Good God Almighty have mercy on us!" They said and fell prostrate on the ground.[92]

Visitors to the prison in these early years also heard the women sing. During a 1912 visit, Mrs. Maude Ballington Booth and company heard women sing in a fashion described by New Orleans' *Daily Picayune* newspaper: "A distinct feature was the singing of the negro women. One woman was the leader and in a clear and penetrating voice, she would line out a verse of the hymn and the women would sing out a line in a chorus."[93]

Despite initial positive reports that occasionally included musical evidence of pleasure and difference, recurring crises and calamities constantly threw the Louisiana State Penitentiary back into a negative light. As a public institution, the state—not the earlier lessees—assumed risk and incurred significant debts. Major floods in 1903 and 1912 hindered the central goals of prisoner custody and financial solvency. In 1910, the boll weevil destroyed the cotton crop, and the state began shifting toward raising sugar cane. In 1917, Warden Henry L. Fuqua controversially laid off most guards in an attempt to save money, moving security responsibilities to armed prisoners.[94] Under the "trusty" system, as it became known, prisoners earned enough trust to be appointed to coveted jobs with less susceptibility to the violence of outlawry and hard work in the fields. In 1921, an expensive sugar mill was built, raising the stakes for Angola's financial solvency. In the 1920s, Louisiana reinstituted chain gangs because the automobile industry needed roads Southern states could not afford.[95] In 1922 and 1927, Angola suffered additional flooding. In 1928, Governor Huey P. Long announced the burden of the penitentiary was costing taxpayers $1 million per year when it should be self-supporting. As governor, he disciplined the prison, ordering a return to abandoned wide-striped black and white uniforms.[96] The Great Depression compounded the economic chaos wrought by ruined crops.

Austerity and discipline marked Angola through the first half of the twentieth century, but accounts of music still made the news. Music punctuated harvests and holidays. The *State Times* covered the Christmas celebration of 1925, reporting on state donations of food and tobacco and a suspension of work at noon on Christmas Eve. The next day was full of music. Angola's top band played on the yard. A radio broadcast Christmas carols and contemporary songs as camp cooks prepared a feast. It made for "good news" reporting that echoed the 1901 Board of Control report: "The prisoners will fare better in most instances on Christmas than if they were free in the matter of gifts and good things to eat."[97]

By the 1930s, Angola had increased visibility. The public was more invested in the issues and Angola's astonishing outward-facing musicality. For prisoners, music likely offered relief and religiosity in off-hours and coveted trusty prisoner jobs. While we have few detailed records of the early musical practices, we have enough evidence to claim various musical practices, including organized church music and a notable jazz band, all functioning within the penitentiary, plantation, and outlawry.[98]

Enter Lomax and Lead Belly

In 1933, an encounter between a folklorist and a prisoner, both interested in music, profoundly affected how Americans came to listen differently to prison music as a distinct type of folk music. The influence of this new way of listening was indelible. The folklorist John Lomax recounts meeting an exemplary musician at Angola:

> We found a Negro convict so skillful with his guitar and his strong baritone voice that he had been made a "trusty" and kept around Camp A headquarters as laundryman, so as to be near at hand to sing and play for visitors. Huddie Ledbetter—called by his companions Lead Belly—was unique in knowing a very large number of songs, all of which he sang effectively while he twanged his twelve-string guitar.[99]

Twenty years Lead Belly's elder, Lomax had expanded his own interest in collecting cowboy songs to American folk music in general.[100] In fact, Lomax was in the process of defining what we now know as "American folk music." Lead Belly was trying to survive the Jim Crow South and make a living with music he learned and adapted to his constantly changing situations.

Lead Belly was a migrant laborer, balancing intermittent agricultural and musical work before getting sent to Angola in 1930 for attempted murder. He had learned to play guitar from his uncles. He had amassed an extensive repertoire of songs, catering to a variety of audiences in Louisiana and Texas.[101] Lead Belly was always learning songs, even while serving time in Texas prisons. By the time he came to Angola, he had developed a powerful singing voice, rhythmic guitar style, consistent musicality, and breadth of repertoire. He knew ballads, barrelhouse, jazz, ragtime, blues, hollers, religious songs, square dances, sooky jumps, topical songs, protest songs, and work songs.

On the one hand, Lead Belly was a consummate entertainer. On the other hand, he, like his contemporary Ma Rainey, the mother of the blues, was engaged in what Nicole Furlonge calls "sonic literacy" with an emerging Black "listenership."[102] Furlonge suggests that performers like Lead Belly had a commitment to a certain kind of embodied listening, tuning their ears to suffering, delight, and triumph and then creating multimodal expressive performances that brought a suffering community together.[103] In other words, Lead Belly could convey powerful and relevant experiences in song to multiple audiences. Furlonge's insight is that they also cultivated a type of aural literacy in their audiences, developing a way of listening for a communal experience. I suspect that Lomax did more than collect Lead Belly's songs. He learned new ways of listening at a time when prison grew in American life and imagination.

The Great Depression had boosted incarceration rates nationally. Policymakers responded to social problems by investing in prisons. From 1925 to 1939, the national incarceration rate climbed from seventy-nine per 100,000 residents to 137 per 100,000. In the first half of the 1930s, Black incarceration rates about tripled those for Whites, as White incarceration rates dipped.[104]

In Louisiana, Governor Huey Long dominated state politics, and his prison system was in shambles. Long and his political followers had pushed Angola back toward pre-1901 conditions. Long loathed spending any money on prisons. Instead, he continued to encourage the well-established policy of prison self-sustenance. Work in the fields began before sunrise and finished after sundown. A handful of prisoners had enough money for a fan and a radio to distract them from grueling life on the farm, but most were poor.[105] Prison records show that between 1928 and 1940, guards admitted to 10,000 floggings.[106] Some prisoners sustained fifty lashes each.

Long appointed R. L. "Tighty" Himes to head the penal system and demanded 100 percent efficiency.[107] During Himes's appointment, an average of forty-one inmates died annually.[108] Austerity resulted in the highest rate of death since 1901. Corruption grew rampant. Money earmarked for feeding prisoners was diverted and food budgets shrunk as small as possible—grits, greens, sweet potatoes, and black strap molasses. Between 1931 and 1936, 194 convicts escaped. The response to escapes was disorganized.[109] While the camps had surveillance, no guard towers lined the levee around Angola. Some died in the strong currents of the Mississippi River, attempting to swim to the other shore. Amidst the tumult, state support for reform or rehabilitation aims took a backseat. A few educational programs, still highly touted, made do with the lack of support.[110]

Within months of his 1930 arrival, Lead Belly worked his way out of the fields to trusty jobs—a waiter in Camp F, a tailor at Road Camp 5, and then at the laundry.[111] When off work on Sundays, he entertained fellow prisoners. Soon he caught the ear of the administration and became an in-demand camp entertainer.[112] Lead Belly developed his reputation as Angola was developing its own reputation as a particularly musical institution. At forty-five years old, Lead Belly was older than most other prisoners. His experience, maturity, and musical ability cemented his status as a trusty prisoner, not as an armed guard but at hand for entertaining guests.[113]

On Sunday, July 16, 1933, John Lomax and his eighteen-year-old son Alan visited. Angola was one stop on a larger mission. He had received unpaid sponsorship from the Library of Congress, a contract with Macmillan Publishers, and a state-of-the-art, three-hundred-fifteen-pound acetate phonograph disk recorder newly developed by Walter C. Garwick and custom installed into the back of his station wagon. The frontier myth reconfigured—horse turned Ford sedan, and lasso turned phonograph recorder—the Lomaxes set out on their tour through the American South to find remnants of a musical past in song. For the sixty-five-year-old Texan, the expedition fit a romantic imaginary. As Richard Slotkin argues, the cowboy myth posits a lone figure moving between high and low classes with ease—courting the banker's daughter while sharing food with the Indians and winning card games with outlaws in the saloon.[114] Lomax's decision to go to Southern prisons was the most extreme act of academic cowboy-ing that he could imagine. He flung his Harvard education into the worst prison system in the country, a place of the outlaw where the poorest of the poor hit rock bottom.

The 1920s and 30s had seen a growth in consumer media technology, and Lomax was both inspired and horrified by the changes the phonograph was bringing to American culture. His mission was genealogical, seeking connections to older plantation songs and, in turn, African work songs.[115] He and Alan searched for music untouched by the church or the popular music industry. Many of these "pure" songs, he thought, might still be behind prison walls, safely away from corrupting modern technologies. Prison loomed large in Lomax's imagination. As Lomax biographer John Szwed explains, he "had grown up hearing stories of men who were broken by heat and dehydration and the dusk-to-dawn work of the prison farms, or who had simply disappeared, lost in the system, incarcerated, 'under the jail.'"[116] He asked prisoners and administrators for "made-up songs," "reels," "jump-ups," and "sinful songs."[117]

Prison farms run by Southern states resembled old ways of life to Lomax. Angola seemed to be an extreme relic of antebellum life.[118] Austerity, outlawry, and distinctive Southern music combined in a promising way. But when he and Alan arrived at Angola, he found that he had to do some additional filtering. The prison walls had not done the work of fending off contemporary pop culture. There was a lot of popular music there, including a well-rehearsed jazz band led by an "influential Italian bartender."[119] They also found none of the work songs they had discovered in Texas and Mississippi institutions. Officials told them that they had ended singing in the fields.[120] "We were in some measure disappointed," Alan would later report. "The officials of the Louisiana prison in their wisdom had decided, all history to the contrary, that Negroes work better when they are not singing. Lead Belly, however, was some consolation."[121] Their goal for collection shifted to singers, and Angola was ready to provide them.

They drove their station wagon through the fields and parked at Camp A. It was a drizzly afternoon. It was because of Sunday—not the weather—that no one was working. Lead Belly met them and presented a selection of the hundreds of songs he had collected over the years. While they all shared a deep interest in collecting songs, John Lomax's phonograph set him apart in many ways. For Lomax, field recording was a new way of collecting folk music, one that provided a more direct connection between a singer and a listener.[122] Lomax championed the technology's transparency, not its selectivity, calling his recordings "sound photographs."[123] It is worth a moment to question Lomax's claim.

Like the accounts of music floating over the fields at night, the phonograph created an ethical distance between the singer and listener. Sound recordings and photographs present what we cannot hear and what we cannot see differently. A picture has a frame. We know that we can't see around it. Field recordings have a less discernible border between audible and inaudible—a gradient horizon rather than a clear and noticeable edge.[124] It is harder to know what we cannot hear in a sound recording.

Furthermore, Lomax's recordings partially captured the multimodal experience of live performance and "sonic literacy" projects that Lead Belly informally developed. Recordings filtered out gestures, body sensations, space, interruptions, smells, and audience interaction. Nonetheless, the distinctive voices emanating from the grooves of a phonograph record had a fidelity that sheet music did not.[125] And because its inaudibility was hard to discern, the recordings gave Lomax's audience a sense of having captured the whole piece. Lomax warns of written transcriptions: "Worse than thieves are ballad collectors," he states in the introduction to one of his collections, "for when they capture and imprison in cold type a folk song, at the same time they kill it."[126] By contrast, sound recordings have verisimilitude. They feel more representative than a page in a songbook. The authority of phonograph recordings helped define Lomax as a "professional" folklorist and present his recordings as truth.

Lomax's work was part of a more significant professional documentary trend of the 1930s born from a concern that news media manipulated their audience.[127] Not only did the phonograph allow the production of voices, but it was a seemingly neutral, clinical way of collecting songs. Leaning on the authority of the technology, Lomax went as far as to tout his own lack of musical ability as a qualification for collecting "pure" representations of Black music. In his words,

I am innocent of musical knowledge, entirely without musical training. Before starting on the trip, I was impressed with a cautioning word from Mr. Engel, chief of the Music Division [of the Library of Congress]: "Don't take any musician along with you," said he; "what the Library wants is the machine's record of Negro singing and not some musician's interpretation of it; nor do we wish any musician about, to tell the Negroes how they ought to sing." The one hundred and fifty new tunes that we brought to the Library at the end of the summer are, therefore, in a very true sense, sound-photographs of Negro songs, rendered in their own native element, unrestrained, uninfluenced, and undirected by anyone who had his own notions of how the songs should be rendered.[128]

The statement may be striking to a contemporary musicologist. But at the time, there was no real precedent for making recordings of American folk music for study and archiving. Early folklorists like Lomax were figuring out how to listen as a folklorist. They distinguished themselves as professionals by listening with a sense of rationalism that used cutting-edge technologies. At the dawn of many professions, practitioners separated themselves from ordinary people by developing specialized ways of listening—think of stethoscopes connected to the ears of medical professionals.[129] Simultaneously nostalgic and modern, Lomax's recordings had the stamp of folkloric authority.

Among the singers that Angola administrators had brought them, Lead Belly was the standout. John and Alan Lomax recorded dozens of songs from Lead Belly. Technical problems with the new recorder marred their 1933 recordings, so they returned a year later for more songs. The product of that encounter was more than an archive of songs. The meeting produced a new way of listening because of what Lead Belly sang and the technology Lomax brought in the trunk of his sedan. The presumed clinical nature of phonograph recording produced a new disposition, a habit of listening to prison music as expressive, tied to the performer's experience. The uncanny listening experience, seemingly direct while being inherently distant, no longer served sonic literacy and was no longer an embodied experience. It represented difference.

When I spoke to Anna Lomax Wood, Alan's daughter, many decades after the Lomaxes' encounter with Lead Belly, I asked her why her father never returned to Angola to collect songs. After all, he famously recorded prisoners at Mississippi's Parchman Farm in the late 1940s and 1959. Anna explained to me that Alan had been too disturbed by what he had seen.[130] Nonetheless, it was these recordings that helped define "prison music."

Curating "Prison Music"

John Lomax's Lead Belly recordings gained national prominence for two complementary reasons: increasing *public interest* in prisons and (in partnership with the growing mediascape of the United States) *shifting labor roles* away from manual labor toward cultural labor. Put simply, Americans were interested, and prisoners had new performance opportunities. Lead Belly's songs became part of a general fascination with prisoners that offered direct testimony and appeals as outsiders. At the same time, the recordings represented only a sliver of the musical life at Angola, defined by Lomax as authentic.

Summarizing his findings to the Library of Congress in a 1934 report, Lomax drew lines around what he called "prison music." He acknowledged Angola's practice of providing Black entertainers for White visitors, distinguishing between urban and itinerant musicians, preferring the collected songs from the latter. He described a Black musical purity that, in his words, grew "in the eddies of human society, particularly where there is isolation and homogeneity of thought and experience." He went on to claim, "These communities of Negro men and women, shut out from the clamor of the world, thrown back almost entirely on their own resources for entertainment, lonely, few with any background of reading, naturally resort to song."[131] In romanticized outlawry, Lomax had discovered American culture worth preserving for music students and sociologists. Thus, Lomax identified a community of convicts—isolated from mainstream America and thus separated from the "unnatural" influence of mass culture.

Lomax knew that the prison was only so effective at keeping out mass culture. He fully understood the grey area between what he called "folk" and "popular." For his 1936 collection of Lead Belly songs, Lomax carves out a selection of songs from Lead Belly's repertoire: "From Lead Belly we secured about one hundred songs that seemed 'folky,'" he states in the introduction, acknowledging that "he knew many more of the popular sort, current presently or was in other years." This unusual mass of folk songs amid his popular repertoire, according to Lomax, was incidental. "His eleven years of confinement had cut him off both from the phonograph and from the radio."[132] But this was not true. Lead Belly had been out of prison between 1925 and 1930, during the first commercial boom of the phonograph. But the book's primary aim was to define folk music, not accurately document Lead Belly's musical life. Lomax wrestles with the definition throughout the introduction:

> We present this set of songs, therefore, not as folk songs entirely, but as a cross-section of Afro-American songs that have influenced and have been influenced by popular music; and we present this singer, not as a folk singer handing on a tradition faithfully, but as a folk artist who contributes to the tradition, and a musician of a sort important in the growth of American popular music.[133]

In this statement is a promise of purity and a danger of contamination.

Lomax found Lead Belly valuable not because he himself was "authentic" but because he could select from a vast pre-existing repertoire. He explains, citing musicologist George Herzog:

> Lead Belly, according to Dr. George Herzog of Columbia University, has inherited the large bulk of his song material. "More than half of these melodies and texts have been published in other collections, in some other version. Others are of white parentage, some are white tunes pure and simple." But since Lead Belly learned them all from hearing other people sing them, and practiced most of them for years in isolated penitentiaries, we may feel pretty sure that his tunes are not precisely like other versions.[134]

In fact, Lead Belly was as much a song collector as Lomax. But they differ in their approach and their positionality. Lead Belly's strategy was to cast a wide net for various audiences. Lomax's strategy was to be selective, fulfilling his role as a professional folklorist and also appealing to the public interest.[135] Lomax authoritatively positioned Lead Belly as his subject.

In his book on Lead Belly's songs, Lomax describes him as a character who, as Benjamin Filene argues, transgresses boundaries but does not obliterate them, fitting an idea of an American spirit to the iconic image of the outlaw.[136] Outlawry, a tributary to Angola, becomes part of the musical representation of prison, adding to murder ballads and other folksongs that romanticize the outlaw living in the "eddies of human society."

Nationally, a broader interest in prisons amplified Lomax's filtered representation of prison music. Bookending Lomax's recordings and songbooks, prison images and sounds flooded through movie theaters and radios, satisfying a fascination with the closed-off world of the prison—then less of a marvel than the penitentiary was 100 years earlier. Film historian Bruce Crowther identifies the early prison film subgenre as an offshoot of the Cagney/Bogart/Edward G. Robinson gangster film genre.[137] *The Big House* (1930) and *I Am a Fugitive from a Chain Gang!* (1932) are representative, both released on the heels of the infamous 1929 Auburn and Dannemora prison riots. The two films primed national audiences, likely including Lomax, for listening to Lead Belly as an outlaw.

Examining the early prison film genre, David Gonthier draws from Colin Wilson's literary definition of "the outsider" to describe the archetypal protagonist. This character, in his words, "cannot live in the comfortable, insulated world of the bourgeoisie accepting what he sees and touches as reality . . . what he sees is essentially chaos . . . he is an outsider because he stands for truth," he is a person "*awakened by chaos* [emphasis added]."[138] Gonthier generalizes the prison film narrative as a series of events that arise from an outsider-prisoner protagonist who looks for order and truth within the prison. But it is elusive because the prison is an "ideologically unstable contested space" only posing as order.[139] Redemptive themes emerge as the alienated prisoner looks inside himself and determines his own free will in search of utopia, a precursor to Jean-Paul Sartre's existential play, *No Exit*.[140]

Gonthier doesn't describe the music in the prison film genre, but I argue that music plays a narrative role that supports Gonthier's description of the prison film narrative. *The Big House* uses music as a counterpoint to the chaos. During a long take of a hallway lined with prison cells, Kent, the protagonist, settles in, out of sight. A song emerges from a singer unseen: Antonín Dvořák's well-known theme from the *New World Symphony*. The song itself alludes to spirituals. "Going home, going home . . ." cuts through the cruel and sinister banter, beginning to rise above the noise. But another prisoner summarily cuts off the baritone singer: "I wish you *would* go home!" Chaos and song battle in a place where outlawry masquerades as a penitentiary.

I Am a Fugitive from a Chain Gang! also uses music for narrative development, but more strongly as a racial signifier. After escaping, protagonist James Allen hides from the law in the nearby city. Jazz scores Allen's apprehensive walk downtown into a boarding house. W. C. Handy's "St. Louis Blues" might seem quaint today, but a contemporary remake of the film might substitute hip-hop to achieve the same effect of using Black music to signal criminality. After his recapture, Allen labors on a chain gang. The other prisoners sing

"Working All the Live-Long Day" to the rhythm of their hammers. The scene opens with a shot of a Black prisoner, hammer raised, belting out the song in a strong baritone (a register that would not carry well for an actual work song). These cinematic representations would give way to Lomax's folkloric definitions. Still, the film sets up "prison music" as something in search of truth and tied to Blackness, generally sung a capella, either alone or with a group of laborers. Soon enough, actual prisoners took over the actors' roles.

Changes in legal and penal philosophy shifted what prisoners did while incarcerated. Alongside continued hard labor, prisoners engaged in more cultural labor than before. The media followed the sounds of this work to actual prisons. Historian Ethan Blue argues that as a consequence of New Deal labor legislation restricting the use of physical labor in prisons, "prison radio meshed with other popular cultural forms, including baseball leagues, rodeos, literary magazines, and newspapers, to retrain prisoners in recreational activities appropriate to the welfare state and a Keynesian economy."[141] Incarcerated musicians became prospective knowledge workers. Fueled by an emerging mass media, a new racial category developed, one that John Dougan defines as a "convict/entertainer," a reinvigorated combination of two stereotypes of Black Americans that had developed in the first half of the twentieth century.[142]

Through the 1940s, radio programs fed public interest in imprisoned singers. In 1938, WBAP Radio in Fort Worth presented *Thirty Minutes Behind the Walls*, featuring musicians from the Huntsville Unit of the Texas State Prison. The show did more than entertain. It blurred the line between media and the prison, bringing potentially redemptive prisoners into living rooms across America. As Ethan Blue argues, the show "capitalized on the economy of mass media, and by stressing correction for select prisoners, was very much a product of the New Deal era's expanding reformist impulse." He continues, noting what I have called music's "astonishing" nature. "*Thirty Minutes*, after all, was entertainment, not torture. Yet its entertainment masked the violence that remained an intrinsic part of incarceration."[143]

San Quentin on the Air followed the success of the Texas program in the 1940s. *Time Magazine* described the unlikely variety from the notorious prison perched on the San Francisco Bay: a twenty-six-inmate glee club, a twenty-two-piece orchestra attempting Rachmaninoff, and vocals by prison songbirds. A quote from Warden Clinton Duffy stressed the importance of music "to help the prisoners in society when they are released."[144] Unmentioned is the influence of composer Henry Cowell, who, during his four years incarcerated there, taught music lessons, led orchestras, and composed original music.[145] Media presented musicality as a natural state of the pained prisoner, a window into a redemptive soul. Acknowledging the institutions that Cowell had built would be to forgo romanticizing the outlaw and accept prison music as institutional and collaborative labor.

Within the media of the 1930s and 40s, Lomax's recordings remained a distinct and dominant sound of prison music, uniquely identifiable and seemingly pure in its racial difference. At the Louisiana State Penitentiary, life went on. Music continued in its many forms in the daily lives of all those confined there as prison music became a quasi-folkloric genre understood widely by national audiences.

After the 1934 trip, Lomax expanded his search across the country. But his selective definition of "prison music" got in his way. Inquiries typed underneath the Library of Congress letterhead shot out to every prison in the country. The response was meager.[146] The wording of his letter was likely to blame. In it, he asked for "songs or ballads current and popular among prisoners or 'made up' by them and passed around by 'word of mouth' rather than by the printed page." A few prison officials mentioned musical activity centered on rehabilitation but noted that it was perhaps outside the scope of the request. In other words, the letters confirm that there was music in 1930s American prisons, but none of that music made it into the Library of Congress archive. Musicologist Velia Ivanova insightfully suggests that, in effect, Lomax's letter made prison officials cocurators of the archive. Prison administrators' understanding of music informed the musical definition of "prison music" by not including more varied musical practices.[147] In essence, the state power of the Library of Congress and state prisons exercised a joint classificatory project. The details of this classification of prison music had a lasting effect.

Lomax turned his many folk recordings into books systematically filled with notated songs. Song classification was no easy task. But it was his way of building an authoritative account of American folk music of many distinct types. These kinds of categories, however, are mostly unstable. A Tin Pan Alley song, for instance, might be adapted to set the pace of unloading boxes at a train yard. Lomax signals this problem in his influential *American Ballads and Folk Songs* compendium, initially published in 1934, which neatly divides songs into categories: railroad songs, chain-gang songs, mountain songs, Creole songs, cocaine and whisky songs, to name a few. Lomax connected song style to song function to accommodate the fluid nature of folk song practice into a rational system, making prison music a distinct form, suiting the particular situation of being Black and incarcerated in a Southern prison farm. As H. Bruce Franklin would later claim, refining Lomax's classification, prison music was a tool for endurance, protecting individuals, and reframing work.[148]

Still, Lomax used stylistic elements. As literature and music scholar Erich Nunn summarizes, Lomax developed three conditions of authentic prison music: Southern in origin, sung unaccompanied, and unpredictable. The rural field holler was an ideal type.[149] Nunn argues that this static stylistic definition had a segregating effect.[150] Prison songs were distinct from popular and art music, an idealized, pure category of "folk" art developed in the wake of Lomax's publications. Lomax understood the stylistic difference as racially pure. His writing reflects ideals of romantic racialism that he likely adopted as a child in Texas, where a version of White supremacy grew out of Victorian assumptions that there were apparent differences between civilized and savage.[151] As Lomax describes his eventual findings, "the folk-songs of the Negro" are "songs that in musical phrasing and poetic content are most unlike those of the White race, the least contaminated by White influence or by the modern Negro jazz."[152]

As Lomax and Lead Belly's encounter turned into a relationship, Lead Belly also took part in representing prison music. He was released for good behavior, receiving one of six commutations signed by Governor O. K. Allen on July 20, 1934. Soon after, he contacted Lomax for employment.[153] Relocating to New York, the singer enjoyed considerable fame, some of his songs becoming staples of the American songbook. Lomax hired him as his driver and booked concerts around the country. Despite their prominent differences, their shared penchant for drinking kept them close, hitting up bars together during travel to and from shows and media appearances, all the while adding to their song collections (see figure 1.6).

In a way, Lead Belly continued his cultural labor after release. Lead Belly gave "prison music" a stronger connection to a redemptive outlaw archetype in live performance. As his benefactor, imagined patron, employer, collaborator, and friend, Lomax created an outlaw to articulate an outsider populism, a definition of American culture that eschewed material success.[154] Detailed accounts of an unquenchable sexual appetite, struggles with temptation, misogyny, attempted suicide, and eventual abandonment in prison gave concrete form to this idea.[155] By dramatizing the musician, Lomax claimed the authenticity of his songs of struggle. Subsequent studio recordings, for

Figure 1.6. Stills from "Leadbelly," in *March of Time*. 1, no. 2, March 8, 1935 (Library of Congress, American Folklife Center).

example, "Angola Blues (Get Up in the Morning So Doggone Soon)" (1935), offered a psychological peek into the psyche of a real convict. In a time before grants and fellowships, Lomax funded his scholarship by classifying and sensationalizing Lead Belly. An eager public listened to a particular kind of musical difference seemingly born from the outlawry of a Southern prison farm under the joint auspices of scholarship and entertainment. Lead Belly fought for payments within the complex revenue stream that flowed through Lomax.[156]

Alan Lomax would expand his father's work in different and impactful ways, inspiring even more people to pay attention to the importance of folk music and folk musicians. Intermittently, folklorists and musicologists continued to travel to prisons throughout the country over the next several decades to record and collect songs. Reasons for their interest varied, but most saw prison as a unique site of music-making as initially theorized by John Lomax.

If it weren't for the encounter between John Lomax and Lead Belly, I wouldn't have been interested in Angola. Their shadows loom over a defined category of "prison music." More broadly, their recordings and subsequent songbooks left an indelible mark. What they curated from Angola played a vital part in defining American folk music. I use the word "curated" to stress that jointly, their project was selective. While they ignored certain types of music at Angola, they contributed to the public image of the prison, along with popular music performed for guests, religious music, and jazz ensembles providing entertainment for plantation holidays, for instance. Lomax and Lead Belly gave Angola a distinctive sound and national attention. But not everyone was astonished.

Musicologist Carl Engel had been chief of the Music Division of the Library of Congress since 1922. In an issue of *The Musical Quarterly*, he tore into Lomax's suppositions and Lead Belly's talent. "Mr. Lomax entertains the belief," Engel writes, "that long confinement in prison cells keeps the singer of folk-songs from influences which tend to contaminate and pervert the 'folky' strains and thus rob these songs of their authenticity. We do not hold to this theory."[157] Engel distanced the sober mission of the Library of Congress from Lomax, criticizing him for sensationalizing prison music.

> It was not long before reporters and publicity-hounds got on the scent of a news-story that savored the sensational. A charming and modest university professor from Austin, Texas, was hoisted to the giddy pinnacle of Manhattan head-lines, hailed as the discoverer of a rank criminal who could sing tender blues as well as blood-curdling ballads.[158]

Engel's points stand. But rather than stopping at dismissing Lomax's work, I hope we can peer around the frame and tune into other senses of a musical encounter.

The prolonged encounter between John Lomax and Lead Belly dulled other senses of listening to music practices at the prison. The polyphony of Angola's complex history seemed to be monophony. This mishearing is the product of a folkloric listening disposition, encouraged by the authority of a relatively new folkloric discipline that selected and classified voices of an imaginary "pure" past. Granted, neither Lomax nor Lead Belly sought to define Angola's music but to collect songs, curate American folk music in general, and make a living doing so. Nonetheless, their encounter set the terms of authentic "prison music" through a type of astonishment: sensationalism. What did we miss when dulled by ideological presuppositions, the limits of recording technology, and racial stereotypes? What did we miss because Lomax was not astonished by the Italian bartender–led Angola jazz band? How do we get back on track toward understanding musical change at Angola, looking for history instead of heritage?

After Lomax and Lead Belly left, there were infamous prison breaks, violent killings, a slew of new wardens, and continued local media attention.[159] A Fourth of July festival began after prisoners loaded cantaloupes on trucks that took them to free world markets, returning to the prison yard to roast a goat that turned the noses of staff members.[160] Was there music that day? Fifteen years later, reformer and journalist Margaret Dixon wrote of the 1949 harvest: "[T]hey tell time by the calendar instead of by the clock. The cane crop this year brought in 10,534,000 pounds of sugar and most of the profit goes to the farm revolving fund. Three carloads a day are shipped and the time and energies of most of the 2000 or so prisoners as well as that of the authorities is devoted to the cane crop."[161] What kind of music accompanied the 1949 plantation holiday?

Expanding from the monophonic folkloric representations, imagine the roots of prison music entangled in the convoluted origin of the prison itself. The polyphony of prison sounds out from its structure: outlawry, the plantation, and the penitentiary. I find this approach—listening to prison—to be a more productive alternative to attending only to individual prisoners. The psychologizing tendency when listening to individuals often promises insight into artistic intent. But that tendency overlaps with what the American criminal justice system does to prisoners—it isolates and pathologizes. If prison formulates people as fundamentally individuals, perhaps thinking beyond the individual is where we might find collective resistance, augmentation, sanity, and continuity with the outside world.

Conclusion

The following chapters may be astonishing: incredible individual achievements amid brutal violence. But be wary of your astonishment. Keep it in sight but peer around it and ask: What enabled the musical encounter? What happened when people went back to their routines? Who capitalized on astonishment, and what were the consequences? Often, the answers lie in ordinary things.

I'll end by returning to Laird Veillon, who helped me shift from wondering why prisoners played music and got me thinking about how they created opportunities to play music. Veillon was the one who sat with me in the circle of folding chairs and was among Angola's most active musicians, the one who hoped that you might be astonished by all of this. Still preoccupied with the individual, perhaps under the spell of Lomax and Lead Belly, I asked him why he chose music. Veillon began his answer by telling me that someone had warned him against music in the beginning. Veillon was the only one I met who had learned to play *after* being incarcerated.

> The little guy that got me started playing let me know that it was like a drug. If I wasn't gonna be serious about it, just leave it alone, 'cause it was going to drive me the rest of my life. And that's basically what it's doing.... I can't

listen to the radio anymore because I'm analyzing everything. I'm not listening to the music, I'm copping licks, I'm studying in my head.[162]

I appreciate the addiction metaphor for its simplicity. There is plenty of testimony in the following pages of loftier motivations: "It makes me a better person." "We provide entertainment and relieve tension in the population." "We're good at setting up sound for events." "It brings me in touch with God." Most of the time, however, incarcerated musicians are motivated by what Veillon admitted—obsession, a commitment to doing it. Musicians make all kinds of excuses just to play. That, to me, reveals less about prisoners than it does the many ways prisons allow for music and how freedoms come from persuasive requests to make music together.

Musicians will occupy the spaces they can claim, taking advantage of any opportunity to play. As we will discover in the next chapter, the openings in 1950s Angola helped collaborative creativity roar into the prison—generating a history of music that shakes folkloric notions of "prison music" and establishing support for musicians for decades to come.

2
Association

Recordings from Angola in the 1950s offer a picture of folk roots—blues, work songs, and spirituals—a limited representation of the music that prisoners made there. These recordings are a poor soundtrack to the era. The years between 1952 and 1963 were years of reform under the leadership of a federally trained penologist trying to answer urgent public demands for change. A broader representation would place jazz at the center of musical life and in the eddies of reform efforts. Plotted through that decade of reform, Angola's musical practice changed too, gradually shifting from minstrel and hillbilly acts to dance-oriented bebop. These transitions, however, were not smooth. Angola was rife with obstacles and inequities. Contemporary jazz developed through abrupt interruptions and strides of regrowth as reform attempts met agricultural demands, entrenched racism, and political pressures.

The folk recordings from the late 1950s provide an entry point. We will start with documented individual tradition-bearers (independent folk singers) and then move on to midlevel prisoner associations (jazz combos). In contrast to the folkloric history of antiquated, rural African American styles, jazz musicians took advantage of unequal opportunities within new penitentiary logic. Outside factors also contributed—increasing drug convictions, increased urban representation among prisoners, and the remarkable efforts of several individual musicians. The music was a shift—not a departure—from existing prison practices. We will listen to the changing polyphony of the prison, hearing new consonances and dissonances of outlawry, slavery, and penance.

Avoid reading a story of progress. Placing prison reform in the near present and atrocities in the distant past obscures how prison continues fundamental violence in new forms and how reform efforts inherently wax and wane.[1] *Listening* to prison allows us to think differently, attending to uncertainty, crossfading, noise, fits and starts, polyphony, and counterpoint.

Instrument of the State. Benjamin J. Harbert, Oxford University Press. © Oxford University Press 2023.
DOI: 10.1093/oso/9780197517505.003.0003

Nonmusical elements undergird these musical changes, and it takes a bit of political theory to get at this.

Before continuing this history of music at Angola in the following chapters, let's ensure that we know how to adopt broader perspectives, keeping our astonishment in view but also seeing the mundane, the ordinary, but no less important aspects of musical life at Angola Prison. This wider position will allow us to consider how astonishment, in its laudatory sense, is a resource for both prisoners and administrators. It will also reveal astonishment in its cautionary sense, accounting for how we, as readers, might be affected by stories of freedom and constraint. It will show us that extraordinary efforts require long stretches of everyday maintenance before change to take hold.

Thinking Beyond the Individual

Recall Alexis de Tocqueville, the French chronicler mentioned in chapter 1, enamored by American penitentiaries (and horrified at the New Orleans Jail).[2] Tocqueville was also an influential observer of American democracy, commissioned by the French monarchy in 1831 to come to the United States. Published in 1835 and based on his nine months of travel, *Democracy in America* interrogates the principles of American democracy. In that work, he marvels at a distinctive American character—the propensity to collaborate, voluntary groups of Americans taking on problems. In his words here, he describes association as a unique and powerful national characteristic:

> If some obstacle blocks the public road halting the circulation of traffic, the neighbors at once form a deliberative body; this improvised assembly produces an executive authority which remedies the trouble before anyone has thought of the possibility of some previously constituted authority beyond that of those concerned. Where enjoyment is concerned, people associate to make festivities grander and more orderly. Finally, associations are formed to combat exclusively moral troubles: intemperance is fought in common. Public security, trade and industry, and morals and religion all provide the aims for associations in the United States.[3]

Association becomes the basis for Tocqueville's political theory: that Americans keep the reach of the government at bay through their own acts of spontaneous association.

Legal historian William Novak reconsiders Tocqueville's claim in a way that will help us think beyond the individual and toward Angola's music associations. Novak finds that American propensity for association is not part of a national character—an unbridled "will of the people," safeguarding the nation from government tyranny—but in the very structures of nineteenth-century law. That legal system, as he finds it, put voluntary association at its center. Laws transferred the power of the state to a variety of citizen associations. According to Novak, the American distinction Tocqueville found, the one that spontaneously formed to remove an obstacle from the road, was not in national character but in a legal system that enabled them to take action together. In Novak's words:

> Nineteenth-century legislators, judges, and commentators defended associations not as alternatives to a legal-constitutional state, but as constitutive components of it. Associations did not arise outside of and immune to coercions of public power as natural counterweights to the artificial sovereignty of the state. Rather they were in fact legally-constituted and politically-recognized delegations of rule-making authority and public resources. Associations often functioned in the nineteenth century as explicit technologies of public action—modes of accomplishing public objectives different from the Franco-Germanic leviathan, but no less essentially governmental. Early American associations were a mode of governance, resting upon an elaborate system of laws, powers, and discriminations.[4]

Legislative proceedings chartered an astounding array of associations—to name several types: academies, agricultural societies, aqueducts, banks, boroughs, bridges, burial grounds, canals, charitable associations, churches, cities, colleges, ecclesiastical societies, ferries, fire companies, fishing companies, governor's guards, highway districts, highways, hotel companies, insurance companies, library companies, manufacturing companies, markets, masonic lodges, mechanics societies, medical institutions, mining companies, monument societies, musical societies, navigation companies, powder house companies, railroad companies, religious associations, saving societies, school districts, school societies, schools, scientific associations, sewer companies, steam boat companies, theft-detecting societies, towns, turnpike companies, villages, and workhouses.[5] The list confounds contemporary sensibilities—blurring divisions between public and private, religious and state, commercial and nonprofit.

Several scholars have brought Novak's insight, now called "associationalism," to a more extended history of overlapping public and private political and economic activity. Highlights of their work get us within reach of twentieth-century Angola. Historian Brian Balogh brings the idea to the twentieth century, arguing that associationalism has made it easier for those suspicious of government involvement to become involved in government initiatives. He details "ways in which Americans have braided public and private actions, state and voluntary-sector institutions, to achieve collective goals without undermining citizens' essential belief in individual freedom."[6] Taking what he calls a "mezzo-level focus," in between the individual and the state, Balogh shows how the government continued to endow associations with intermediary roles, distributing public entitlements through private associations.[7] Political scientist Eldon Eisenach identifies what he calls "parastates," highlighting the importance of intersections between state and society.[8] In so doing, he shows how the state grants "stateness" to a variety of associations.[9]

Associationalism, alongside accounts of free Black mutual aid societies in nineteenth-century New Orleans, reveals additional ways associations and the state negotiate shared power and responsibilities. Fatima Shaik's history of New Orleans' Société d'Economie et d'Assistance Mutuelle, a venerable site of activism, political debate, civic aid, and music, describes one of many benevolent societies that were as political as they were social.[10] To move beyond thinking of the individual, envision a history of association between the state (whether enabling or coercive) and the individual, an account particular to New Orleans and general to the United States.

To varying degrees, prisoners suffered continued outlawry and the legacy of an idealized self-sufficient plantation. Associationalism is key to understanding collaboration at Angola—how musicians survived inescapable absences of state power at Angola. Powerful and independent wardens strategically, pragmatically, and sometimes unwittingly granted liberties to prisoners. In the 1950s, many liberties came in the name of rehabilitation, a descendant of penitentiary ideals. It's a clunky term, but "carceral associationalism" can help draw attention to how prisoners form groups, argue for change, provide administrative labor, and other forms of activity between the individual prisoner and the prison administration.

Carceral Associationalism

Associationalism reveals how groups of individuals negotiate shared power with the government through the legal entitlement of chartering, suretyship, bylaws, eminent domain, legal protection, and tax exemption. Association in the nineteenth century was the basis of a kind of citizenship—providing a suite of rights and responsibilities granted through an array of chartered associations.

Pivoting to twentieth-century Angola, prisoner clubs, which include but are not limited to officially designated bands, are granted control over membership, use of space, relative freedom of movement, budgets, and protection. In prison, these conditional freedoms might seem to be "privileges" developed as part of progressive reform in the 1890s.[11] And in a post–prisoners' rights era, courts make distinctions between rights and privileges. But before prisoners gained rights and access to courts, liberty came through negotiation—often in collaboration with other prisoners. The concept of privileges misses a critical insight—that the prison administration is never totalitarian, that prisons require a degree of cooperation with prisoners.[12]

Associationalism's insight—that seemingly spontaneous collaboration has roots in the laws and procedures that give power to people to associate—provides an essential window into musical activity. Associationalism reveals how music can be an integral part of associational life. Prisoners at Angola lose most rights and freedoms as a legal consequence of their conviction. Musicians gain back certain momentary liberties through working together.

Angola operates through remarkable prisoner cooperation, epitomized by the trusty system, to make up for the perennial absence of staff and continued austerity. Association maintains operation for the administration, but it also becomes a way to preserve what few rights prisoners can gain in prison. From the outside, many of these don't seem like extraordinary rights. But being able to have privacy through a closed-door rehearsal, raise money at a public event, choose colleagues, and even wear a T-shirt with your club's name—these are rights gained as much as they are revocable privileges.

Making music through official clubs seemed strange to me initially, an overly formal sanctioned means of coming together. I am used to more spontaneous musical partnerships, like forming bands with friends. At first, when I learned of the bureaucratic structure, I rationalized it as a technical necessity—a rigid prison administration accommodating musical needs as a privilege. But my perspective changed when I learned how African American benevolent societies do much more than parade during Mardi Gras. They also assist communities in ways that the state won't. They receive tax breaks, are allowed to fundraise, and offer dignity through collective action. My understanding of musical association was provincial. Add to that the narrow definition of prison music as a lone spontaneous individual singing expressively. "Prison music" was blinding me to music in prison. Slowly, but crucially, I began to see music as a way of establishing and maintaining rights collectively.

So much literature and so many media representations pit the prisoner against the jailers.[13] Prison is a metaphor for struggle. What's more, as the nation struggles to combat a social justice issue of mass incarceration, now acknowledged as a substantial part of structural racism in the United States, it is easy to privilege struggle and antagonism.[14] Music is a means to protest conditions of oppression in general and incarceration more specifically. There is plenty to acknowledge here. And I am not, by any means, arguing that prisoners *want* to be in prison. But I am suggesting that prison life includes antagonism *and* association in a way that is more nuanced than solely mapping those two modes to dissent and acquiescence. Many of Angola's reforms struggle to take hold, but the associations preserve these reforms, holding together rights and responsibilities despite austerity, violence, abandonment, indignity, and pain endemic to life at Angola.

Carceral associationalism describes the fraught political space between the state and an imprisoned individual. The constant negotiation of shared power in prison is the key to understanding the importance of musical activity and conditions for musical freedom. In other words, music highlights carceral associationalism. Because music coordinates human behavior, it offers a unique way of understanding a broader prison experience, one centered on negotiating rights, sharing time, and overcoming the atomizing effects of prison.

The broader interconnections with music—such as labor, bureaucracy, administrative operations—challenge an American tendency to romanticize music in prison as primarily a voice of freedom, protest, or redemption. The disturbing pains of the carceral system and inspiring voices rising to power are noteworthy, but they should not distract us from understanding the subtle workings of the prison. Yes, Angola can crush an individual. But it also is full of associations that work complexly, sometimes in service of an individual and sometimes not. Musicians there constantly negotiate institutional frameworks through volunteer prisoner clubs. By following the associations at Angola, the rest of this chapter will examine—as Novak did with Tocqueville—the structures that support and ultimately produce conditional collaborative freedoms. Music is astonishing, but it is also ordinary and woven into the most mundane and bureaucratic aspects of Louisiana State Penitentiary. That was something that folklorists missed.

Songs of the Gunmen

In 1957, a letter arrived at the Library of Congress in Washington, DC, addressed to Rae Korson, Head of the Archive of Folk Song. It was from thirty-three-year-old folklorist Harry Oster. The letter requested more audio tape to complete the recording of what Oster described as "representative examples of the major types of Negro folk singing now going on in Louisiana."[15] Based out of LSU's English department, Oster had already recorded twenty-five hours of regional talking blues and other types of local folk music. And thanks to John Lomax before him, prisons promised more folkloric music. Oster was not interested in institutional reform or the sociology of the prison. He was collecting cultural relics for study and safekeeping. With modest support from the Library of Congress and his university, Oster looked north to Angola.

A psychologist who had worked in prison referred Oster to the Louisiana Board of Institutions.[16] His request worked its way to Warden Maurice Sigler, who approved the project and put him in touch with the recreation department. Upon arrival, Oster listened to a Black choir sing spirituals and then asked members for leads on work songs, trying to get deeper into the prison to hear what he envisioned as prison music. The referrals took him to Camp A, where he found most of the musicians he recorded (see figure 2.1).[17]

In a professional folkloric manner, Oster distinguished "improvisers" from "verbatists." The older generation were improvisers. In the liner notes to *Southern Prison Blues*, Oster describes Guitar Welch by his age and his musicality simultaneously, saying that he "has the most archaic style."[18] Welch was sixty-three. Roosevelt Charles, another musician Oster documented, was a longtimer, having arrived at Angola in 1937. According to Oster, the improvised "talking blues" was a folk process—something rare, living within the older musicians.

Figure 2.1. Men singing for Harry Oster (photograph by Harry Oster, courtesy of the Arhoolie Foundation).

Prisoners in the camps unwittingly helped Oster define an ideal blues musician—one steeped in older, rural traditions. Oster's job was not to represent musical life there fully. It was a salvage mission. "Since most of the prisoners are in their early twenties," he wrote, "they are accustomed to getting their entertainment from radio, television, and motion pictures rather than from folk sources. . . . There is, however, a minority of older prisoners, who are still a rich potential source of folk songs, especially blues, and in much lesser degree spirituals, and still less group work songs."[19]

In Camp H, Oster set up a makeshift recording space in the tool shed. Musicians Robert Pete Williams, Hoagman Maxey, Roosevelt Charles, and Guitar Welch volunteered. As he recalls: "The authorities would assign me a room and I found enough work song material to do a record. I had to stage it in [the] sense of putting them together."[20] Searching for the tradition that barely existed, Oster looked in unlikely places and developed appropriate recording strategies. Oster reported,

> I recorded some unusual things such as men singing while operating a stamping machine which makes kinda musical sound. I also visited the women's section of the prison. I heard there were women singing as they

were working on sewing machines. I included a couple of tracks of a woman singing as she works.[21]

On the back of one of the several LPs he produced, Oster acknowledged that reforms were changing prisoners' conditions, but, for the sake of establishing continuity with the past, he stressed lingering problems: "Although conditions at Angola . . . have been improved in recent years, the dominant feelings remain largely the same; wherever Negroes suffer injustice, frustration, and loneliness, there is a need for blues like these."[22]

Oster's recordings astonish in both the laudatory and cautionary sense—they are exceptional and distracting. Robert Pete Williams's song "Louise" is hauntingly sublime, with birds audible in the background. Song and microphone work together to create a whole world out of the guitar's detuned resonance—like when the sustain pedal on a piano lets all strings vibrate freely. The song mostly, but not totally, masks the distant environmental sounds of the farm. In a cautionary sense, I wonder what else sounded in the acoustic horizon, inaudible to a folklorist.

Oster knew about other music, but he was interested in the music of poverty and dejection. In his liner notes, he wrote:

> Among the 3800 convicts in the desolate flatland of the prison farm at Angola, Louisiana, there was a surprising number of talented performers, most of whom did not have musical instruments. The authorities did their best with the limited funds at their disposal to encourage musical activity; they supplied two progressive jazz ensembles, two hillbilly bands, and a rock-and-roll band with instruments; they arranged rehearsals and performances of two choirs and several vocal quartets. The few other instruments available were in demand among the hundreds of convicts hungry for harmonicas, guitars, fiddles, trumpets, etc.[23]

But he didn't record them. The only outlier to blues, spirituals, and work songs is a single track on *Southern Prison Blues* by an unnamed rock 'n' roll group. And in the liner notes, Oster encourages listening to their music as folk music. "Although the underlying beat and the general style of the band belong to rock-and-roll," he writes, "the warm sincerity and restraint of the singer, also the sensitively moaning lead saxophone are testimony to the continuing vitality of the Negro blues tradition."[24] He leaves out the innovation and the possibility that prisoners might want to listen to the newness of the sounds.

Oster was of his time. The study of music was just beginning to draw from the social sciences. He researched like his contemporaries: understanding songs as objects, people as receptacles, and traditions as disappearing. Ethnomusicology was just getting on its feet in the late 1950s. It would be a while before music scholars looked at musical practice as ritual, musicians as part of political economies, and music as part of systems of power, for instance. Alan Merriam's game-changing *The Anthropology of Music* wouldn't be in print until 1964. We can, however, connect Oster's work to that of a budding sociologist who overlapped with Oster at Angola. They seem to have never met though both were from Louisiana State University.

I like to imagine a car ride shared between the English professor/folklorist and the graduate researcher in sociology, Joseph Mouledous, the two driving up Highway 61. Filling the hour-long drive, Mouledous might have remarked that the musicians Oster was recording were at the lowest end of the prison hierarchy. Their conversation may have drifted to their shared support for civil rights efforts. Both, after all, expressed common sympathy for the powerless Black prisoners in Camp A. Mouledous might have suggested that Oster's recordings were a soundtrack to injustice. This imaginary conversation would unfold as jazz musicians elsewhere began to articulate Black nationalism, as Ornette Coleman decolonized jazz at the Five Spot in New York, on the eve of Eric Dolphy's wailing saxophone solo in "Fables of Faubus," imitating painful cries of political frustration.

Joseph Mouledous was a graduate student in sociology at LSU who the House Committee on Un-American Activities had just identified as a communist.[25] The thirty-one-year-old scholar-activist took a classification officer job at Angola as an opportunity to conduct fieldwork from 1957 to 1960. Eventually, he wrote a substantial master's thesis entitled "Sociological Perspectives on a Prison Social System."[26] While he didn't write about music, the study helps put the musicians on Oster's records in perspective and in relation to the jazz musicians we will meet later.

Mouledous noted a peculiarity about Angola. There was less tension between prisoners and security staff than he had expected. Perhaps he was primed to look for an inevitable revolt, given his Marxist assumptions. It may also have been because sociologists mainly studied Northern prisons. There, the staff focused on maintaining absolute control of the prisoners. As a result, the prisoners posed a threat of working together: rioting, striking, or attempting escape. Angola was by no means free from tension.

But tensions operated differently there—spread out across a complex social structure. Mouledous identified large strata of what he would later call "interstitial groups"—those with statuses in between the most powerless prisoners and the administration.[27] This observation bears a resemblance to associationalism's perspective in general and Brian Balogh's "mezzo-level focus" mentioned earlier, on the political space between the individual and the state.[28]

At Angola, Mouledous found a complex social organization that had developed out of the camp system, itself a relic of the plantation and convict leasing, that split prisoners between "gunmen" (those who work the fields under the gun) and "inmate guard-trusties" (the prisoner-guards who held the guns).[29] Trustys maintained the peace, motivated by self-preservation (see figure 2.2).[30] Any disturbance threatened their individual position of power, more comfortable work, and prestige.[31] Over time, Angola's social hierarchy had developed into a continuum of power spread across all the jobs required to maintain security and a reform-minded penitentiary tasked with being self-sufficient through forced agricultural work. Trusty assignments included being a clerk, a cook, a garbage collector, an educator, a sports manager, a barber, and, as we can imagine for our purposes here, a

Figure 2.2. A trusty guard on duty, 1955 (*Life Magazine* archives).

professional musician. Each position had different and complex ties to power and responsibility.

Bringing Mouledous's theory of interstitiality to Oster's folkloric work reveals the lived experiences of gunmen that Oster recorded. Musicians used limited tools for relief and psychological escape from the power hanging over them—not only from the administration but also from the trustys. Power formed in the chaotic fields, where outlawry blended with the pressure of the plantation. Oster's recordings are powerful cultural documents of human testimony. Songs like "I Had Five Long Years" and "Let Your Hammer Ring" accompany well Mouledous's description of a gunman's life:

> The majority of the gunman inmates were marched daily from their camps to the fields to labor. Generally, they remained in the fields all day, receiving the noon meal from a food cart. . . . [A] common practice was to place each man on a row of cane, cotton, or some other crop that required weeding, harvesting, etc. The job would then begin like a footrace: fifty or more men each with his own row to work and the last five to reach the far end of the row would be whipped.[32]

As Mouledous describes this "slave-style" brutality, Oster offers a soundtrack. The songs are of isolated individuals, left with little hope and almost no power. What about the other musicians? What sounds developed in what Mouledous called the interstices of power?

A significant renewal of penitentiary ideals has entered Angola in the 1950s, coexisting with the power of the plantation and the trusty system. The changes were not immediate, and they did not necessarily last. It took years to build new facilities to replace those left over from the plantation. Reforms disproportionately affected White prisoners. Resistance to policy changes created a dynamic and unpredictable prison even if it trended toward reform ideals. Week by week, the prison newsmagazine *The Angolite* documented sporadic changes, providing snapshots of organized musical activity—outside big band jazz performances, vaudeville shows that toured the various camps, jazz combos working out Miles Davis songs.

Finding Swing in a Prison Newsmagazine

While scouring archived copies of *The Angolite* for any reference to music, I discovered how prisoners gradually transformed a Black-performed minstrel practice into jazz by occupying Angola's many associations. I read about remarkable musicians who navigated complex laws, policies, and economies and secured resources to practice music at a high level. They tell a different, but just as important, story about music at Angola. The prisoners who once played in and provided services for these bands are long gone. I have pieced together their contributions from reading music coverage in *The Angolite*, the mimeographed prisoner-operated weekly that had developed out of the reform in small runs. Additional research led to a few arrest reports and obituaries.

A few caveats on the data. The accounts in *The Angolite* skew toward representing prisoners who had access to and support from the new associations. And since the publication was an outward-facing medium, prisoners were aware of how they presented themselves. Degrees of self-awareness held by *Angolite* contributors bring out certain things: more aspirations toward professionalism, attempts to connect to outside readers, strategic requests, and careful reportage of events. The articles often present prisoners as their best selves.

Nevertheless, it's important to respect and consider these presentations as claims for dignity, not to dismiss them as solely coerced statements. They exist within complex gradients of power. Often, these best-self presentations are strategically within the logic of reform ideals—about rehabilitation, professional development, and altruism. Usually, people serving time are seen as their worst selves. The articles in *The Angolite* show a very real reflexive aspirational attitude.

For all the freedom given *The Angolite*, the editor had a particular role and perspective. William "Old Wooden Ear" Sadler was on his second sentence. Having experienced Angola in the 1930s, perhaps the most violent era of the prison, Sadler was a vocal champion of the new reform efforts of the 1950s.[33] Furthermore, the optimistic tone of this early era of the uncensored newsmagazine reflects Sadler's cautionary stance. Appreciative reviews of events helped ensure the newsmagazine's continued support from the administration. Negative reviews risked future opportunities.[34] Positive spins do not simply make *The Angolite* an administrative mouthpiece. Selective positive coverage of prison activities also provided tacit encouragement for particular policies. Noncoverage might achieve the opposite. (For this chapter, let the unspoken accounts of violence and indignity linger. Testimony in chapter 3 will fill in what life might have been like for these pioneers.)

Sadler's Whiteness was a limitation. It distanced him from Black views. Likewise, he had little access to the women, who lived in Camp D. Staff writers managed to piece together life in what they called "The Forbidden City," drawing from female prisoner correspondents about hairdos, birthday parties, and visits to the camp.[35] Regular reports from Camp D and the Black camps, a mail column, and submissions of creative writing carve out some space for underrepresented voices.[36]

For its incarcerated readers, divided and spread across the 18,000 acres of the prison, *The Angolite* provided valuable opportunities for dialogue and reportage to prisoners.[37] Prisoners in one camp could vicariously experience and comment on an event. Thick descriptions of food and music helped pull readers into the accounts. The writing was also an act of resisting or mocking representations of inmates as illiterate, self-interested, irredeemable convicts.[38] Portrayals emphasize variety, literacy, generosity, and collaboration. In print, prisoners creatively reimagined themselves as audiences of film, music, theater, and dance performances.[39] The accounts of music of *The Angolite* reveal how prisoners and administrators blurred their relationships and worked in complexly concerted ways—they show how music was an integral part of the emerging midlevel associations.

Change in prisons happens glacially. Nevertheless, the story of jazz musicians that develops through the pages of *The Angolite* shows real musical and associational development born from newly gained small powers. Simultaneously ordinary and remarkable activities drive the story—getting a guard to unlock a door, purchasing reeds for saxophones, meeting for rehearsals in private spaces, compelling a warden to tap his foot in the women's camp. In the attempt to play jazz at a professional level, small actions established new shared routines and more predictable days, weeks, and months. When the prison collapsed into outlawry in the 1960s, the musicians of the 1950s left examples of possibility, a precedent of complex interassociational relationships. As we go back to 1951, we will listen along gradients of power, often contested and conflicting. In doing so, we will hear a broader musicality of the prison.

A Sudden Call for Attention

Often, a musical sound does not originate musically—a clenched muscle, an inhaled breath, an idea. In this case, it started in February 1951 with an act of self-mutilation. The Heel String Gang, as they would come to be known, was a group of White prisoners fed up with conditions at Angola. A few had been sent to the most powerless place on the farm, the Red Hat Cell Block in Camp E, reserved for only the most incorrigible. Prisoners competed with the rats for their dinner each night—trustys threw leftovers from Camp E onto the floor of the dark cell. Inside, a solid steel door blocked the exit. The only other opening was a square-foot opening near the ceiling. Warden Easterly ran the prison with a firm hand and mind and was determined to step up his crackdown on the protests. That evening, the prisoners in the Red Hat Cell Block acted together in protest.

Waking up the following day, Nurse Mary Margaret Daugherty had the unique task of reattaching thirty-one Achilles tendons. She fought off trusty guards attempting to exact punishment on the self-crippled protesters as she worked. It was these trusty guards who might face trouble from Warden Easterly for the mass act of protest and the resulting loss of labor. The Heel String Gang had coordinated their self-mutilation to bring attention to the conditions on the farm. After six more from Camp H joined the gang in the days following, Nurse Daugherty helped break the story to the press and submitted her resignation letter. In it, she described Easterly as an "arrogant, uncouth, narrow-minded, unprincipled bigot."[40] A flood of reporters arrived in the wake of Nurse Daugherty's departure. *Collier's* soon published a story titled "America's Worst Prison."[41] The exposé nationally broadcasted Nurse Daugherty's accusation: Louisiana failed to run its penitentiary. Her words from the article:

> I have seen almost seven thousand men discharged from this institution . . . and I have never seen a man discharged . . . who was as qualified (for a place) in society as he was the day he was admitted. . . . Degenerates of every type, . . . psychopaths and neurotics, are huddled in bedside companionship with the new arrivals, in huge dormitories that, as one inmate described to me, . . . "stink like the hold of a slave ship." There is . . . no trade school, no handicrafts or arts—not even a library. A man sentenced here who cannot read or write leaves here the same way. . . . No effort . . . is made

to help him stay out of the penitentiary once he obtains his release.... Their only choice is to steal or beg.[42]

In this account, the state's neglect of penitentiary ideals let the plantation and outlawry overtake the state institution. Angola hadn't received this amount of negative media attention since Major Samuel James' convict-leasing days of the 1880s.[43]

With the bad press of the heel-slashing landing on the eve of a gubernatorial election, the political consequences were swift. All eight candidates promised to appoint a trained penologist at Angola. Robert Floyd Kennon Sr. won the election in 1952 and put Angola at the top of his priorities. Angola received new funding, new leadership, and a new mission. The legislature increased the prison's operating budget by $700,000 with a separate $250,000 for hiring guards. An unprecedented $4,000,000 bond issue paid for construction and improvements. Governor Kennon brought in professional federal penologists to leadership positions at Angola. Maurice Sigler was appointed as the new warden of Angola, effectively putting the control of the prison under an outsider—a professional federal penologist trained in what was then called the "new penology."[44]

Warden Sigler expressed his philosophy, incidentally an update of Edward Livington's jurisprudence (described in chapter 1), in an interview with *The Angolite*: "We are going to shape Angola so that its inmates, men and women, will leave the penitentiary as citizens. That's our sole aim and purpose: men and women who have been bettered; who will not come back to this or any other prison."[45] The revised articulation of the penitentiary model stressed that prisons work best when prisoners are allowed to set up their self-governing systems.[46] In effect, the principles of associationalism became part of Angola's shift back to a penitentiary. Angola's new policies granted certain powers to individuals *through* prisoner-led associations. A practical benefit of this strategy dovetails with the trusty system: saving money and blurring power relationships by running certain prison operations through so-called voluntary prison labor.

Eager to play music, musicians cultivated the support of new administrative departments, primarily education and recreation. Capitalizing on the principles of Warden Sigler's reform effort, musicians found ways to argue for access to musical instruments, education, rehearsal space, mobility, and performance opportunities. New volunteer associations like the Inmate Council and the Inmate Lending Fund were just as essential. Each association offered unique but overlapping support for musical activity.

Perhaps the most fundamental of the new groups were those supporting representation and banking. Nationally, inmate councils were proliferating. Sociologists advising prison officials had determined that cracking down on informal prisoner associations only produced riots and protests.[47] Consequently, soon after Sigler became warden, *The Angolite* reported that "an election will be held in which all the offices will be held by convicts, and all the electors likewise convicted felons."[48] Once established, Sigler met with each council regularly.

One of the early accomplishments of the council was to help indigent prisoners with legal fees and money upon release. Angola prisoners still used cash brought from home, supplied by families, and even given $5 bonuses after notable harvests. Anyone from New Orleans might have understood the council as something similar to a mutual aid society. These longstanding African American voluntary organizations made up for the lack of public entitlements. At Angola, small donations trickled in from individual holdings into a unified fund held at a bank in nearby St. Francisville.[49] The Inmate Lending Fund became the financial backbone for other prisoner associations.[50] The fund grew to finance things that the state did not cover.

Musicians partnered with the new political and financial institutions in three main ways. First, voluntary prison clubs financed shows through the Inmate Lending Fund, covering supplies, free security staff overtime, and food. Second, to gain influence, musicians could hold elected council member seats. Third, musicians could propose fundraising events for the Inmate Lending Fund during holidays and create additional performance opportunities for themselves. The social order, however, was still rooted in the plantation-oriented camp system of division and agricultural production.

Hillbilly to Jazz in Camp E

In the wake of the heel-slashing, the White hillbilly bands of Camp E waned as the jazz orchestra waxed. More new arrivals came from cities, torn from developing professional and industrial jobs. Young urban representation affected interest in more contemporary urban musical styles. And the new rhetoric of rehabilitation was more in line with jazz.

The last of the hillbilly groups was the Top Hillbillies, an eclectic bunch who revolved around guitarist Douglas Catt. The musical saw, trumpet, fiddle, steel guitar, and other random noisemakers swarmed into a cacophony that provided entertainment. It also offered a jestful punching bag for *Angolite* commentators. Hillbilly bands were fixtures in prisoner-vaudeville camp shows.[51] Angola's variety shows, likely predating Warden Sigler's arrival, were local versions of the decades-long American vaudeville practice that would move into television shows such as *The Milton Berle Show* (1948–1956) and even *Late Night with David Letterman* (1982–1993). Angola vaudeville included acts that prisoners brought and developed. A charismatic emcee strung together an unrelated series of performances that often included comedic cultural representations. The symbol of the hillbilly could simultaneously romanticize and stigmatize. In doing so, the bands addressed the tension between a rural past and an industrial present for Angola's prisoners and staff.[52] Arguably, the White rural style would feed Angola's country bands, White professional bands that would gain prominence in the late 1960s (covered in chapter 4). But in the early 1950s, the hillbilly genre was in decline.

At Angola, the image of the hillbilly was the opposite of the new 1950s prisoner. As presented in *The Angolite*, they were cartoon musicians—foils to the noble ideals of rehabilitating prisoners for society. There was plenty of strange activity ripe for commentary. A report entitled "Candidate for Hillbillies: Man Invents 'Coke-a-Phone'" describes someone in the camps playing with water-filled Coca-Cola bottles with a steel wand. Playfully recommending him to the Top Hillbillies, the author describes, "out comes a variety of what is alleged to be music. He's at 'liberty,' as performers euphemistically put it."[53] *The Angolite* published a more forceful article in the form of a public service announcement. In "Hillbilly Music Is a Disease," the editors suggest that the music "is like oysters, olives and okra. It requires a taste for the bizarre which often borderlines hysteria and psychosis. . . . Probably a hundred years from now they'll wonder how we stomached it. Just as we wonder today."[54] In contrast, the sound of the new penology was jazz—sophisticated, urban, collective, and virtuosic.

Angola's jazz renaissance developed where modest entitlements began to take root—the crowded White Camp E. A handful of newly appointed free personnel—not trustys, but new hires with clear professional credentials—took over space in the buildings, led key institutions for music, and encouraged prisoner leadership. Warden Sigler committed space, community, and time to the new rehabilitative-oriented programming. Music classes offered practical training, taught music literacy to musicians, and provided music appreciation classes for general students. Rosters of prisoners helped distinguish professionals from apprentices. A new charge for music at Angola was expressly in service of rehabilitation.

White prisoners with higher-level jobs received education and vocational resources first because a circular racial logic underpinned prisoner classification for plantation labor and lingering notions of who deserved rehabilitation. Classification officers assigned White prisoners to Camp E—the central hub of agricultural processing and distribution—because of segregationist policy that relegated them to industrial and clerical jobs. Tasked with sugar manufacturing and export, the cannery and sugar mill provided alternative jobs to the grueling fieldwork. Residents of Camp E seemed more amenable to programming, partly because work there had certain structural advantages. They had more time to think about and discuss things like music-making because of the nature of their jobs. They also had more access to the prison administration because they were involved in the advanced tasks of Angola's agro-industry.

Warden Sigler had hoped to provide rehabilitative opportunities without disrupting the well-established revenue-producing agricultural practices, expanding trusty jobs to bookkeeping, procurement, and work coordination.[55] After all, he built his reform changes on a still-functioning plantation. The musicians in Camp E took advantage of wider communication channels between administration and prisoners, reformist goals, and trust—repurposing reform to organize complex music. Jazz became part of Angola's turn toward voluntary chartered clubs as musicians began to collaborate with a suite of emerging associations like Alcoholics Anonymous, the Methodist Men's Club, and the Dale Carnegie Club. Recreational sports, dance, and music associations developed alongside other clubs through officially sanctioned events.

Multi-instrumentalist Les Winslow emerged as a leader during these early days of reform. A check fraud conviction brought him to Angola in 1952. Originally from Monroe, Louisiana, he was adept on horn and piano. Some even said that Winslow toured with venerable entertainer Bob Hope.[56] At thirty-five, he was older than most. Soon to be known as "The Profile," he quickly found a leadership position within the developing education and recreation programs as a music teacher and band leader. Over the coming years, Winslow trained musicians to play in a big band jazz ensemble (see

Figure 2.3. White jazz orchestra rehearsing in Camp E (Special Collections, University of Louisiana at Lafayette).

figure 2.3). The Cavaliers developed into a touring group, representing new Angola in the sound of big band jazz to the general public.

Angola's new reform mission created a new value for music. The Cavaliers provided relatively cheap and seemingly authentic public relations for the new administration as Warden Sigler continued to make his case for changing the status quo.[57] White musicians became public ambassadors. The 1950s public perception of a prisoner was precisely that—a White man with a shared larger sense of morality.[58] Despite the folkloric authenticity of John Lomax's representation of Lead Belly, the White makeup of The Cavaliers suited the racialized role of redeemable prisoners—not outlaws, but redeemable men who perhaps had fallen on hard times, who had made life-altering, but ultimately forgivable, mistakes.

The Cavaliers received positive reviews in local papers. Performance requests picked up, and the band became an emblem of progress. A *State-Times* article in June 1952 surveyed the prison, noting modest but real improvement, citing "the two bands, White and Negro, which provide music not only at the camp functions but are in great demand for outside performances, and in the general esprit de corps."[59] The Cavaliers traveled throughout the state, a visible and aural metaphor for the new Angola. They entertained audiences at the new American Legion Hall in Clinton, the Simmesport High School Junior-Senior Prom, and the Central Cattlemen's Association Meeting at the Blue Moon Nite Club in Bunkie, playing their arrangements of popular dance songs. Prison jazz astonished audiences, if even just for moments, narrowing public attention to the idealism of revived penitentiary goals.[60] And yet, sometimes the Cavaliers were simply an affordable alternative to a free-world band. They played for dances, beauty pageants, boat races, gala events, and dinners sometimes programmed around novelty acts from the local community.[61] Most of these were community organization-sponsored fundraisers. The Cavaliers billed as "The Angola Band" were musical laborers aligned with free-world community altruism. But not everyone was thrilled.

Just outside Angola, a community organization formed, ostensibly to protest a rash of escapes even though escapes were on the decline. Members of the West Feliciana Parish Citizens Committee, including the West Feliciana sheriff, started putting political pressure on the prison, accusing it of having become "a damn playhouse."[62] For local critics, prisoner events made the prison look like a country club, straying from plantation models of hard labor and outlawry models of punishment.[63] To skeptical free-world audiences, music signified idle time. What's more, jazz had lingering associations with drug use and criminality.

In November 1953, Louisiana Assistant Attorney General M. E. Culligan announced a halt on the traveling bands.[64] In his opinion statement, he declared that "state laws fail to open penitentiary gates for convict bands to play for parish fairs, rodeos, and patriotic and hospital dances."[65] He countered Director of Corrections Reed Cozart by saying that he had no legal authority to let prisoners out—even though they had been doing so for decades, especially in partnership with the East Louisiana State Hospital, the nearby mental hospital.

The Cavaliers played their last show on October 17, 1953, at the Bunkie Elementary School, a community dance organized by the American Legion to raise money for Christmas gifts for needy children.[66] Unable to travel and gradually losing members to release, The Cavaliers disbanded. They played a few shows at the camps. Perched on a truck nearby an intercamp baseball game, now a mere quintet, they were a shadow of the big band they were the year before.[67] Winslow would leave Angola before forming another group, but he left a precedent. The education program now had resources for music. Newcomers could envision prisoners as professional jazz musicians supported by administrative and associational structures.[68]

The Rhythm Makers of Camp A

As *The Angolite* lauded Winslow's jazz efforts and playfully ridiculed hillbilly music, musicians in the other camps took notice. Despite being spread out, the sounds of the camps influenced each other. Bands from different camps shared the makeshift stages at all-camp festivals and intercamp tours. The success of The Cavaliers, however, was not replicable everywhere. Each camp had a distinct population, segregated by race and job classification. Each had different resources.

Reform seemed to have passed over Camp A. The vermin-filled buildings reserved for Black prisoners were the decrepit old quarters of the convict lease days. The infrastructure barely supported the five hundred Black inmates who worked the fields from sunup to sundown. It may have been the place at Angola that most looked like nineteenth-century convict-lease housing. (Perhaps the setting played a part in drawing folklorist Harry Oster there.) Plantation appearances aside, the demographics had shifted with an increase in young urban arrivals. Drug convictions were to blame.[69] Narcotics raids and car searches throughout Louisiana revealed stashes of drugs, interrupting the careers of many professional musicians—many of whom had come to New Orleans for work prospects only to find themselves at Angola eventually.

In spring 1953, Leroy Dukes, with his distinctive goatee, returned to Angola on his second armed robbery charge and was assigned to Camp A. He was twenty-two years old.[70] Dukes had caught his first charge soon after relocating to New Orleans from California. Back home, the Santa Monica native had played with Dexter Gordon as a teenager in Los Angeles.[71] At the time, Los Angeles was a hotbed of musical exchange. Many African Americans had migrated from the South to escape Jim Crow and secure jobs during World War II. Some of the musicians in Los Angeles were from New Orleans, actively forging new music that would become rock and roll. If Dukes was in New Orleans on a pilgrimage—a reverse migration to find the source of the new music—he found Jim Crow laws entangled in the musical roots.

Dukes had played in a minstrel troupe during his first stint at Angola in the late 1940s. Black prisoners dressed in prison-striped tuxedos entertained fellow prisoners and occasional guests. It was a relic of the stereotype-driven shows of the nineteenth century. But on his return for a second conviction,

Dukes saw new possibilities. The prison had begun to change. In Camp A, he met two new musicians, pianist Isaac Cole and bassist Oscar Crummie. In 1952, Cole and Crummie had recorded with the legendary jump blues singer Wynonne Harris on his King Records release "Bring it Back / Bad News Baby (There'll Be No Rockin' Tonight)." The two had been traveling with the Sonny Thompson Orchestra when they were pulled over and caught with narcotics.[72] Together at Angola, Dukes, Cole, and Crummie put together a lean combo, eventually adding guitarist Floyd Richard.[73] Their musical skills were undeniable, and the whole prison began to hear them.

The Rhythm Makers became the first prominent Black jazz group in 1950s Angola. Unlike the Cavaliers, Duke's combo played more inside the prison— performances at holiday festivals and variety show camp tours. Their music was modern. Jazz in the 1950s had overlapped with emerging R&B. New Orleans musicians recorded with Fats Domino, Big Mama Thornton, and Little Richard, for instance, when they weren't playing with leaders like Art Blakey (who had given bebop strong backbeat grooves with an infectious swing). Urban Angola musicians were increasingly versed in these musical shifts.

Dukes and his combo had their debut performance on the Fourth of July, 1953. It was one of the most extravagant holiday events Angola had seen. *The Angolite* attributed the event to the generous license granted by the new administration.[74] All of Angola came to Camp E, even those in the women's camp and the B-Line (the separate housing area reserved for families of staff). Attendees cheered on boxing matches, enjoyed T-bone steaks, rooted for their teams in an integrated all-star baseball game, and laughed at a White minstrel show, perhaps put on by the Top Hillbillies.[75] The Baton Rouge radio station WXOK—a new voice in African American radio—sent up one of their house bands to play. But they were no match for Leroy Dukes and his Rhythm Makers, who played through the entire event.[76] Soon after that day, every camp on the farm wanted a visit from the new jazz combo from Camp A.

Summer was busy. Dukes and his quartet toured the camps, granted mobility through recreation department support. With mobility came visibility. Coverage from *The Angolite*, which dubbed their "hot jive" to be incredibly popular among prisoners and free people alike, described detailed reviews of the shows.[77] Reports announced when the Rhythm Makers teamed up with other acts or featured a particular singer from the population for a popular song. The coverage was mutually beneficial. The Rhythm Makers gave *The Angolite* rich events to describe and progressive ideals to champion.

The 1953 Labor Day festival was even bigger than the Fourth of July event, with over two thousand prisoners, staff, and their families attending.

The Rhythm Makers played throughout boxing matches, magic acts, and female impersonation performances. Attendees ate hot dogs and drank pink lemonade. *The Angolite* reported, "many of the spectators went home with peeling noses and red faces, caused by over-exposure to 'Old Hannah' [the sun]."[78] A female vocal group from Camp D gave Dukes's combo a break that turned into an affair. Ida Mae Tassin, Evette Simmons, and Lula Mae Martin received multiple encores after their set, threatening to prolong the show beyond its allotted time. Yet the constant sound throughout the day was the music of the Rhythm Makers, intermingled with the crowd. There is no mention of repertoire, but given the various acts showcasing their talents, they likely played popular music that resonated with prisoners from all the camps (see figure 2.4). In review, *The Angolite* declared that the program was "the best ever produced on Angola under the new prison management," tacitly encouraging the new administration to support jazz across the camps.[79]

Figure 2.4. Outdoor festival performance. Louisiana State Penitentiary (LSP) Museum Photograph Collection, University Archives and Acadiana Manuscripts Collection, Edith Garland Dupré Library, University of Louisiana at Lafayette, LA UAAMC COLL-0522, Box 017, Folder s094.

Dukes continued to lead the Rhythm Makers through 1954, and by all accounts, they continued to be busy. They were the core of the "Black and Tan Review," a vaudeville show that brought music and comedy acts to all the prisoners.[80] For a year, they helped bring other groups like the Pinetop Quartet out of Camp A for intercamp tours.[81] The combo even took outside invitations, mainly substituting for The Cavaliers before the Attorney General's travel ban.[82] In June 1953, a radio station broadcast their show in Ferriday, and the group began to get requests for playing their own outside shows.[83]

Through all their activity, the Rhythm Makers expanded support for voluntary associations in Camp A. Musical life there was finally growing in partnership with the reforms. As musicians requested license and sponsorship to play, they developed stronger footholds for securing space, instruments, educational resources, mobility, and performance opportunities. The recreation department began to reach beyond Camp E.

Eventually, the education department expanded into Camp A. Trumpet player Joe Tate began teaching an official class in music reading with an enrollment of fifteen.[84] With the activity of the Rhythm Makers and a developing stable of musicians, the music scene at Camp A began to resemble the rich scene at Camp E. Other camps took notice. The Rhythm Makers developed an intercamp circuit, cultivating intercamp associations and connecting prisoners across the farm through centralized recreation, education, religious, and civic-oriented organizations.

Then, in August 1954, an incident ground things to a halt. During a fight at Camp A, prisoners used instruments as weapons. Warden Sigler swiftly confiscated them and, in a concession to the Rhythm Makers, transferred the group and their instruments to Camp I, a Black trusty camp down on the southern bank of the river.[85] While the camp may have had more privileges, the Rhythm Makers' performances were more constricted.

Their remaining shows took them only as far as Camp F, the other small Black camp.[86] By the end of the year, the group dissolved. Oscar Crummie and Floyd Richard went home in November. A final tour of the camps fell through for what *The Angolite* simply called an "unexpected reason."[87] Dukes tried to fill the empty slots with newcomers but couldn't. His band had ended.

This loss is more detrimental than it may seem. When a named, and essentially *chartered* band, fails, musicians lose access to liberties once accessed through the group. After all, individual prisoners gain power through sanctioned associations. Being in the Rhythm Makers had afforded the musicians mobility, access to equipment and space, the ability to fundraise, and a clear purpose for being with each other. But that wasn't the end of jazz.

The All-Stars Start in Camp H-2

Racial segregation was one of the most pernicious institutions blocking musical activity. Official policies would last at Angola through 1978. Racism was woven into its fabric—work classification, camp assignments, and Jim Crow policies. When he arrived, Warden Sigler's attempts to rehabilitate Black prisoners did not go over well with sections of Angola. "I was not welcome here," he reflected decades later. "This was a deep segregation time. You just didn't do anything for black people. But I had my own ideas and I believed in these [rehabilitation programs] because that's the way I was raised and trained."[88] The nation's debates over desegregation were intensifying. In summer 1953, Baton Rouge Minister T. J. Jemison led the first civil rights boycott of bus segregation.

Integration efforts did not go unnoticed in *The Angolite*. Discussion of integrating the baseball team was largely in favor of the effort. In an April 1954 editorial, the editor of *The Angolite* made a plea for integrating the entire recreation department, claiming a long history of racial harmony among prisoners: "For years, negroes and whites have worked together on Angola as they do today. Side by side, in the field, factory and shop, there has never been the friction so often common in similar situations in the North. There has grown, through these years, a mutual understanding and respect."[89] Keep in mind that it was in the interest of *Angolite* editors to seem aligned with Warden Sigler. Musicians also took interest. With *The Angolite* echoing the warden's stance and the success of intercamp jazz performances established by the Rhythm Makers, some prisoners built on a scattered and perhaps imagined project of integration even though most voluntary associations and administrative positions were White controlled.

By and large, bands were segregated, partly by administrative segregation but also through self-segregation. A handful of White jazz musicians found the color line a hindrance. Thirty-year-old Adrian Ballam felt this acutely. Before Angola, Ballam was an active saxophone player and bandleader. In spring 1953, his career was cut short after a raid of Tommy Garrett's luxurious apartment on the corner of Esplanade Avenue and Burgundy Street in New Orleans. Ballam and his wife had been there discussing music that he was going to compose and arrange for Garrett's upcoming magic show. After bursting in, the narcotics squad found Ballam and Garrett's wife in the bathroom, desperately trying to flush nineteen joints down the toilet.[90] Not only was he caught red-handed, but Ballam also had prior arrests for attempted armed robbery and auto theft. The judge was unsympathetic.[91]

At Angola, Ballam was loath to play with just the White groups. Before Angola, after all, he played with Charlie Barnet, one of the first New York bandleaders to integrate his bands.[92] But at Angola, Ballam's Whiteness kept him from the bustling jazz scene that the Rhythm Makers were developing at Camp A. He was assigned to Camp H-2, far from the jazz scenes. Guitarist Douglas Catt had the most prominent group there, the Top Hillbillies. Joining the Top Hillbillies did not suit Ballam's training.[93]

In his first few months, Ballam managed to sit in with the Cavaliers for a June 1953 intercamp show to wide praise.[94] About the same time, jazz musicians from Black Camps A and F put out feelers for permission to hold an intercamp jam session.[95] Ballam was at the top of their list. In *The Angolite*, Ballam expressed deep gratitude for the invitation, making a point at the end about the importance of career continuity for musicians. He drew on rehabilitation-driven penitentiary logic: "You see, when a man is received here he usually is put on a job that fits. He may thereby 'keep his hand in.' However, a musician, like myself, is out of luck for there are no jobs playing music. So he doesn't get the practice he needs like a welder, an electrician, or a driver."[96] Ballam's inspiration may have been the trade school that Warden Sigler had just opened, but his rhetorical ploy was to swap penitentiary ideals for plantation policies. Pushing a bit farther in that same letter, Ballam rallied support for forming a regular intercamp combo of, in his words, "competent men who have devoted their entire lives, as I have, to the study and presentation of modern music, . . . able to present listenable, interesting concerts to the inmate population."[97] Appealing to cost-effectiveness, he suggested that music could help inspire or replace some of the recreational activities that had been flagging: "As baseball and other sports activities are now practically at a standstill I think the entertainment would be appreciated. Am I right? I'm sure that if we all show our interest and seriousness our good officials (who are interested in our rehabilitation) will give us the go-ahead."[98] The administration granted his request.

Adrian Ballam's All-Stars was the first interracial and intercamp musical group. Visually, they offered an alternative to Angola's racial and camp divisiveness. Musically, they were the top players on the farm, period. Drummer

Charles Burton had played with the Joe Liggins Band.[99] If people hadn't known Cole and Crummie from their preconviction recordings, they surely knew them from their Rhythm Makers shows. Leroy Dukes joined up as well. They were versatile players from different camps: E, H, A, and C.

Versatile as they were, Ballam refused to play any hillbilly music on principle. Speaking on behalf of his group in *The Angolite*, he wrote, "We regret we are unable to play any hillbilly tune as this band is made up almost completely [of] professional musicians, but any other type of music—well, you name it and we got it!"[100] They crafted sets of popular jazz numbers and managed to get security escorts to rehearsals. The All-Stars debuted at the hospital and Camp D, the women's camp.[101] Then, all of a sudden, for reasons unknown, they were swiftly shut down.[102]

Ballam's public struggle to reinstate the group is revealing. In *The Angolite*, Ballam argued for continued opportunities to play, developing a logic of interracial meritocracy. "We received a wonderful reception and were classed by our audiences as the most entertaining group formed on the farm," he wrote directly.[103] Adding to Ballam's plea, the editors advocated for the All-Stars, publishing a letter from the women's camp, which had both Black and White prisoners due to the relatively small number of women at Angola.

> Dear Sir: Last week the girls at Camp D were entertained by the "All Star Band." We sincerely feel that it was the best entertainment that has been displayed here in some time. Lately we have heard the unit is to be discontinued. We feel that we are in a position to comment on this as all our entertainment and recreation such as movies, etc., is for both white and colored inmates of this camp. Since the band was composed for the inmate entertainment, we would like for you to give a great deal of consideration to and before disbanding the unit.[104]

Below Ballam's statement and the reprint of the Camp D letter came an editor's note: "The above are two of the many expressions received by *The Angolite* against the disbanding of the 'All Stars.' Some of the expressions were from the free personnel."[105] We ought to be careful in reading this support as fundamentally integrationist. The free staff was less interested in symbols of progressive politics than they valued access to a good band.

Prisoner bands were some of the only entertainment options for the free personnel and their families. This particular audience had grown under Warden Sigler. He had been able to increase free staff positions with his augmented budget. Lin Sharpe, who grew up on the B-Line in the 1950s, told me why she liked prisoner bands: "Since we all lived in such an isolated place, we were excited to have something to do on Saturday nights." Undeterred and encouraged by some, Ballam continued practicing and fighting for a music career on the farm.

By February of 1954, he received interest from King Records to cut sides at the prison—likely through Cole and Crummie's contacts.[106] Though the album never seems to have made it to release, the story spread through *The Angolite* for weeks—a marker of success for an integrated professional group of their own.[107] Ballam kept at it. Just because the All-Stars lost their sanctioned status didn't mean that efforts to integrate the bands stopped.

The 1954 Fourth of July festival at Camp E became a real intercamp celebration with Ballam, now an established leader, running the music. The *Angolite* plugged the event with promises of notable singers. All camps had representation through an intensive scouting effort. Rehearsals began two weeks ahead of time in Camp E's recreation building.

At 8:00 a.m., July 4 began with a fried egg breakfast. Attendees moved on to doughnuts and iced drinks as they shuffled between boxing matches, variety shows, and an all-star baseball game on the athletic field.[108] Musical acts crowded onto two flatbed trucks for a forty-five-minute variety show. Napoleon "Nappy" Fontaine was the emcee for a mix of music, comedy, and dancing. But Ballam's playing stole the show. His small combo offered a newer lean bebop sound—a product of intercamp and interracial collaboration. If you tuned into it—there was a sound of social change. "Hats and Coats" McElroy made a guest appearance to sing in "rare scat style" and then threw off his crutches to dance in a "spectacular buck and wing on his one leg."[109] *The Angolite* registered the significance of old and new Angola on display: "The customers knew they were watching a trouper from way back, and the ovation they accorded him threatened to stop the show. 'Hats and Coats' comes from Camp I, but all Angola claims him."[110]

Ballam's show had combined a modern integrated jazz band with a nostalgic minstrel troupe leader performing a precursor to tap dance on one leg. Is the reading political unity or a White *Angolite* reviewer claiming cultural ownership over a Black performer? The answer might be both. Ballam's intercamp and interracial group provided audible evidence of the possibility of moving beyond the camp system through collaboration. With no reported incidents, *The Angolite* contended that cooperation and a suspension of strict control were the keys to its success—direct principles of the new penology. The music temporarily defeated the camp system in grooves, laughter, and spectacle. The plantation festival that had been established decades earlier as cyclical relief for harvest work now resonated with new ideas.

Adrian Ballam would remain at Angola for ten more years, playing in numerous bands and eventually taking over the music education program in the 1960s. In his early years at Angola, he was ambitious—not only playing high-level bebop but also subverting racial and camp divides. Ballam's performances relied on support from voluntary associations and administration. But music also served the new collaborative practices by exercising relationships and setting a precedent. Producing music meant approving events with documents needing several signatures, typing up and circulating rosters for formal music classes, scheduling the recreation department's rehearsal spaces, coordinating dates with the Inmate Council, and financing shows through the Inmate Lending Fund. In this way, associated musicians helped prisoners hold on to limited freedoms by creating a plethora of everyday activities that furthered musical goals.

A year after Ballam's 1954 intercamp Fourth of July festival, former minstrel troupe leader "Hats and Coats" McElroy remained at Angola, but he took up the upright bass, became the barber in Camp I, and replaced his wooden leg with a prosthetic one.[111] He and "Sonny Boy" Williams took on a project of reconditioning a Civil War–era piano donated to the prison, repurposing it to "beat out late be-bop."[112] The legacy left by The Cavaliers, the Rhythm Makers, and the All-Stars was gathering force.

Minstrelsy to Jazz with the Nic Nacs in Camp A

By the middle of the decade, incoming Black musicians at Camp A saw space for up-to-date jazz on the older vaudeville stage. Unfortunately, they had no access to instruments. With considerable effort, a handful of new and older musicians revived music at the dilapidated camp through a series of intercamp variety shows.

In March 1953, at a bar in the French Quarter of New Orleans, Lester "Big Noise" Thompson was less than a year into his parole and got into a fight.[113] He chased the man around the corner and stabbed him to death. Thompson returned to the farm, where he had completed time for stealing several musical instruments from a car in 1949.[114] Angola must have looked a bit different to him. Changes initiated by the 1951 heel slashing had modestly improved some aspects of the prison. The paid free staff had grown (though trusty guards remained), money had been committed to improvements (about $8 million over the past two years), and a new classification staff was finding ways to separate first offenders from the general population (a reform urged by the Prison Reform Association fifty years earlier).[115]

Still, many of the changes had yet to affect Camp A. The prisoner population was on the rise. At more than 440 beyond capacity, the entire prison was about to break a record. It was also business as usual. Angola's agriculture was cutting edge with the latest high-tech sugar cane crops. Field Captain Eli Landry was planning on introducing a new field of Irish potatoes. Fifty acres was enough for a test run of the new crop.

Thompson didn't care much for farming. Nevertheless, he was assigned fieldwork for all of 1954. He knew other prisoners secured local "parole sponsors"—farmers who would take on a parolee in exchange for free farm labor. As far as he was concerned, that was no option. He claimed to have over a decade of professional experience sharing stages with Joe Turner, Lloyd Price, Fats Domino, and T-Bone Walker.[116] He was set on returning to New Orleans to play music.

Talk of a Black band starting up way over at Camp I dispirited Thompson. He published an open letter in the late February 1955 issue of *The Angolite*: "I am a musician of lots of experience and can play well. I am on the edge of flipping my wig because I can't get my hands on a horn. Please somebody help me. Just give me a chance to play a little something. My horn will do the speaking for my ability."[117] Instruments were still banned at Camp A since the fight six months earlier.

It must have frustrated Thompson that his horn was stashed somewhere on the farm, out of reach. When he had been granted parole in the spring 1952, he had left his $200 saxophone behind.[118] A month after publishing his first open letter, Thompson wrote again, this time offering his local credentials: "I am credited with being responsible for the start of the minstrel show that used to entertain the farm." But what Thompson wanted to play was jazz, the latest and the most innovative.[119]

Thompson's role in minstrelsy—a practice mentioned above as a tributary to Angola's vaudeville shows—deserves more backstory. The legacy of stereotypes in blackface minstrelsy is far longer and more damaging than those of hillbilly music. Minstrelsy was a powerful musical force in America, emerging in the mid-nineteenth century. White performers blackened their faces with burned cork and performed professional routines in derogatory imitation of Black musical practices. After the Civil War, many Black entertainers found professional opportunities on the minstrel stage. Eventually falling out of favor, remnants of minstrelsy remain in American musical life. Cleaned-up minstrel songs like "Oh Susannah," "Camptown Races," and "Buffalo Gals" still resound around campfires and in Warner Bros. cartoons. Yet the continuation of minstrelsy into 1940s Angola was anything but cleansed of its racial import. Black prisoners doubly performed exaggerated stereotypes of themselves—as African Americans and convicts (see figure 2.5).

At first read, it is startling to imagine minstrelsy continuing into the mid-twentieth century in a Louisiana prison—Black bodies doubly bound by a criminal justice system and lingering derogatory cultural tropes. In figure 2.4, note the tuxedos made of prison stripes, the white makeup exaggerating African lips, and the three prisoners in drag. Lester Thompson is likely somewhere in the photo with John "Hats and Coats" McElroy, more recognizable by having only one leg. McElroy had played in numerous bands before being incarcerated and led Angola's minstrel troupe in the 1940s.[120] In his book *Slaves of the State,* Dennis Childs sees in McElroy a "musical slave" and provocatively asks, alluding to the well-known 1951 heel-slashing, "does not the black captive's last-resort effort at securing a tenuous and always already incomplete reprieve from the penitentiary's innumerable other staging

Figure 2.5. 1940s Camp A Minstrel Troupe (*The Angolite* archives).

grounds of punitive terror through painting a mask of black self-immolation represent an act as desperate, injurious, and vexing as self-mutilation?"[121] Indeed, McElroy's bleak prospects were crushing.

Recovering fragments of McElroy's activity through the pages of *The Angolite* shows additional ways he navigated Angola. As an active musician, his participation in developing bebop gave him relative musical liberation from his minstrel persona in the 1940s. McElroy, working within the associations of the mid-1950s, widened, if only by degrees, what Ralph Ellison might call "freedom within unfreedom," budging the vaudeville stage closer to what I will cover in the next chapter: radical jazz of the 1960s.[122] A decade of descriptions of Black intercamp performances in *The Angolite* reveal that at Angola, bebop developed *within* minstrelsy before displacing it. McElroy and Lester Thompson were prime movers, drawing on the modern avant-garde exemplified by Charlie Parker and Dizzy Gillespie. It could be that on his way out of prison, McElroy, like early-century entertainer Bert Williams, appropriated the right to perform Blackness, only to carry Blackness so far into jazz that he surreptitiously discarded the minstrel mask in the commotion.[123] We know that Lester Thompson seized upon all available performance opportunities. While he continued the effort to play jazz, mention of minstrel performances in *The Angolite* decreased.

In spring 1955, Thompson threw together a trio with McElroy on bass and "Shorty" on conga.[124] On a visit to a Camp C event, they borrowed instruments and played. The review was ecstatic: "These people dealt a selection of hot vibrations that left the rafters tingling half the night after they had gone."[125] Later, Thompson got his hands on a horn again when Adrian Ballam's group blew through Camp A for a show. Ballam invited a few Camp A musicians to the stage for a jam during their matinee show, and, as *The Angolite* reported, it "was easily the finest musical output ever heard in this bailiwick."[126] But again, Thompson's hands were empty afterward. He had played Ballam's horn, which left with Ballam and his group.

Thompson was finally able to collaborate more fully when he met Fuzz. Louis "Fuzz" Surgent had learned the clarinet from his grandfather while in grade school.[127] By age fifteen, he was playing in a youth orchestra that would host visiting artists. (Once he played with Duke Ellington when the maestro came through New Orleans.) As he became more dedicated to the saxophone, he followed the sound of Charlie Parker to New York City. There, he joined a combo with legendary drummer Cozy Cole. Drug use began recreationally—a sniff of heroin in the green room with other players.

86   INSTRUMENT OF THE STATE

Surgent was busy gigging and making good money at college and society parties before going overseas to fight in the Korean War. Like many veterans of the time, a causal relationship with heroin became a dependent one. The needle offered a quicker route to self-medication. Fuzz brought his heroin addiction back home to New Orleans, where, in spring 1955, one capsule got him a ten-year sentence. By summer, and now at Angola, he partnered with Lester Thompson to figure a way to play again.

Thompson kept writing to *The Angolite* as he folded Surgent into the effort. Surgent began composing new music and writing arrangements. The two rounded up musicians and made a renewed case through yet another *Angolite* letter. Now writing as a combo, they requested access to instruments, leaning on the kind of penitentiary logic that Adrian Ballam had used a year earlier. "We hope we are not asking too much," they wrote. "After all, each and every man should be given a chance in life. Someone can make us very happy and feel like we are modern prisoners. Please do."[128] In essence, Thompson and Surgent centered their request on their unique skills and prior (musical) work experience. To develop vocationally, they required access to rights: mobility and association, good mental health, and self-expression. By July, Thompson, Surgent, and a few others found free personnel to provide their security.[129] That was crucial. Security sponsorship granted them movement among the camps and provided required security detail during performances. In prison, performances disrupt the ordinary custody routine, needing additional and often unpaid hours from staff.

In August 1955, weeks away from Labor Day, another prisoner from Camp A made an ambitious request. He asked the Inmate Lending Fund to organize another Labor Day event, hoping the precedent set by the All-Stars the year before would sway the administration, promising, "The entire inmate body, working together, should be able to put on the best show ever held here."[130] He asked each prisoner to donate a dollar to the ILF to finance the event, including fees for the top Black and White musical groups and female singers from Camp D and cash awards to boxers. Education Director Charles Eldridge went for it, and so did the ILF committee.[131] There wasn't much time to organize the event.

As the boxers began to train, Thompson's musicians waited for a promised return of the instruments from Camp I.[132] Within a week, they arrived. A few musicians from Camp I tagged along. Leroy Dukes and Isaac Cole (formerly from the Rhythm Makers) had jumped at the opportunity to join. It was a big group: tenor and alto saxophones, guitar, piano, bass, drum set, and bongos.[133] These musicians were versatile enough to compose and arrange popular songs and modern jazz numbers. With Fuzz's up-to-date styles and the addition of former members of the Rhythm Makers, Angola had a whole new sound.

Calling themselves the Nic Nacs, Thompson's group shared the 1955 Labor Day stage with two other groups that had formed in the Rhythm Makers' wake: the Play-Boys from Camp I and Ballam's new group, the Tune Toppers, as well as, perhaps embarrassingly, yet another iteration of Camp E's Top Hillbillies, now led by "Speedy" Bratcher.[134] The Hillbillies presented acts aimed at attracting the attention of outside radio producers with unconventional arrangements and trick effects. But the Nic Nacs just played. And in doing so, they stunned all of Angola with their skill and cutting-edge material. Surgent and Thompson returned to the barren Camp A that night, again without instruments but with the visceral memory of playing.

The Nic Nacs Occupy the New Prison

In November 1955, contractors finished building a new state-of-the-art facility in the middle of Angola. Dubbed the "new prison," it looked nothing like the camps (see figure 2.6). Long open-air walkways connected dormitories, each named after a tree. A physical plant, kitchen and mess hall, ample yard space for recreation activities, and offices for associations and administrative departments were all waiting for a new flow of life. It was a modern facility with more space and updated facilities that were part of the $4 million bond issue the Louisiana legislature passed in 1952. The opening met great anticipation for more follow-through of reform goals. Adding more than improved living conditions, a centralized facility promised collaboration without the hindrance of camp divisions. It was tempting to imagine how the new prison might change the social structure.

The camps were more than segregated housing. They were a pernicious system of control. The old management system was built upon instituted harvest competitions—camps rewarded or penalized for their relative crop yields—that bled into intense rivalries in sporting matches and general antagonism. Divided and conquered. With the opening of the new prison, the shift away from the camp system was not abrupt, nor was it total, because it was part of the longstanding social fabric of Angola. Nonetheless, the coming

Figure 2.6. The new main prison, 1955. "Bad Prison Goes Straight," *Life Magazine* 39, no. 24, December 12, 1955, 55.

of the new prison tilted practices toward a penitentiary model. The camps became symbols of the "old" Angola.

The Angolite offered hope and caution in an editorial entitled, "One World—One People."

> With the passing of the camp system here, one by one will also go (we hope) the old rivalry which existed and was fostered by previous administrations.... We shall be doing ourselves and our fellows an extreme disservice by carrying over this asinine rivalry to new quarters. Let not the trap born of the old days be sprung again.[135]

There was precedent for unity. Ballam's intercamp groups and the Nic Nacs' recent Labor Day show had already demonstrated prisoner solidarity through music and dance. Eventually, prisoners moved in. While the new prison didn't bring immediate social harmony, it did bring new possibilities for musical collaboration. It took time to reestablish jazz there.

Prisoners transferred to the new prison generally had privileged status (officially and unofficially). Those with little political power stayed at the decrepit camps. Granted, no one wanted to be at Angola at all, but there was palpable excitement about the new facility.[136] Moving from Camp A into the new building must have felt like moving forward through time. Still, the new prison had new challenges for associated musicians. There were more gates to be unlocked, requiring new security procedures. Segregation remained. Modern architecture was no match for racism. Jim Crow remained throughout the new prison, despite modest administrative and prisoner efforts.[137] Even so, the vestigial camp identities were eroding thanks to prisoners' actions, print articles, radio commentary, and musical performances.

The design of the new prison accommodated prisoner associations—radio, education, recreation, and *The Angolite*. For musicians reliant on associations, clubs and council members were all within close reach: a walk away, albeit with a few turns of keys. As musicians found places within the new prison, they made some changes audible.

By summer 1956, the new prison had a closed-circuit "radio" station expressly for prisoner entertainment—the first iteration of WLSP radio. The recreation department set up an intercom system with linked speakers and patched in distant radio programs and broadcasts of local performances. Prisoners DJ'ed from 7:00 a.m. to 10:00 p.m. using a homemade record player broadcasting from a studio on top of the education building. Strauss waltzes, Basin Street boogie, and bebop played through speakers wired up in work areas, the cafeteria, and the walk.[138] Program schedules appeared in *The Angolite*. Listeners would often print their thanks in the same pages, likely aiming their appreciation of WLSP at DJs for their efforts and Warden Sigler for his allowance.[139]

The station attracted donations through requests in *The Angolite*, outside media, and networks to external contacts. A gift of two professional turntables drastically upgraded the station.[140] And when three prisoners spoke on WDSU-TV in New Orleans, the television station sent WLSP seventy-five records.[141] At the request of an Angola minister, a private donor sent more than a hundred records.[142] Stations throughout the state began donating more. The records were a boon for musicians hungry for new music.

WLSP became a resource for the bands forming in the new prison. By 1957, WLSP partnered with the education department to set up equipment in the library. There, DJs recorded bands and broadcast the performances around the prison. When it was too cold to perform outside, recordings kept the sounds of local talent audible.

Though closed-circuit, WLSP was in a tradition of multivocal radio programs as described in the last chapter—unpredictably mixing penal discipline with cultural representation and entertainment.[143] Warden Sigler found an administrative use for the radio. Each week, he hosted *Facts not Rumors,* a fifteen-minute show in which he answered questions sent in from prisoners.[144] In an everyday sense, WLSP helped break the monotony, provided more reliable information from the administration, and gave hope for continuing reform amid looming threats of budget cuts.[145] The station was one of a few institutions for musicians within the new prison.

While the new Director of Education position suffered high turnover, each free-staff administrator was an advocate for music. The first director was a musician himself. Director Mark McWaters established a performance class and taught lessons to an initial class of three dozen Black and White students. He called for two new bands to form at the new prison, one White and one Black. Along with the new bands, new instrument purchases replaced the old worn-out ones from the camps.[146] McWaters purchased saxophones and clarinets and reconditioned two pianos.

Most of the music resources went to the new prison. But in general, music was not an administrative priority. The program was always precarious. McWaters produced the 1956 Fourth of July event at the new prison cafeteria and showcased the new prison's latest bands. The show was a disappointment, and by August, McWaters left his position.[147] For the rest of the year, musical activity slowed. A baffled contributor to *The Angolite* wrote, "It was expressed that during off hours on our days off we would be entertained by our local musicians and their mellow music. Could you tell us, the inmates, why a fine plan has fallen through? . . . No use to have horns and drums if no one can enjoy its purpose."[148]

Eventually, pianist Fred Nesbit began teaching piano. Older than most at thirty-eight, the New Orleanian was beginning his three years of "hard labor" for marijuana possession.[149] He was a Bourbon Street entertainer, playing regularly at Show Bar and La Lune, and a piano arranger.[150] Nesbit put his skills on stage at the 1955 Christmas show.[151] He took McWaters's teaching position soon after the performance, a welcome alternative to working the fields. *The Angolite* later voiced approval: "Fred Nesbit, stylish man of the ivories is doing a wonderful job tutoring those who wish to learn to play the piano. . . . The professor, one of the finest in his field, is a true artist."[152]

He quickly rose to become the vice president of the Dale Carnegie Human Relations Program, securing yet another foothold in the new prison.

Meanwhile, stuck at Camps A and I, the Nic Nacs renewed their request for musical instruments. The administration finally responded, giving them the option of transferring to the new prison and joining the new Black orchestra.[153] Transferring prisoners was more straightforward than moving instruments.

Once transferred, Lester Thompson and Fuzz Surgent had to adjust to the new regime. Questions loomed. Would camp tours still make sense for the Nic Nacs? Would the plantation holidays still be a site for intercamp cooperation? Would moving musicians through the labyrinthine dormitories help or hinder regular rehearsals? Who would compete for power and space?

The Nic Nacs' debut in the new prison was lackluster. Playing on the fenced-in walkway that connected the dormitories got them little attention.[154] Thompson wrote, frustrated at the lack of *Angolite* coverage and general support, "We have a small combo and band and in this condition of being incarcerated it takes a lot of effort, what with all the practicing these cats do."[155] The developing associations filling the new prison were primarily White. So the Nic Nacs kept searching for their niche. An opportunity soon opened in an unexpected place.

In March 1957, the Inmate Council approved a measure mandating that 10 percent of all financial transactions, even transactions among inmates, would go to the Inmate Lending Fund.[156] In essence, it was a sales tax to build the ILF beyond its donation-driven support. With the opening of the new prison, the camp inmate councils consolidated, and all eyes were on the future of the ILF (see figure 2.7).

Fuzz Surgent had become a council member and worked out a deal in which the Nic Nacs would play an all-camp and new prison tour as an ILF fundraiser. Music would help publicize and boost the new political and financial structures. To produce such a tour, Surgent needed to enlist more administrators than ever. Security was more complicated with the new prison. Plus, they would need to move a significant amount of money around the camps if things went well. For a few months, Surgent got the support of the new Director of Education, the Superintendent of Industries, and the Inmate Council. But the proposal got cold while waiting for the approval of Warden Sigler.

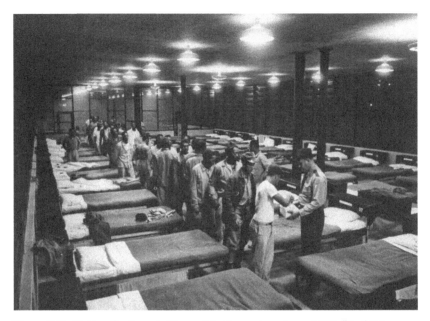

Figure 2.7. Voting for Inmate Council in the main prison, 1955. "Bad Prison Goes Straight," *Life Magazine* 39, no. 24, December 12, 1955, 58.

Thompson wrote another open letter, appealing to fellow prisoners. No doubt, his letter resonated. The Nic Nacs' stale proposal was like many other stalled promises at the new prison.

> I want to ask all the inmates that are likers of good music to try to the best of their ability to support us, musicians, and the Disck Jockey [sic] we have been promised some things that have never happened. We, the musicians were told that we would have the pleasure of playing music at all camps with the inmate lending fund, as our sponsors, it has been taken before the Board and approved, but it looks like for some reason beyond our knowledge, someone has chocked our wheels. If you have eyes for some entertainment of all description see your inmate council, ask for what you want. That's the only way to get what you want, we want the inmates to know that there isn't anything we would like to do better than to play for them, and a little freedom too.[157]

With no action, the Nic Nacs resigned themselves to playing on the walk when the weather allowed.[158] With help from the WLSP DJs, they also managed to record in the library. When it was too rainy, their music blared out of the speakers drilled into the cinder block walls.

The Warden's Band

By May 1957, the Nic Nacs got approval to play the intercamp tour. (For reference, this was the same year Harry Oster secured magnetic tape from the Library of Congress to record folk songs.) The Nic Nacs had come far from Camp A, relocating to a modern facility, gaining the support of WLSP, *The Angolite*, the Inmate Council, and the Inmate Lending Fund, and, in their final crucial step as a prison band, became the Warden's band.

The tour began in an unlikely place—Camp D, known locally by the men as the "Forbidden City." On the yard of the decrepit women's unit, the Nic Nacs played an hour-long set. Given how rare it was to play coed and interracial events, the songs likely had an unusual potency that Saturday evening. B. B. King's 1956 "You Upset Me Baby" was solid dance music, but its repetitive line, "Well, like being hit by a fallen tree, woman, what you do to me," lingered with many of the women after the show.[159] In the following days, the Nic Nacs continued through the camps, hospitals, and the new prison, but Camp D was a highlight. In their regular column in *The Angolite*, the women thanked Warden Sigler and L. G. Knox, the chairman of the Inmate Lending Fund, for "making the happening be" and the Nic Nacs for "making it be a happening."[160]

Soon after, the women moved from the Forbidden City to the Willows. More simply known as Camp F, the rat-infested fire-trap dormitory had been refurbished, and the chicken coop became a workshop space. The impetus for the move may have been to achieve equity with the men having the new prison. Or perhaps it was because the hog pens built next to the Forbidden City had been more acceptable for habitation than the women's quarters—"like a Bowery skid-row flop-house," as described in *The Angolite*.[161] At the Willows, the women formed a separate inmate council.[162]

Musical opportunities were different for incarcerated women.[163] There were no jazz ensembles at the Willows. Formal group singing was predominantly religious. Black women also sang in the sewing factory and fields. Some of that singing was likely similar to blues that scholar Sarah Haley describes as a distinctively Black challenge to the terror of incarceration.[164] Harry Oster would eventually record Odea Matthews singing "Something

Within Me" at her sewing machine. Fifty-six years later, Dennis Childs would hold Mathews's performance up as an "act of sonic redress [that] expresses the burdened, dispossessed, and terrorized collective predicament of the living dead through the very act of sounding claim to a modicum of individual freedom."[165] The women at the Willows found other collective uses for music.

While the women could not go to the new prison, they managed to bring its sounds to them. It is no small feat to initiate a music series in prison. Their access to the administration helped. Many White women worked in the warden's office. Secretarial work was a convenient way to merge penitentiary philosophy (developing job skills) with the mandate for self-sufficiency (a lack of paid administrative positions). As a consequence, these women had the warden's ear while engaged in daily prison operations. Warden Sigler's wife, Francys, also led a church music group, accompanied by an organ.[166] Working closely with the administration had perks. The women managed to turn the first Nic Nacs' show at Camp D into a monthly series at the Willows.[167]

The Nic Nacs, now the most talked about band at Angola, played the Willows in June and then again in July.[168] The diverse sets had something for everyone, and the band unleashed their songs at unbelievably quick tempos, reflecting the event's excitement. The lyrics "And I am once again with you" from "Stardust" and "Embrace me, my sweet embraceable you" from "Embraceable You" no doubt got everyone imagining. In a review, one woman reported that the jump blues classic "Let the Good Times Roll" reached "whatever part of the listening body that had remained unmoved." The words, "Come on baby, let the good times roll . . . roll all night long . . . feels so good . . . when you're home," reminded them of good times before prison—left behind, hopefully waiting after release, or just within the imagination of the moment. Jazz standards "Sweet Georgia Brown" and "Half Nelson" showcased virtuosic solos. By the July show, the Nic Nacs incorporated original songs, debuting Surgent's "Mood for Mex (Desire for Travel)."

In September, the Women's Council held a meeting and requested the Nic Nacs to perform for them yet again.[169] In response, Warden Sigler put them on a bi-monthly schedule. At this point, they brought guest singers and took requests. "Pennies from Heaven" was a regular request. Sitting in on vocals, Ben "Since I Fell for You" Stewart crooned, "The streets outside are paved with gold."[170] While there is no concert recording, Harry Oster's unreleased 1960 recording of the Nic Nacs might come close to substituting.

It's unclear why Oster recorded the Nic Nacs. Maybe the blues scholar was humoring the group and had a few reels of tape to spare. Maybe Odea Matthews convinced him after he recorded her while sewing. Fortuitously, the recordings give a sense of the music—a dance-oriented mix of standards, current bop, and original songs played by musicians of uneven experience. Among the twenty-eight songs on the reels, "Sweet Georgia Brown" and "Half Nelson" are ones the women report hearing throughout the Nic Nacs' 1957 Willows series. The recordings are refinements of what they had played for the women. But during the recording session, instead of playing to dozens of women, the Nic Nacs had a thirty-six-year-old LSU English professor and his stereo microphone as their audience.

Nonetheless, "Half Nelson" busts out in breakneck bebop tempo, adding chromaticism to the original head. Saxophones fill the arrangement with busy added passages and then split into harmonies at the end. A drum fill abruptly stops the song—as if the rug was pulled from underneath. "Sweet Georgia Brown," also on the Willows set, is a well-known jazz standard born from a 1925 popular song. But Fuzz sneaks in a more contemporary quote from Charlie Parker's virtuosic "Ornithology," laying on yet another level of bebop reference. The melody returns to the original but can't shake the Parker-esque inflection that Fuzz introduces. Imagining these recordings intermixed with ballads and occasional crooning along with the shows described in *The Angolite*, it's safe to say that the women brought life to the Willows by managing to book the Nic Nacs.

The Nic Nacs quickly reached acclaim with secure footing in the new social and administrative regime, filling pages of *The Angolite* with ample details of their performances, reviews, and updates on band members—evidence of their continued support from the Director of Education and Warden Sigler. Their progress, however, was not smooth. Attrition through release had always been a threat to prison groups. When Arsia "Streamline" Harris was released, the Nic Nacs lost their piano and sax player.[171] And not all their requests were approved. Supporting a recording session request on behalf of, in his words, "one of the biggest outfits on Angola, the Nic Nacs," a prisoner in the new prison wrote:

> They are a group of inmate musicians who serve as great morale boosters (eh, Willows) for the entire population and a key part in Rockin' Charlie's talent shows. Under the fine leadership of Louis (Fuss [sic]) Surgent,

cutting a few sides would really prove to be a fine move by the Recreation program.[172]

No one ever approved a request to record. Members of the Nic Nacs were still prisoners, and things like cotton harvesting always took precedence.

Associations did provide degrees of liberty. Surgent joined the education staff at the new prison to teach music.[173] Like Les Winslow before him, Surgent could scout for and train musicians to keep the Nic Nacs fresh (simultaneously avoiding the backbreaking work in the fields). Musicians aspired to join the Nic Nacs. *The Angolite* offered frequent encouragement through published asides like, "F. Kaugman is doing a good job playing his saxaphone [sic]. Keep it going, you'll make the Nacs."[174] Jam sessions also helped create opportunities for new musicians to catch Surgent and Thompson's ears. Sometimes auditions turned into full-fledged shows. According to *The Angolite*, one audition day was "such a sensational success last Saturday that the audience joined in to create a floor-shaking jam session. This occurred three times during the afternoon."[175] These degrees of liberty had a catch.

Music wasn't only for prisoners' ears. Because Angola and the surrounding small towns weren't quite a cultural hotbed, free staff and their families relied on the bands for entertainment. In a macabre way, the employees had professional New Orleans musicians in artist-residencies enforced by the state. Lin Sharpe, who grew up in the B-Line housing at Angola, remembers this simply as one of the perks of her dad's job.

> We all headed to the dances in the "A" building which was a part of the "new" prison. The guards would have to let us through two locked, barred doors into the large room where the bands were set up on one end of the room and tables for the free people were set up on one side.... The bands played current popular music and I always thought they were very good. The jitterbug was the predominant fast dance and their selections were a good mix of fast and slow songs. The girls were all crazy about a guitar player named Rocky and that's all we knew—he was a guitar player and he was cute in a tough, convicty sort of way. The age range attending the dances was amazing in that there were small children all the way up to grandparents ... and everyone danced![176]

Music brought various people together, but temporarily and conditionally. When the music stopped, the Nic Nacs returned to being conscripted laborers in a plantation power structure, a step away from other prisoners put to use at Angola as cooks or house boys.[177] Thankfully, there were other connections to hold on to when the music stopped.

All the work surrounding the Nic Nacs helped create and sustain collaborative opportunities and build resources throughout the prison. For the next several years, the Nic Nacs and their supporters kept busy, playing for prisoners and free staff alongside Ballam's All-Stars, the Chosen Gospel singers, and the emerging rock and roll groups like Jimmie West's Rock 'n Rollers, the Marvin Loveless Rockabilly Band, and the Jones Boys.[178] Guest singers sat in with the Nic Nacs and developed notoriety. The Nic Nacs had a standard repertoire of popular songs but always needed to create new arrangements and keep things fresh and current. Media attention in *The Angolite* could reach sympathetic readers on the outside. Theo "Nubby" Jack published a favorable comparison of the Nic Nacs to innovative players on the outside: "Nice work, 'Cool,' your sounds are more like [Gerry] Mulligan, and 'Buddy' kicks like Max Roach."[179] The attention like this brought a sporadic but reliable influx of donated records from outside readers to WLSP, providing critical up-to-date sounds for musicians to study.

In February 1959, prisoners built a stage recreation of a New Orleans nightclub for a show after Mardi Gras had wrapped up far away in New Orleans. Noting the whole music and dance procession, an *Angolite* reviewer marveled at the effort and success: "After many hours of preparation, Art Davis and his fellows put on a show for the spectators who had never seen the Indian Pow Wows executed exactly as done in 'The Easy' in Mardi Gras."[180] It was almost as good as a street session with full costumes. With music's powerful reference to the world beyond prison, the Nic Nacs and their dancing audience probably didn't seem to be from Angola. Maybe that was the point.

The structure of the prison that provided support for jazz would not last. Reforms that began with the pain of self-mutilation and Nurse Daugherty's vocal resignation in 1951 started to unravel with a whisper in 1958. Warden Sigler had staffed his office with a female prisoner named Penny Kent. That was just what State Representative Lloyd Teekell needed to turn a whispering campaign about Sigler into an official report. Teekell and other representatives of surrounding rural areas criticized the new Angola, applying political pressure to local distrust of the federal penologist's leadership. Voters were already wary of outsiders running the prison. When they found out that prisoners like Penny Kent were being considered more qualified for administrative positions than civilians were, they were outraged.[181] *The Teekell*

Report, based on Representative Teekell's initial visit to the institution in 1957, urged expanding the plantation—primarily the sugar and cotton crops. Warden Sigler's allies argued that agricultural jobs were already drying up in Louisiana and that the expansion of agriculture would impede efforts of rehabilitation programs.[182] But the committee countered that mechanization and a rising convict population resulted in idleness and surplus labor. At its heart, however, the whispering campaign was part of an assault on the new penology. Rumors insinuated that Penny Kent's background as a stripper was the real reason she was working as Sigler's secretary. Some even said she was pregnant.[183] Presented as a legitimate indictment of Angola's leadership, *The Teekell Report* altered statements taken from prisoners to discredit Sigler. The effort succeeded.

Amidst the attack on his policies and character, Warden Sigler resigned. The day after, over 2,000 prisoners protested by refusing breakfast and not working.[184] The Board of Institutions nominated Victor G. Walker, a staffer since 1954, one of the Federal employees brought to Angola. He oversaw the women's relocation to a new facility in St. Gabriel, south of Baton Rouge, in 1961. Walker managed brief continuity with established reform until he left in 1963. The battle over old and new Angola blazed in the legislature. The conservative-leaning *Shreveport Times* blasted legislators who were trying to essentially legislate for outlawry, accusing them of believing, in their words, "that a prison sentence is intended to place a man—or a youth—under conditions of cruelty and hardship making it impossible for him ever to be a trustworthy citizen again."[185] The penitentiary, plantation, and outlawry models continued to play against each other in and outside Angola. Free staff members left after Governor Davis slashed the prison budget by a third in 1962. Some programs continued only because prisoners stepped up to run them.[186] While the end of reform and defunding had a detrimental effect on the associations, the fundamental aspect of interstitiality—gradients of power that ran through prisoner roles—would remain at Angola and continue to affect music. The structures that supported creative collaboration withered, but the decade of jazz, in particular, set a precedent for others. The musicians had forged a legacy out of penitentiary logic. Following 1963, musicians moved the degrees of freedom established by leaders like Les Winslow, Leroy Dukes, Adrian Ballam, James McElroy, Lester Thompson, and Louis Surgent into new spaces that would continue to cultivate them.[187]

Listening to Jazz in Prison

In 1959, as reform at Angola began to unravel, German jazz scholar Joachim-Ernst Berendt came to the United States on a three-month jazz research tour. He hired fashion photographer William Claxton to document the trip and the musicians they encountered. Berendt's *The Jazz Book* (1953) was already an authoritative general history of the genre (and continues to be updated as jazz develops).[188] In New Orleans, Berendt met Harry Oster, who suggested they take a side trip to Angola to hear the blues. John Lomax's folkloric notions still haunted the scholarly imagination of "prison music." Oster pitched to Berendt that Angola was a musical time machine, containing the roots of what they were hearing in the contemporary New Orleans jazz clubs. Berendt took Oster up on his offer.

In Berendt and Claxton's account of the visit, there is no mention or photograph of the Nic Nacs or Adrian Ballam's bebop group. Dramatically, Claxton describes finding "authenticity" in (what we have been calling) outlawry that lay beyond steely local gatekeepers.

> The morning we arrived at the prison gates, the guard was stern but obliging and had us ushered through to the warden's office. The warden listened as Joe [Berendt] explained that we wanted to photograph and record some of the jailed musicians. He took a puff on his cigar and asked which "side" we wanted to visit: "The nigger side or the white side?" Joe quickly replied, "Oh, the Negro side. Aren't there more musicians there?" The warden gave us an icy look and said, "Okay, but I can't give you a guard escort; we're short of men. You are on your own." I got a lump in my throat, but I kept quiet.[189]

From what we know through this chapter's account, it seems as if Claxton was in another prison. The warden, Victor G. Walker, was a federal penologist desperately holding together the reform efforts in Warden Sigler's wake. He was anything but gruff and indifferent. And though the prison was segregated, there was no Black and White "side." But it sets up the idea that they made a choice when they arrived. However the trip unfolded, they missed the active, contemporary jazz at Angola.

Oster took the German musicologist and the fashion photographer to Camp A. Hoagman Maxey, who Oster had already recorded, played for them. (From this chapter, we know that most of the younger musicians with connections had managed transfers to the new prison.) Claxton continues:

My fear disappeared and we actually enjoyed ourselves, as did the prisoners. After leaving the prison, I got a delayed reaction to being surrounded by a thousand or so prisoners with no guard. It was a bit unnerving. The music and stories that we heard were both depressing and inspiring, but above all authentic.[190]

The story exaggerates. There were nowhere near a thousand in Camp A. But more interestingly, the account, together with what we now know about Angola's jazz and its related associations, shows how the folkloric gaze persisted. The ways of thinking about "prison music" didn't account for the swell of younger urban prisoners, for the importance of staying current with musical changes developing in the outside world, or for collective and collaborative efforts that blur the power relationships between prisoners, administrators, and guards. Judging for authenticity got in the way of listening to incarceration.

In a *New York Times* interview about the trip, Berendt said of the Angola blues, "This is the true jazz and poetry, not the things the beatniks do."[191] But there was jazz there. When I first read about this visit, it was after I had pieced together the Nic Nacs story. I couldn't help but wonder: Had they heard the Nic Nacs play in the new prison, would it have seemed authentic to them? More to the point: How might they have listened productively to jazz at Angola? I would later discover that Oster had indeed heard them.

As mentioned earlier, Oster did record a small amount of jazz. He recorded the Nic Nacs and the All-Stars on two-track tape on five occasions in 1960: February 6, April 10, 11, 25, and June 1. The twenty-eight unreleased jazz songs include standards like "Scrapple from the Apple," "Half Nelson," and "Straight, No Chaser," as well as a few original compositions. To my ear, these recordings provide evidence of association. They are an audible claim to professionalism. The style reveals the urge to return to the flow of life back home in New Orleans and Baton Rouge. The music is evidence that drug convictions increasingly ensnared young African Americans, those on the forefront of jazz and caught up by racial profiling in the Jim Crow South. This way of listening to music in prison is outside the scope of most folk music collections.

I received copies of the reels thanks to Adam Machado at Arhoolie Records, the small venerable folk- and blues-focused record label in El Cerrito, California, that acquired Oster's recordings after his death. I felt like it was a prison break, perhaps more of an archive break, getting the sounds past the label's president Chris Strachwitz, who perhaps saw little value in Oster's recordings of progressive jazz.

When I listen to the recordings, I listen for the sound of the space, for interactions among the musicians, to various personalities, for evidence of the aspiration, and as best as I can discern, to the agendas of different players. In short, I listen to how they fill their space. The acoustics give a sense of the physical space. The large ensembles drown out the sounds of the farm that are audible on many of Oster's other recordings. The short but prominent reverberation gives a feeling of activity in a closed space. These are not studio recordings of studio musicians. As field recordings, they expose technical flaws and lack of recording experience in some of the musicians' performances (minor flubs easily forgotten in a live setting). The arrangements accommodate a range of abilities and are at times ahead of the playing skills of the performers. But the flaws reveal aspiration. Each missed note shows knowledge of what the musicians are *trying* to accomplish, a work-in-progress, and a legacy with roots in Les Winslow's classes in Camp E. This carceral associationalism gave prisoners small degrees of power together, more than they could find working under the gun as individuals.

James Khoury, a former student of mine and a jazz musician, offered this sympathetic take on the musical unevenness after studying the recordings and the history of music at Angola that I have presented in this chapter. He writes, "The failure to clearly, definitively, and crisply play technical passages in their entirety, intonation issues, articulation discrepancies, incorrect chord tones during a solo, and other shortcomings are *part of a collective, accepted by all of the players within this shared convention* [my emphasis]."[192] He identified things he knew well as a jazz student—sticking close to a shared ideal arrangement of a song while also searching for innovative voice-leading, interpreting musical form, quoting recordings, and the audacity of developing whole-cloth new compositions.

Despite the artificiality of Oster's recording situation, the musicians probably felt excited to be recorded by an outsider—even if he was an English professor. The excitement is audible in the successful musical moments. Soloists take their time to find a musical niche or groove, and when they do, the band responds. Fuzz Surgent leans in with astonishing prowess on his horn. The uncredited piano player asserts an unwavering St. Louis style with laid-back chord blocks in steady train-like rhythms. The guitarist's comping is understated. It has a veteran's simplicity, making room for others while keeping the music fit for dancing. Whoever did the arrangements dropped in moments of *sforzando* surprise and unpredictable rhythmic interpretations of the standards. The original compositions don't sound like Angola. They sound beyond Angola.

Musicians incarcerated at Angola negotiated the flows of an ideological and material change in order to keep playing, each group using musical footholds established by their predecessors. Over a decade, jazz performances by the Cavaliers, the Rhythm Makers, the All-Stars, and the Nic Nacs helped erode Black minstrel and White hillbilly acts of prison vaudeville. By eliminating vaudeville, the scene that the Nic Nacs eventually represented challenged the stereotype of an uneducated, unskilled prisoner. The dogged persistence of the musicians was one factor in their success. But they also relied on the occasional but crucial administrative support from the warden and even more vital support from the associations that developed out of a reform idea convenient to Angola's mandate for self-sufficiency: that prisons work best when prisoners are allowed to set up their own systems.

Along with Warden Sigler's departure in 1958, Angola suffered a lack of funding and further erosion of reform efforts. Drug convictions continued to bring in new musicians, young players who began to develop a politically charged sensibility in the leadup to and aftermath of the Civil Rights Act. The next chapter shows how the Nic Nacs would press on through 1967, adapting to a changing prison. In the violent austerity of a prison farm, a new version of the Nic Nacs would become an association that expressed Blackness through musical style, develop an intellectual community, and hold on to fragments of liberty.

3
Politics

It was a bit past five o'clock, December 16, 2008. Leotha Brown prepared for the cold, bundled in a gray hoodie, jean jacket, and dark watch cap. Brown had just clocked out from his daily job as a transportation clerk and had collected his saxophone. Clutching the worn instrument case, he left the band room of Camp F, the trusty camp located at the northernmost border of the prison. Mainly, the country and the gospel bands used the band room, keeping their equipment locked in the plywood cabinets they had built. Brown didn't play in a group anymore. But others made space for him. He had plenty of respect as a veteran member of the musicians' community. As part of his usual routine, he took time to play music by himself before dinner began.

Brown walked his instrument case from the band room toward the barbed wire fence, placed it on a metal picnic table, and opened it up. His soprano saxophone rested in the black felt. I watched him assemble it with his calloused fingers. He turned to the fence and, as it seemed to me, prepared to play to an invisible audience on the other side. But I had it wrong. He didn't imagine an audience at all. He wasn't transforming the picnic area into a stage. He was putting himself somewhere else, somewhere indefinable, past the storage shed and over the fields. "I look outside," he told me afterward, "beyond the fences. I look beyond the fences because, really, that's where I am when I'm playing. I'm beyond any type of confinement, any type of restraints."[1]

Occasionally, a few other prisoners shuffled behind him on the gravel path without looking, familiar with his routine. His playing continued, busy and exploratory, shifting from a straightforward rendition of Nat Adderley's jazz standard "Work Song" to free and extended modal departures awash in Coltrane-esque sheets of sound. Postbop innovator Yusef Lateef played the same song when he was with the Adderley Brothers Quintet in 1964, the same year Leotha Brown came to Angola, the same year that the Civil Rights Act passed.

Well before that historic legislation, when Nat Adderley was a child, he watched a chain gang out his window. He listened to them sing as they paved the street in front of his family's Florida home.[2] He drew from that experience when he eventually wrote "Work Song," a musical commentary on the history of bondage. In the original 1960 recording, Adderly initiates call-and-response melodies with his cornet. Guitar (Wes Montgomery) and cello (Sam Jones) answer back. Loud resonant snare hits (Louis Hayes) imitate a hammer, hoe, or ax, sounding out otherwise monotonous labor, decisively framing each call, each response. In a way, Adderley had archived a troubling childhood experience and updated it by turning it into jazz. The choruses break from the imitative head arrangement and shift into a slippery four-on-the-floor sixteen-bar blues that seems like a twelve-bar cycle until you give up counting and just start feeling—quintessential hard bop of its time. The final moment in the 1960 recording is Adderley slowly recapitulating the melody alone.

Leotha Brown's 2008 rendition is another thing altogether, bringing Adderley's transformation of bondage into the early-twenty-first-century prison. It's as if he takes Adderley's final statement in the 1960 recording as a hand-off and keeps developing it. In Brown's continuation, the voices of the unnamed men in Florida that Adderley had resurrected in a jazz tune now sounded over the fields of a Louisiana prison farm. Brown took it farther out, breaking up the structure to dwell in the push and pull of notes, exploring a sound, allowing himself melodic and rhythmic freedom to find new takes on the original. The performance wasn't just astonishing. It was principled, guided by deeply felt knowledge of music and politics. Brown's playing matched his demeanor—refreshingly self-assured and centered, not needy, wanting, or strategizing to get something out of our encounter.

After Brown carefully packed his horn, we sat on a bench nearby. I had developed enough trust with my security escort that she walked off to attend to other things. (Or it could be that the officer was simply less interested in music than we were.) I was still in my early trips to Angola, learning, listening openly, allowing conversations to go where they would go, and following leads. Several musicians had pointed me to Brown. They told me he was the closest I could get to a music historian at Angola. His qualifications: forty-four years of incarceration, his proven dedication to music, and his clear memory.

I asked him about the song he had just played. Admittedly, I thought it might lead to actual work songs, like the ones John Lomax and Harry Oster recorded. "Years ago," he began, "they would work, and they would sing songs and more or less keep the rhythm while they're working..." But soon, Brown pivoted back to jazz, shifting from third person to first person to describe his earliest memories of Angola. "When I found out they had a music room where they were making music, I went to the band room," he remembered. "This is when I met some musicians. They all had their instruments and so forth. They had bands already formed."[3] In this way, Brown led me to Angola's jazz legacy.

At this point, I was unaware of the Nic Nacs, the Rhythm Makers, and the Cavaliers. I only knew of Angola's musical life through the Lomax and Oster recordings. I still thought of prison as a site where a state power acted on an individual and that music was the voice of that impossible struggle. It took me a while to understand how the 1960s prison farm had been alive with innovative, politically minded jazz. For a few years, I continued to talk with Brown about his experience and ideas, triangulating music, violence, and association. He had become a member of the Nic Nacs within a few years of his incarceration.

Brown died before I had done enough research in *The Angolite* to know the 1950s precursor to his early musical scene, before I understood the significance of being an alumnus of the Nic Nacs. So I was left to follow a lead: I remembered when he put his hand on that worn instrument case one day and told me, "This came from a very special friend of mine, Charles Neville of the Neville Brothers. He and I played together up here. He taught me more about music than they ever did in school."[4]

This chapter untangles what Leotha Brown presented all at once when he played Adderley's "Work Song" through the fence into the fields. It describes the fields as a place of outlawry and slavery, but it also connects the fields to a more significant space for associated musicians: the band room. The violence in the fields inspired some musicians to search for principles of musical politics collectively, not through work songs, but rather, through getting out of the fields and into the band room. Avant-garde jazz, practiced in relative safety, was an escape to a place of learning and resistance. As musicians learned how to improvise, they developed musical and political ideas. We'll pick up where the last chapter left off, forty-four years before I met Leotha Brown, when any hopes of reforming Angola had evaporated. State funding had decreased as violence increased.[5] A young musician landed in Angola on a drug charge.

Singing Out-of-Law

When twenty-five-year-old Charles Neville arrived in 1964, the music scene was in retreat but still semifunctional. This was the least of his problems. Officially, newcomers received thirty days of work exemption, but because it was harvest season, no one was exempt from working in the field. The young saxophone player, adept at R&B and, to an increasing degree, jazz, found himself holding a bag in a cotton field early in the morning. Someone somewhere blew a whistle. Neville looked around, began yanking at the cotton, and dropped what came off into the bag. A moment later, he felt the sharp blow of an ax handle against his head. "Goddamn nigger, you don't know how to pick no cotton!"[6] The trusty guard, mounted on his horse, turned from Neville to the others and commanded, "One of you boys, come here and show this boy how to pick that cotton!" A nearby prisoner walked over and emptied Neville's bag, filled with useless green parts of the plant.

Neville developed new skills quickly, learning to twist the base of the cotton to pry it from the sharp green triangular boll. His fingers hurt, and he struggled to keep up. People continued to help that first day, even though it was against the rules. Apprehensive, Neville had heard macabre stories while nervously awaiting Angola in the parish jail about the consequences of receiving help from strangers. Aside from his exceptional horn playing, Neville was pretty representative of the demographic trend arriving at Angola—young, Black, urban, and knowing little about picking cotton and cutting cane.

Decades later, Neville would tell me that the musical life he developed at the prison grounded him. He devoted himself to study and practice in the musical association and eventually managed to articulate a political musicology. It took him a while to get there.

I met the legendary saxophonist in 2016. We participated in a music symposium at Angola. He brought his experience, and I brought my research. Weather canceled the event right after we touched down at the Baton Rouge airport, so we spent the week together at a hotel outside the prison. A second trip for the rescheduled event brought us into the prison to discuss music with an audience of prisoners and visitors. I invited him to Georgetown University for a week-long residency a year later.

On that early morning in the field in 1964, however, Neville's mind was not on singing. He was actively navigating the complex situation of forced farm work—the technique, the timing, the social dynamics, the fatigue, and the expectations. He was so focused on skill acquisition that he didn't even remember if anyone was singing. Fellow prisoner Albert Woodfox's insight, developed in those same fields in the mid-1960s, describes Angola's plantation logic: "In prison, you are part of a human herd. In the human herd survival of the fittest is all there is. You become instinctive, not intellectual. Therein lies the secret to the master's control."[7] Neville had to develop his instincts before getting back to music.

Neville needed new instincts when his work detail shifted from cotton to sugar cane. On his first day in the cane fields, Neville jumped off the hootenanny, the string of wagons pulled by a tractor that carried workers to the site, alert to conform to the motions of others. Four lines of men formed, two on either side of the hootenanny. Everyone prepared to collect the cane. Neville and the others walked on each side, keeping the pace of their cut with the moving vehicle. It took a while to adapt to the work. Reflecting on the experience decades later, Neville laughed at himself for not knowing how to swing a blade to cut sugar cane properly. His first hit sent the blade bouncing back and left the cane uncut. (You have to hit it at an angle.) But he was also laughing at the indignity and the impracticality of the situation. The joke—to spell it out—was how absurd it was, in 1964 Louisiana, to be a Black man stuck in a sugar cane field as a consequence of holding two joints of marijuana.

In time, he cracked jokes and told epic stories to build camaraderie in the field. He finally tuned in to his fellow New Orleanians singing old Indian tunes to pass the time, relieve frustration, or feel at home together.[8] As detailed systematically by folklorists, many older work songs kept the pace of the work, allowing workers to regulate the speed of group labor.[9] Work songs were pragmatic and political. Folklorists during the 1960s developed the idea that work songs forged solidarity—a powerful image during the civil rights movement. But the songs were disappearing in part due to mechanization and prison reform. Folklorist Bruce Jackson argued that work songs were disappearing in Texas prisons about the same time Neville was following a tractor with a cane blade at Angola.[10]

As Neville and I sat over coffee fifty years later, him in his signature tie-dyed T-shirt and beret, he continued the story of his early days at Angola with a mix of humor and horror. Discussions with Neville about the field kept questions alive in my mind. Were there songs he heard ones that we might connect to a larger tradition? Can we challenge the death pronouncement that folklorists gave to "pure folk song"? There is a little Lomax in me, but through conversations with Neville and other men forced into the fields like Neville, I learned how the violence and chaos of the fields connected to avant-garde jazz. Tracing that line requires understanding the extreme difference between the must fields and the band room. The fields contained outlawry, and the band room housed associations with the power to create by-laws: mutually determined, semipredictable collaborative procedures.[11] Musicians searched for different pockets of individual freedoms as they moved between these spaces. Though distinct, the field and the band room haunted each other.

Outlawry of the Field

One way to stay alive at Angola was to get out of the fields. But unless there was a medical reason, a prisoner's first job was in the fields. It didn't matter what skills they might have brought with them. Most tried to last ninety days without an infraction to be eligible for a transfer to another job. Follow-through, however, was inconsistent, and petty infractions kept most prisoners in the field, especially during harvest. The official logic held that the work was good for the prisoners. But for prisoners, the field's violence was far from logical. It was insanity. Given the lack of accountability out-of-law, everybody was a potential threat.

The competitions of the old camp system had given way to individual competition among the work lines. Some competed to see who could get work done the fastest. Yet they all had varied experiences. Some had worked on relatives' farms or picked up agricultural work in their teens. Most had not. Neville recalled the "bullies," those who took masculine pride in what prisoners called "bullying the crops." Aggressive approaches to agricultural work gave some a feeling of superiority over weaker prisoners. Jerry Courvelle expressed his attitude, linking it to his rural background: "We've been raised around fieldwork and horses all our lives. It's sort of in our blood. So, while most people would think of all this as bad work, we take it as bread and butter. There's nothing to it."[12] Others, like Neville, were from larger cities like New Orleans and had no experience with agriculture. They had to learn on the fly.

Financially, the work still kept Angola solvent. Agricultural work turned profits, and it also helped manage custody with minimal staff. Work was a way of occupying the prisoners' time. Major Dixon, who supervised work during this period, said, "The primary task is to keep the men busy. If there are periods when there is little to do in the field, we'll put them to work in the ditches, cutting grass, and working the roads."[13] There had been nominal reform by 1964. Shifts were now eight hours, an improvement from the days of working dawn to dusk in the 1940s. But miscounts of prisoners could keep them out in the field longer. The uneven procedures of work and custody were still rooted in the trusty incentive system, tied loosely to slavery (and explained systematically by sociologist Joseph Mouledous in the last chapter). When work wasn't monotonous, it was confusing. Most of the guards during this time were trustys and therefore caught up in the tangled power dynamics of the prison. The supposition of a "system," in fact, obscures that outlawry, the lack of law, defined the prisoner experience.

The prisoners who worked in the 1960s fields called it "the desert." As far as they were concerned, the work was fundamentally punishment and abandonment. When I talked to them about the experience, any discussion of singing was peripheral to their descriptions of the suffering and confusion. The cold of winter and the heat of summer worsened the poor conditions. Cotton stalks grew so close that they embraced each other and hid snakes. Southern copperhead, western cottonmouth, and canebrake rattlesnakes were the poisonous ones. Prisoners learned to identify them from the two dozen species in the area. Stress triggered unexpected fights, which are more dangerous when working with long sling blades. If a guard even perceived an infraction, he might immediately lash out, adding to the unpredictability of surveillance. Some prisoners tried to avoid or slow down work altogether by playing sick. But roving "technicians" pushed back with instant diagnoses, threatening to write up any false claims as infractions. Organized protests could result in being placed on lockdown or outright attacks from trustys and free staff.

Death lurked around every corner. Some prisoners were worked to death. Some died at the hands of each other. The stakes of fights rose when guards tied opponents' wrists together with a bandana.[14] Sexual assaults were commonplace. Rapes were more common when picking okra because the size of the crops kept things out of sight. "The heat and the work doesn't keep the men's mind off sex," Major Dixon coldly admitted in the 1970s, mistaking violence for sex.[15]

The rampant institution of prostitution throughout the prison heightened danger in the field. Accepting favors might provide an opening for coercion. Neville remembers a young piano player wrongfully convicted of rape who let down his guard. "He let some guy talk him into letting him help him and letting him get him stuff. He said, 'Okay. You owe me for all this stuff, and there's one thing I want . . .'"[16] In a swift series of moves, he was raped. By Angola's unofficial logic, the pianist then became the property of his rapist and afterward called a "gal-boy." He could be bought or sold in the sexual marketplace. "And so, they got him like that," Neville continues, lamenting the loss of a promising piano player. "That ended his career in the band because then he had his old man having him turning tricks at the out camps. He became a gal-boy once he became a bitch. That was it. He had no rights." Ending the arrangement was a challenge. The only way to get out of the situation was to kill your owner. Neville recalls how a guy named "Minnie the Moocher" got out of being a gal-boy.

> He caught the guy lying in his bed sleeping and had one of those shanks made out of a file, what they call a "black diamond" file. He went up there and put his hand over his face at the top of his head. [cutting sounds] Everybody in the dorm looked at him. He turned around after he killed that dude and said, "Alright, you motherfuckers. One of you all call me a bitch again, you know what's going to happen." And that was the end of him being a "girl."[17]

The stories I heard about Angola's 1960s fields reveal less about "dangerous predators" than they do about how the state can assert power through the suspension of law—outlawry.[18]

In the fields, the mind did its best to deal with unpredictability, stress, violence, and the monotony of the work. Sometimes prisoners drew on music's ability to stabilize or redefine relationships, substituting musical relations for legal relations. This is the work of music when practiced out-of-law.

Music of Outlawry

On a visit to Camp F, I asked a group of older prisoners about working the fields in the 1960s. They all burst into laughter.[19] They weren't musicians, so I didn't have the rapport, but still, it wasn't the reaction I expected. "A lot of them songs inmates sang, I couldn't talk about it. It wasn't right," one said, to which another added plainly, "It wasn't civilized." I pried a bit, "So guys were singing songs that *I* would be shocked about?" "Sure would!" he said. "Bet you would." They insisted if someone like Harry Oster (or I) had brought a microphone to the fields in the 1960s, he wouldn't have found anything. The administration wouldn't have allowed the kinds of talk rampant in the fields with an outsider around. They told me that it wouldn't have made much sense even if someone managed to record it. The talk was often coded. Prisoners spoke in pig Latin and slang (angering guards who couldn't understand it).[20]

I asked Neville about my interview with the men in Camp F, trying to get at what had felt like stonewalling. I asked why they laughed, and he replied, "Because *everything* went on in the field."[21] It was the kind of lost-for-words laughter that war veterans use to reflect on the insanity of war once they have a safe distance. As I would learn through dozens of interviews, chaos was the key to understanding music's role in the field. Without the protection of the law, work was unpredictable, dangerous, and disaffecting. Prisoners used every available resource to get out of the situation. Music became a repurposed skill, part of a set of tools that mitigated the chaos, the intense physicality of the labor, and the precarious position of being isolated. Music helped in two main ways: music lent structure to the experience and helped people get out of the field.

If outlawry tore apart the social fabric, music stitched some of those pieces back together by creating improvised social activities. Be careful not to romanticize it, though. Music had limited use and, as the men in Camp F told me, not always dignified. Abuse, trickery, fighting, and brutal labor dominated. Listening to music takes attention away from hearing potential threats. But in the right moments, prisoners told jokes and stories, played games, and sang.

Songs mixed with toasts, African American traditional heroic tales. Neville often told versions of "The Signifyin' Monkey," adapted from versions he heard as a child from his uncle and his friends while they played checkers:

> They said the fourth of May was a hell of a day. But the Fifth of May was a hell of a night because that was the last time old Brock saw the light. See now, Brock started across Eighth Street about half-past eight. When he got to St. Louis Place, he thought he was about fifteen minutes late. He walked in and say, "Hey bartender, you got any scotch to sell? If so, give me a fifth..."[22]

The tale could stretch into an hour of development and layer upon layer of jokes.

Not everyone remembered music being part of the field, but everyone remembered the loud rhythmic sound. Each cane stalk slice made two simultaneous sounds: a forceful blow to a hollow reed and a resonating metal blade. The long metal blade allowed for a low cut to the cane stalk and rang slightly longer than the reed because of its length. The distinctive sound punctuated a soundscape of rustling cane leaves and scattered conversations. Samuel Stark, who arrived in 1965 and worked in the cane and cotton fields for a year and a half, remembers finding and following group rhythms to guard against the swift consequences of lagging behind other workers.[23] Keeping rhythm wasn't musical to him. It was a way of not being heard. Being out of rhythm could attract unwanted attention.

Some listened for musicality in the soundscape for mental relief. "Music was coming from that blade, *'Whack!'* " Jimmy Johnson explained.[24] Some remembered when a musical rhythm caught on among the laborers. Given the unpredictable and uncoordinated work, the musicality didn't always last. "Sometimes in the field, they just go to singing, but they didn't have no direction to go in," explained Walter Quinn.[25] When it would catch, music gave relief to the inescapable labor. "It seemed to make the work a lot easier in the fields when everybody is just singing," said Leotha Brown. "It's something that you know you *had* to do, so let's get a little enjoyment out of what we're doing."[26]

When singing, prisoners mostly adapted contemporary songs. But using songs learned from the radio in the field was like using a butter knife as a screwdriver. It worked, albeit in a limited way, to pass the time, establish a fleeting sense of community, and maintain the rhythm of work. Older songs, now in folk song collections, were tailored to particular types of work. Songs born from manual labor matched song style to work needs. For example, the tempo of group cross-cutting ax songs matched the speed and weight of the axes. Sung verses were short and repetitive to guard against distraction (and accidents) when chopping down trees.[27] Newer commercial songs were not organic to manual labor like the old songs. But that doesn't mean that they didn't work. Elements of African American popular music—call-and-response, improvisation, and double-speak—have roots in work songs and can still coordinate labor, provide psychological relief, and establish community.

Fitting songs to work, most people drew from what they knew already. Fragments of songs from Ray Charles or Bobby Bland were typical, but there were also songs that didn't come from the radio. Some sang spirituals. Some made up songs or reworked old songs. Neville often sang the gospel hymn "How I Got Over," famously performed by Mahalia Jackson at the 1963

March on Washington, applying the song's sentiment to his own situation. Neville sang me a snippet of another he remembered learning in the field, swinging the eighth notes and pushing the F♯ a bit sharp for a blues feel (see figure 3.1).

Figure 3.1. Transcription of "Rumor Enough," sung by Charles Neville. Interview, 2016.

Lyrical themes reflected shared discomforts: "Oh Lord have mercy, the sun's so hot," "I need a drink of water," or "Waterboy, walk slow."[28] Some songs were specific to agricultural cycles and already well instituted. One Neville remembers well is "Tone the Bell," recorded by the Golden Eagle Gospel Singers in 1937 for Decca and perhaps distantly related to "Tone the Bell Easy," documented by Zora Neale Hurston and Alan Lomax in 1935. Neville sang it for me like this (see figure 3.2):

Figure 3.2. Transcription of "Tone the Bell," sung by Charles Neville. Interview, 2016.

People sang this version at the end of cane harvest, anticipating the ringing of a bell after someone cut the last stalk of cane, the one marked with a red bandana tied to the top. With that, harvest was over, and a prison-wide plantation holiday would follow. There was still work the day after the holiday: shaking stubble with a hoe for the next crop, cutting ditches, and cutting grass back with a blade.

Singing was part of the affective labor that filled the social void and eased the psychological terror of outlawry.[29] Music boosted spirits, validated each other's feelings, and salvaged human connections, even if in a transactional way. Prisoners who could sing well often described what they did as a type of labor with exchange value in Angola's complex unofficial economy. Larry Wilkerson remembers discovering the importance of knowing the lyrics to so many songs. It enabled him to carry a tune someone else might start but not be able to keep going. It also helped that he sang well and knew how to sing harmony. He quickly gained notice in the field. "By them knowing that I sing," he recalled, "they start to [ask], 'Hey Larry. Man, won't you sing one of them songs that you sung last week?'"[30] Even when not in the mood to sing, he accepted requests in exchange for cigarettes or a sandwich when they returned to the dorms. These transactional musical interactions helped stabilize relationships within the outlawry of the field. It also created broader connections.

Having a recognized musical ability could help someone get out of the field. Work reassignment required connections (Black prisoners were generally at a disadvantage). Therefore, music's ability to build relationships made it an important resource. Neville found his way out of the fields this way. Lester "Big Noise" Thompson of the Nic Nacs was going home. Neville's reputation put him first in line to replace Thompson. Leading the Black activities of the band room and playing horn with the Nic Nacs was a way of getting back to both music and safety, getting back in-law. But Neville was still not totally safe. Angola's fields were on the extreme end of outlawry, but outlawry exists wherever the prison exerts the power not to look. The by-laws of the music associations would provide relative freedom from outlawry.

Associations/Cliques and By-Laws/Muscle

Music alone can't protect anyone. Independent musicians at Angola might find a little respect to reduce their vulnerability, but it wasn't failsafe insurance. Musicians still had to prove to the yard they could defend themselves, fighting off assailants, defending reputations, or acquiring weapons. For

Neville, the structures around music-making offered supplemental protection. The band room became a stronghold, and the association of musicians became muscle.

Unofficially, Angola was organized by what are still called "cliques," social groups often defined by where people were from.[31] A few dominant friends led each one. Subordinate members were dependent "little kids" and sexual partners. Each clique had distinct personalities, identities, and projects. It's tempting to think of musicians as free from this social order, but music-making was simply one of the many group identities that defined hundreds of cliques. Nonetheless, the music cliques were distinctive. Musicians had a history of administrative access, specialized skills (music-making), and legacy.

Musicians in the band room looked for two things when searching for new members: strong players and strong fighters. As saxophonist Charles Venardo explained, the two skills intermixed in his musician clique:

> The guys in the band, they're going to make sure that don't nobody mess with you.... I had guys in my group that they was [physically] weak, but they would sing like angels. We backed people off them. We said, "Hey, find somebody else. He's in the group. We got him in the group." And he could sing and play good or do whatever that he can do good. It's like getting in a family. When you get in the group, you come under protection and everything. The group did look out for you. They take care of you. If you don't have this, don't have that. You need soap, deodorant, food stamps, or whatever.[32]

Once protected from outlawry through a band room assignment, musicians could survey the prison for other musicians, securing power and security.

Every Thursday was "fresh fish day," a crucial moment for finding new members. As new prisoners walked from intake into population, trusty guards left them to the onlookers. The loud voices from the first row intimidatingly promised to "turn out" newcomers. "I got you, boy!" "You're for me." "Look at that ass."[33] Hiding the fear in their eyes, newcomers searched for any friends behind the first row. In the band room, there was a promise of safety for those who might be a good fit.

Before Neville took over in 1964, the old guard from the 1950s had been holding the musicians together. Consider the following description of the activity in the band room, a montage that I have culled from various *Angolite* reports throughout the year before. It had been an active year, even if they had been more limited to the band room than they were in the 1950s. Well-worn instrument cases lined the room, some waiting for newly minted musicians who had completed music appreciation and theory courses with Kibby Ballam, Frank West, and Willie Judd. A new arrangement of a Charles Mingus tune was in the works. Ballam, formerly of the All-Stars, wrote original experimental songs and arrangements, now that he was adept on alto, tenor, and baritone horns. There weren't many instruments, but there were enough to outfit a half-dozen bands. Sixty-four new musicians had learned to read and could successfully play through current dance band arrangements.[34] Ralph "Rabbit" Howell and Norby Aias hovered over an electric guitar, working out songs for a rock band despite objections that it was a simpleton's music. The Jazzmen, Inc. and the Starlighters were two of the new groups, ready to replace the old guard. They shared rehearsal space with the Nic Nacs, still led by Lester Thompson and Fuzz Surgent. Even though musicians were segregated, they all shared a single band room. Some old players from the 1950s scene still crossed the color line to play jazz. Multi-instrumentalist Russell Sweet, for instance, played trumpet with the Black musicians and drum set with the White country musicians. Visual artists dropped by from the art room. Napoleon "Nappy" Fontaine created images inspired by jazz from materials easily sourced: duotone coffee and sugar on canvas.[35]

By Neville's account, the music scene had already shifted when he took over for Lester Thompson. Musicians were more constrained, but pockets of freedom remained. The Nic Nacs were no longer the warden's band. With Warden Sigler long gone, reform efforts had evaporated.[36] And because the administration acted less through the voluntary prisoner associations, it was harder for musicians to use reform-minded penitentiary logic to advocate for music resources. Bands waited for state holidays and plantation holidays to perform. Occasionally, Neville set up the Nic Nacs on the walk, accepting donations from the dormitories.[37]

Because of the lack of support from the administration, musicians were free from administrative oversight of their music. During band room jam sessions, musicians were free to explore new ways of making music. And when not playing together, musicians practiced intensely, studied music, arranged songs, and managed personnel. Thankfully, collaborative opportunities beyond the band room still existed. Many prisoner associations stayed intact through by-laws. Each association's formal and informal rules preserved certain freedoms gained in the 1950s. By-laws helped codify membership and procedures and gave groups legitimacy in the eyes of the administration.

Neville inherited an active network of associations—primarily the education department, WLSP, and *The Angolite*. Radio and newsmagazine staff were entirely White, but jazz provided a shared undertaking with the musicians.

WLSP carried the sounds of the bands throughout the prison, still a closed-circuit "radio" station with equipment maintained by volunteer prisoners. On Sunday nights, WLSP live-broadcast performances. The Nic Nacs set up in the library after hours with a single microphone (placed just right) to broadcast their new jazz arrangements throughout the main prison, often following an announcement in *The Angolite*. DJs still brought in donations of new albums, essential sources for outside sounds.[38] Soliciting contributions through the mail from their cramped office in the main prison, WLSP secured a steady supply of LPs from sympathetic Baton Rouge radio stations. Norby Aias hosted the *Jazz Record Show* every Sunday. After the new tracks debuted on his show, Aias, also a musician, brought the records back to the band room for closer study.[39] And when WLSP was down for a stretch in 1964, *The Angolite* carried the torch by printing updates on the latest hit songs.

The prison newsmagazine continued supporting musicians. By 1963, Frank "Bloody" West (pronounced Blow-dee) became the band room spokesman for *The Angolite*. He was a talented multi-instrumentalist rumored to have sung with the doo-wop group the Velvetones in 1955.[40] In his regular column, "Music Room Sounds," West offered general accounts of the local music scene, aired listening tests with musicians, and explained new music to its readers.[41] Arriving at Angola in 1958, he was a link to the tail-end of the reform period.

With only modest administrative support in the education department, the musician associations fended for themselves.[42] Music theory classes developed fresh cohorts that fed the music scene. Bands played in the band room, offering plenty of informal opportunities for learning during jam sessions. But few free officers liked the adventurous jazz that Thompson, Surgent, and bassist Willie Judd had been developing.[43] So without reliable administrative support, bands lost the mobility and security necessary for performances.

Neville used his leadership role and growing connections to book the Nic Nacs and prepare them for shows. An occasional private party in a dormitory meant his musicians walked away with tobacco, food, or even a pair of shoes. Families sent money from outside, and a flow of stamps (money had become contraband) and account transfers through the Inmate Lending Fund kept the musicians afloat. They pooled money to buy and maintain instruments, and Neville made purchase requests for books and manuscript paper, coordinating mail order purchases.[44]

In mundane, everyday ways, Neville and his musicians kept safe, adding muscle and by-laws to the remaining interassociational support from the 1950s reforms. In the band room's confines, musicians studied music to stay sane. Individual study and solitary practice ensured that group efforts could continue when administrators or guards split people up for custodial reasons. Neville remembers when this kind of thing helped trumpet player Russell Sweet. Put in solitary confinement, the jail within the prison known as "the dungeon," Sweet emerged days later able to play Charlie Parker's "Ornithology," a notoriously complicated bebop melody.[45] It's an astonishing story that illustrates how musicians, even without musical instruments, can use nothing but time, knowledge, and intellect to untangle musical puzzles. Sweet's accomplishment, however, isn't only one of individual accomplishment (and subversion of punishment, we should note). Sweet's story is a powerful synecdoche of the jazz that Neville oversaw during the early 1960s: Isolated and suffering from arbitrary punishment, musicians focused on musical ideas free from the burden of entertaining wider audiences. This free space is familiar to many musicians. In jazz, it's the jam session. At Angola, it was the band room, the by-laws within outlawry, and practicing freedom within unfreedom.

The New Feel

It was no surprise that current musicians would bring new musical approaches into the prison. It is, however, remarkable that Fuzz Surgent and Lester Thompson were able to *leave for others* a space for growing new ideas and honing musical skills. They left the Nic Nacs.

Bands at Angola aren't necessarily what we often envision on the outside as natural units of musicians, drawn together solely through affinity, chemistry, and friendship. Technically, they are chartered organizations. Bands are associations granted a place with administration, security staff, and other prisoner associations. Just like members of the Rotary Club have a certain standing in a community despite an ever-changing lineup, prison bands maintain missions, equipment, by-laws, and the use of common prison space. Critically, however, bands need new members as much as they need to preserve existing structures. The 1960s brought many new musicians to Angola.

A narcotics crackdown in the city in the mid-1960s had an outsized effect on musicians, often traveling and working in public, and often idle while waiting to play. Pseudo-scientific studies of the era linked drug use, socioeconomic categories, and race, targeting young, poor Black people as narcotics users.[46] Jazz musicians were easy targets, especially those breaking Jim Crow laws to play in racially mixed ensembles or to mixed audiences.[47] As a result, the cadre of new musicians brought to Angola in the 1960s was the most star-studded in the history of the prison, perhaps of any prison in US history. What devastated communities and music venues throughout America invigorated Angola's band room.

Frank West's column in *The Angolite* during the mid-1960s was exciting to read (and, of course, simultaneously depressing) as it welcomed well-known musicians to the farm. It is like reading a jointly published *Down Beat Magazine* and police report. Saxophonist Charlie Maduell arrived in 1964, convicted of obtaining morphine through fraud. West enthusiastically wrote that a "REAL musician" was on his way. "Good musicians," he continued, "are so few and far between here, that we are really looking forward to having him around. All that we have to keep up with the newer musical trends are a few old, beat records and somebody that knows what's happening, fresh from the world, is a rare treat."[48] Maduell played in Dr. John's band, whose members were as well known for soulfully mixing New Orleans jazz, R&B, funk, and blues as they were for their narcotics activities.[49] People like Maduell and Neville energized the band room. It became *the* place to encounter music on a high level.

For a long obsessive period, Neville would settle in the band room and begin repeatedly dropping a needle down on the same John Coltrane album, studying the grooves laid down by one of the inscrutable masters of jazz.[50] The record jacket, perched on a stack of other LPs shared with WLSP, only had so much information. Neville and the others listened to Coltrane blow, returning the needle to specific sections of his solo, asking: "How does he do that?!" For a genre so strongly associated with feel and embodiment, access to new ways of *thinking* has long been part of the practice of jazz even if underrepresented in the writing on jazz.[51] As a consequence of Black musicians' lack of access to conservatories and omission from standardized music theory books, jazz thinking developed into idiosyncratic, inventive systems that generated new sounds and feelings.[52] What Michel Foucault calls "subjugated knowledge"—unofficial, local, and seemingly incomplete ontologies—is the fabric of jazz thinking, a shared archipelago of theories that, when sounded and felt, challenge dominant, accepted ways of listening. Neville, at that time, was new to thinking in jazz.

Neville was adapting to a new horn. Thompson, counting his last days on the farm, had the tenor, forcing Neville onto the alto. So he finally took the advice that bebop legend Sonny Stitt had given him years before: learn to read music and practice scales. Neville was working from a simplistic method book, *My First Arrangement*, to write parts for the Nic Nacs, relying on the piano to check by ear. He found relief from all this hard musical work by picking up the alto and playing what felt good.

In one of these moments, he closed his eyes and began playing the nostalgic jazz standard "I'll Remember April" until a voice broke his flow: "Oh man! You must have smoked a lot of weed in your day!" Neville looked up and saw John Probst at the piano across the band room, squinting through his thick Coke-bottle glasses. Probst continued, "I can tell by the way you play. Your playing is too diatonic. You don't have any vertical structures in it." New to music theory, Neville had no idea what that meant. But, he was intrigued. Whatever a "vertical structure" was might nudge him to sound more like Probst.

The New Orleans pianist was practically blind and spent much of his time in the band room. When he first arrived, a classification officer questioned the "legal" definition of his blindness and put him in the field. When Probst swung at a horse's leg, mistaking it for a cane stalk, classification reassigned him to the band room.[53] It was a better fit. Professionally, Probst had played with the Pete Fountain Sextet in New Orleans and with Boots Randolph and Rosemary Clooney. When he arrived at Angola, he was fresh from recording "Yakety Sax," a well-known 1963 novelty instrumental. Intellectually, he was part of a cohort of New Orleans musicians who took Dixieland and applied modernist harmonies, phrasing, rhythms, new instrumental techniques, and collective improvisation.[54] He knew how to stay in the pocket for club gigs and how to get loose and adventurous for after-hour jam sessions.[55] By calling Neville out on his playing, Probst transformed Angola's band room into a jam session.

Rather than take "diatonic" as a slight (plenty of misunderstandings at Angola lead to violence), Neville pushed him to explain the term. In hindsight, being called "diatonic" may have been an insult. It meant that he was fundamentally conflicted. Composer and jazz theorist George Russell used creative etymology to criticize the major scale for being "diatonic," taking "di" as the Latin "two" and "tonic" as a sense of melodic rest. Being diatonic meant Neville's improvising wasn't settled. He was stuck between two resting points, even though the notes felt comfortable. Probst had opened the door to a whole new way of thinking about music, which would lead to another door about politics. First, music.

Freedom in a New Unity

Soon after calling Neville "diatonic," Probst recommended that he order George Russell's *The Lydian Chromatic Concept of Tonal Organization*.[56] The education department's connection to Louisiana State University helped Neville purchase one of the most radical revisions of tonal harmony. Now, the influence of *The Lydian Chromatic Concept* is well documented in influential jazz theory texts and in celebrated jazz albums. The book planted the seeds for modal jazz, most famously cultivated by Miles Davis, Bill Evans, John Coltrane, Art Farmer, and other midcentury innovators who played in the wake of bebop. Similarly, Russell's book transformed jazz at Angola. With no recordings, we only imagine how the book impacted the Nic Nacs. Neville's testimony and the music criticism in *The Angolite* will inform our imagination. Further testimony comes from many older prisoners with whom I spoke. Those incarcerated in the 1960s remember hanging out in the band room just to listen, taking in the new music.

Once all the Nic Nacs had digested *The Lydian Chromatic Concept of Tonal Organization*, they began writing music based on Russell's concepts.[57] The ideas helped solidify and organize the range of styles the group employed—"everything from steamy R&B to cutting-edge bop, and all stops in between," Neville recalls.[58] Before examining the concepts of the Lydian Concept, it warrants a pause to think about the role of music here.

Jazz intellectualism is missing in the documented history of music at Angola Prison, which has focused on vestiges of nonliterate blues and work songs. As discussed in the previous chapters, "prison music," narrowly defined and represented by folkloric recordings, centers on pity and out-of-law suffering. In contrast, Neville's engagement with Russell's book reveals ways the band room connected with radical political thought and new jazz practices. The developing modernism of the Nic Nacs mirrored African American musical-political ideas of their time, the sound of a risky political lunge toward a future amidst the hardship of the present.[59] It was principled and communal while carving out space for individual freedoms.

The Lydian Chromatic Concept of Tonal Organization gave improvising musicians new ways to think about improvising. Russell encourages thinking in two musical dimensions: an interrelated sense of "horizontal" and "vertical" musicality. Neville knew the horizontal: carrying a melody from start to finish, developing tension, and releasing it. Understanding the vertical, however, required some rethinking. If you are not comfortable with technical aspects of music theory, I'll walk through two nongraphical ways of understanding Russell's point: existentially and musically. But first, I'll need to start with an x-y graph. On sheet music, pitch is represented on a vertical axis while time is on the horizontal, moving left to right (see figure 3.3).

Figure 3.3. Horizontal and vertical illustrations of music.

The left part of figure 3.3 shows a few measures from the ending of "I'll Remember April," where collections of different pitches (chords) change over time. If played, you would hear those notes as a cadence, musical change that leads your ear to a resting point in the fourth measure. Horizontal thinking links these notes and chords, left to right, as steps toward an ending. In contrast, the right part of the figure is a complex chord, with nothing before or after it. If played, you would hear it as a sound with specific characteristics—complexity and perhaps an emotional connection. If you have an instrument and can read, you can select individual notes from the chord and play them at liberty, separately, or in combination. The difference between each side is that the left encourages your attention to *progress through time*. The right draws attention to the *relationships among the pitches*—toward different feelings of relation among the notes, like gravitational pulls within a system. Listening horizontally may be more common in music: anticipating a change, feeling resolution at the end of a passage, or counting on a repeated phrase, for instance. Vertical listening is less common. Now, consider nongraphical explanations.

Applying vertical thinking to horizontal thinking was liberating. Russell's vertical listening is like being aware of living in the moment, a value deeply embedded in American modernist philosophy from William James to Herbie Hancock. Being in the "now" rather than anticipating the "next" means attending to new possibilities, feeling the uniqueness of that particular chord as a unique sound. The Concept gave musicians choices. The 1964 edition of the book even included a pull-out musical slide rule for measuring and exploring degrees of vertical difference. For an example of music centered on verticality, listen to Miles Davis's *Kind of Blue*, mainly how he takes his time introducing notes, revealing relationships among them, dwelling on the note at hand rather than anticipating an end point or remembering a clear starting point. If you hear that, you're listening to George Russell's ideas.

Some collections of notes (scales, modes, or chords) encourage vertical listening over horizontal. One of Russell's insights is that an underused, perhaps forgotten collection of notes actually encourages vertical attention: the Lydian scale (see figure 3.4). Why Lydian? I'll spare you the long answer.[60] For that, you can read Russell's book. And if you have studied jazz at school, you'll find the roots of what you learned about how scales and chords relate. (Russell's theory was later adapted by David Baker and used in countless university programs.) According to the Concept, the short answer is that the Lydian scale expresses unity.

Figure 3.4. The major (Ionian) and the Lydian scales.

Figure 3.4 shows the difference between the more common major (Ionian) scale and the Lydian scale. I have spread them out horizontally not to show time but to make it easier to see. Observe that only one note differs between the scales. In the Lydian, the fourth note is a half-step higher, affecting the feel of the whole. The difference in this fourth note is significant. When I first heard a musician use the Lydian, I was at a small concert in college. My ear went straight to the guitarist, who had started playing in the Lydian scale.

Instantly, it created a world of sound in which to dwell. I was so struck by that moment that I stayed after the concert to ask him what he had done. His answer: Lydian. The sound was exotic to me, an appealing departure from what I knew, but it was also a musical concept with a name, scale, and distinct expressive nature. Meeting the Lydian was like meeting someone new, someone strange and alluring. That concert was my introduction to modal jazz and my first time hearing what I would later identify as Russell's reorientation of music theory. I found it in college. Neville found it in prison.

Decades later, Neville and I could indulge our penchant for music theory and our mutual appreciation for the Lydian when he visited Georgetown University as a visiting artist. On campus, scribbling dots on a chalkboard five-line staff, we could get into fine details of how the major scale contains two resting points: the first and fourth notes of the scale. The major scale, the most favored in American and European music, is therefore in a constant state of tension between two competing resting places. On the other hand, the Lydian scale relates all its notes to its fundamental first note. Its essence is unity.[61] Its seven notes establish tendencies among all the notes, like forces of gravity within a field of discrete pitches. A chord is merely a facet of these notes—one side of its character, discovered through playing, listening to, or even imagining the ways notes interact. In his book, Russell goes on to show species of related scales, applications of the scale, and analyses of music with vertical development, from Bach to Bird (Charlie Parker).

The Lydian Chromatic Concept is a way of thinking about and creating jazz expansively: in the moment (vertical) and relating to other moments (horizontal). Neville could now play through the chord changes of a song while retaining the liberty of following discoveries made along the way, taking time for a focused excursion into the relationships of notes. In Neville's hands, it became a textbook for developing a more modern sound of early-1960s cutting-edge jazz. Neville worked through the concepts, completed the exercises, and discussed the theory with other musicians in the band room. At Angola, the book enabled the freedom to think comprehensively in jazz. As its influence spread, the Nic Nacs used the book to solve musical puzzles, reconceptualize melodic approaches to old standards, and compose new works based on fundamental principles. Neville's playing became less "diatonic" and more free.

The impact of a book about musical freedom, as you would imagine, was markedly different for Neville at Angola in 1964 than it was for me at Wesleyan University in 1991. As I read about music theory in a mahogany-paneled library reading room named after an antebellum university president, my newfound freedom found in the Lydian scale may have brought me in touch with a sense of independence from home and childhood. The musical independence for Neville existed within pockets of freedom left over from musicians who had transformed a 1950s Southern prison farm minstrel spectacle into a bebop stage. They were moments of future-oriented joint creativity claimed within a brutal institution that triangulated a convoluted mission felt as penitentiary pressures of conditioning, the plantation pressures of laboring, and outlawry pressures of alienation. For Neville, following Russell, musical thinking led to political thinking.

Transforming the Listenership

Like much of Afro-modernist theory of its time, music theory applied to more than just music. As jazz scholar Ingrid Monson argues, this moment of jazz intellectualism, rife with utopian thought and discipline-breaking rigor, claimed that becoming one's own theorist was part of a larger project of self-determination for African American artists.[62] Jazz was a sonic consequence of collectively rethinking freedom. The theory was understandably messy. Russell unified what, at that point, was a mixed bag of jazz theories. But he also made room for eclectic abstractions that had already defined jazz theory.[63]

Technically, Russell's book provided new strategies for connecting melodies to chords on the spot. Politically, it gave musicians an African American vision of liberty. Neville remembered the effect. It started in jam sessions. In one memorable session, he remembers when playing within a key no longer seemed like a strict rule of law: "Someone was playing and singing, and they said [of the piano player], 'Whup! There he goes! Somebody get him. He's going to E♭!' He'd sing the verse or chorus, he'd come in on another key, so we'd say, 'Oh! Catch him!'" Without worrying about key, their new principle was *playing together*. They didn't reprimand the piano player for changing keys. They followed him. "It was just movement, liquid movement," Neville recalls. New expressive potential opened up. "Instead of playing the notes," he continues, "he played these sounds of a black man screaming. That was part of what was in the 'new music.' They were breaking the boundaries of what was set by the classical composers and the classical music theory from Europe." Thinking jazz was thinking politics.

The *Lydian Chromatic* was at the center of a new intellectualism that caught Angola up to Miles Davis and Ornette Coleman, but it had additional resonance among prisoners in Angola. It took some work, however, to get it to resonate. Neville had to develop a listenership by writing about the new jazz in *The Angolite*.[64] The first of his articles, published in June 1966, pointed out the overlapping goals of musical and political liberation, both of which take work. To other prisoners, Neville admitted that the new music might be hard to listen to, but the challenge was to break free from imposed European ways of listening.

He starts with the image of an unrestricted essence: "A sound is developing that must be true to itself and not to any falsely imposed restrictions."[65] Then, in a twist of George Russell's thinking, Neville redefines "wrong notes." Rather than thinking of the notes being wrong, the sensation of wrongness is, in fact, aural evidence of breaking European-derived rules: "Mainly, the New Thing is abandoning the conventions handed down through European tradition. [New jazz musicians] are producing a music without tonal centers that resembles other non-western forms (Indian Raga, for instance)." New jazz didn't sound "bad." It was freedom from the abusive listening habits acquired from a kind of musical colonization.

Other voices began to chime in. Crism, another frequent *Angolite* columnist, wrote an article linking jazz greats from Fats Waller to Albert Ayler. Uplift, he argued, could still be found in the free playing of the avant-garde: "Let him turn to Ornette Coleman who may uplift him with beauty, affirmation and hope, or demolish him with the twisted, growling shrieks of a tortured soul."[66] And it was "esthetic destruction," according to Crism, that expressed the feeling of Black nationalism at that moment. In that article, he explained:

> Coltrane's music is related to the mood of American Negroes, and particularly the just-awakened and deeply frustrated young members of that group. Some performances should be heard, felt and reflected upon by every politician, police official, psychologist, social worker, editorial writer, and perhaps by every American, for if there were a documentary film on the Watts riot, John Coltrane is the man to score it.[67]

Sporadically, *The Angolite* added to an expanding forum for articulating socio-political music theory. Angola (and the Jim Crow South) was a place filled with seemingly arbitrary rules and people there who had broken laws.

New understandings of freedom sprang from Russell's book: jam sessions in the band room and published music criticism, all discussed in an emerging counter-public sphere. Like archeologists, Neville and his collaborators dug for freedom buried underneath sediments of cultural norms, economic systems, and legal apparatus. Part of recovering subjugated knowledge was calling out minor laws in favor of principles.[68]

The Lydian Chromatic Concept offered political possibility by distinguishing principles from rules. Recall that the major scale encourages horizontal motion. That's a principle. The notes, felt as a key, set up the possibility that some notes may risk unproductively stopping movement toward a harmonic goal if that is the only aim of the improviser. Avoiding "wrong notes," playing in the "wrong key," or using the "wrong scale" adheres to rules. Knowing theory in a different way can open things up.

In Russell's words, "These *principles* of music shown in the Concept offer better guidance than *grammatical rules* of standard music theory texts. Understanding tonal gravity is a different way of knowing that, for instance, two melodies ought not to move in parallel fifths."[69] Indeed, music theory has a bad reputation for rulemaking. In Russell's theorizing, however, there are no rules. Principles enable thinking on a higher level. Principles grant freedom through . . .

> . . . an attempt to organize all the tonal materials that the jazz improviser deals with, so that he may choose for himself on the basis of his own aesthetic needs. The concept provides the possibilities—it is for the musician to explore these possibilities. By analyzing his choices, the musician may broaden his taste vocabulary—and possibly find his own concept within this one.[70]

The project of reconciling minor laws with universal principles became central to Neville's emerging politics. Though seemingly complex, the Concept offered clarity. It proved that musical principles superseded stylistic rules by including diverse jazz innovators alongside Western classical composers. In a general sense, it obliterated the idea that different rules should apply to different people.

Neville developed a listenership that could hear political thought in radical music. New musicians at Angola were the conduit. They were already hip to Ornette Coleman, Albert Ayler, Charles Mingus, and Cecil Taylor. "They were known amongst the musicians," recalled Neville. "That was the time of the Black Panthers and the Black Power Movement, and *they* [the avant-garde musicians] were the voice of that movement." And then, the musical-political counter-public sphere got a boost in 1967 when a conviction for heroin possession sent drummer James Black to the farm.

Adding Rhythm to the Concept

With James Black's arrival, Neville continued to use *The Angolite* to defend the radical new jazz approaches by blurring the line between musical and liberatory racial politics. And Black simply suffered no fools. He had a forceful yet unpredictable presence both on drums and in person. Idris Muhammad once described him as "a cold-blooded jazz player."[71] The drummer was well versed in Black nationalist thought, New Orleans rhythms, and the kind of principled playing that Neville was exploring.

Born and raised in New Orleans, James Black crafted his musical style deep in the local jazz scene and amidst the city's second-line tradition. He started on trumpet and piano in school and later studied music briefly at Southern University in Baton Rouge. He eventually switched to drums, and by his early twenties he began supporting prominent local artists. Black recorded with Cannonball and Nat Adderley on their *In The Bag* album in 1962. The following year, he played with Ellis Marsalis at the Playboy Club in New Orleans and later played on the Ellis Marsalis Quartet's album *Monkey Puzzle*, composing four of the seven songs himself.[72] By the time he landed in Angola, Black had command over a new, freer jazz, fresh from touring and recording with Yusef Lateef.[73]

By the time Black arrived at Angola, he was hip to new jazz thinking. Lateef worked with George Russell's theories. Black learned to accompany in a way that similarly pulled away from horizontal, goal-oriented playing—adding surprise elements developed from bebop, reorientated downbeats, and textural explorations that mimicked the vertical approach that the *Lydian Chromatic Concept* gave to melodic improvisation. Free as he was, Black still had an anchor in the groove.

Black's connection to New Orleans rhythm distinguished him within the musical world of avant-garde players. His syncopations came from the streets. You can hear them clearly on Eddie Bo's "Hook and Sling" (1969), recorded after his release. The drum part stands shoulder-to-shoulder with Clyde Stubblefield's groove on "Funky Drummer" (1968) or Gregory Coleman's locked freneticism on "Amen, Brother" (1969). Especially in a jazz context, Black could settle you into a groove only to eventually reveal that he'd led you astray, and yet, somehow, you'd still be with the beat. He may have had uncanny control of a groove, but he couldn't make sense of Angola.

Neville remembers the challenge of getting Black safely to the band room:

> When we heard James Black was coming, we thought, "OK. We got a drummer who can play anything. We gotta be [ready]." When he came, picture Yusef Lateef with his turban. So, James Black came in, and when he got here, he was going to be a Muslim, a Black Muslim. We told him, "Don't be talking that *salaam alaikum* shit. Cause the White boys don't play that shit in here." He was kind of arrogant. "[I'm not going to do] that 'yessir boss.'" [And I said,] "Oh yes, you are!" And when we explained to him, "If you don't, they will kill you," he got it, kind of.
>
> But still, he was different. He wasn't a common criminal. He was a world-famous musician. So, he didn't have to behave like everybody else. When he got to work out in the field, he was always asking, every time he would come in, "Get me out of the field." [We'd say,] "We're working on it. We're working on it. There's no opening in the music room, but I can get you in the education building." So, we got him a job teaching English. So, they got him out of the field into the education building until the next cane harvest. He was back there. We were all back there that year. But then, when we did get him into the music room—I guess the next year, we got him in there. He and I were the two prisoners who were actually in the music room the whole time.[74]

Neville got Black to the safety of the band room, but he also knew that he had to prepare his listenership for the new jazz that Black brought. True, Black couldn't hide the influence of second-line drumming in his playing, a recognizable soundmark of New Orleans, and he had credibility as a successful touring musician. Nonetheless, Neville couldn't trust Black to speak for himself regarding politics and avant-garde jazz. So he took to *The Angolite*.

Neville wrote as if he was introducing a legend to the stage: "The only thing I have lacked, until now, is the chance to play the music with someone who is hip to what's happening.... Now, in the person of James Black, I have met a man who has played and lived the 'New Thing' over the past few years. His presence here is going to add some new dimensions to the sound of music at Angola."[75] Black joined the Nic Nacs.

In the band room, the music spoke for itself. Immediately, jam sessions took on another level of musical freedom by adding something not covered well in *The Lydian Concept*: rhythm. Neville remembers the changes well.

> He was one of the people who was suggesting things, different kinds of music to learn, different things to do that we hadn't been doing, things we hadn't been listening to, like some of the Coltrane stuff that was happening at the time, Yusef Lateef and Archie Shepp, those guys ... Albert Ayler. Also playing, getting the musicians who weren't that good up to speed on being at least able to play the melodies, the tunes with us. If their soloing wasn't up to the level of the song, that was cool. Then they could only play the melody and help them play solos. I'd improvise and make it sound good.[76]

Black took forceful liberty with time signatures, keeping musicians attentive to the "now." Neville explains, "When James Black came along, the same freedom that tonal instruments were taking, he would do that with the rhythms. He's keeping time with the drumming, and then, all of a sudden, the thing would shift. 'Oh shit! Where'd he go?!' ... He had switched the downbeat one beat over until everybody got lost, and then he'd put it back." For the rest of the Nic Nacs, *The Lydian Chromatic Concept* had provided a logic that became important for folding in such a drummer. Without it, they may not have been able to follow the principles. Black's influence, as you might suspect, was not just musical.

In 1967, James Black had no patience for lingering Jim Crow. Neville tells a story that at once illustrates Black's unapologetic approach and Neville's never-ending problem of keeping him safe at Angola.[77] Before Black's arrival, new laws in the Civil Rights Act had technically forced the desegregation of the education building's bathrooms. Neville remembers watching an orderly paint over "WHITE ONLY" above the bathroom nearest the band room. The orderly caught his eye and said, "By God, y'all better remember where those damn signs was!" Years later, after Black had arrived, Neville walked toward the band room and heard Black shouting, "Charles Neville!" He rushed in and found Black pinned against the wall. The captain on duty had caught him in the same bathroom with the painted-over signage. Apparently, when the captain had accursedly asked, "What you doing in here??!!" Black replied, "I'm taking a shit." Neville managed to diffuse the situation by assuring the guard that he would make sure it wouldn't happen again.

Russell's book gave tools that associations have often needed—an internal refinement of by-laws based on a clear-eyed mission that articulates public good.[78] Perhaps the concept of a higher principle offers some relief from keeping track of disorganized collections of rules. For musicians in prison, daily negotiation involves constant consideration of multiple agendas among the many musical stakeholders. "Will the administration like the music?" "Is the music presenting us as redeemable felons?" "Will White people dance to it?" "Does it align with *The Angolite* agenda of resisting prisoner stereotypes while not running afoul of the warden?" Restating Russell's theory from earlier, adhering to principles allows a player to legislate musical rules rather than simply follow them.

The new jazz of the Nic Nacs was part of a more extensive national claim for natural rights. They were contemporaneous with the formation of the Black Panther Party in Oakland and George Jackson's Black Guerilla Family in San Quentin Prison. With James Black driving the rhythm and attitude, the Nic Nacs became the sound of liberatory thought.

The Long Arm of the Band Room

Despite all that was happening in the band room, plantation logic ruled Angola when harvest season rolled around. The field always threatened to whisk people away from secure positions. But during harvest season, all hands—including staff, free officers, and trustys—went into service of the cotton, sugar, and soy. Tensions were higher given that more people were involved and work demands were more intense. As an established group, members of the Nic Nacs could keep much of the outlawry at bay. They carried the muscle and influence that they developed in the band room into the fields. But with relative peace of mind, boredom crept in. Tedium can lead to invention.

Neville still relied on music when returning to the field, but differently than before. He took back the monotony of labor to provide himself the mental space to develop ideas that flowed from musical-political principles while at the same time adhering to prison's plantation rules. Neville had conceived plenty of musicological pathways down which his thoughts could wander, exercising new habits of the mind. Now literate, he didn't need his saxophone to create. So Neville spent his time running through John Coltrane's complex melodic permutations in his head.[79] He reflected on jam sessions with his new collaborator James Black. He explored ideas from the book that John Probst had introduced him to nearly three years earlier.

The Lydian Chromatic Concept is like a workbook in certain places. It offers musical exercises Neville carried around in his head: setting goals for memorization and creating new mental habits for improvisation. Addressing the reader, Russell gave Neville musical challenges: "Construct your own ingoing vertical melody based on the chords of the test on the following page."[80] "Identify the parent scale and two other Principal Scales based on the parent Lydian Tonic of each chord."[81] Neville worked through the solutions, occasionally developing the ideas into flowing silent improvisations, all to the rhythm of his labor.

In some respects, Neville's new approach to fieldwork was similar to the field hollers recorded by folklorists.[82] Field hollers, uniquely African American music accompanying solo labor, did not pace group labor. Instead, singing laborers capitalized on the rhythmic freedom of unpaced work to improvise melodies, play with timbre, and invent rhythmic stresses.[83] It's similar to doodling with a pen in the margins of your notes—a separate and often more compelling space parallel to your primary work.

Folklorists understood field hollers as preserved African songs, categorically distant from European traditions. Folklorist Ray B. Browne, recording field hollers in 1950s Alabama, psychologized the singers to create even more distance for White readers. He suggested that the distinctive and disappearing field hollers "afforded them a much-needed mode of self-expression. The 'holler' was as natural a call as the song of the bird, a spontaneous overflow of the poetic urge. Under these conditions, communication with other persons was only secondary."[84] I'll take what Neville told me about thinking jazz in the field to suggest that hollers may be better understood not as a naturally expressed African sound but as a skilled and principled intellectual activity that may have been *in search of* something essential. Perhaps hollering never died out. Maybe it was always moving forward. Links between Neville's account and folkloric descriptions show that the folklorists didn't have it all wrong.

Alan Lomax, John's son who carried on prison recording, made an unusual connection between prison singing and seemingly more systematic musical traditions. Lomax writes about Benny Will Richardson, identified as "22," singing on a 1947 recording they made in the fields of Mississippi's

Parchman State Penitentiary. In reflection, Lomax admits that his written description...

> ... only approximated the intricate pattern of the "new style" that 22 and his bunch were weaving together. It was tricky and highly syncopated, allowing the singers to improvise rhythmic breaks in opposition to the main beat. Where work-song stanzas are generally brief, these ran to a minute or a minute and a half, like an art song or Far Eastern improvisation or a bop solo.
>
> This poetic style seems to me conceived and practiced according to a *vertical* [emphasis original] model, which considers the several simultaneous parts of a black choral rendition and allows space for all present to contribute to the entire effect: here the sonorous and verbal aptness of all the interjections is essential to the whole. Such compositional style is difficult for Europeans, especially north Europeans. To perform or even to perceive—at least without the aid of a diagram or a musical score. But it comes naturally to people raised in the black African tradition.[85]

It's the end that Lomax may have wrong.

Lomax, speaking as someone of Northern European descent, believed that the singers expressed something intrinsically "African." But perhaps the musical difference he sensed came from the singers *naturalizing* new musical ideas, rehearsing to develop agile and inventive musical gestures. Certainly, field hollers drew on what singers knew. But they also innovated in ways similar to the mental exercises that Neville practiced. From this perspective, field hollering produced countless fragments of new musical ideas that became lost to the fields. Benny Will Richardson's complex musical sketches could have grown if given the opportunity, except his only rehearsal space was carved out from brutal agricultural labor. By contrast, the Nic Nacs returned to the band room at five o'clock.[86]

Neville described how he and the other musicians salvaged ideas they developed in the field and put them to use in the band room. The formulations were often radical, created free from the burden of an audience.[87] The Nic Nacs used the field to harvest their own musical ideas. Neville recalls singing phrases while working "and trying to keep that thing in your head while you go on with the rhythm of whatever you're doing. And then get back and write that down or play it."[88] The sound of an animal in the field or the sounds of the work might trigger an idea that would develop according to musical principles.[89] The rhythm of work could keep it in memory. In this way, sometimes thoughts turned into actual songs.

In some respects, James Black's "Dirt Dauber" could have fit the pages of folkloric books, a teasing song born from forcing humor on a violent situation in a coded manner so as not to attract attention.[90] "Dirt Dauber" was a nickname the prisoners gave a field boss who surveyed the cane lines. Like a dauber, a type of wasp that builds nests from mud, the field boss was filthy, as if his rail-thin body had just crawled out of a muddy hole. He was aware of his nickname and was notorious for severely beating anyone who used it. This predictable violent reaction led to a constant prank that many remembered from their first day in the cane field. If a newcomer asked you a question, the gag was simply to point to the mounted field boss and say, "Go ask Mr. Dauber over there."

"Dirt Dauber" became a staple in Nic Nacs sets. James Black kept the joke going from the field to the band room by writing a song that turned "dirt dau-ber" into a three-note melody, similar to how Dizzy Gillespie used "salt pea-nuts" as a motif in his 1942 hit. Prisoners cracked up at the inside joke whenever they heard it played on the yard or in a jam session.

Inventiveness kept collaborative music alive *despite* the field. Exercising the skills from Russell's book helped salvage something from the forceful plantation practice. Neville emerged from the field like Russell Sweet came out the hole knowing how to play "Ornithology"—as a better musician and collaborator, reaching for Tonal Unity with each whack of the blade and with new ideas from harvesting creative ideas in the field. Music didn't stop the suffering, but at least it sounded nearby.

Echoing principles from Russell, Neville linked suffering and principled pursuit, distilling his discoveries in an *Angolite* article written after harvest season. "A cat who turns out to be great sets his goals very high and is determined not only to accept the pain necessary to achieve them but to stamp out much of it along the way. He actually conditions himself to be impervious to certain kinds of suffering."[91] The Nic Nacs used their time in the field to innovate and improve as best they could. When they hit the stage again, everyone heard it.

The New Nic Nacs

By 1967, the Nic Nacs were a new group with new attitudes on jazz and politics. It took more than just playing to keep them together. Neville's daytime work in the band room included scheduling, instrument maintenance, sorting through the custodial issues (how to move musicians through security from dormitories and work sites), and negotiating equity for Black and White musicians sharing space. He wrote to LSU and other universities to source manuscript paper, educational texts, and sheet music. Visits to the WLSP radio station office kept the record collection fresh. And visits to *The Angolite* ensured that all of Angola knew about upcoming shows. Nighttime was another kind of busy. Musicians with regular work assignments could elect to study and play music only after work, so the band room filled with rehearsals starting around five. Some rushed to the band room as quickly as possible with precious musical discoveries lodged in their heads, eager to test out modulations, phrases, variations, new rhythms, or inventive melodies. Small audiences formed, curious about the new sounds. Neville had managed to secure some of the best players from New Orleans.

Pianist James Booker arrived that year, bringing the Nic Nacs to a new level of showmanship. He was on a one-year sentence for heroin possession.[92] (His habit had evolved from a morphine prescription he was given as a child after being hit by a speeding ambulance.) Booker mastered Liberace's performances as a child while simultaneously playing the organ at his father's Baptist services. He moved quickly through the Xavier Preparatory School's music program and took up playing blues and gospel organ on New Orleans radio WMRY. His slippery organ playing charted nationally with "Gonzo" for Peacock Records in 1960. Burning the candle at both ends, he balanced college coursework with session work for Fats Domino and B. B. King.

Booker's flamboyant stage presence on New Orleans stages may not have adapted so well to the Angola stage had it not been for his fierce command over his instrument. Arthur Rubenstein, floored at hearing him play in New Orleans during a 1958 tour, once exclaimed, "I could never play that... never at that tempo."[93] And while prisoners were used to "real gals from the streets" (transgender prisoners) at variety shows on the yard, Booker's expressive gay sexuality was indefinable—he was his own essence, in Russellian terms. Booker added flexibility, deep musical knowledge, and energy with his syncopated piano playing that had already changed the modern New Orleans sound.

Young Leotha Brown, who initiated this chapter with a solo rendition of "Work Song," saw an opportunity in the band room upon arrival. But unlike the others, he hadn't developed a musical portfolio before coming to Angola. He had just started college before a terminal wrong turn. Brown was from a middle-class family and full of professional promise. After his first year of college at Southern University, a summer job had gone wrong after a racially charged altercation escalated. Convicted of killing an unruly White patron at the bar where he worked, Brown came to Angola in 1964 and managed to get out of the fields by landing a job in the education department teaching musicians how to read music.[94] By 1967, he was playing trumpet in the Nic Nacs. But to fully be in the band, he needed to learn to play without having sheet music in front of him.

The Nic Nacs band was as much a school as it was a band. The musicians helped Brown learn jazz, relentlessly calling out his mistakes and presenting him with unexpected musical situations. Brown remembered one performance at the A Building in particular.[95] Upon arriving, he searched desperately for his sheet music to no avail. He panicked. The other members replied, "Ah, don't worry about that. Just play what you think you're supposed to play." They had intentionally hidden his music. Brown remembered that as an important, albeit unconventional lesson in jazz: "Once I began playing, the music came back. I was playing exactly what was on the sheet music. It fascinated me. I didn't know that I had been developing to that stage until they put me in that position." Other times, the unexpected lessons presented more urgent responses in the middle of a show. "Okay, we're gonna come back in on four," James Black would say, and after "four," everyone but Brown would stand up and cross their arms, leaving an unsuspecting Brown to play alone. "Like throwing you in the water," he remembered. "You either going to swim, or you're going to drown." The 1960s introduced Brown to many excellent musicians he later remembered as mentors. It also toughened him up by giving him a sense of independence in collectivity. As the Nic Nacs, Neville, Black, Booker, and Brown became a formidable quartet.

Singers often dropped into jam sessions. Chris Kenner, or "Sick and Tired" as he affectionately came to be known at Angola, was arrested for statutory rape and started his three years at Angola in the band room.[96] His big hit in 1961 had been "I Like It Like That," cowritten with Allen Toussaint. He had also recorded with Eddie Bo and Candy Philips. Neville remembered others: "We had one cat, Bug Juice, doing 'Drown in My Own Tears' sadder than Ray Charles and another singer singing 'I Pity the Fool' bluer than

Bobby Bland." "Smiling George" was another regular. The Nic Nacs were the core of a music scene.

In his last year on the farm, Neville earned the nickname "Maestro." One day, leafing through a music supply catalog, he saw a picture of a baton. He had learned basic conducting in school. Although conducting was atypical of the jazz he played, brandishing a baton could signify his leadership. The baton became a part of his status as music director, a high-visibility position. Neville coordinated music for annual festivals and club events. And the band room was as close as they could get to the late-night jazz sessions at storied places like The Five Spot in New York. They pushed each other's abilities and repertoires.

Led by the unifying perspective from *The Lydian Chromatic Concept*, they developed new approaches to show tunes, jazz standards, rock, soul, zydeco, and Dixieland. Outside the band room, they still played what the job required, often dressed in prison outfits when playing for outsiders. They met the needs of each gig. "Usually, when we played on the yard," Neville explained, "we were playing for some kind of function. . . . We played for football games. We played for parties in the dormitories. We played the shows, the Easter show, the Christmas show, the Fourth of July show. We played the rodeo show." They even played a high school prom held on prison grounds. "For that, we had to play what was expected, stuff that wasn't too far out." Neville remembered the arrangement as familiar: White people hiring low-wage Black musicians for good entertainment. The audience, however, had no idea that, at times, they were dancing to Lydian chromatic concepts.

The Nic Nacs managed to slip in a few nods to the avant-garde when the music grooved. *The Lydian Concept* brought it all together. Stylistic rules fit under an umbrella principle of Tonal Gravity, inward and outward motion. As Russell explains in his book, "The concept is of a jazz origin, but by no means is it applicable only to jazz music."[97] Russell's elevation of jazz, taking the practice from ghettoized music to stand toe-to-toe with venerable European composers, established a musical principle of universalism. One could be style-agnostic, following higher musical principles, and still participate in playing the needs of any prison function.

Musically, no one could touch the Nic Nacs. I mean that in two ways: in the colloquial sense that they were competitive players and in the physical sense that they had infused their collective bodies with recognized musical value. Music was a type of sonic armor from violence. Neville explains this more directly: "Because the [Nic Nacs] brought diversion and pleasure, the prisoners wouldn't let anyone fuck with us. We played holiday parties for the general population as well as affairs for the administrators and free people. Everyone wanted to book the [Nic Nacs]. . . . We were cooking with gas. Given the chance, the [Nic Nacs] could have competed with any band of that era—Cannonball Adderley, Horace Silver, Art Blakey, even Miles."[98] The Nic Nacs brought joy to a place with no joy. Consider that in prison, the prisoners provide most of the emotional labor. That kind of labor is complex in a complex place like Angola.

Neville developed shows for the whole audience while working with what he had. "I expanded our repertoire and used a white guy, a comic-showman, to emcee, giving us a Vegas vibe that everyone dug. I also started writing charts of Broadway show tunes. To add sugar and spice, I had a real girl from the street [an originally transgender prisoner], who sang like Billie Holiday, sing 'Strange Fruit,' followed by Sabu, another real girl, an exotic dancer with more moves than Gypsy Rose Lee."[99] Music was at the center of all-prison talent shows. There, the Nic Nacs would back amateur singers. These were good opportunities to gain connections with antagonistic groups. Neville remembered getting a request from a White inmate about to go home. He asked the band to back him for the sentimental "A Lot of Livin' to Do" from the 1963 film *Bye Bye Birdie*. The lyrics were promising: "There are girls just ripe for some kissin', and I mean to kiss me a few! Oh, those girls don't know what they're missin'. I've got a lot of livin' to do!" Neville didn't know the song but put together a big band arrangement for it. He rehearsed it with the Nic Nacs, fleshing out a big band with musicians from the band room. It was a success. The amateur singer sounded and looked good. As a result, Neville earned respect from many White audience members. Some even asked for lessons despite lingering Jim Crow rules.

Neville's success posed a problem for other prisoners' worldviews. A curtained dining hall, dormitories, exercise yards, camps, and bathrooms remained segregated. By contrast, the meager resources for education, art, and music meant that White and Black musicians shared the space. The band room was not free from conflict. Segregation from the yard seeped in. Neville recalls several times when the White musicians were playing country LPs loudly on one side of the room while Black musicians battled them with jazz records.[100] The noise signified the impasse—John Coltrane's "A Love Supreme" and Buck Owens' "I've Got a Tiger by the Tail," on one occasion, played at maximum volumes on opposing speakers.

A breaking point happened when an aspiring White musician approached him, one who had always been standoffish. He sat down and laid his makeshift knife on the table. "Truce," he said to Neville. "Man, I think I owe you an apology." "Apology for what?!" Neville replied. He proceeded to confess to Neville:

> I'm beginning to realize that I've been given some bad information in my life. I'm thirty-three years old from Corpus Christi, Texas. I have never attempted to have a conversation with a Black person before in my life. I've spoken to Black people, "Hey boy, go over there . . ." But it never occurred to me to have a conversation because I was taught by my family, by the school, by the church, by everything around me that Black people weren't really animals, but they weren't really people either. I was taught that the Black man didn't have the brain capacity of the White man and was incapable of thinking on the same level as a White person. I'm a White person, and I've been struggling, trying to play this goddamn guitar. And here you come in here and been teaching people that got better than me. So, if your brain capacity is [supposedly] so much less than mine, something is wrong.[101]

The conversation led both men to reflect on how they were subject to more extensive ideological influences and sets of false rules.

The rigor of music and the audible capacity to learn, in a sense, opened an opportunity for presenting oneself outside the stereotype. Neville recalled, "He was taught that all Black people were one thing. I was thinking the same thing. This poor guy is a victim of this shit just like we are, just like the Black people are." With that social barrier cracked open, things began to change in the education department.

In moments, the intellectual mission of the band room helped break apart false essentialism, an excuse for moving above racialized rules. "A couple of days later," Neville continued, "the White guy who was over the art department—Red, he was called, he had been there a long time, older guy—he come into the music room, he's got this book." Neville knew him from spending time drawing in the art room but had never really interacted with him. Red said, "I've been noticing you've been trying to draw. Look, take this book here. It'll teach you all about perspective and the horizon. Learn this, and you can make your drawings three-dimensional. You'll learn it." Soon after that, Charlie Davis, the other White guy in the music room who used to blast country music at them, walked over to Neville and James Black. He offered them cake and cookies baked by his mother. They began talking. After that, White guys kept asking for lessons even though it remained forbidden.

Pause now to consider Neville's pathway from the field to desegregating the band room. He was delivered to cotton and cane fields and developed agricultural and self-defense skills. Discovering that music gave him affective skills in the fields, he seized on the fortune of filling an empty job in the band room, learned to read music, discovered the Lydian Concept, and turned it into a musical-political campaign. Through a White-run prison newsmagazine, he published his adaptations of George Russell's ideas to create a listenership. And on top of that, he maintained a creative space that could be a haven for others. Neville's four-year effort required navigating the infrastructure kept in place by prisoners simply to secure life and liberty. Consider the effort required simply to stay safe and sane as a consequence of holding two joints one day or, more pointedly, being Black and playing music for integrated crowds in the Jim Crow South.

Coda

Charles Neville left Angola later in 1967. Then he fled the South to play music in New York, struggling with drug addiction that Angola had only exacerbated. Eventually—and it's a story for another book—he got the support of his family and became a member of the internationally renowned Neville Brothers. Their 1978 self-titled debut LP is in the Cultural Gallery on the top floor of the National Museum of African American History and Culture in Washington, DC. A guard tower brought up from Angola is five floors below in the exhibit "Defending Freedom, Defining Freedom: The Era of Segregation 1876–1968." We toured the new museum together when he did his residency at Georgetown in 2017, invited by the museum. One of the curators took us on a private tour early in the morning, before the opening hours. Neville had already been awake for hours doing his daily tai-chi exercise. The public had filtered in when we made it to the room on the museum's top floor that held the Neville Brothers LP. He agreed to pose with a few star-struck fans. As we drove back to campus later that day, he said, "I never thought that such a variety of people would be interested in all that."

James Black picked up his music career in New Orleans after leaving Angola in 1967. But he began to play less often through the 1970s and

1980s. Ellis Marsalis still brought him on stage, as did young Harry Connick Jr., an up-and-coming piano player whose father was district attorney of Orleans Parish. Black managed to mentor a new generation of New Orleans drummers and secure two fellowships from The National Endowment for composing before dying of a drug overdose in 1988. His body lies in an unmarked grave in New Orleans.

After release, also in 1967, James Booker continued to tour and record music despite suffering deteriorating mental health exacerbated by Angola. He found some relief from racism and homophobia in 1976–1978 while in Europe. But on his return to New Orleans, work dried up. Self-medicating with alcohol and heroin for too many years, he developed renal failure and died alone in a wheelchair waiting for help at Charity Hospital in New Orleans in 1983.[102]

Leotha Brown, the youngest member of the Nic Nacs, became the longest living prisoner in Louisiana. He carried on the jazz scene after Neville, Black, and Booker left. He also became a member of the seven-man Prisoner Grievance Executive Committee when desegregation finally got under way at Angola in the mid-1970s, at first meeting secretly with White prisoner leaders to broker a balance of racial power to curb violence and demand representation with the prison administration.[103] He also became Chairman of the Negotiating Team, Prisoner Representation in the Inmate Council General Assembly. Brown successfully negotiated certain liberties that prisoners still exercise today, holding the administration to their commitments to reform. Still dedicated to music, he hosted a jazz program on WLSP called *Jazz on the River* on Mondays after the station became a low-wattage over-the-air station. And as I said at the beginning of this chapter, he became the de facto jazz historian.

In his final years, Brown lived in Camp F, the trusty camp, although he was careful to call it his "housing assignment," not his home. There, he continued to play the soprano saxophone that Charles Neville had left him. He played jazz alone, folding his newer interest in Kenny G into the unity of the Lydian scale as he practiced near the fence. Occasionally, younger musicians would ask him to play with their gospel groups. "I've sometimes been considering playing with them," he once mentioned. "'Amazing Grace,' things of this nature. I will play that as an expression of my faith, but as an expression of me as an individual, I prefer playing jazz." He died at Angola in 2009 of pancreatic cancer. His body remains there, in the prison graveyard.

The Nic Nacs refined the associations developed in the 1950s in a space under less administrative scrutiny. The association Neville stewarded provided something outside the self, measuring humanity against a higher calling, carving out a space beyond the laws of survival. Measuring up to the principles of jazz had three main outward-facing effects. First, the prisoners distinguished themselves as a cadre of musical laborers who could readily handle the task of entertaining and networking with the whole prison. Second, jazz as an *intellectual* pursuit made the notion of Black political identity audible years before the Black Panther Party formed at Angola. Third, the musical mission could counter the logic of racism that defined social relations, even if just a little. Music never melted away differences by itself. Plenty of people lived in rules: following, resisting, negotiating, establishing, abusing, and evading. But the Nic Nacs created musical events that had the potential to get people thinking about principles instead.

George Russell's take on music theory equally describes the principles that remained seeded in the musical soil at Angola: "A truly objective theory of music should preserve that which in the past was dedicated to excellence, integrity, innovation and beauty, and preserve and shelter that which in the present is dedicated to those same qualities, accommodating, inspiring and preserving those attributes in future generations."[104] As Angola moved into an intense period of violence in the 1970s, the musicians carried what they had built in the band room out to public audiences and free-world political associations.

4
Surfaces

The Pure Heart Messengers were good at talking to outsiders. They were the prison's premier gospel quartet and one of the first groups I met at Angola in 2008. The four men had many years of experience as outward-facing musicians, walking that fine line between performing meaningful music and meeting the needs of the administration in exchange for performance opportunities. Any working musician is familiar with the complex management of band members, audiences, and clients, but in my early days there, I still saw prison music as something fundamentally different from the outside. During our first conversation, I asked them, "Is there a certain song you sing that has illuminated your situation here?" I was getting at well-worn themes in ethnomusicology—how music becomes meaningful to individuals in a social context and how music can provide new ways of understanding the self. I was trying to probe deep into human experience, unaware of how significant surface experiences were at Angola.

Ray Jones answered first, enunciating carefully with a calm voice that always seemed to be revealing a secret. He told me about how he had adapted "Wind Beneath My Wings" for free-world audiences. It's a well-known song with many versions. Lou Rawls brought one version to the R&B charts in 1983. Gary Morris topped the country charts with another that same year. Bette Midler's 1989 pop version is perhaps the best known, featured in the 1988 melodrama *Beaches*, starring Midler herself. "It touched a lot of people," Jones said about the gospel version he developed for the annual Angola rodeo. "By this touching other people, and by which it has touched me, we'll build upon emotions."[1] But the song wasn't only cathartic, he explained. He chose it strategically and crafted it meticulously. "You want to make it professional," he continued. "We bring the product.... We'll make an environment of our actual experiences."

I appreciated rediscovering the song, but it wasn't what I was after. Like John Lomax writing his 1934 request to prisons for songs "'made up' by them and passed around by 'word of mouth,'" I was narrowly selecting for authenticity. I wanted to get past Bette Midler and find deep senses of the self, musical epiphanies, and unscripted uses of music. Perhaps the problem was in my wording. As I often do, I had articulated the question poorly. Jones thought my phrase, *illuminated your situation*, meant what *brought his situation to public attention*. Nonetheless, I stumbled on something more interesting than authenticity.

"Wind Beneath My Wings" has an uncanny way of relating to people. Jones's song choice was smart. Its lyrics encourage the listener to adopt the singer's or the addressee's position.[2] It's as relatable as a Hallmark card. In fumbling my question, I had discovered more than this particular song. I became interested in how incarcerated musicians developed, navigated, and used surface interactions, like the rodeo performance Jones described and even the very interview we were having.

Prison is a study of surfaces: constricting walls, high fences, and loud gates that enclose and delimit, watched by officers and prisoners alike. At first glance, surfaces can seem false, superficial, or inauthentic. But prison surfaces are dynamic, complex spaces. They can be vital spaces in which to be heard. They can also be transactional and riddled with agendas. I thought more about Ray Jones's stress on music touching listeners and what exchanges occur in passing encounters.

My reconsideration of surfaces made me rethink prison's borders. Despite the interview taking place in the middle of an 18,000-acre prison farm, in a room only accessible through a sallyport and several locked doors, I was still on the surface of the prison. The fences and guard towers are just one part of a boundary. Angola's practice of letting people into the prison reconfigures its boundaries and creates new ones.

Popular culture makes many of these surfaces alluring. The law makes them enforceable and impenetrable. But the negotiation of the law also makes these boundaries flexible, for instance, when prisoners speak or perform outside the prison and when visitors enter. Prison surfaces have a little give and also a degree of magnetism. In these complex spaces, the prison still operates, dividing people legally bound to the institution from free people. Prisoners study the surfaces to gauge possibility. As much as they constrict, the edges of prisons offer hope for eventual release.

Herein lies music's critical role in prison. Music creates a surface, reconfiguring the ordinary place of the prison. Music is an interaction. And when it happens between prisoners and free people, it takes on characteristics of prison's legal boundaries. Music can augment difference, it can present an image of a suffering or redeemable prisoner, or even establish a feeling of commonality. The musical surface of the prison is far from simple. Instead, it has a jagged texture made by cultural imagination, legal realities, and the personalities of everyone present.

My own experience visiting Angola took place on peripheries created by music. Laws may establish these prison boundaries, but boundary surfaces can become places where incarcerated artists create persuasive and meaningful art. A musical surface might be an interaction across a social or political difference, a shared but configurable barrier, an audible canvas, or a performance of suffering. By considering music as a surface, we might understand the role performance plays on the border and how music can provide a limited but genuine reconfiguration of boundaries. These complex superficial spaces that I encountered at Angola developed during the 1970s following a period of upheaval. Violence and political action created a desperate need to cultivate Angola's reconfigurable and superficial borders.

War Zone

The late 1960s and 1970s developed many uneven opportunities for public engagement. White country musicians played for the developing prison rodeo, television shows, and outside invitations. Black prisoners expanded opportunities for making and sustaining alliances through club banquets held in the main prison. Musicians made money. They also asserted control over the public perception of prisoners by providing a soundtrack for encounters with the public. Allies in the growing prisoners' rights movement listened to prisoner needs. At the same time, Warden C. Murray Henderson defended his stewardship of the prison after riots erupted and new legal challenges mounted. Public audiences allayed their fears of violent prisoners by watching them compete in a rodeo ring as they listened to the prison band and by watching them on television.

Angola was becoming extraordinarily dangerous as outlawry gained on the other missions of the prison. *Angolite* editors Wilbert Rideau and Billy Sinclair described the environment as a war zone: "Death duels were waged on a near-daily basis—and they were fought with homemade but high-quality knives, hatchets, swords, and occasionally with zip-guns and handguns. For battle gear, the inmates constructed sophisticated helmets, shields, and chest armor."[3] Angola led the nation in violence and escape attempts. A quarter of the prisoners were "gal-boys," forced into sexual slavery after being raped.[4]

146 INSTRUMENT OF THE STATE

Racial segregation was still the rule, further disadvantaging Black prisoners who couldn't find protection in the prison's safer jobs. Power overlapped and intermingled in the cliques, the administration, and White-controlled voluntary associations. The continued reliance on trusty guards only exacerbated the violence. As killings and stabbings dramatically increased, many slept with phone books strapped to their chests to ensure they would make it through the night. And if they could get on to them, prisoners found safety on surfaces.

The Rodeo Surface Redraws Boundaries

In 1963, the New Orleans Chamber of Commerce established the Greater New Orleans Tourism and Convention Commission to promote and coordinate the tourism industry. Tourism spread through the state and eventually took hold at Angola. Today, trusty prisoners work as docents at the prison museum and accompany bus tours for evangelical groups. The prison's investment in tourism, however, began with a rodeo.

Historical accounts of Angola's rodeo are peppered with touristic marketing copy and outrage commentary from journalists, making it a fraught subject. But it's safe to say the rodeo began with prisoner initiatives and games with farm animals.[5] Officers and prisoners channeled boredom and rural masculinity into an informal amateur rodeo event for two or three years. Then in 1965, prisoners suggested holding a public rodeo to raise money for the Inmate Lending Fund.[6] The Inmate Council and administration jointly coordinated the event.

The first rodeo open to the public took place in October 1966.[7] Twelve hundred prisoners outnumbered the five hundred visitors, all braving rain. Professional rodeo announcer Billy Duplessis kicked things off, and the 007 Continentals backed the event with music. They were the White version of the Nic Nacs, led by Russell Sweet, a fixture in Angola's jazz scene. Charles Maduell, from Dr. John's band, and Charlie Davis played saxophones. Eddie Wold played guitar, and Basil Harris played bass. These were the White musicians who had been crossing the color line to play jazz in the band room with Charles Neville, fluent in all styles but rooted in principles of jazz. They played with the country musicians to maximize their playing time.[8]

After Duplessis's introduction, the 007 Continentals launched into the Confederate anthem, "Dixie," as another prisoner tap-danced in the ring.

Rodeo participants marched out and offered a presentation of colors. As the rodeo got under way, Hot Rod Dantzler joined the Continentals to sing a mixed fare of standards and country songs, structuring and setting the show's pace and dramatizing events like bull riding, the wild mule scramble, and bust out. Despite minor injuries and challenges, Angola prisoners pulled off a spectacle and raised money for necessities that the state didn't provide. There was a promise of making it bigger next year.[9]

In spring 1967, a professional arrived. Rodeo star "Cadillac" Jack Favor had been sentenced to two life terms for two murders. Upon his arrival, classification officers spared Favor from work in the fields due to his health issues and a general sense that he was innocent of his crimes. (It also helped that he was a famous White rodeo star.) He laid low at first, working in the hospital and library. In time, members of the clubs reached out. His connections and influence were a potential boon for groups setting up programs and soliciting outsiders. Eventually, Favor joined Alcoholics Anonymous and the Methodist Men's Club, boosting membership and programming. One of Favor's jobs became breaking-in horses for officers and herding cattle.[10] His work connected him to officers and other prisoners on the job. While working, ideas flowed.

Favor had been to a prison rodeo at Oklahoma State Penitentiary in the 1950s. He explained how Oklahoma had been presenting a state-wide prison rodeo since 1940, run with assistance from the Oklahoma Roundup Association and dozens of other organizations in the state. Outside professionals, like Favor and the prisoners who were former cowboys, had put on exhibitions of bulldogging, riding, and roping. The other prisoners had entertained as rodeo clowns. Favor's description of the Oklahoma State Penitentiary rodeo gave them all an idea. Favor could bring professionalism to Angola's small-time local spectacle.

James "Boss Dick" Oliveux, free-staff head of the cattle operation at Angola, did what he could to help Favor develop the event.[11] He had known Favor from his rodeo days and believed he was innocent. With an eventual $5,000 allocation from Governor McKeithen, Favor began overseeing the construction of a bleachers framework to fit 5,000 people. Favor's work didn't stop with the completion of the arena. Once it was open to the public, his stardom helped draw crowds.

Dangerous events featuring untrained prisoners transfixed the crowds. Favor developed new, prison-specific events like "Guts and Glory," in which prisoners try to retrieve a poker chip tied to the wildest and meanest bull in the ring.[12] Music helped normalize the outlawry on stage, scoring risk and fear with improvised sets of crowd-pleasers. Favor's role grew as he traveled the state (with staff members) for TV and radio appearances to promote the rodeo. With effort, it developed into an annual public event, drawing significant crowds and dollars for the Inmate Lending Fund.

The rodeo dramatized inside-outside connections, creating a controversial spectacle about which many have written.[13] Criticism has focused on coercive institutional pressure. Favorable news coverage has presented incarcerated participants as volunteers and prison officials as benefactors. But if William Novak's concept of associationism (discussed in chapter 2) teaches us anything, it is that state power flows through volunteerism. Following Novak, I offer a third possibility—that the rodeo is a subinstitution of the prison, one with a related yet distinct mission that provides some freedoms within a severe power imbalance. A Faustian bargain for an individual.

The public debate over the treatment of individual participants fuels conversations about criminality, justice, and the unique ways Louisiana does things, keeping dollars flowing to the prison's voluntary associations. Imbued on the surface of the rodeo is a productively confusing set of forces, ethics, and images. I have sat within earshot of tourists attending the rodeo, discussing the event in passionate but predictable ways, debating ideas of outlawry ("they deserve it" versus "it's cruel"), penance ("it instills values through challenge"), and slavery ("it pays the bills"). But I've never heard them talk about how much money they spent on their vacation in the same breath. I would hear about that from the musicians counting proceeds after the rodeo.

The rodeo developed into a surface, a temporary space that could sustain fleeting interactions, where members of associations could interact with the public and draw profits, ultimately making up for the lack of state support. What strikes me is how the rodeo gave associations the power to let the public into the prison.

Usually, we think about prisons keeping people inside. But prisons also keep out people who might be curious or helpful. Events like the rodeo reconfigured the surfaces of Angola. Legalized physical prison boundaries include fences, walls, guard towers, and the threat of fines and jail time for trespassing. Statutes against trespassing on prison grounds are state laws that effectively grant prisons discretion over enforcement. With the establishment of the rodeo, subtle legal boundaries of the prisons shifted. The state gave power to the administration, who, in turn, gave power to the voluntary prisoner associations to invite the public onto prison grounds. Granted, this is not a geographic boundary. No one could leap to freedom across a cafeteria to a group allowed in on tour. But in a quasilegal sense, prisoners could temporarily redraw the legal boundaries and bring the public onto the surface of prison, something that Michel Foucault understands as prison's veil of secrecy, cloaking the mechanisms of punishment.[14] But when positioned on that veil, on that border, prisoners have a little more control over interactions, impressions, and relationships. To eventually get out of Angola, Russell Sweet and his band clung to Angola's new rodeo surface and held on tight as the media continued its coverage of Louisiana's most distinctive rodeo.

The Westernaires 1.0

By the time the rodeo developed, multi-instrumentalist Russell Sweet was a musical force and still only in his early twenties. (Sweet was the one who, as described in the last chapter, mastered "Ornithology" while in the hole.) He played trumpet in integrated bebop bands for the first few years of his thirty-four-and-a-half-year sentence for armed robbery. When pressed at a show, he sometimes sang. A 1966 *Angolite* review of a show testified, "Russell doesn't sing often, but when he does you don't forget it."[15] Perhaps his Yankee voice offered rarity—a New York flavor set in the fields of a Louisiana prison farm.

Sweet's proximity to the Nic Nacs's intellectual project kept him learning and made him stylistically flexible. That was crucial for him because country music, and all the opportunities Whiteness afforded it, didn't need a trumpet. So he switched to drums, learned by practicing on the bottom of his shoe.[16] From the drummer's throne, he soon led Angola's premier country band. Sweet shifted his weight onto another foothold of freedom by changing musical styles.

The Westernaires, under Sweet's leadership, spring-boarded from the 1966 rodeo into statewide media and free-world performances. Sweet swapped out members of the 007 Continentals with five other White musicians who had more country music experience and then renamed the group. Like many White prison bands, they suffered from having too many guitars—four, in their case. But they designated bass guitar, lead guitar, and strummed acoustic guitar roles, and had insurance in case they lost a guitarist for unexpected (but inevitable) security reasons or release. Most had short sentences for theft and burglary convictions.

They played covers exclusively—songs by Merle Haggard and Buck Owens, representing a strand of country that would eventually be called "outlaw country," an alternative to the commercial Nashville sound with a cultivated outlaw persona.[17] They even tossed Johnny Cash's "Folsom Prison Blues" into sets, giving his song an eerie dose of authenticity.[18]

Eventually, the Westernaires caught the ear of Bill Black, better known for his television persona, Buckskin Bill. Black had been a fixture on WAFB television since 1955, distinctive in his fringed buckskin jacket and cowboy hat. His two daily shows, *Storyland* and *The Buckskin Bill Show*, were his pulpits for advocacy. Throughout the 1960s, for instance, he encouraged donations to build a zoo by signing off each day's show with the phrase, "Remember, Baton Rouge needs a zoo," until it received enough donations to open in 1970.[19] Many local education causes also got boosts from Buckskin Bill's attention.

Black heard the Westernaires play at the second annual rodeo—the first to be professionalized by rodeo star Jack Favor (see figure 4.1). The rodeo tapped something in him. Perhaps it brought back memories of working as a

Figure 4.1. The Westernaires at the 1968 rodeo (State Library of Louisiana Historic Photograph Collection).

rodeo clown to put himself through college in Arkansas. Black sympathized with the prisoner associations pitching for contributions to support their missions, and then an idea formed: The music of the prison, articulated through the Westernaires, was something he could bring to television. Buckskin Bill's showcase of astonishing prison talent might boost educational efforts at Angola.

WAFB agreed to air *Good Morning—Angola Style* on Friday mornings. Black found sponsors and personnel to help him produce the program from inside the prison.[20] For two-and-a-half years, he and his friend Sid Crocker (the voice of Señor Puppet on *The Buckskin Bill Show*) drove up to Angola to audition, rehearse the musicians, and plan the show with prisoners and staff. "The show is my way of encouraging new rehabilitation programs in our prisons," Black later said in an interview.[21] Like raising money for Baton Rouge's zoo, Black called on the public to support penitentiary ideals and donate to educational programs.

Why not simply fund the rehabilitative programs through state budget allocations? And why not reduce sentences for prisoners who volunteer to work for and develop rehabilitative programs instead of giving them hope for a pardon through participating in a television show? In a way, donations and volunteerism provided cover for state power. Historian Brian Balogh suggests that the associative state (governance through granting power to associations) survived into the twentieth century by providing a kind of sleight-of-hand. State support (tax breaks and other entitlements) of midlevel associations made them a proxy of the state—providing, distributing, and administering that support. Americans could feel like they were keeping a large, centralized government and taxation at bay while local organizations manage various civic entitlements.[22] Public entitlements then seem to flow uninhibited from generous donors to deserved individuals, obscuring the many other midlevel associations involved in the transfer. Thus, a commonwealth tradition and a classical liberal commitment to individual rights stay intact.[23]

The rodeo, WAFB, and the prisoner associations did the work of supporting rehabilitation efforts that seemed to spring from a direct connection between a benevolent donor and a redemptive prisoner. The rodeo musicians, now on television (and in regional newspaper coverage), created an astonishing public image: redemptive White individualists burdened by prison and poor life choices.[24] The music drew attention away from the disproportionate increase of Black prisoners at Angola and frequent organized prison riots.[25]

The Westernaires became Bill Black's house band for *Good Morning—Angola Style*. In exchange, the television appearances gave the band members positive attention. Several secured pardons from the governor, who had come in contact with the music of a familiar White cowboy presented within a framework of benevolence and redemption. This framework, cobbled together between the state and the prisoners (the administration, Attorney General Jack Gremillion, WAFB, and a variety of prisoner associations), gave the musicians access to hope in exchange for public relations for Angola's rehabilitative programs. Appearances also generated some revenue for the band, but it wasn't enough.

Prisoner donations to the Inmate Lending Fund made up for any shortfall of outside contributions to the Westernaires. A blood drive raised money for a special fund for guitar and drum purchases. Officer Billy Ulmar, who sponsored the group, often lent them money when donations weren't enough to pay for the cost of travel. With funding, the Westernaires leveraged their recognizable brand (developed through television appearances) and their professional status (secured by sharing the rodeo stage with major recording artists) and began taking live performance requests. By granting them travel while still committed by the state, the administration extended the prison out into the state. This more dynamic boundary was conditional, imbued with privilege, trust, and exceptionalism.

Given the variety of needs for a country band, they accepted a variety of performance requests. In 1968, the Westernaires played the Amite Fair in Tangipahoa Parish and were invited back for the following year.[26] When the first state geriatrics hospital, Villa Feliciana, opened in Jackson, they played the open house, also featuring prisoner art. "In order to attract a crowd, there will be an art exhibit of paintings by inmates of the Louisiana State Penitentiary at Angola," promised an advertisement.[27] In 1969, they arrived at Livonia High School, a two-story brick building in a town of about six hundred, to play in the gymnasium. They provided music for a male beauty contest put on to fundraise for a new park to be shared with the neighboring town of Lottie.[28]

The interstate highway system, a massive public works project initiated in 1957, was nearly complete, providing the Westernaires' bus better access to the state from the remote confines of Angola. After the twenty-mile drive from the gates to Route 61, the new roads became the backbone of a new touring route. By May 1969, the Westernaires knew the circuit well. In addition to their weekly appearance on *Good Morning—Angola Style*, they played three outside performances per week.

On the way back from a performance at a Methodist school in Ruston, about two hundred miles northwest of the prison, the band's bus broke down about thirty minutes into the drive. The band was a slightly different lineup, spaces filled after musicians had finished their shorter sentences or received pardons from Governor McKeithen. (At this point, more than two dozen musicians had been Westernaires.) While several worked to fixed the bus, new band member James MacDonald slipped away. He made it to the nearby town of Monroe, where he stole a car, only to be captured a few days later and returned to Angola. The failed attempt had repercussions. McDonald went from being a Westernaire back to convicted forger, now facing additional charges for escape. It also meant the end of the Westernaires and the narrow pathway that they had created outside Angola in hopes of release.[29]

The Westernaires 2.0

Soon after taking over from a series of wardens in 1968, Warden C. Murray Henderson expanded public events on prison grounds (while Russell Sweet's Westernaires were still traveling the state). Tourism brought dollars. Outside of the rodeo, the first major event was a 1969 summer music festival featuring Black and White prisoner bands with the expressed purpose of raising money for recreation programs for children living in Angola's B-Line.[30] The Jaycees' Angola chapter produced the show. Musicians provided a significant part of the labor, setting up equipment and performing. Continued reliance on musicians for public events gave prisoners with specific musical skills value in the eyes of the administration.

By 1970, Angola expanded rodeo stadium seating to 8,500.[31] Big-name cowboys traveled to share the ring with prisoner contestants. National musical acts like Flatt & Scruggs, Jeanne Shepherd, and Charlie Louvin—country and western groups exclusively—added Angola to their touring circuits.[32] Music by these acts drew even larger crowds to the remote arena. Admission was one dollar. Outside the ring, hobby-craft sales added new revenues to make up for the reduced prison budgets. Given Warden Henderson's problems with both solvency and image, prisoners had a partner in developing for-profit spectacles.

In spring 1971, several Supreme Court cases in favor of prisoners' rights to sue prisons had opened the floodgates for prisoner legal action.[33] In part, the case was made when a group of attorneys from the American Bar Association had visited Louisiana on a reform mission for US Chief Justice Warren Burger and criticized the conditions as that of outlawry—in their words, "archaic," "medieval," and "pure squalor."[34] Though the new women's prison in St. Gabriel wasn't Henderson's responsibility, guards there had repeatedly beaten and gassed female prisoners.[35] Running the prisons was further complicated by the increasing free-staff turnover, likely due to the poor conditions and danger inherent to the job.[36] And the state legislature earmarked a paltry 2.2 percent of the Department of Corrections budget for education.[37] Amidst all that bad news, Warden Henderson received a phone call.

Henderson must have been relieved when he discovered that it was a girlfriend of a new prisoner on the other end of the line. She was concerned about her boyfriend, who had recently arrived with a life sentence for aggravated kidnapping.[38] He and a friend had held two police officers hostage after a bank robbery and shot them in a field. She told Henderson that he was more than just a convict. He was an excellent guitar player.

After Warden Henderson hung up the phone, he made his way to the cell block on the Big Stripe side to size up Bud Wilkerson, the new guitar player. Reunited with the Nashville Telecaster electric guitar he had brought to prison, Wilkerson effortlessly demonstrated his prowess. Henderson asked for his word that Wilkerson wouldn't run off if placed in the traveling band. He swore he wouldn't.

I met with Wilkerson in 2013 at Camp F, the trusty camp where I had listened to Leotha Brown play modal jazz many years earlier. Wilkerson had suffered a stroke and lost his right thumb in an industrial accident. He walked me through how he had launched an integrated country band, an updated version of the Westernaires. When we finished, Wilkerson asked me to wait and returned with fifty songs recorded in the 1970s spread out over three cassettes. Had it not been for his girlfriend, he may not have ever been able to record them. By now, it was a familiar story: the warden granting musical freedom in exchange for musical labor.

Warden Henderson, after accessing Wilkerson's skills, took a gamble. He immediately transferred Wilkerson from the cellblock of the main prison to Camp F and asked him to assemble a band. At the time, Camp F had no fences. Hence, Wilkerson was free to wander the farm as a newly minted trusty, scouting for talent.[39] After a time, he managed to put together a solid group of five or six musicians who were up to the task of playing the expanded rodeo. They were all reassigned to Camp F, and the band got busy learning a list of popular country hits and Wilkerson's original songs that, as Russell Sweet had done two years earlier, flung the new iteration of the Westernaires from the rodeo to the outside world (see figure 4.2).

Dora Rabelais remembers scheduling their trips while working for Henderson. "They were really a hot band and everyone wanted them."[40] She supervised security officer Bobby Howard, who provided the security detail for the band. With budgets tight, a booking required payment to the prison in advance, covering travel costs and overtime pay for Officer Howard. Angola caught stride with the increased statewide economic shift to tourism. Most engagements were in Avoyelles Parish, just west of Angola (home to the Cochon de Lait Festival, an annual celebration of roasted suckling pigs). Parades, parish fairs, state fairs, and special events made up the majority of performances. Buckskin Bill even picked up the new Westernaires for a feature on his Saturday morning show.[41] The Westernaires developed a reputation despite not being heard much in the prison except for the rodeo.

Wilkerson remembers spending only a few nights per week at Angola. The other nights, the Westernaires slept in parish jails scattered along their

Figure 4.2. Westernaires playing an outside show (Angola Museum).

performance itineraries. (This may explain why many of the older prisoners I met knew the name but didn't remember the music.) Officer Howard took them on tour. It was an all-encompassing job since the band was on the road most nights of the week. One of Howard's perks was sitting in and playing saxophone with the band. He would take them to the grocery store after shows. Band members would take their share of the kitty and spend it on food. Theft of personal food stashes was prevalent in the dorms, so gigs helped keep them stocked with enviable consumable goods.

It's hard to know if the people who called Dora Rabelais knew that the Westernaires were now an entirely different lineup or if they even cared. Fundraisers like one for the Annual Occupational Therapy Picnic for the hospital in Jackson again coupled the Westernaires with curated artworks from Angola, adding works from state hospitals and public schools.[42] Fundraisers like this were creative ways to keep state institutions solvent—collecting money through touristic means. Economically, the 1970s were a period of growth for the state despite Governor Edwin Edwards's mandate to shrink the government with his arrival in 1972.

Local fairs had hosted Angola bands for decades. The state legislature had begun allocating funds to encourage fairs in the 1950s (another instance of the associative state). Fairs date back to medieval marketplaces, link with antebellum camp revivals, and maintain regionally distinctive destination events today. It's hard to imagine any of these fairs without music. These events, however, from state to parish to town, have offered more than mere entertainment. Fairs have given local associations a platform to make symbolic impacts, to contribute to public conversations. Because the Westernaires represented Angola, band members walked a fine line to maintain touring. "We didn't have no fights," Wilkerson said, recalling the care they took to retain the trusty status that kept them eligible for outside performance and rodeo events. The rules were pretty clear. "No alcohol" was one of them.

With a mix of trust and threat, Warden Henderson folded the Westernaires into an administrative effort that he initiated with Elayn Hunt, the new Director of Corrections, redrawing prison's boundaries to allow prisoners temporarily out of prison and into schools, community groups, and parish law enforcement organizations. It was no secret that the warden had a political stake in the performances.[43] Music and handpicked "authentic" speakers provided a cheap and convincing means for educating the public about prisons and assuaging an increasing public anxiety over the unraveling of society.

Silencing the Black Panthers

Prisoner activism developed within Angola's chaos. In 1971, a chapter of the Black Panther Party formed, initiating a vanguard political action group that stood for rights. Angola's was the first chapter to form in a prison. One of the founders was Albert Woodfox, who had a skull and crossbones underneath the word "DEATH" tattooed inside his right arm, inked with pen and needle by Charles Neville years earlier.[44] Neville and Woodfox, both in the New Orleans clique, had come through mid-1960s Angola discussing political thought in fits and starts. Their soundtrack was Nic Nacs jazz. Woodfox remained at Angola after Neville, James Black, and James Booker left. He remained committed to education, change, and principled action around issues of unsanitary conditions and exposure to violence, sexual and otherwise. It was an internal effort concurrent with outside legal initiatives.

In mid-April 1972, months into organizing, chaos ensued. A yard concert (with a rare performance by the Westernaires) preceded a prison strike, and shortly after, free-officer Brent Miller, raised on the B-Line as a child, was stabbed to death with a sharpened lawnmower blade in the Pine 1 Dormitory. Another officer was lit on fire. Without any evidence, leaders of the Panthers were accused of the murder.[45] The administration cracked down on prisoner organizations and cliques. Free guards took matters into their own hands, terrorizing the population. Mayhem ensued. One consequence of the violence was a two-year ban on large gatherings, including concerts. It was the end of Angola's radical organizing. Panther leaders like Woodfox would each spend decades in solitary confinement.

The tumult of Angola led many musicians as far from the depths of Angola as they could get: the surfaces. They were still in prison but operating on the contorted border to find safety and hope for release. The Westernaires, and others who managed to retain some freedoms, did what they could to get far from the violence. It was the end of the jazz era.

Free-World Surfacework

The new formation of the Westernaires played on the yard again in 1974, when Warden Henderson reinstated prison-wide events. But they were more focused on playing to free-world audiences outside, in part because they were safer on the road, but also because their music was designed for surface interactions. Wilkerson crafted a distinctive style with his relatable tenor voice and lead guitar. His original music obliquely engaged the complex public rhetoric of White incarceration of the 1970s. About prison and *from* prison, his outlaw country songs centered on redemptive themes of regret and pain. On battered cassette tapes that Wilkerson handed me in 2013—toilet paper replacing the felt pads—studio recordings were all that was left of his work. As I listened to Wilkerson's 1970s songs, I imagined the effect that they had on audiences.

I imagined that if the sociologist Erving Goffman attended a show, he might have understood the performance as part of a social ritual. In scholarship, Goffman's concept of "total institutions" is part of the bedrock of sociological thinking on incarceration.[46] A Westernaires performance, however, might have prompted him to rethink concepts he developed outside his sociology of prisons, concepts he developed for ordinary free-world interactions. By taking time to think through outside performances as a multifaceted ritual with many participants, we can appreciate the labor that musicians did during these shows and its cultural effects. I'll rework and reapply Goffman's ideas to show the complexity of surface interactions between band and audience. What he dubbed "facework" and "stigma" offer keen insights into how the concerts operated socially. After revising Goffman, I'll incorporate an old American practice of "showing scars" to round off a comprehensive way of thinking about a Westernaires performance that I will call "surfacework."

Seeking to find commonality among different cultural norms, Erving Goffman proposed that we manage social approval by making a good showing of ourselves. "Saving face," a term he coined, is one of many strategies that he identifies as "facework," defined in his words as, "the actions taken by a person to make whatever he is doing consistent with face . . . to counteract 'incidents'—that is, events whose effective symbolic implications threaten face."[47] At a party, for instance, we might demonstrate our fluency with social norms and manage our faux pas with a representation of ourselves, our "face." Whenever someone breaches conventions, blunders a social situation, facework comes into play. Goffman describes facework as part of a social ritual that he breaks into four phases: *challenge, offering, acceptance*, and *thanks*.[48] (I'll keep these in italics over the following several pages to keep the ritual structure in mind.)

In Goffman's original use, perhaps at a dinner party, sitting down at the head of the table as a guest might *challenge* patriarchal norms. Once recognized, by noticing a surprised look from the host or a hush from the company, a verbal "I'm sorry, it looked so comfortable" would be an *offering*. Laughter and "Why don't you take this seat here" would be the *acceptance* from the host. And "Thank you" is the *thanks* that restores the acknowledgment of social norms surrounding traditional seating arrangements.

At a Westernaires show, adapting the structure of facework, Goffman might suggest that the band members arrived with the *challenge* to social norms already hanging over them. Wilkerson's songs, if understood as authentic, would begin the *offering* phase of a ritual. As he intoned into the microphone, apologetically:

> Take all I have to give to offer you for as long as I live.
> Take the tears from these eyes that can see only you.
> Take the pain from this heart that is so sad and blue.
> This is all I ask for, all these things I offer you
> Take this life I give you, and teach me how to live.
> But darlin', don't take part of me,
> Take all I have to give.[49]

In another song, submissively:

> You know you can have me whenever you want,
> Or if you don't want me at all, I'm yours, yours alone, I'm yours from now on.
> I'm yours. I'm at your beck and call. . . .
> You know if you need me, I'll always be there. I'll be there. I have to crawl.[50]

And in another, reflectively:

> I was too blind to see what I was losing until she was gone.
> She was just too good to me. She never asked me to change how I lived.
> Heartaches that won't let me be.[51]

Apology, submission, and the country trope of "looking in the mirror" help convert country songs into an *offering*.[52] In Goffman's description, an *offering* demonstrates "that he is thoroughly capable of taking the role of the others toward his own activity, that he can still be used as a responsible participant in the ritual process, and that the rules of conduct which he appears to have broken are still real and unweakened."[53] A musical *offering* of redemptive White prisoners dramatized Angola's penitentiary mission through songs of penance set to a country twang.

The *acceptance* phase may need a little tweaking from Goffman's original use. The incidents he describes as requiring facework are relatively innocuous—like spilling a drink or telling a tasteless joke. Westernaires concerts, however, were grander affairs, and the elephant in the room was that the musicians were convicts. Thus, as a ritual, the prison musicians' *offering* needed more than a host's *acceptance* of an apology. Everyone in the room had to address the social stain on identity that the Westernaires brought to the stage, a phenomenon that Goffman developed elsewhere.

In 1963, Goffman coined the term "stigma" to mean an "attribute that is deeply discrediting."[54] In fact, he wrote an entire book on it. Stigma is visible in symbols. As one of many examples he gives, "the handcuffed wrists of convicts in transit" become visible identifiers.[55] Much more so, the Westernaires, donned in prison chambray and accompanied by an officer, slightly hunched and careful with eye contact, presented an array of stigma symbols.[56] Bringing Goffman's two concepts together—facework and stigma—a Westernaires show reveals different ways that free audiences could react to the spectacle of incarceration within the ritual of performance. Goffman points out that people react differently to the same stigma. So if we bring stigma into the process of facework, then we can acknowledge that the performance might not affect everyone in the same way, and that the concert was an effort to change hearts and minds with no guarantee of *acceptance*.

At a hypothetical Westernaires concert, in the back of the Legionnaires Hall, everyone in the performance space would orient around stigma in three categories that Goffman calls the *own*, the *normals*, and the *wise*.[57] The *own* would be members of the Westernaires and any other prisoners, those who bear the stigma of incarceration.

The *normals*, perhaps sternly unsympathetic, would be the people who have not given *acceptance*. They might be unmoved by Wilkerson's song "The Loser's Hall of Fame." They might revel in the spectacle and understand themselves to be better citizens. Perhaps they simply enjoy the cheap entertainment.

The *wise*, however, would be those sympathetic to the plight of the stigmatized. Music caters to the *wise*. And conventions that help audience members relate to downtrodden characters are baked into country music. Country music makes carceral stigma relatable with its trope of the socially disengaged "fool," an ideally imperfect figure lost in his own past.[58]

The increasing popularity of outlaw country in the 1970s (Johnny Cash and Merle Haggard), in fact, brought country music's relatability to the doorstep of prison.

Audience reactions to the Westernaires would identify them as Goffman's *wise*. For example, a hardware store owner might choke back emotion over the line, "Share our guilt and shame. In this place, we're all the same," when triggered to think about an employee, maybe the son of a family friend, whom he had fired for grifting cash from the register. Anyone drawn into the facework of the stigmatized Westernaires' *offering* might flip from *normal* to *wise* once their *acceptance* was asked for. Audience members could visibly signal *acceptance* of the prisoners' *offering* by tapping their feet to the music and shaking Bud Wilkerson's hand afterward, feeling his callouses.

Expanding the stigma-driven ritual of facework further, consider that the *challenge* also flowed in the other direction, that the breach of social norms was that the prisoner's suffering was beyond acceptable norms. Facework, then, is in service of a compassionate audience feeling uncomfortable with prison conditions. If seen this way, the ritual begins with a presentation of the pains of punishment, proof of the prisoner's burden. Thinking of Wilkerson's songs as a surface brings out another meaning of the term. The prefix "sur-," a variant of "sub-," means being underneath an additional burden (like a "surcharge"). A surface, in the context of prison, is an added burden of the prisoner, evidence of a cruel and unnecessary punishment. This helps describe how prisoners often use music as a way of performing the pains of incarceration in expressive yet superficial ways. There's an old American practice at the heart of this reversed facework.

Performing pain to show a breach of the social code has deep roots in White audiences' liberal commitment to human rights, except initially, it was a visual performance. In antebellum practice, those who had escaped enslavement could gain sympathy by revealing their scars to sympathetic abolitionists.[59] Adapted from slavery to prison in the late nineteenth century, lash marks continued to be powerful images. Scars became symbols of the urgent need for prison reform. Adapted yet again, nearly a century later, the practice of showing scars adapted well to music, particularly within the sense of authenticity the singer-songwriter developed (a musical form that developed in popular music in the early 1970s). Outlaw country performed by prisoners was a pointed showing of pain.

The detrimental effect of prison on prisoners was an emerging debate in the media in the 1970s.[60] Music was another space where a public could engage these issues. Scars feature prominently on Wilkerson's musical surfaces in the form of separation and estrangement:

> The loneliness I feel is more than I can bear.
> If it'd only happen where my dreams could all come true,
> I'd be there at home to spend this Christmas Day with you.[61]

Or the awkward but concise stinger, "I'm in misery where you're not."[62]

By showing scars to a partially receptive audience, Goffman's phases of social interaction then flowed like this: The *incident* was Wilkerson's presentation of lingering carceral pain. Audience members likely gleaned Angola's *incidents* from the many reports of mismanagement, riots, prisoner lawsuits, and escapes. The audience might then make the *offering,* asking forgiveness by digging in a pocket to put a dollar in the kitty, resolving to initiate a donation drive with their church group, deciding to be more attentive to politicians' stances on prison reform, or just feeling time together with the prisoners. The *offering* acknowledged the need for change, wishing that Angola could get back to working order as a penitentiary.

The acceptance might happen when the Westernaires nod to those who drop money into the kitty, or when they say, "Thank you for having us play. Goodnight." Acknowledgment does the double-work as *acceptance* here and *thanks* in the original characterization of facework, where the audience recognized the stigma and forgave the social breach of their crime. An audience of the *wise* leaves thankful and feeling better about themselves. Moral order seems to return as some in the audience feel sympathetic.

The scarred surfaces of Wilkerson's songs didn't beg listeners for the same assistance that lash scars did abolitionists. Formerly enslaved people showed scars and received sympathy in the form of food, money, and shelter. Tweaking the practice to a 1970s prison country band, the Westernaires accepted donations as the warden argued for reform, state funding, and outside volunteerism. The administration was part of the Westernaires' performance even if they weren't present for a show. Revealing the lingering evidence of pain ritually reaffirmed a commitment to the humanitarian goals of the penitentiary by seeding discontent over the brutality of slavery and outlawry.

As a two-way ritual rooted in stigma and scars, my analysis has stretched Goffman's term too far. The work done by the Westernaires is unique and consistent enough to differentiate it from Goffman's sense of facework. Instead, *surfacework* better defines the work of the Westernaires, acknowledging the imperative social role of showing the prisoner's burden and retaining the notion that began this chapter—that the surfaces of prison developed into complex, superficial, creative spaces.

Bud Wilkerson wrote songs for this two-way ritual, showing scars and offering atonement in the form of a sad, slow subgenre of country music.[63] As he told me decades later, "I didn't listen to the radio. I just made up my own stuff." He wrote the music, assembled and led top-notch musicians, and managed to record his songs at the prison in 1974. The songs extend the reach of the musicians, the surfacework he did for himself, the other prisoners, the administration, and increasingly, for *wise* audiences.

Flipping part of the *normal* audience into the *wise* did only so much for the prisoners. Audience members were primarily *passive wise* outside of their contributions to the kitty. The only potential *active wise* sat on parole boards or behind the governor's desk.[64] As a perpetual *offering* to the public, music provided only limited hope for release. Most members of the Westernaires actually left Angola when their short sentences ended. Primarily, outside concerts kept them safer from the violence inside the prison because it required them to be on the road so much of the time.

Wilkerson's band presented a sympathetic view of the prisoner based on notions of White commonality, a theme that country music had inherited from hillbilly music.[65] Race was central to the surfacework of the free-world Westernaires concert. In our adaptation of Goffman's ritual, a free-world White listener's *acceptance* could seem to restore social norms by making them *wise* to the ideal-imperfect of White working-class society: "We've all done something wrong, I suppose." But in an audience of all White people, "we" is conditional. The performance also drew the audience's attention away from media depictions of rioting African American prisoners in the 1970s, those not asking for forgiveness but agitating for change.[66] Black musicians, then, were doubly unrepresented—not eligible to play in outlaw country bands and seen as violent (and therefore less redeemable) in the press. Practically and symbolically, they were unable to participate in the kinds of ritual performances that the Westernaires did. As it happened though, it didn't last long for Bud Wilkerson and his band anyway.

The Demise of the Westernaires

When I talked with him, Bud Wilkerson struggled to get the words out to tell me about his privileged first few years at Angola. His stutter and missing thumb were not scars brought to do surfacework with me. They were just scars, nonperformative consequences of aging in a place that offered meager medical services. He told me about playing at private parties in the 1970s, when he spent more time on the road than in the prison. These performances, usually held in upscale residences, were his favorite. He accepted good food offered by hosts and rubbed elbows with outsiders who might offer good connections. His visible and audible leadership of the Westernaires gave him more hope for support during an eventual parole hearing. A memorable private party was in 1975 for Attorney General William J. Guste at his house in Alexandria. Bud caught eyes with a woman at the party that eventually led to marriage—one of the small gains that prisoners' rights efforts had made.[67] The surfacework of a touring prison band, however, is precarious.

Music can come off as an undeserving entitlement granted to the stigmatized. Many might wonder, "Why do convicts get to have fun playing music?" Smiling onstage while receiving the adoring looks of a young girl could easily cause trouble. Ultimately, the person responsible would be the warden.

To mitigate Warden Henderson's risk, the selection process for the Westernaires became more rigorous. By the mid-1970s, the band had become part of a broader semiofficial public relations campaign—less like the independent contractors for playing parties, events, and festivals they had been before. To participate in outside programming, prisoners had to be recommended by the Chief of Security and staff. The Secretary of Corrections in Baton Rouge would also need to sign off. Gradually, musicians lost out to a handful of boxers and members of the Angola Jaycees as the official travel program shifted into speaking engagements—less risky events than concerts with dancing, alcohol, and fun.[68]

A single incident killed off the Westernaires, already in disfavor, again in 1976. They had finished playing at a private party where they had managed to get a bit drunk. (The hosts had plied them with whiskey.) Hoping to continue the party, Wilkerson stashed a bottle in his guitar amplifier. Arriving back at Angola's gates, officers followed the smell of Wilkerson's breath to the hidden bottle. He spent that night in administrative segregation and went to prison court the following day. Stripped of trusty status, he was transferred to Camp I. It was his last outside gig and was also the end of the Westernaires.

The administration couldn't fill the empty slots because few qualified musicians could get the votes to travel. Associate Warden Peggi Gresham, who booked the band then, said that the administration "preferred seeing the band die rather than fill the vacancies with prisoners whom they had doubts about."[69] Warden Henderson, who sponsored the band in the first place, also left that year, and the new warden, Ross Maggio Jr., had less incentive to use the Westernaires for public relations. At that point, Louisiana had lost control of the prison. Angola fell under a consent decree and federal receivership, a story we will pick up in the next chapter.

For Wilkerson, there wasn't much to the story after the bottle of whiskey was found. The band continued to play a bit within the fences—the Angola banquet circuit and some yard shows. He formed another band called Barbed Wire, but without the affordances that the Westernaires had, he felt they never became as good. Other bands would eventually take the outside gigs after musicians regained trust in the 1990s. But reflecting on current bands playing outside, Wilkerson said to me, "They ain't as good as we was."

The legacy of both versions of the Westernaires is in the way they exploited surfaces. The rodeo, the use of administration for booking frequent outside shows, and their appearance on media brought the surfaces of the prison to free-world listeners. The surfacework did the double-work of astonishing audiences with an intertwined ritual made more potent with Bud Wilkerson's original outlaw country songs of carceral pain. By offering redemption and showing scars, the performances accomplished a few things. They gave limited hope and freedom to prisoners, provided a safer space to be on the road, produced a public ritual of *offering, acceptance,* and *thanks,* and, perhaps most fundamentally, provided opportunities for prisoners to be musicians.

The Westernaires also gave the administration an effective tool during a time of chaos and public debate over Angola's failures. When large corporations make mistakes, they often use their budgets for advertising campaigns, employee training, or community reparation. The state used prisoner volunteerism to merely signal a commitment to reform. Publicity drawn from the rodeo gave Warden Henderson access to media that could put a "good news" story first. Interviewed during an event, he could explain the financial or infrastructural state of the prison. For instance, in a 1970 *Times-Picayune* feature, Henderson argued that violence is a product of neglected infrastructure and inadequate staffing. He articulated his rehabilitative mission, noting the importance of offering prisoners jobs to give them skills for release, the need for psychological services, and the importance of having people from universities doing fieldwork there. "One of the ironies of prison life is that when you isolate a man from society, he is cut off from these values that you want him to incorporate."[70] In the article, Henderson's quote mixes with photographs of staff and prisoners working together and a half-page picture of the rodeo preparations in the arena.[71] Other profiles read more like advertisements for the event: "Remember, any Sunday afternoon this September is prison rodeo time—Louisiana style!"[72] Stories stressed volunteerism—arena construction and event development—which bolstered penitentiary ideals of preparing a White prisoner for reentry through self-organization and hard work. The image, of course, traded on spectacle, the thrill of watching a more dangerous version of a local rodeo set to music. From prisoners' perspectives, there are limits to the Westernaires' outlaw country rhetoric.

Reflecting only on individual wrongs, the Westernaires' songs never identified collective problems. They didn't sing about policy changes that were being negotiated by prisoner collectives with the administration in the early 1970s. Wilkerson's songs were centered on the individual. What's more, they supported racialized rehabilitative ideals. White prisoners have inherited an image: prison as the mortification of an individual who, through penance, can be reborn as a citizen. Black prisoners inherited the image of plantation workers: prison as a collective mass best brought under control by the whip. Unsurprisingly, Black prisoners had a more challenging time occupying the stage of redemption. It would take years for gospel musicians to develop different but related strategies (described in the next chapter), dramatizing *spiritual* redemption in support of penitentiary ideals and allaying fears of an out-of-control violent mass.

When I spoke with prisoners who were there in the 1970s, especially Black prisoners, few remembered the Westernaires. The Westernaires' legacy is felt most among the former staff and the children who grew up on the B-Line. Like touring bands who hit a national circuit that pulls them away from home audiences, the Westernaires weren't heard much in the prison. They played outside Angola every night of the week and slept in vacant parish jail cells. Even if they had played in Angola, their redemptive surfacework might not have registered in the same way with Black prisoners struggling under a different weight of incarceration.

Banquets

Despite budget cuts and violence, music programs persisted through the 1970s at Angola. But it was harder to find places to play. Plantation festivals were on the decline in part because the economy changed. The price of raw goods produced at Angola had begun slipping in the 1960s. The lower market value of sugar eventually led to the sale of the sugar mill to a Guatemalan firm in 1976. Deindustrialization was slowly transforming the entire region. Shifting from big holiday shows, musicians operated within the recreation and education departments, club support, and religious activities. Club banquets became the new venues for bands inside Angola after a policy shifted music performances from the yard to the clubs.

The band room was active, and there were plenty of musicians and equipment. The Inmate Lending Fund gave Angola's micro-economy a degree of stability. Income from the rodeo and media appeals for donations also helped. By some measure, musicians had strong resources. From another perspective, the lack of performance opportunities meant that Angola had a musical labor surplus. Leotha Brown explained that the recreation department created a policy whereby bands "were required to play for [the] inmate population at least twice a month or else you would lose your practice time in the music room."[73] There were so many bands that there were small shows on the recreation yard every weekend.

These shows were some of the few bright moments of life on the farm for Michael Lindsay. Reflecting from the perspective of a musician in the early 1970s, Lindsay explained,

> At that time, they had a whole bunch of homosexuals here. And they'll pile up and get together and dance, which made it more enjoyable for the musicians because it let us know that people were enjoying our music. . . . They'll get out in the yard and dance, have fun, second-line. . . . Most people from New Orleans love second-line, so that was like the highlight of the show. . . . The homosexuals at that time were dressing up somewhat like women, to a degree. It was just dancing and having fun.[74]

But the media coverage of sexual and physical violence made these mass gatherings a liability for the administration's safety and public relations concerns. Warden Henderson associated the yard shows with violence, the sex trade, and immorality. Henderson reflects, "There was no useful purpose to be accomplished by men dressing up as women and trying to be seductive to other prisoners."[75] Fights over gal-boys and a firmly entrenched sexual economy bred violence and unpredictability.

Warden Henderson had a slew of problems, and few could be fixed with a country band. The academic and vocational programs, the ones aligned most with the penitentiary model of rehabilitation, had dried up. In his own accounts, Henderson describes singlehandedly marshaling the Department of Education to revive the programs.[76] The less dramatic story is that he channeled state penitentiary power through voluntary associations.

Henderson handed over a degree of control to the prisoner clubs to make up for losing rehabilitative program funding. Clubs created more events around their missions. They offered custodial stability, and by now there were more of them: the Jaycees, Vets Incarcerated, the Angola Amateur Boxing Association, Full Gospel Businessmen Fellowship International, Alcoholics Anonymous, and the Lifer's Association, to name only a few. Events provided incentives for joining. Membership was a prerequisite for attending association-sponsored events that included music, food, and outside guests. In exchange, robust club memberships offered the administration more predictability than the cliques. The optics were also good. The social activity of the prison seemed less recreational when led by altruistic volunteer associations. And finally, concerts moved indoors to more mission-driven banquets that the clubs sponsored and organized. By delegating power to the associations, Henderson solved several problems at once.

In this book, our framework for understanding music at Angola should be clear now: the administration chartered voluntary associations (including bands), granting them limited powers to run certain aspects of prison operations. But why not simply hire subcontractors or pay for operations through state budgets? Part of the answer is that the public can't stomach images of large bureaucratic state initiatives, especially ones that require additional taxation. Looking at American governance in the twentieth century may shed light on the unique ways that free-world and prison voluntary associations became integral to life at Angola.

Historian Brian Balogh argues that Americans have kept associationalism alive because it keeps state power hidden from sight, when in actuality, state power flows through associations—intermediaries granted power, privilege, and resources through the state.[77] Bringing Balogh's insight to Angola, Warden Henderson's support of prisoner associations, especially those tied to outside free world associations, could fulfill the penitentiary mission through volunteer groups. For instance, the Alcoholics Anonymous club worked with chapters in the state as well as in Mississippi and Texas to organize events.[78] Henderson may or may not have strategized this, but it was the effect of his stewardship, and it was a means for bringing outside volunteers into the prison—a circuitous funding scheme that hides forms of state support as much as it cuts costs.

Voluntary organizations like church groups and political action groups receive tax shelters, donations, grants, and access to state resources, reinforcing the sense that the state is only coordinating individual initiatives and trusted intermediaries. A similar thing happened under Henderson. Albeit with a different rationale, Henderson explained that "because trained salaried staff was in short supply, a lot of professional organizations were called upon to fill the gaps—the Jaycees, Dale Carnegie, Great Books clubs, Mensa, and various religious groups with outside sponsors."[79] The groups didn't just get permission. The administration coordinated the effort. They provided scheduling and security (paid through operations budgets) to enable these organizations to do some of the work of the state—primarily custody and rehabilitation. Sponsorship gave associations the ability to have administrative coordination, security, spaces for meetings, movement of prisoners through the prison, and the flow of outside goods and services for projects and events.[80] Angola's clubs had as much in common with the free-world associations that Brian Balogh details in his wider writing on associationalism in the United States, but that is not the whole story of associative persistence.

Mutual aid societies have a distinguished history in Louisiana. These societies developed in the late eighteenth century because of an absence of state support for African Americans. Some argue that they are rooted in West African institutions that had been given more freedom under French rule.[81] Joined together, members offered financial aid and space for cultural expression to those who needed it the most. Not only did they provide essential services that neither the city of New Orleans nor White voluntary associations offered (for example, financial, medical, or funeral services), they also articulated an ideology of uplift and unification that developed in the Second Great Awakening of African American social thought.[82] New Orleans benevolent societies organized the parades that mark second-line traditions. If there is a legacy of these in Angola's associations, it is this legacy of cultural expression and political action, transplanted from New Orleans streets to Angola prison in the 1970s.

By the 1970s, Black businesses had taken the place of most mutual aid societies like the Société d'Économie et d'Assistance Mutuelle and the New Lusitanos Benevolent Association. But they stayed active culturally, contributing second-line performances during Mardi Gras, most visibly. It was not lost on New Orleanian prisoners that Angola's associations were influential organizations akin to mutual aid societies. As practiced at the prison, they offered aid and spaces for music, art, and dance.

It's tempting to romanticize these institutions. As Wilbert Rideau, the first Black editor of *The Angolite*, cautions in a 1978 article, there were plenty of self-interested reasons for joining clubs:

> For the politically ambitious, clubs offer an opportunity for leaders to exercise political maneuvers, rising through the ranks of the club structure. For those who possess an itch for tyranny, clubs provide an opportunity to engage in ruthless power struggles. For the criminally corrupt, clubs offer a means to steal and rip-off the profits made by the club's concession. For the believer in God, clubs offer an opportunity for him to preach and spread God's word. For the teacher, clubs offer classes in a variety of subjects. For the homosexual, clubs provide an opportunity to meet a lover. Regardless of the motive, clubs provide an invaluable way of convicts to cope with their caged life.[83]

Despite the many motivations for potential members, clubs provided opportunities for social action and made their missions known through charter and through sponsored events. Clubs gave structure to community action, even if individuals were driven by love, tyranny, or religiosity. A venerable club like the Jaycees (US Junior Chamber), for instance, was based on and stood for civic organization, tasked with addressing community issues within and outside of the prison.[84]

Angola's associations proliferated in the 1970s: sports and recreation leagues, religious groups, self-development programs, community service, and musical groups. As the prison desegregated and ramped down its plantation practices in the 1970s, associations began to structure power throughout the prison. Clubs influenced change and preserved incremental gains even though they were subject to the unpredictability and opacity of prison authority. The growth in clubs coincided with a new opening of prisoners' rights.

The successful litigation of *Sinclair v. Henderson* in 1971 upheld the Eighth Amendment right to be free from cruel and unusual punishment and the Fourteenth Amendment right to due process, ruling against the "hands-off" policy (outlawry) that had been in place since 1948.[85] *Sinclair v. Henderson* set a precedent for Federal judicial intervention. Centered on prisoner litigation, this new "open door" era did less to open a door than to develop new surfaces inside prison, ones on which prisoners worked with advocates. Prisoners used power granted to clubs by Warden Henderson and US courts to establish connections with the outside. Some club members took speaking engagements at local schools and community groups, colleges, and antipoverty programs. Some took on fundraising projects for charities and advised on crime prevention programs. In return, prisoners found ally associations who might help them out of prison.

Surfacework of the clubs brought together prisoners, staff, and outsiders, potentially creating alliances. Clubs could initiate a reason for travel, and club members could be known and trusted candidates for representing the prison.[86] Club connections to the outside were sustained through inviting related groups to prison events. Approval, however, was never guaranteed. Many visitors were denied access at the gate or notified by mail that they could not attend. But chartered associations and free-world allies had better chances if under the auspices of participating in a banquet. Since music was part of the events, musicians found increased opportunities to play for club banquets. Music helped develop the banquet surface, one with a different texture than that created by the Westernaires outside Angola. The participants were different.

Outsiders included free-world lawmakers, family members, activists, religious leaders, motivational speakers, and musicians. Allied prisoners and visitors collaborated to secure prisoners' rights, release, and rehabilitation. Fundraisers often included outside people, families, state representatives, and guest speakers. Music gave this charge a feeling and was part of the draw. Prisoners dressed up, paid admission, and enjoyed food, music, dance, and speeches. Every banquet had a band.

A 1978 profile of banquets in *The Angolite* expresses the importance of the winter banquet season:

> The only events which make prisoners voluntarily leave their warm dormitory patterns are the annual winter banquets sponsored by the various prison organizations. The banquets mean good food, loud music, and free world guests. That spells a break in boredom and an escape from hopelessness. It's a time for the best: pressed Levi's, shined patent leathers, and polished gold earrings, watches and necklaces. It's a great moment for wall-paper pimps, yesterday-sharp players, and the plain regulars. Each is there to promote a special, selfish interest. False-airs, city-bred deceit, and prison-drunk smiles flow like they do at a Washington yankee party.[87]

Beyond self-promotion, however, banquets provided associations energy and action. Meetings presented minutes, updates on legislative efforts, personal accounts of incarceration, group prayer, shared food, and lots of handshakes and hugs. The combined legacy of White volunteer associations and Black mutual aid societies developed a robust social space of civic action and cultural expression in the associations. *The Angolite* continued its role of presenting these events to prisoners unable to attend and to a growing free-world readership. Banquets were best in person, however, because musicians could bring a diverse audience together in song. In other words, with the right selection of song and musical style, they could establish a common groove, make people dance, and offer testimony. This was the work of the banquet musicians. When not paid in dollars, the musicians accepted food and maybe even extra helpings. Musicians could sometimes get people on a list to get in for free.

Each banquet was different. The Human Relations Public Speaking Club produced an Easter Festival with a dancing contest and track and field events.[88] The Social, Economics, and Athletic (SEA) Club regularly offered a culminating event to cap the music classes they sponsored (along with chess, public speaking, and group therapy). Monday evenings provided regular games, business discussions, and refreshments. The SEA 1974 Christmas banquet brought gospel music from the Culpepper Trio, an outside group. Local Reverend A. U. Hardy and his two daughters sang afterward.[89] Many other clubs also had enough outside links and powerful enough administrative sponsors to bring in outside guests and entertainment.

While the associations appreciated musicians, there was the sense that the prison administration had abandoned them (likely because the administration was effectively letting the associations do the work of organizing music). In his "Sound of Music" column in March 1974, Thomas "Twin" Wiltz wrote, "Apparently there seems to be no interest in the music department on the walk. Musicians are similar to rolls of tissue paper here at Angola. They are occasionally discovered." Despite Wiltz's legitimate complaint, the musicians were constantly asked to play for social gatherings by the clubs. His issue was that there was little direct state support for music that required, in his view, "long hours of playing and practicing." In the same piece, he made a case for state allocation: "The Department of Corrections does not recognize music as an honest trade; however, it offers one of the most rewarding futures to an ex-convict. There are no college certificates required, just the will and the ambition to want to make it in this cruel world."[90] Wiltz's call for administrative state support fell on deaf ears. Warden Henderson had already set up an associative state within Angola. Music was subject to the patronage of the voluntary clubs, which were less at risk of public outrage over frivolous expenditures on convicts.

Sublime Surfaces

A detailed description of the 1974 Lifers Association banquet will show a type of surfacework done for clubs inside Angola. This banquet is well documented because it was the first major event to follow the ban on large gatherings following the violence, the murder of a guard, and the elimination of the Black Panther Party in 1972. I also draw from my interview with Edwin Cook, who came up from New Orleans on his own accord as a teenager to perform. The event I will describe shows how music developed a shared sense of being impacted by the criminal justice system.

Visiting banquet audiences drove up the twenty-six-mile rural highway and went through many stages of security protocol, confirming their names, presenting identification, waiting in sallyports, and eventually taking a seat in the cafeteria or prison chapel. These audiences were, in Erving Goffman's terms, the *wise*. The game at banquet performances was less to flip *normal* to *wise* than it was to share a burden. Music's role was to create a surface and investigate what lies beneath that surface together. Goffman's description of ritual is less useful here. Ralph Ellison's understanding of ritual and surface, however, gets closer.

Ellison, a late modernist and contemporary of Goffman, also looked for social ritual. But where Goffman saw systematic processes, Ellison saw an ungovernable depth. His reflection on the artistic process pointed him to surfaces, ritual, and the imperative of reckoning with what lies beneath. Ellison was an astute observer of jazz and drew many connections between music and writing, not just writing about jazz but writing *as* jazz.[91] His thinking helps frame the work musicians did at banquets. Here, he describes a discovery of depth while wrestling with structuring his first novel:

> I began by trying to manipulate the simple structural unities of *beginning*, *middle*, and *end*, but when I attempted to deal with the psychological strata—the images, symbols and emotional configurations—of the experience at hand, I discovered that the unities were simply cool points

of stability on which one could suspend the narrative line, but beneath the surface of apparently rational human relationships there seethed a chaos before which I was helpless. People rationalize what they shun or are incapable of dealing with; these superstitions and their rationalizations become ritual as they govern behavior. The rituals become social forms, and it is one of the functions of the artist to recognize them and raise them to the level of art.[92]

Ellison's image of ritual here, of a surface, draped over a stable framework amidst underlying chaos, identifies a role of the artist: *to reach beneath the surface*. Elsewhere, he explains his artistic process as creating a surface—not as the art itself, but as a way of setting the stage in order to reach below. In his words:

[I]t was not enough for me simply to be angry, or merely to present horrendous events or ironic events. I would have to do what every novelist does: tell my tale and make it believable, at least for as long as it engaged the reader's sense of reality, his sense of the way things were done, at least on the surface. My task would be to give him the surface and then try to take him into the internalities, take him below the level of racial structuring and down into those areas where we are simply men and women, human beings living on this blue orb, and not always living so well.[93]

The way I think of it, Ellison adds another dimension to ritual surfacework. Our revision of Goffman's ideas of facework and stigma cast an outside Westernaires show as meaningful superficial motion across surfaces, a ritual of redemption and forgiveness flowing in two directions. Now, with aid from Ellison's idea of peering below surfaces, we can include a third dimension to depth—a shared commitment to looking into the irrational chaos of life. Banquet surfacework involved club and association efforts across Angola's borders, attempting to solve problems involving prisoners' rights, community aid, fundraising, and self-empowerment—a remnant of the kinds of projects that mutual-aid societies had supported.

We ought to be cautious of starkly racializing these distinctions between outside shows and banquets. Indeed, for some attendees, connections at Westernaires shows went deep into the irrational chaos of prison experience. And more than a few Black audience members at banquets remained on the superficial threshold between *normal* and *wise*. But structural differences are apparent. More African Americans had connections to the criminal justice system. More recognized that the system was broken and far from principled. And the idea of the stigmatized self was well developed in African American intellectual thought, given the persistence of racism.[94] The community burden of incarceration on the Black community was growing, and it begged for collective action.

Originally founded as a social club, the Lifers Association had become one of Angola's most influential Black self-help associations, but Louisiana's changing sentencing laws shifted the association's mission in the mid-1970s.[95] From 1926 until then, most Louisianans with life sentences could count on the "10-6 rule," meaning that after ten-and-a-half years, they were eligible for parole and an automatic recommendation from the warden. A life sentence based on indeterminate sentencing, then, was simply the state's rare option to hold someone until they died, a maximum on a continuum. In the early 1970s, so-called truth-in-sentencing laws emerged in response to national political pressure to curb increasing violent crime, restricting judicial and custodial discretion over sentence length.[96] Though Louisiana's 10-6 rule was officially abolished in 1979, changes in the makeup of the Board of Pardons occurred in 1974, effectively ending the practice.[97] As Lifers Association member Eddie Hall explained, "This caused us to change our goals and policies from one of socializing to the business of just trying to get out of this place. . . . we have to gear our efforts in the judiciary. We have to gear our efforts toward becoming more knitted together as a group and find the information and the facts we need to get out of here."[98] The work of the Lifers became confronting the prospect of never-ending confinement at Angola and supporting each other's court cases as "life" became *life*.

In 1974, the Lifers Association was a strong point of contact with prisoners' rights activists, including outside state legislators and religious leaders. They produced a rival to *The Angolite* in 1974, addressing the fact that Black editors could not join the all-White *Angolite* staff. *The Lifer* reported more directly on pains of incarceration, prison reform efforts, news from the free world, critiques of Angola's White-controlled associations, minutes of meetings, and plans for upcoming banquets.[99] With robust membership, media, and a new mission, the association became a reinvigorated force at Angola.

The Lifers Association banquets reflected the retooled association. In March 1974, State Representative Johnny A. Jones and Reverend Cato Brooks Jr., outspoken advocates for prisoners' rights, accepted the Lifers invitation to be distinguished guests at their annual banquet. Association members then envisioned a prison-wide event that might bring a more extensive array of constituents, something bigger than a banquet (but still called a banquet to couch the request in familiar terms). It would take the entire summer to plan. John Guidry, an active member of the Lifers, pitched the idea to the administration. He suggested that the Pro-Fascinations, a new R&B group from New Orleans (that happened to include two of his sons), should perform at the banquet along with local Angola groups. The Lifers already had a successful history of bringing outside entertainment—like the Southern University Jazz Band—to banquets.[100]

But there was still strong opposition to large music events among administrators and security officers. They were afraid that the concert might spark violence again.[101] State Representative Johnny Johnson of New Orleans, who had developed a relationship with the Lifers Association, put additional pressure on Warden Henderson and the Director of Corrections, Elayn Hunt. Providing a tipping point, Security Major Richard Wall, a newer free-world hire, broke with the uncooperative security staff and volunteered his shift to help produce the banquet as a concert with bands. It was the first time in the prison's history that a security shift (instead of an administration) offered to cosponsor a prisoner-hosted event. The Lifers got to planning.

In early fall, Edwin Cook of the Pro-Fascinations drove up from New Orleans to sing at the banquet.[102] Cook was sixteen years old and had already distinguished himself as a musician in the Desire Projects in the Ninth Ward. Many men he knew from home had been driven up the same route to the penitentiary only to find themselves working in the fields soon after. Rohillion and Wayne Guidry, singers in his group, would soon see their father, John Guidry, who had originally pitched the banquet on behalf of the Lifers Association. As I spoke to Cook about his connections to Angola, he tried to remember if their uncle was also imprisoned there.

There were plenty of free people in the dining hall, where the event took place. State representatives Johnny Jackson and George Connor attended and when introduced, received sustained applause from the crowd. Representative Jackson had become a leader of the New Orleans delegation after organizing community activism in the 1960s. He had been director of the Desire Community Center, where he famously negotiated a standoff between the Black Panthers and the New Orleans police.[103] After moving into the State Legislature as its third Black member, he helped found the state's Legislative Black Caucus. Representative George Connor made history when, as a high school basketball coach, he set up the state's first interracial basketball game, which would eventually unite Louisiana's Black and White athletic organizations. Both Jackson and Connor had been working on prison issues. Other notables included George Vinnett, a well-known civil rights activist and New Orleans DJ on WYLD who had recently started his nationally syndicated variety show, "Get Down" on WGNO. When one of the prisoner bands played "Jungle Boogie," it was a bit of a nod to Vinnett. Kool and the Gang's use of "Get Down" was a reference to Vinnett's program.

The Guidry brothers took in the scene but managed to hide any emotion when they saw their father. Cook told me that he himself was relatively unfazed. In contrast to Johnny Cash's powerful 1968 recorded encounter with Folsom Prison, Cook's experience neared ordinary. He wasn't nervous because, as he said, "I was used to that environment." Cook knew some of the people incarcerated there from growing up in the Desire Projects. It was more like a reunion, especially given Johnny Jackson's presence. Just as Cook had distinguished himself at the Desire Community Center Showcase, he had the respect and encouragement of a community that championed him. "Good for you" in the Desire Projects became "Don't do like me" as he met prisoners gathering for his performance at Angola.

When the Pro-Fascinations took the stage, administrators and staff were alert for trouble. It was in everyone's interest to show that concerts could be peaceful. Cook and the Guidry brothers sang their original "Do I Baby" and a mix of popular tunes. Cook remembers that everyone was extraordinarily well behaved as they sang. But that doesn't mean it was lifeless. For prisoners, it was refreshingly familiar—current pop songs, laughter, children, and men and women not in uniform. A review of the event in *The Angolite* describes the life that the banquet created with "singing, dancing, beautiful girls, young children running here and there with cold drink splattered over their little tummies and joyous inmates."[104]

After their set, the Pro-Fascinations cleared the stage for the Kennedy Sisters. The five sisters sang and danced their distinctive slow soul and R&B. The 1970 Stax crossover hit "Mr. Big Stuff" playfully taunted:

> Mr. Big Stuff, who do you think you are?
> Mr. Big Stuff, you're never gonna get my love.
> Now because you wear all those fancy clothes (oh yeah),
> And have a big fine car, oh yes, you do now,
> Do you think I can afford to give you my love (oh yeah)?
> You think you're higher than every star above.

And another Jean Knight hit, "One Monkey Don't Stop the Show," had a slightly different resonance for an audience of felons:

> A thief in the night, he stole my mind.
> Breaking lover's hearts should be a crime.
> But he'll return to the scene of the crime.
> I'll set a tender trap. He'll be unaware.
> I'll wear a smile down the aisle,
> 'Cause he's the father of my child.
> Stick-up, highway robbery,
> Stole my love from me—it's a case of grand larceny.
> Stick-up, highway robbery,
> It's a felony—heartbreak in the first degree.

They closed with Gladys Knight & the Pips's "On and On" and then an encore of the same tune. Yvonne Kennedy then said to the crowd, "We are here to let you know that we care and that we have not forgotten you." Emcee Darryl Evans, a gregarious emerging prisoner leader who had come off death row into the general population two years earlier, presented all female participants with crafts made in the prison's hobby shop.[105] The Kennedy Sisters cried as they heard the individual stories told by the members of the Lifers Association. The music held the event together as they collectively peered into what a life sentence now meant following the suspension of the 10-6 rule. Attendees danced, laughed, and sang along, allowing musicians to do their intersubjective work of turning "I" into "we."[106] The collaboration between outside and inside musicians was not only relief and inspiration for the incarcerated musicians. It formed a musical community that transcended the prison, albeit momentarily.

The banquet set off testimony, discussion, and dancing. I find it helpful to bring in cultural theorist Paul Gilroy's notion of the "slave sublime" in understanding the event, adding to Ellison's suggestion that surfaces provide a vantage point from which to examine an irrational and chaotic depth. In African American practice, Gilroy describes a type of artistic strategy that uses music, dance, and scars in the struggle to understand the traumatic past of slavery in solidarity.[107] His adaptation of the European concept of "the sublime" describes art as the engagement of threshold experiences, continual discovery, and accepting the indefinable as inherent to the mode. We may not come to an understanding of a hidden and fundamental truth, but we can reckon within what he calls a "lower frequency where it is played, danced, and acted, as well as sung and sung about."[108] Adapting Gilroy's concept to the banquet, music engaged a deep chaotic unknowable that held a lingering slave sublime at Angola. Now more devastating in 1974, the *prisoner sublime* was an unfathomable prospect of dying on a former slave plantation. Events like the 1974 Lifers Association banquet all offered degrees of emotional work, augmented by musicians ready to take the gigs.

Interviewed after the banquet, Officer Wall thought the event was a success. As reported in *The Angolite*, he "expressed the belief that the cooperation between the inmates and his officers represents a move to tearing down the long withstanding barriers barring meaningful communication and that he is looking forward to more such joint efforts in the future."[109] The show reopened the opportunity for concerts. The Pro-Fascinations and the Kennedy Sisters played another few concerts together at Angola over the next few years. The success of the banquet gave trust back to music events, which also became tinged with the collective feeling of activism.

Two years after the 1974 Lifers Association banquet, Wilbert Rideau, founding editor of *The Lifer* and eventual editor-in-chief of *The Angolite*, wrote an evocative review of an unsponsored concert in front of the Big Stripe band room, something unimaginable during the performance events ban. As he describes, the Scientists of Soul transformed the space outside the recreation department into an outdoor concert (see figure 4.3). Hundreds lined the railing to listen to a funk group that could never have subbed for a Westernaires performance or been featured on *The Buckskin Bill* show.

Rideau described the effect of the music: "Dominating their emotions, the funky music reached deep into the hidden places where each of them lived, yanking to the surface all of those secret emotions that had long craved expression but denied an outlet—until now, until the music.... dragging us across the threshold, a world where our keepers could not follow."[110] In Rideau's description, there is more than a little of Ellison's call for the artist's use of surfaces.

The banquets continued through the 1970s as clubs took on expanded roles in the prison. They linked prisoners to the outside and became more financially sound through the strengthening backbone of the Inmate Lending Fund. Emcees often led the events. A glowing review in *The Angolite* praised one emcee: "Joey Norwood started it rolling with a professional monologue that ranked with many of the monologues we have seen on the Ed Sullivan Show."[111] Some of the most important outside guests at the banquets, as you could imagine, were families.

Figure 4.3. The Scientists of Soul perform in front of the Big Stripe Band Room, 1976 (*The Angolite* archives).

When I discussed the music of the 1970s with horn player Charles Venardo, he first lamented not being part of a successful outside band. But when he brought up the banquets, he lit up as if remembering career highlights. For Venardo, music at the banquets was a way of mending family separation:

> The last song I played at a banquet was "Come Morning" by Grover Washington, and my mother was there, . . . man, that was joy. To see all the other mothers, all the other families, . . . just seeing the expression on her face, I had let her down. But now I'm doing a little something positive, and just the expression on her face was worth it all. . . . And she was there just looking at "my son." "My son." Even though I'm incarcerated, even though I'm going through all these trials and these tribulations, it's still like a little bright spot. For me, it helps me make it through.

The musicians benefited from the relative formality of the banquets as well. It was different from everyday Angola, and music was part of that. Venardo told me how the musicians valued the stage: "Guys just enjoyed going and being there and playing. With the music, it's like a form of escapism. When you get off into the music, you just get away from it all. . . . When you get off into the music, you're back in another world, man. You're oblivious to everything else."[112] Whether contributing to the serious surfacework of the prisoner sublime or just offering an enjoyable a break from ordinary incarceration, music at banquets was invaluable. Ironically, perhaps, escaping into the banquet experience was the volunteer work of musicians, playing the role of effective state laborers, supported by the administration's transfer of limited power to the associations.

Voluntary associations grew under Warden Henderson's arrival, significantly impacting daily life at Angola.[113] According to Henderson, clubs added to "the peace and security of the institution by balancing the prison's subcultural power structure."[114] The 1970s also saw a racial balancing of the clubs. Leadership positions gradually became filled by the increasing Black population, following statewide incarceration trends and slow desegregation of the prison.[115]

Lingering Surfaces

Angola's surfaces continued to mutate and adapt, desegregating and becoming more important under the tightening grip of the state. While many musicians got out after serving shorter sentences or receiving pardons, Bud Wilkerson and Leotha Brown both died at Angola. Had 1970s attitudes on incarceration been different, they may have gotten out.

The end of the 10-6 rule governing life sentences had no grandfather clause. Those who had not completed their ten-and-a-half years before "life" became *life* would eventually form another association: the Ten-Sixers, an aging group of men given life sentences between 1963 and 1973 who lobbied unsuccessfully to secure release. The mid-1970s were a perfect storm for the Ten-Sixers. Overcrowding at Angola led to a mandated expansion of the prison system. As Louisiana built new prisons throughout the state, District Attorney Harry Connick of New Orleans initiated a well-financed "tough on crime" campaign. Now able to house more prisoners, the state issued more life sentences and made less use of parole.[116] Angola's population grew older. When I arrived to study music there in 2008, the prison's gravedigging had picked up its pace as the Ten-Sixers continued to fight in court. Musicians continued to use music to strategically preserve opportunities to play and to connect to the outside.

Returning to the interview that opened this chapter, the one that surfaced the Bette Midler song, "Wind Beneath My Wings," Jewell Spotville sat next to Ray Jones, thinking about my initial ill-crafted question, "Is there a certain song you sing that has illuminated your situation here?" Spotville, also a member of the Lifers Association, understood that I was looking for a certain authenticity that original songs could only deliver. His song, "When Will I See

You Again?" was a go-to for his gospel group, the Pure Heart Messengers, when they performed at the rodeo. He explained its significance:

> It's about your mother who started coming to Angola to see you and telling you about the grandkids and telling you about the children and everything. It was time to go [from visitation]. She had to leave. She was sick, and you're trying to tell her, "Don't come," but she kept on coming. This song fits everybody here.

For many, especially those with life sentences, mothers are the last among family and friends who continue to visit. Getting news of your mother's passing is one of the most devastating moments in a prisoner's life. He described when he got the news and how he put the feeling into his song:

> I went to the shed, and I was playing basketball, and they called me for a visit, and this happened to me. This song here touches my heart. There's no bounce to it, but it's real—the situation that we in now—and it touches people's heart. I sung it at the rodeo, and the people was touched and Ray say, "You sung that song, and you left them in a sad mood." He had to bring them back up! This song . . .

The others encouraged Spotville to sing it. He cleared his throat and began singing. "When will I see you again? I want to know y'all." The others joined in, humming in harmony, and he continued:

> When will we meet again?
> Sometimes, I don't want anything to eat. I just lay in my bed.
> I just can't sleep. Tossing and turning all night long.
> Sometimes, ah, sometimes I just lay awake. I wonder why.
> I wonder why. Why must my loved one leave me, leave me, leave me wondering.
> Oh, when, when will I see you again?
> When will we meet again?

And with that, Spotville explained that music and testimony were both part of the delivery when they perform:

And that's when I go into the testimony, and I start telling my testimony. In 1973, I came here serving a life sentence, and at that time, all the persons coming to see me was my mother. I get emotional about that song...[117]

Choking up, he couldn't continue.

It's hard to watch someone weep—especially hard in these circumstances, a grown man expressing pain over losing his mother, the only remaining love for him in the outside world. Ray Jones gently placed his hand on Spotville's back and spoke for him: "Because it's true events. A lot of time, what Pure Heart does, we take it, and we'll make it our environment of our actual experiences." It was a palpable moment, revealing testimony of the pain of incarceration along with an explanation of artistic process.

I included this encounter in a paper I once delivered at an academic conference.[118] I added power by playing the audio from the interview in my talk. I instinctively knew it would move an audience of liberal academics while providing insight into mass incarceration. I set up the quote and then let the grain of Spotville's voice do the work of illustrating the relationship between music and state violence. I later theorized what he told me in my dissertation.[119] But only after knowing the history of the rodeo and banquet performances did I understand that those fleeting, emotional encounters with people like me were part of prison's economic and moral economy of music. The superficial spaces at the border of the prison may not have represented the depths of life at Angola, but they were vital, complex, and historically rich.

Spotville was adept at showing scars, expressing redemption through gospel songs, and articulating penitentiary ideals. It gave him access to hope during a period when violence decreased and sentence lengths increased. Four years after that first meeting, I sat with Spotville again along with fellow Pure Heart Messenger Emmanuel Lee in the back of the chapel. We had watched the first screening of my film *Follow Me Down*, on music at Angola, the Louisiana Corectional Institute for Women, and Elayn Hunt Correctional Center. Spotville, Lee, and I had arranged security clearance to linger afterward and discuss the film in depth following the general Q&A session with four hundred prisoners and a few staff members. There, Spotville drew out something he gleaned from the film, what I now understand as the associational aspect: "It's different personalities," he explained, "and you got to make five or six people come into one mind doing the same thing. No big 'I,' no big 'you.'"[120] Spotville told me he could also find that aspect in most other music

I had featured. "I like country," he admitted. "I come up in that era. . . . I know the work that they put in." And then he offered a rare critical take, directed at the metal band I featured at the end. They were from Hunt, south of Baton Rouge, a newer prison that held a younger population without the legacy of musical practices that Angola had developed.

In the film, the interracial band Tribe plays a song inspired by prisoners' rights martyr George Jackson called "Blood in My Eye." The song's title is a direct lift from Jackson's book title, completed days before his assassination at San Quentin.[121] Like Jackson's 1971 book, the 2012 song directly addresses racism and incarceration but with heavily overdriven guitars and downtempo hip-hop–inflected vocals. There are nods to themes and legacies that overlap with Spotville's 1973 start at Angola, a time of agitation and protest, but the seventy-year-old gospel singer found only a slight resonance in the song.

> The guy was singing at Hunt about "blood in my eyes," and I'm feeling what he's saying . . . but we got too many young people coming in now. They younger than my grandkids, and I'm looking at their whole concept. Their whole principles are different from our principles. Sometimes you really gotta get out the way because right to them is wrong to me, and vice versa.

There was a generational difference, for sure. Spotville had worked to uplift through music, a value many of his generation held. But there was also a fundamental difference of how the music worked on the surface of prison. The unapologetic truth of the hip-hop generation is less adaptable to triangulating alliances out of outsiders, administrators, and prisoners—especially the older ones who led the associations.

Spotville kept hope. Part of that hope was in his maintenance of a tenuous prison border that had developed out of the 1970s radical reconfiguration of Angola's boundaries. He couldn't stretch them far enough actually to leave—dying there in 2014—but a shadow of him remains on the surface of my film, testifying after singing with the Pure Heart Messengers in the recreation yard of the main prison. "I'm waiting on my blessing," he says to the group (and also performing for the camera). "I believe by faith, God going to deliver me out of this place. Me, I'm not just singing it. I mean this by *faith* that I sing this song. I got a blessing coming. My delivery is right there."[122]

There was an ever-present rehearsedness when Spotville answered questions and sang for me, one we can think of as a legacy of a violent prison that fostered collaboration, the big "we." But Spotville also had a personal use for music in an institution rife with surveillance and providing very few ways of being alone. Performance helped him maintain privacy. Like manners, surfaces gave him what doors give to others—privacy from the embarrassment of incarceration.

Prisons have the power to deny privacy in many ways—through surveillance and coercion, with architecture, and by bringing in visitors like me. In the absence of privacy, rehearsed responses can satisfy the needs of the exchange without really having to submit to invasive questions. The use of surfaces in prison provides prisoners relief from the constant pressure of having to answer for crimes or to tell others what it is like to face a life spent in prison. Music allowed him to toggle between private and public engagement.

Spotville arrived in prison at a time of great upheaval, when the boundaries of the prison were instrumentalized for gaining public attention and partnership. Once the violence diminished and modest policy gains took hold, music became an essential resource in its ability to engage a broad constituency. As we will see in the next chapter, Spotville would develop his voice after the prisoners' rights era, when the prison population rapidly increased.

5

Inflection

It is tempting to point to the warden known as "Boss" Ross Maggio for initiating the major change that started in 1976. Certainly, Warden Maggio was a swaggering public figure. But had it not been for the prison coming under federal receivership in 1975, itself a result of prisoner litigation, Maggio might not have been tasked with solving its problems. It's often convenient to identify a warden of a prison as a single-handed force of change, but Angola's efforts were part of a national prisoners' rights movement beginning in the mid-1960s, advancing the claim that prisoners ought not be enslaved. From then until the mid-1990s, Southern prisoners and allied organizations took the government to court to try to eradicate the Southern prison farm, end racial segregation, eliminate the trusty guard system, and ban agricultural stoop labor (challenging agricultural work done in a sustained squatting position).[1] The efforts at Angola made strides in some of these areas, though those strides took time and went against national currents.

During these two decades, social policies shifted from funding social entitlements toward emphasizing individual responsibility. In the 1960s, President Lyndon B. Johnson had initiated legislation and an expansive social welfare campaign informally known as the War on Poverty. Prominent examples of related programs include Medicare, Medicaid, food stamps, and Social Security. But in the 1970s, public awareness campaigns began characterizing social issues as products of individual "pathologies" like drug use, nutrition deficiencies, and teenage pregnancy.[2] This intensifying focus on the individual (something already baked into penitentiary logic) did little to address structural racism embedded in unequal access to health care, daycare, education, and the labor market. Public concern over pathological "criminal minds" and increasingly violent depictions of prisons in media gave ammunition for so-called truth-in-sentencing laws, leading to more incarceration and longer sentences in Louisiana.[3]

At Angola, the combination of modest prison reform and an unprecedented prison population shifted outlawry to interminable penance. The horror of prison was less physical violence than it was the endlessness of warehoused felons. Publicly, the changes at Angola seemed to be evidence of improvement.

We can investigate the discord of reform and expansion by listening to the musical changes at Angola following 1976. Songs of political struggle are often topical and contextual. But individual songs that encapsulate a galvanizing moment don't reveal much. It may be more helpful to think more broadly about post–prisoners' rights music. Examining music after prisoners' rights wins helps make sense of how people use music in the wake of critical moments of change—following the resonances of that change, tracking its dispersion, and acknowledging the daily maintenance of structural changes.

In the grand scheme of things, prisoners' rights happened quickly. In 1971, *Sinclair v. Henderson* set a precedent for upholding constitutional rights for prisoners.[4] *Williams v. Edwards* (1974) set the stage for a federal takeover of the prison by identifying a litany of Eighth Amendment rights violations at Angola.[5] While important in their own right, these cases only initiated a slow but lasting change, requiring active maintenance and negotiation. Think of them as inflection points, shifts in lived experience.

With every change came follow-up effort. After segregationist policies ended, prisoners had to sort through Angola's messy and lingering racism. In the years after sensationalized media coverage of prisoners' rights agitation (Attica being the most famous), the public needed to understand Angola's prisoners differently. After the use of prisoner-guards was prohibited, new kinds of trusty classifications granted power to prisoners who exercised authority differently: working on legal efforts in the law library, securing access to outside movement, and participating in the widening touristic opportunities developed by the prison. And following prisoners' rights activism, the plethora of organizational alliances grew and changed the nature of the prison's voluntary associations. All combined, the terms for playing music at Angola shifted.

The impact of mid-1970s court successes created an inflection point. If that moment was impactful, the next twenty years followed an inflected trajectory, a bend toward change despite the continued gravities of the penitentiary, plantation, and outlawry. The story of music in this chapter begins with a musician who honed his craft in Angola by finding musical freedoms in prisoners' rights gains. The rest of the chapter follows how musicians navigated a post–prisoners' rights era. I'm less interested in how musicians and their music demonstrate newfound rights. I want to track how these limited and tenuous rights inflected the music. We often think of music as a mirror of social phenomena, a reflection of a nonmusical belief, reality, or struggle. I use *inflection* to acknowledge that music doesn't simply conform to change but more often bends toward it, filling the gap between ideals and reality.[6]

Like the omnibus term "surface," "inflection" can mean several interrelated things that can help pull our understandings of music and prison together. Musical inflection describes changes to pitch or timbre, often subtle ones. Musicians at Angola inflected their playing to accommodate requests, make sense of social changes that followed policy changes, and find new performance opportunities. These tiny modifications in playing or singing are crucial to sounds we consider emotive, distinctive, or representative of a particular genre. Inflection makes something sound naturally "human." Musicians can tinker with inflection while playing. Similar to speaking differently to shift register or imitate a dialect, inflection can bring out different meanings, signifying regional, racial, and formal differences. As Angola's musicians played to post–prisoners' rights audiences, they used inflection to shift from genre to genre, develop into versatile players, and become musical chameleons who sometimes made hybridity their main feature.

Developing the theme of inflection moves our investigation between thinking about minuscule timeframes, musical changes within the beat of a song, and glacial timeframes of policy change. New questions flow from trying to tie these perspectives together. How might changes in musical inflection be part of a change in sentence lengths? How might a musician's ability to inflect his playing to sound like a particular genre be useful when gauging a newly desegregated audience? How does group singing change when harsh labor in the field becomes less harsh? Listening to the long aftermath of intense prisoner litigation reveals a work-in-progress, gains under threat, a world in which prisoners only have access to the courts if they can afford them, and the uneven effects of legal and policy changes.

The Promise of Otis Neal

Otis Neal became a young, respected R&B singer by the time he left Angola in 1978. In the eyes of many prisoners who had survived a violent and austere decade, Neal represented the promise of prisoners' rights. He had started at Angola in his late teens, convicted in 1971 of an armed robbery at a gun shop. It hadn't gone well. While waiting outside a hospital for his friend to receive medical treatment for his wounds, the police found him covered in blood in a getaway car.[7]

Once at Angola, facing a fifteen-year sentence, Neal found the band room. And as he moved into his twenties, the associations provided Neal with relative stability and community. Neal's growth as a musician was astonishing. He navigated Angola's most tumultuous era of violence, along the way learning from musicians who informally took charge of arranging education, rehearsal, and performance of all music at the prison. For many, his adept voice became the sound of hope. Everyone knew he was an accomplished musician and singer, comparing favorably to others who had developed names for themselves after release like Lead Belly and Charles Neville.

By 1978, Neal was a member of the Dixie Blue Boys, somewhat of a supergroup that had emerged from the recent investments in prison programs. They had an extensive repertoire. In the 1970s, American popular music had moved to ever-increasing niches of narrow genres—new wave, funk, disco, progressive rock, and country-pop, for instance. Angola's musicians kept stride. In many ways, the members of the Dixie Blue Boys were successors of the Nic Nacs. But the legacy left from the 1960s wasn't jazz. It was universalism. Many of the most prominent groups of the late 1970s through the early 1990s developed eclectic sets and incorporated diverse musicians.

As the name would suggest, the Dixie Blue Boys started as a country band, a local version of the Westernaires (who were too in demand outside to play inside the prison). They fulfilled primarily White prisoner appetites for popular songs like Ronnie Milsap's 1976 number one hit, "Let My Love Be Your Pillow." But with desegregation beginning in the aftermath of the *Williams v. Edwards* de facto class-action lawsuit, Black and White musicians found it easier to play together and mix styles.[8] By the time Otis Neal became the bassist for the group, the Dixie Blue Boys could equally deliver a KC & the Sunshine Band song.

It may be tempting to listen to stylistic variety as evidence of successful racial integration—for instance, when a country band slips a Curtis Mayfield song into its set—but music is rarely just a mirror of social phenomena. Musical styles meet needs. Bands in the post–prisoners' rights era were adapting to mixed audiences at yard shows, competing with other bands for different association banquets, predicting musical tastes among expanding free-world rodeo attendees, and taking on musicians across the color line. Otis Neal learned to be adaptive in the band room, to hold down the rhythm section in any style and to sing to any audience. His versatility and talent put the Dixie Blue Boys in great demand.

Don Notte, a prominent member of Veterans Incarcerated, took on the task of managing the Blue Boys and became an advocate of Neal's. Veterans Incarcerated was an association that grew in the 1970s with support from Vets Outreach in Baton Rouge and the VA in New Orleans.[9] Club leaders like Notte used existing outside connections to widen their outside networks through letter writing, phone calls, and producing banquets. He was chairman of the external job placement committee for Vets Incarcerated and founded a prerelease program of his own. For Notte, Otis Neal wasn't just a versatile musician. He was the sound of possibility.

Supporting Neal and the band, Notte worked his outside connections and lobbied Warden Maggio to invite a Studio in the Country talent scout to the prison to hold auditions. Neal was a central focus. In general, the unique talent held by prisoners at Angola was now recognized statewide. Their reputations drew from the precedent set by the Cavaliers, the Nic Nacs, and the Westernaires, earlier bands who toured extensively in the decades before, making headlines throughout the state. Notte leveraged a certain mystique that had developed in the silent pause of prison music heard since the travel ban and the end of the Westernaires. Without outside performances, you had to go there to hear Angola's music.

It was a two-and-a-half-hour drive from the recording studio in Bogalusa. The studio already had success—national at that. Most recently, they had recorded two of the pop-prog outfit Kansas's multiplatinum albums, *Leftoverture* (1976) and *Point of Know Return* (1977). Recording engineer Bleu Evans had started Studio in the Country in the image of other Southern studios like Muscle Shoals and Stax, attracting artists seeking the authenticity of rural Southern isolation. The studio was positioned to be part of the Southern studio strategy that countless national and international musicians used to record unique albums away from the bustle of New York, Los Angeles, or London. Evans brought Willie Nelson, Stevie Wonder, and Kansas—national acts who might appreciate Louisiana's unique musical history. The studio was rooting around the prison for musical talent like folklorists John Lomax and Harry Oster, but only for flavor, not for the main course. The studio had a gap in their schedule, and one of the engineers needed training, a perfect opportunity to take a risk recording unknown potential studio musicians.[10] Nearly every musician at Angola found a way into a band that audition day.

After the auditions, Studio in the Country promised contracts to three singers and three bands, including the Dixie Blue Boys. After the audition,

Lt. Col. Walter Ponce, the officer who sat in on the sessions, said, "They're floating so high right now that they could probably all get loaded off the same piece of bubble gum."[11] Four months after the audition and soon to return home, Otis Neal was in an excellent position. He had impressed the producers at Studio in the Country with his versatility, musicianship, and professionalism, and they had offered him session work upon release.[12] Manager Don Notte couldn't have been more pleased. A profile in *The Angolite* on Neal ahead of his release stated, "Success generally eludes most Angola ex-cons who chase it, primarily because of lack of exposure and opportunity."[13] It went on to detail the music career awaiting Neal on release and to promote his last show (hopefully) at Angola.

The gains of desegregating Angola under federal control brought new opportunities for Black musicians, epitomized by Neal's story. The Dixie Blue Boys' integrated rodeo debut in 1978 was just that. Watching the events and the crowd from the crow's nest, the band broadened typical rodeo country and western fare, improvising songs to rodeo events using snippets of style from a range of popular music. They offered "something for everyone," proclaimed *The Angolite*, "a real demonstration of their versatility."[14] To prisoners, they were an audible symbol of a change. To new rodeo audiences, the range of styles helped them feel welcome at the event, making the music good for business.

Rising tourism in the region was part of the continuing state-wide economic turn to tourism. Outside New Orleans, plantations-turned-resorts and parish festivals drew the masses. While Angola competed with other regional draws, it had the distinction of being a prison. Angola's musicians were part of a unique service industry that produced events to raise money for what the state continually refused to fund. The bands could draw a range of people now that the rodeo was desegregated. A variety of people meant a variety of musical styles—for instance, country, R&B, swamp rock, funk, and an occasional gospel hymn. For the administration, the audible and visible racial diversity also had the potential to draw larger crowds to a prison that again made national headlines for violence.

Warden Maggio used the rodeo as a backdrop for speaking to the public, as had Henderson before him. But Maggio cultivated a cowboy image that worked well on television and in the papers. In his cowboy hat and floral shirts, he was the image of independence over the farm—a strong man with charismatic Louisiana flair. Elsewhere, he was notoriously strict. Most musicians with whom I spoke don't remember him fondly. Maggio could not be convinced that Angola's bands should play outside the prison walls. Prison musicians made do through playing prison events while the image of the prison developed outside. The rodeo was as far as Maggio allowed music to travel. And that's where Otis Neal said goodbye to Angola.

On the rodeo band stage, Otis Neal, with his large afro and Fender bass guitar, got to play with top-notch outside musicians (see figure 5.1). Notable acts headlined the 1978 rodeo for the allure they provided for the event. Local swamp rocker Everett Brady was one of these. His big regional hit was "I Almost Called Your Name" (1975), a genre-bending mix of rock, country, and Cajun music supporting Brady's rasp-tinged crooning. Otis Neal moved set-to-set, playing in his inside and outside projects: the Dixie Blue Boys, his newest band, Storm, and with Brady's band, Capricorn.[15] Neal's versatility was a good fit for Capricorn. And in a few days, he'd join Brady on a cross-country tour.

Neal left with a signed contract to play and record with established outside acts, having arrived at Angola as a teenager. It wasn't just his doing—and that is crucial for understanding that hope was rooted in collectivity. The associations and gains of prisoner lawsuits removed some obstacles that a prisoner might face alone. Neal, however, was an exceptional individual. Most others kept following hope but never got out. The years following Neal's

Figure 5.1. Otis Neal, left, 1978. "A Star Is Born?" *The Angolite*, July 8, 1978, 10.

release would see varying degrees of uneven improvements, increased statewide incarceration, and longer sentences. Otis Neal's story offers an inflection point. The remainder of the chapter doesn't get to triumphant endings. It follows inflected paths, less dramatic trajectories that bend toward ideals, even if they never arrive at them. Music reveals incremental change, hopes, and new collaborative missions.

Uneven Reforms of the Field

The fields did sound different in the post–prisoners' rights era. Angola's prisoners' rights movement and ensuing federal receivership eased agricultural labor, but it did not eliminate problems for workers. The decommissioning of the sugar mill and the end of trusty guards resulted in less strenuous fieldwork, relieving degrees of both physical and mental stress. Despite these gains, there was still a need for music. Singing distracted prisoners from mindless stoop labor, and professional free-personnel guards and other prisoners could still be cruel. Listening to the field's music reveals partial gains and the unevenness of Angola's reforms.

In 1976, the end of sugar production made field labor easier. That was the year when the state of Louisiana sold Angola's sugar mill to a Guatemalan firm.[16] The rigorous work of cane cutting and processing had reigned supreme since 1911. It had been a primary target for many prison reformers, a specific part of brutal labor practices, and a general reminder that Angola was still an operational plantation. Nationally, agricultural prison labor was under scrutiny. After forty-five Freedom Riders (including John Lewis and Stokely Carmichael) spent thirty-nine days at Parchman Farm in 1961, the link between prison and slavery had become a prominent activist theme. While Northern efforts drew on slavery as a metaphor, Southern ones cast the continued use of the prison farm as an everyday living legacy of slavery and set out to abolish the practice.[17] For Angola's activists, the sugar mill was a potent symbol of oppression and the actual engine of grueling cane harvesting. The attempted uprising in 1972 (described in the last chapter) had included plans to burn the mill to the ground.[18] The mill's demise, however, was less dramatic than it could have been. It was merely decommissioned under market pressure.

Americans were buying less sugar. Nationally, consumption had been down for nearly a decade. Consumers started to link sugar to obesity, diabetes, and heart disease. The Federal Trade Commission and the Food and Drug Administration launched investigations into sugar's safety, and large sugar manufacturers countered with public relations campaigns. Artificial sweeteners like saccharin and the steady rise of diet sodas reduced demand.[19] Market prices dropped, and, eventually, Angola switched crops.

Agriculture was still substantial, and it took consistent time and effort to plant, grow and harvest 3,200 acres of soy, 850 acres of cotton, 300 acres of assorted vegetables, and 400 acres of corn.[20] Switching to less grueling crop and refinery work, the labor got easier and policies relaxed. In the field, work began at 7:00 a.m. (instead of sunup) and lasted until 3:00 or 4:00 p.m. (instead of sundown) with a thirty-minute lunch break. Workers no longer had to eat in the rain.

For John Henry Taylor, who arrived in 1970 and witnessed the changes, the sale of the mill and Warden Maggio's removal of the leaders of the most violent cliques coupled to improve conditions.

> When they stopped the sugar mill, stopped the cane. They were cutting cane here. Most of that was cut out. A lot of guys that was here, [Warden Maggio] moved them out. Well, thank God that they did move the majority of them fellas out of here because they were very . . . ooh, I couldn't find the word to say . . . I won't even say the word that I want to say, but they were terrible. God had found a way to spread them out, send them to another satellite somewhere here. 'Cause, they were very disturbing here.[21]

Eradicating the trusty-guard system decreased violence because it reduced the outlawry of the field. As we learned in chapter 3, brute force had filled the vacuum of law, rules, and procedures.

Trusty designation was older than the prison, a relic of the James plantation practice of posting prisoners with murder convictions in the big house. Trusty power had grown into all spaces of outlawry, anywhere no one cared to look or report from, reinforcing the ingrained practice of sexual slavery. But once Angola had budget allocations for hiring professionals and a federal mandate to do so, the trusty prisoners were essentially demilitarized. Though many new hires abused their positions or turned callous eyes, professional officers were more apt to write up offenses or likely to receive a visit from a supervisor or the warden, bringing a modicum of due process to the field. By 1977, violent deaths had dropped to only one per year. Prisoners were as likely to die from natural causes or execution as they were at the hands of each other.[22] According to those I interviewed about work in the field in the 1980s, administrative oversight (shifting to professional guards) led to increased trust among prisoners which then led to new opportunities for group singing (see figure 5.2).

With less stress over personal safety and fewer risks of being "turned out," prisoners relied on each other more. Michael Dyer, who arrived in 1980, recalled that camaraderie eased the hard work. "In actuality, the time didn't move any faster, but it seemed that way because we was singing and having fun. We were working, but it helped us get through the day."[23] Most described

Figure 5.2. Fieldworkers after the decommissioning of the sugar mill, ca. 1989 (*The Angolite* archives).

singing as spontaneous and collective. Stanley Lindsay described a typical day.

> Once somebody starts singing and hit a certain note, and somebody else joins in, [then] somebody *else* joins in, and the next thing you know, we've got like a choir, an R&B band, whatever you might want to classify it as. We had fun doing it. It was like a daily thing.[24]

Rather than being on guard all the time, Lindsay felt free to seek out people with good voices.

> It became a habit-forming thing. You look for certain guys out there to harmonize with because you know they're going to start singing. You want to work close around them so you can just get your mind off the work.[25]

When speaking to prisoners like Dyer and Lindsay, who arrived after 1976, I did not hear the kinds of horror stories that those who worked the fields in the 1960s had told me. Fieldworkers in the post–prisoners' rights era used music more to find degrees of freedom from the work than to mitigate violence.

Lindsay, who arrived in 1978, recalled lots of group singing. They chose familiar songs, mostly popular music, and used what they could remember from their childhoods in church to harmonize. Focusing on relatively complex singing helped to distract.

> We'd be working, and all of a sudden, somebody would come up with a song, most times, it would be an R&B or a gospel song. Somebody else would join in on the harmony side. One voice, and then before you know it, we've got four- or five-part harmony on it. Before you know it, we done finished the little row we're working on, 'cause it gets your mind off of exactly what you're doing. Your body's still working, but you're also concentrating on staying on your note while singing.[26]

With bodies safer and the pace of work less breakneck, fieldworkers could afford to distract themselves.

The repertoire of the field changed post–prisoners' rights, not because of the work needs (rhythms coordinating group labor) but because of who was assigned fieldwork. Fieldworkers were younger prisoners and still skewed

Black. Desegregation had opened up more nonfield job opportunities for Black prisoners. But it was the older, more connected prisoners who secured the better jobs. Daniel Washington explained that changing work assignment policies and an influx of new prisoners had a gradual effect on repertoire.

> Back around the mid-eighties, a lot of older guys that was working in the fields, they found their way out of the fields. Back then, they had a thing they called duty status, and if you get a duty status, you don't have to go in the fields. The only ones really going in the fields was healthy youngsters and the ones that didn't know how to get out of the fields. So, I can tell you a lot of that stuff was lost probably that way because wasn't nobody out there to carry it on.[27]

Older songs were lost to the changing demographics of the field. But the songs Washington thought were lost were not ones you'd find in a folkloric songbook. The older Black prisoners took classic R&B hits from the 1960s out of the fields with them when they found better jobs. There were some exceptions.

Dyer, arriving in 1980 at seventeen years old, sought out the remaining older prisoners because they knew older songs. "One of the field farmers at that time, Mr. Jay," Dyer explained, "he was a real big B. B. King fan. He used to get a bunch of guys to sing B. B. King and stuff. I was too young for that. I don't know enough about B. B. King. He would have guys sing Otis Redding. Songs of that nature." Dyer wasn't just interested in old songs, he also learned new ways of making music.

Improvisation was central. "If it was a good morning and we had a good count and everything," Dyer explained, "we just make up songs. The songs that we made up, it was like happy songs. Something to be content about because work was really rough at that time."[28] Often, spontaneity was a result of people not knowing entire songs. When someone only knew fragments, things could get interesting. Lindsay described,

> What they did was improvise, and whatever they did, we'd laugh. The thing about it was, again, even though they make up a lot of lines, the background will fall in with that made-up line. That made it all so *squeezy*—you know what I'm saying? Because it's like making a new song out of the old song. Even if it was a song that was out at that particular time, a lot of people didn't know all the words to the song or the lyrics.

Matter of fact, back then, you had a lot of people that couldn't read and write to be honest with you.... We did "Amazing Grace" a lot. A lot of dudes didn't know all the words. They'll sing the first stanza and then the second one there. Come up with something like, "I once was lost, but now I'm found. Was hungry, but now I see." [laughs] They'll put the wrong word in, and we'll fall in and say the same thing on the side and just have fun doing it. Say, "Man, you don't know that song. Why are you singing that song?" He'll say, "Man, that's what I feel right now." That's why we went with it.[29]

No matter how they sang it, most of the repertoire was R&B.

When he arrived in 1980, James Marsh went to the field and found the singing unfamiliar. "Mostly, it was the old Smokey Robinson type stuff," he said in hindsight, trying to remember the songs. "Was it 'Tears of a Clown'? That song came up. I remember 'Firecracker,' Ohio Players, maybe?" It was actually the 1979 hit song by the funk/disco group Mass Production, but the point is that Marsh had never listened to any Black music before.

Even though the prison had desegregated, the field still sounded Black. Kool and the Gang and Lionel Richie accompanied the labor in the early 1980s. "You never heard somebody out there singing 'Ring of Fire,'" Marsh continued, noting that Johnny Cash, the White outlaw country musician who had famously recorded in California prisons, had just played a concert at Angola when he had arrived. But Cash's music did not carry onto the field. White prisoners who would have kept humming Cash's songs after the concert generally had other jobs. Marsh pointed out that White prisoners came to prison with certain advantages. "The majority of your White guys had a better education going into this thing, and they ended up with the clerk jobs and the kitchen jobs. Yeah, you had Blacks everywhere you go, but at the same time, the predominant [laborer] out in the field was Black. So, you didn't have a bunch of George Strait sing-alongs."[30] Deep and dispersed racial structures limited the effects of new colorblind administrative policies.

Whether the songs were familiar or not, singing while working long, degrading days still gave emotional relief. Marsh adapted to fieldwork as he learned R&B hits. Holding a heavy sling blade—a hooked steel blade attached to a forty-inch wooden handle—Marsh cut brush with the other prisoners. Working in rows, spaced out to prevent getting hit by someone else's stray blade, the group developed a rhythm that prisoners called "rolling." Teams led by experienced workers set the pace in lead rows. Usually those in the front, acclimated to the work, sang and joked. In the back, a "drag guy" kept others from falling behind, replacing the use of the whip by pushing them verbally. Relatively small and inexperienced, Marsh had to learn fast.

> I'm a young White guy. I didn't know what a ditch plank blade was to save my life, and I'm more concerned about not cutting my arm off than I was with the singing. This fellow [next to me] can rock all day long with the ditch plank blade and sing "Goose the Moose" right along with it. But in the environment I was in at the time, there wasn't a lot of that. Every now and then, somebody would joke around and kick off something, and everybody would kind of get in on it. But remember, back then, I didn't really sing. Didn't know I could.[31]

When talking to Marsh, who now leads a prominent trusty-status country band, I pressed him on how he developed a musicality out of unfamiliar work and repertoire. I asked, "But eventually, you were out there working to Lionel Richie in time?" "Yeah. It works," he explained,

> It don't matter. All of a sudden, it doesn't matter what kind of music comes on. . . . It breaks the monotony. It sweeps the time by because all of a sudden, you feel like you're in the rhythm. As being a musician from a child, from a young guy, it kind of helps the rhythm of things. I mean, you look back to the times you was beating on the railroad and beating rocks on the side of the road, humming and singing.

There are echoes of folkloric descriptions in what Marsh told me: "When they would sing to a rhythm, that would keep everybody on the same pace so that then nobody could be seen as being too slow. . . . You're kind of following along with them, watching what [the lead workers] are doing. And you find yourself, like you say, in a rhythm."[32] Many ways that music was used in the field remained, even if the repertoire had changed. Beyond music from the radio, Marsh remembered what he called "military cadence songs" or "little make-up songs." These sometimes developed out of the rhythm of the work but were commonly an informal part of marching to the work site. Passing song fragments among members of the group, a few might join into some repetition, often poking fun at someone in the group.

Marsh was careful not to overstate music's presence or romanticize its power. "It wasn't every day," he explained, acknowledging that some conditions could be too hard for singing. "Some days was monsters. Some days you're neck-deep in mud and trying to figure out how to get out of this."[33] Focusing on the complex reality of being in prison could inhibit group singing and even make it irrelevant.

In summary, the prison farm remained during the post–prisoners' rights era despite efforts to eradicate it. The predominance of African American repertoire reveals a less overt racism still governed who went to the field. But the presence of newer popular music reflects how older, better-connected Black prisoners were able to get out of the work more easily. The complex ways that people sang together reveal the effects of easing of outlawry with professional guards and the elimination of the sugar crop—defining aspects of the field up until 1976. And the need for music to ease labor and distract from hard work shows that the lingering types of stoop labor were still difficult. Music in the field was neither a direct continuation of nor a clean break from earlier practices. It was an inflection, revealing at once reform efforts and their ineffectiveness.

When I interviewed Marsh, we were near the same fields that introduced him to Kool and the Gang. "You don't hear too much [music] now. The mood's changed, the type of inmates changed here," Marsh said, now with a gray beard and more weight to his frame.[34] Assigned to Camp F, the trusty camp, he is as far from the field as he can be. But he hears occasional snippets of music whenever he is in earshot of younger prisoners there. He told me that he had heard prisoners singing gospel to pace their work a few days earlier. That was rare. More often, rap now sounds from individual workers, still overwhelmingly Black, performing uncoordinated stoop labor that, to Marsh, seems less grueling than his work was in the 1980s.

Time Factor

The recreation yards of the main prison, just outside the dormitories, were places to walk, congregate, and exercise. People had more time to congregate there due to increased time after work assignments. Compared to the field, the recreation yards were teeming with diverse styles of music. When bands set up on the yard in the post–prisoners' rights era, they had a newly desegregated audience in front of them. Bands worked on how to engage and understand such a diverse audience when they went back to the band rooms to rehearse for shows. The new, stylistically eclectic groups were a product of musicians having increased freedom to mix but also the challenge of playing for the entire population, sorting through the confusion of desegregation.

By the late 1970s, the education department had lost administrative support and funding. So the Human Relations Club took over much of the programming.[35] Musicians found organizational support for performances through the clubs. They accessed rehearsal space through the recreation department, which accommodated bands with four partitioned band rooms in the back of the gym. The rooms were arranged like a railcar, divided into groups practicing country, R&B, zydeco, and blues. They were cold in winter. In summer, the loud but weak air conditioners competed with hot vacuum tubes in instrument amplifiers.

When Stanley Lindsay found the band rooms on his arrival in the late 1970s, he saw a way to reclaim some of himself. "I feel like I had lost a lot," he said of his first days on the farm, "until I came in seeing that they had music in here. Leaving the street, playing music was part of your life. Coming here, you don't know what you're facing. Young as I was at that time, approximately seventeen going on eighteen."[36] He was seventeen years old with a head full of stories of violence at Angola he had heard while awaiting transfer from the parish jail. In the evenings, after days of working in the fields, he began to explore. "The first time I walked into the band room," Lindsay remembered, "I stood there and listened. Man, it was just like, 'We got a lot of good musicians in prison!' I didn't know prison had this kind of talent."[37]

After Otis Neal's Dixie Blue Boys folded, the biggest band in the main prison was Time Factor, established and led by guitarist Terry Deakle. Similar to the Blue Boys, Time Factor played it all. Their stylistic prowess enabled them to take any inside gig. In concert on the yard, their ability to shift styles with ease made groups like Time Factor exciting. Lindsay began meeting musicians and following the groups. Every weekend, they played on the yard as a condition of using recreational equipment and space. One day, dropping by a rehearsal, Lindsay started talking to a band member.

> The dude asks me. He says, "You play?" I said, "Yeah, I play a little bit." So, he gives me the guitar. He says, "What song you want to play?" I said, "Anything ya'll play." He started playing some song. I can't remember exactly what it was, but I fell right in, and they really enjoyed it. Then they had an audition for a group that I just told you about, Time Factor. Another dude named Jerry Bell, we went in competition trying to get the spot. For some unknown reason—and he was good—they gave me the spot.

It was no small achievement. Fellow guitarist Daniel Washington remembered that bands had strict criteria. "To be a part of one of those bands," he explained, "you definitely had to have something to offer. . . . If you was a guitar player, you had to be able to play guitar, to carry, because a lot of times, you might have only had one guitar player in a band, so you had to really be a good guitar player."[38] You also had to prove that you were dependable, a good fit with the band dynamics, and not prone to trouble—a constant liability for any group. Otis Neal had set a high bar in all those categories.

Musically, the most valuable attribute was stylistic flexibility, the ability to inflect your playing so that you could navigate the band's shifts in musical style throughout a set. The band room became a school for Lindsay, granting him an opportunity to build on what he brought to Time Factor.

> I grew because I was playing with top-notch musicians. You weren't going to come in there and [not] know your chords. You had to know your musical scales. You had to know your chords in order to sit there and play with them because they was good musicians. They weren't no rookie musicians, like coming together for a jam session.

Bands like the Nic Nacs had mixed different styles before. But what had changed since Neville's time was that segregation was officially over. Desegregation opened new possibilities of incorporating top musicians across the color line. By extension, Time Factor's mission was to play all styles of music, each at a high level.

When Robin Polk arrived in 1982, most bands played a hybrid, up-to-date repertoire. A keyboard player named Spiderman took him to the band room. "Had a band called Time Factor down there," recalled Polk. "They were playing all your new country music. They was playing all your new pop music, whatever . . . rock."[39] Lindsay, who by then was well established in Time Factor, explained, "We was a mixture. We was an R&B band disguised as a country band." Polk worked hard to get into the band. He needed to become proficient and well rounded. But he couldn't simply take a bass from the band room to his dormitory. It wasn't allowed. All his learning had to take place in rehearsal and performance, and access to that was competitive.

Though there were four band rooms, up to fifteen bands were scheduled back-to-back. "It was kind of hard to get in the music program then because everything was tacked down," Polk explained. "So, you gotta look for a spot."[40] He worked his way into the band rooms by forming and joining minor-league groups.

> I bided my time, doing my thing, and I played a little bit with a guy there called Jimmy Johnson. He had a little country gospel band. Him and Russell Gotland [and] I played a little bit of that with them. And I always tried to create, so we would take little gospel hymns and turn them into country-sounding stuff. I'd do that for a little while, and then somebody else would want me to play with them. But at that time, I wasn't up to par to get with the hard hitters, [which] is what we call them.[41]

Eventually, Time Factor's bass player left, and by then, Polk was ready. In auditions, he beat out a jazz bassist who had been playing with Leotha Brown, formerly of the Nic Nacs. While Polk didn't have jazz fluency, he had developed an aggressive electric bass sound that could be used strategically in the group.

Like Lindsay's musicianship, Polk's developed through the multistylistic demands of the band. "I elevated from when I got here," said Polk. "When I came here, the music was basically your typical Kool and the Gang, Bryan Adams, and a little bit of blues, . . . Muddy Waters, up-tempo stuff, modified and stuff. Not much jazz. You have a little bit of jazz. You have a little New Orleans style, the Neville Brothers style."[42] While each genre might be simple, mastering all styles, not only the notes but the feel, was a study in musicality and a freedom to become any musical sound.

Playing different types of music on one instrument requires command over several subtle nuances—the quality of the attack of a note, the microtiming of a beat within a rhythm, listening for cues from another instrument, or the strategic use of an equalizer to shape the timbre of a guitar, bass, or keyboard. Most of these things develop through playing with others and talking to more experienced musicians, remembering along the way which slight musical inflections combine to signify different musical genres.

Time Factor sets were a study in genre-fluidity, shifting gradually to hit any style that might resonate with someone in the audience. "The songs kind of threaded together, so you didn't go from one extreme to the other extreme," explained Polk. "Try to choose those type of songs where there's country-rock, so if you're playing them, you can go from this to this, and it won't be such a drastic change like from a 1950s song to a rap song."[43] Songs had value if they could easily pivot from one style to another. Through the set, Polk would see what affected the crowd.

> And that was satisfaction to me: if it's just one, if it's two, or it's however many. They don't even have to clap. I can watch them, and I can see them patting their foot. I know I got them. . . . But if I'm doing it and he's not enjoying it, and he's talking to Tom, Dick, and Harry, and he's not interested in what I'm doing, either he's not interested in what I'm doing, or I'm not doing what I should be doing to get his attention.[44]

Bands could also get prisoners to break out into second-line dance, a nod to the strong New Orleans presence at Angola and a visible display of that regional sense of unity. But Time Factor wasn't only playing for the general crowd during the yard shows. They also hoped that prisoner leaders might be impressed and invite them to play for a club banquet.

Clubs had grown since Warden Henderson and the prisoners' rights era. Desegregation gave Black prisoners more access to associations and gave the Black associations more access to administrative support and sanction. As described in the last chapter, the more robust club activity developed missions beyond self-betterment and became crucial ways to meet potential outside advocates. This made banquet gigs more attractive to musicians who could gain entry and attract good attention. Guitarist Daniel Washington of Utopia Urumba, a Time Factor rival, remembers being busy in those days. "We played every weekend for four months straight in the A Building," he said. "This was where all the functions and the outside guests came. We got a chance to play for audiences, like outside people" (see figure 5.3).[45] The infrastructure for secular music was robust because clubs had continued to proliferate. As guitarist Myron Hodges recalls, "Back then, the music scene was hot because it was secular, and there were a lot of secular clubs."[46]

As club members listened to bands perform on the yard, they heard samples of what might work well for a banquet. Like A&R representatives scouting talent at a music festival for a music label, prisoner association leaders could listen, size up the impact on the crowd, and judge professionalism. The ability to play New Orleans styles was imperative. Not only did that music resonate, but with desegregation, Black dance groups were now more eligible for official charter and could be programmed into events. Dance troupes Disco Jazz and Black Jumpers developed a relationship to associations like the musicians had, reminiscent of second-line's emergence

Figure 5.3. Photos from a 1983 banquet (*The Angolite* archives).

with mutual aid societies in the nineteenth century. They created participatory events that broke down audience divisions through call-and-response and dancing.[47]

Second-line was a ready-made activity, connecting people and practices who had been brought to Angola. In New Orleans, the practice fills the streets with sound, dance, laughter, and spectacle, reclaiming urban space as a fluid set of relationships (instead of zoned real estate) and turning tight spaces into mobilized areas.[48] The use of second-line in the Ninth Ward's Desire Projects in the 1980s set a precedent for community action at Angola and participation with organizations.[49] With the swell of new prisoners from the Ninth Ward, second-line became more prominent as it became part of activist efforts. The Lifers' Association regularly featured music and dance at the end of meetings, following updates on Governor Edwards's pardons and legislative efforts.[50] Occasionally, dancing would be inexplicably banned by security. But children visiting at banquets, oblivious to any restrictions, would still dance as attendees, and staff often smiled when they did.[51]

Outside of the banquets, bands also played for the major public events. Plantation festivals, less prominent after the sugar mill was decommissioned, shifted to touristic festivals. Time Factor managed to play the rodeo stage, the biggest of prisoner fundraisers, but to get there, they had to pose as a country band. It was a lucrative gig. Individually, musicians earned $25 for the show. The influx of rodeo attendees had created a demand, and prisoners petitioned to expand public engagement in support of the Inmate Lending Fund. The stylistically mixed bands worked creatively to suit the expanding rodeo stage—not always successfully.

The problem for many Black musicians was that the rodeo was modeled on White rodeos. Despite the existence of many Black rodeo traditions, Angola's rodeo drew on racialized traditions of White rodeos, like country music.[52] It was (and still is) celebrated as being born of rodeo star Jack Favor's efforts. And while the rodeo incorporated African American music, Black musicians were essentially guests in the lineup, subject to being deemed inappropriate.

Officer Bobby Howard, the musician who had been a free-personnel sponsor for the Westernaires, oversaw the rodeo production. Howard would come by the band rooms with his saxophone to jam occasionally. He was somewhat a part of the scene. Stanley Lindsay recalls how Time Factor tried to stretch the genre boundaries of rodeo music during an early morning soundcheck at the arena. "We was playing a song called 'Gloria Estefan' and Bobby rode up on his horse and said, 'That's not country music! Ya'll go and cut that off.' And his wife was dancing, so that sure done made him mad!"[53] Limited to the yard and the banquets, bands with a more eclectic fare looked for opportunities similar to the rodeo but without the restrictions. The clubs and sixty individual hobby crafters successfully pitched a new public initiative.

The new Annual Arts and Crafts Festival began in 1979, and there were enough musicians around to bill the event as a music festival. The inaugural one was advertised as "Angolafest." A single dollar admission granted access to the off-season rodeo grounds, filled with tables of prisoner-made crafts from the hobby shop and a rotating lineup of Angola's bands. Kids under six got in for free. A review in *The Angolite* describes the scene: "Festival goers got to listen to good music while they browsed through the display of prisoner-made products: paintings, wood sculpture, leathercraft, jewelry, crocheted scarves and ponchos, etc."[54] To shoppers, the goods sold at the Arts and Crafts Festival were not neccesarily "outsider art." They were bargains. It was cheaper to pick up a chair, jewelry, or a duck call from Angola than at the Shadows Arts & Crafts Fair in New Iberia, for instance.

The Festival opened a market for individual prisoners selling wares and additional fundraising opportunities for clubs. Given the austerity of state prison budgets, the Arts and Crafts Festival helped, in a sense, to further fund Louisiana's largest prison. It also became a new public concert stage that highlighted groups like Time Factor, unbound by the stylistic demands of a White rodeo and adept at playing a broader range of music.

After a few years, Time Factor lost key members to release and started to dissolve. Polk took advantage of his access to the band room and worked on scales—woodshedding while he kept an ear out for opportunities. New musicians continued to arrive as Louisiana increased incarceration rates and filled beds in its new prisons around the state. At Angola, new musicians filled shoes like Lindsay's and Polk's. They also brought in new styles.

Def Posse

Despite hip-hop gaining popularity nationally, rappers had a more challenging time integrating into Angola's organized music scene. Rappers had to find pockets of opportunities within the existing multistylistic bands of the 1980s. Michael Dyer's mixed success in establishing rap from within the band scene reveals its incompatibilities with the musical economy of the prison.

Dyer started in the Versatile Variety, a band in the main prison who, as their name implies, played every style of popular music. They aspired to Time Factor's status. Dyer was relatively young, sentenced to life without parole in 1980 at seventeen for aggravated rape. The same year as his conviction, Kurtis Blow released the album *The Breaks* and was the first hip-hop artist to appear on national television. It was also the year when Blondie recorded "Rapture," introducing rap to a White audience. By 1986, Dyer was twenty-two, and hip-hop was picking up steam. Run-DMC's *Raising Hell* brought the genre to MTV with a dramatized melting-pot video featuring Steven Tyler and Joe Perry of Aerosmith. As Black artists moved onto MTV, Black men were also being swept into prisons at increasing rates.

A series of legal changes are to blame. President Ronald Reagan's "War on Drugs" led to the Omnibus Crime Bill of 1984 and the Anti-Drug Abuse Act of 1986. An effort to get tough on crime introduced a staggering disparity between cocaine in powder and solid forms. For instance, possession or trafficking of five grams of crack cocaine held the same penalties as five hundred grams of powdered cocaine.[55] A racial preference for cocaine use in solid form became a serious liability. The effects in Louisiana were noticeable, with its relatively large Black population. Before the War on Drugs,

Louisiana had the thirteenth-highest incarceration rate in the nation. By 1986, it ranked fifth and then in 1990, third.[56]

While Dyer's conviction was not representative of the types that led to the wave of 1980s mass incarceration, he was the earliest of the hip-hop generation entering prisons then. Born just after the passage of the Civil Rights Act, his parents' generation fought against discriminatory laws, articulated Black nationalism, and sang adaptations of spirituals for uplift and solidarity. The post–civil rights generation was different. They struggled with the promises of self-discovery while stuck between White expectations of racial conformity and older Black hopes for political and cultural unity.[57] The hip-hop generation had a distinct worldview, musical culture, and set of issues. Dyer, on the cusp of this generation, was not only of the post–civil rights generation but also of the post–prisoners' rights population at Angola.

In the post–prisoners' rights era, prisoner associations and outside associations increasingly worked together to challenge violations of Eighth Amendment protections against cruel and unusual punishment. Dyer arrived after litigation pressured the state to follow through with promises. By the time he got his bearings, the clubs had shifted toward more activist goals and were established with the administration. The post–prisoners' rights newcomers had the task of navigating this crowded and constantly shifting landscape of church groups, self-help groups, civic organizations, and special-interest groups that, when they held banquets, created performance opportunities for musicians.

Dyer, a multi-instrumentalist, found his way into the band rooms. With Versatile Variety, he managed to get clearance and access to a band room for rehearsal. His group would have been competitive had they been any good. As Dyer explained, "We wasn't good drummers or good bass players and all this. But we would work it out to where guys told us [how to play]."[58] It was collaborative and one of the few safe places to make mistakes and take criticism. With an ear for the stylistic eclecticism championed by top groups like Time Factor and Utopia Urumba, Dyer started to notice newcomers rapping. Some were good. He hatched the idea of trying it out with the Versatile Variety. Hip-hop could be another style in their pocket and perhaps a way of distinguishing themselves within the crowded field of bands.

Dyer and friend David Robbins started rapping themselves, developing a repertoire on their own. Musically they set themselves in line with groups like L. L. Cool J and Run-DMC. Once they gained confidence, they pitched converting Versatile Variety into a rap group. But the older, established musicians wouldn't go for it. So, Dyer and Robbins peeled off and formed Def Posse. They found a few performance opportunities like the bands, playing on the yard and getting hired for a spot at a banquet that would pay in things like popcorn, cold drinks, and hot dogs. But despite rap moving into the mainstream outside Angola, the new free-world hires that comprised the security staff had not developed a taste for it. Overall, there was little support for hip-hop from the staff and prisoner associations.

The attitude toward rap drew on generational fault lines that were growing at Angola. With truth-in-sentencing laws now keeping prisoners at Angola beyond the ten-and-a-half-year parole eligibility, an older group of musicians remained, along with their older tastes in music and their control of the clubs. Derision from older prisoners toward rap came in many forms. Jewell Spotville, an established gospel singer by the 1980s, recalled poking fun at younger rappers. "We used to do a skit about listening to that rap music: What's going into your brain is just like drugs going to your brain," he said with an air of concern not uncommon with critics. "It gonna affect you some kind of way down the line."[59] The younger, less-established musicians had trouble convincing the associations to feature rap at banquets.

Dyer faced three other obstacles as he tried to establish rap in prison. First, the equipment (turntables, samplers, and drum machines) would have required investment from the recreation department, education department, or the Inmate Lending Fund. And even if they had secured turntables, prisoners could not go to record stores for vinyl to spin. The price of entry may have been low outside. But inside it was prohibitive, and the infrastructure of the band room had already been built from the needs of the Cavaliers, the Nic Nacs, and the Westernaires. Occasionally, bands would hold down grooves for Dyer and Robbins to rap over, but they did so only for moments, returning to funk, jazz, or rock songs.

The second challenge was that truth-in-sentencing laws had converted life sentences to their maximum of natural life. Musicians were no longer going home. Therefore, spots in the band room tended not to open up for someone younger like Dyer. Stagnant band room positions kept a music scene less flexible.

Dyer's third obstacle was associational needs. The music scene at Angola was distinctly made up of interrelated associations, catering to outsiders and administrators. Had Dyer been in New Orleans, he might have pressed into a musical niche and let audiences come to him at clubs. But with the venues available at Angola, he couldn't specialize. If he wanted gigs, he needed to be part of a stylistically flexible group to meet audience needs. A few musicians, however, eventually saw possibilities in Def Posse.

Larry Wilkerson and Myron Hodges had arrived in 1985 on separate second-degree murder charges. Already strong musicians, they quickly received invitations to join bands. Wilkerson was a confident R&B singer, and Hodges a guitar virtuoso. On arrival, Wilkerson was more interested in initiating something new, building a group from the ground up. So he waited.

One day rehearsing in the gym, Wilkerson overheard Dyer and Robbins's attempts to incorporate rap into other styles of music. Since they couldn't get clubs to accept entire rap shows for banquets, they had been testing how rapping might fit into different genres, focusing on creating original material. "Hearing it live when we were practicing in the gym," Wilkerson explained, "was my first time in it. They had a pretty good group. . . . I wasn't about no rap, but I didn't down it either."[60] Where others heard noise, Wilkerson and Hodges heard possibility.

Hodges was intrigued by what he didn't know about rap, about its rough edges. "They were way ahead of their time as far as rap is concerned. They were unprofessional. [But] in some kind of way, it all came together."[61] he recalls. While rap alone didn't suit the musical needs of post–prisoners' rights banquets, it could be a strategic musical inflection, a reference to what was happening outside in youth culture. On Angola's stages, rap soon found moments in songs: during a bridge, a special appearance couched in what musicians had already been playing. Largely unincorporated into the music scene and its supporting associations, rap also developed in informal spaces: the cafeteria, the fields, and freestyling on the yard. Megasound used rap as another way to direct their music to new audiences.

Megasound

When Larry Wilkerson and Myron Hodges began talking to Michael Dyer about rap, they had already been planning something new. Wilkerson had declined an invitation to sing with Time Factor, and instead launched a new project with Hodges. It was already a crowded music scene and hard to know what kind of band could compete. The most active existing bands were outfits like Time Factor, Utopia Urumba, and the Jambeaux Band, acts that could take just about any gig in the prison. Two gospel groups and two second-line dance groups rubbed shoulders with the musicians, competed for booking, and collaborated with other bands at the banquets. Wilkerson and Hodges's new band, Megasound, would become the premier band in Angola, managed by keyboardist Kevin Hayes, who had played with Charmaine Neville before Angola. In a sense, it was a reshuffling of top players. Megasound incorporated the musicians left behind when Time Factor lead guitarist Jerry Bell was released from Angola.[62] They sold themselves on their ability to play all styles in a group.

The stories that musicians tell about learning new styles and recombining them for yard shows illustrate the unfinished work of prisoners' rights during a time when the definition of "prisoner" was changing. Music was an important tool for redefining identities. Once convicted of a crime, a person's conviction can overwhelmingly define them. And once imprisoned, people lose the ability to self-define through the family, career, neighborhood, consumer goods, and other free-world amenities. Instead, prisoners become defined by the worst thing they've done. Additionally, the criminal justice system is still partly driven by penitentiary ideals, forcing or incentivizing prisoner self-reflection.[63] Expectations of atonement and confession can weigh heavily, especially in public engagements. In music, audiences often expect the authentic reflective voice of the prisoner. Here's where music became useful for broadening audience expectations. Genre-mixing provided leeway for prisoners, chances to redefine and subvert expectations of what a prisoner was.[64] In doing so, Megasound stressed group proficiency over individual transparency, skill over authenticity, flexibility over fixed definition.

Megasound distinguished themselves from other bands by folding rap into their performances, bringing what Dyer and Robbins were doing in Def Posse into a live band. They did what New Orleans brass bands would eventually do in the 1990s, finding overlaps between hip-hop and second-line, primarily rhythm, improvisation, and call-and-response.[65] Megasound was a musical sponge. Banquets for the Pentecostal Fellowship, the Methodist Men's Club, and Church of God in Christ, for instance, required a band to back up a gospel quartet. Megasound was that band. The steering committee of the Human Relations Club might need a less interactive affair after highlighting a series of prisoner speeches and so request popular R&B tunes as a backdrop for dining.[66] Equally, they delivered. As Megasound, the band developed a reputation for being able to play anything. In a sense, the musicians were in step with the jazz-fusion approaches of the 1970s spearheaded by Miles Davis, Weather Report, and Sun Ra.

Meanwhile, Robin Polk honed his bass playing in the band room after Time Factor had ended. He had secured a job as the band coordinator for the recreation department. One day, Kevin Hayes ran into the band room. "Man, I need your help. Magic done got locked up." Megasound's bass player was in administrative segregation, the jail within the prison. Polk remembered that day clearly. "I said, 'Again?!'" laughed Polk as he described joining Megasound:

> I said, "Well, come down and just breeze through the songs with me. I've heard your songs before, so I'm pretty familiar with them. Just breeze through some of the intricate changes." . . . this is like R&B stuff. "A Fair-Weather Friend" [by] Freddie Jackson and stuff like Earth Wind and Fire, Commodores. . . . The next day we was on the yard. I'm out there in my short pants, I ain't had no shirt, I have my shirt wrapped around the top of my head 'cause it was smoking [hot] out there. That was an all-Black band except [me], the bass player, . . . I'm the only White guy standing playing out there.[67]

Polk relished being in an integrated group as he and Megasound became a musical force for all prison events. Playing in an integrated band allowed Polk to surprise audiences, especially outsiders. "One time, we was playing at this A Building function. This lady said, 'Man! You really got it! If you put a curtain up in front of you, you'd think you was Black.'"[68] Being the one White musician afforded Polk a provocative *non-belonging* that helped shake audience assumptions about him, especially outside audiences at banquets.[69]

Prisoners have few resources for self-expression through clothing or consumer goods. While Polk's aural racial passing rested on essentialized notions of racial authenticity, they also helped him transcend them. Polk's strategy was not unique among musicians in the newly integrated bands. (Androgyny might have worked as well, except for the hypermasculine environment of Angola and the legacy of sexual violence.) Stunning audiences with an unexpected range of racially aligned styles helped expand the presentation of the self. It meant being more than what one appeared to be.

Crossing over racial barriers was perhaps easier for Polk than for his Megasound bandmate Myron Hodges. Hodges had become a versatile player by following Jimi Hendrix's footsteps through rock, blues, and R&B and then, after coming to Angola, advancing through the eclectic fare of Megasound. As a mission, Hodges sought out guitar styles that fell outside

Black stereotypes, like country, bluegrass, and heavy metal.[70] He told me he learned country styles on the guitar partly out of boredom. But he became more determined when overt racism blocked him from learning country styles.

> After seeing these two guys play—Freddie Johnson and Charlie Le Flor—at a rodeo, I realized that was a style of guitar that I wasn't clicking with. I couldn't understand what they were doing, and it was very intriguing to me. I just went out on a mission to try to meet one of these guys in person and try to join their band, so I could try to learn some stuff from them. . . . Then I met the country guy. . . . Well, I kind of asked him in a roundabout way, "Well, I'd kind of like to learn to do that. I'm a guitar player." He wasn't very hospitable—a little arrogant. I just stayed on him about it. Every time they had a band practice down here, I tried to just be present. Keep showing up and keep asking the guy.

The issue was that some players refused to teach Black musicians. Instead of explaining techniques that would help him inflect his playing toward country, White musicians told him that he didn't have a feel for it. "It used to baffle me," he said, laughing. "I'm trying to figure out how do you *feel* country? How am I going to make myself *feel* country? I don't know anything about country!" Undeterred by racism, Hodges lingered outside rehearsals, out of sight and studying by ear.

During our discussion in 2012, he picked up a guitar in the band room to explain his eventual epiphany after struggling to figure out country guitar style. "The thing about country is this. Stuff like this, if it was a blues lick, you might do a lick like this, say, in the key of G." Hodges played a run-of-the-mill blues phrase midway up the guitar neck. "Then country, for example, that same G would probably be like a 'cowboy' G." He plays the kind of open chord most guitarists learn in the first few weeks. "In the intro, rather than starting on [fret] five, like blues . . ."[71] Hodges finished his sentence with his guitar, playing a similar phrase down the neck, open strings ringing, getting a bright, overtone-rich sound out of the increased length of the strings. Little had he known before his epiphany, country guitarists used the same melodies as other styles. They just fingered them on a different position on the guitar neck. After that, he had a new trick up his sleeve.

After proving himself proficient at country in strategic moments of Megasound sets, Hodges took slots in rodeo bands and expanded his musical fare to cater to broadening tastes and confound racial assumptions of rodeo-goers. He continued learning under the mentorship of established Angola singers and guitarists John Storms and Freddie Johnson (who once was a guitar player for Freddie Fender).[72] Back in their supergroup, Polk and Hodges could inflect their playing to shake audiences out of racial essentialisms and aim Megasound at every prisoner's taste in music.

Officially, race no longer mattered at Angola. Realistically, it only became more complicated when everyone was forced to mix. Through their music, Megasound presented a musical utopia for post–prisoners' rights audiences. Megasound could symbolically stand for a certain kind of diversity, creating what cultural historian Josh Kun calls an *audiotopia*. Kun coined that term to define a space "within and produced by a musical element that offers the listener and/or musician new maps for re-imagining the present social world."[73] Listening *for* difference presents a cultural plurality, something that DJs do with a fader, and Megasound could do with planned segues from country to R&B to metal to zydeco. This type of plurality contrasts with the American "melting pot" theory of diversity. Through music, they demonstrated the possibility of heterogeneity. Differences among styles offered a more accurate sonic portrait of difference on the yard.

By all accounts, Megasound shows were remarkable. On the yard, audiences pressed up to the front, and music resonated with a bevy of racial, regional, and historical sensibilities. But as much as they helped people to look at where they came from, they encouraged people to look to where they were going. Like Otis Neal, who left for a recording and performance career in 1978, Megasound asserted that they were relevant to the outside marketplace. They made that claim musically, with undeniable skill. They could get the New Orleans prisoners to break out into a second-line dance (without the umbrellas, of course). They could induce head-banging, hip-shaking, and group singing through call-and-response. They could turn a collection of fragmented "I"s into a plural "we." Smiles broke out in the stylistic whiplash caused by their eclectic sets. A mix of familiar covers and original songs kept them distinctive. Members of Megasound wrote original songs not because they articulated a sense of being authentic to prison but as demonstrable proof that they were as good as any free-world band.

Big River Band

When Warden Maggio left, new opportunities opened for traveling bands. Outside opportunities had continued to grow with the expanding tourism economy in the state, but a post–prisoners' rights new emphasis on prison as punishment inflected prisoner bands' rhetoric. According to public opinion, rehabilitation ceased to be the state's responsibility. Self-rehabilitation marked public post–prisoners' rights expectations. It was the prisoner's responsibility to choose to be better. Accommodating this shift, when bands began playing outside the prison again, they used their versatility differently. Instead of representing audiotopia, switching genres was like switching spoken registers, using musical inflection to present to the public strategically—as redemptive, cautionary, empathetic, and capable of rehabilitation. The musicians were ready to take just about any outside gig once they became possible again.

Warden John Whitley became warden in 1990 after several others came and went. Whitley had a penchant for music and was a reformer with prison credibility. Over twenty years, he worked his way from security officer to warden. Before coming to Angola, Whitley was warden of one of the newer prisons, Elayn Hunt Correctional Center. There, he had a traveling band. "I thought it would be good for morale to get one started here,"[74] he said. But he also saw value in public relations, stating that music could "show people on the outside that we have some inmates up here who are human."[75] Reviving a traveling band was a risk for Whitley. It could bring bad publicity. Moreover, the Attorney General might again rule that the administration had no authority to take prisoners outside the prison. Whitley mitigated risk, assembling band members with short sentences and nonviolent charges. He figured that if he got criticism from the public, he could say that they were about to go home anyway.

The Big River Band debuted at the 1990 rodeo. Drummer Templer "West Coast" Johnson led guitarists Terry Deakle and Roland Pittman, bassist Jimmy Booker, keyboard player James Byrd, and trumpeter Robert Marshall. After a successful debut, they played at the East Louisiana State Hospital on the first of December and a week later at Greenwell Springs Hospital. Officer Bobby Howard was not only the sponsor. He also played saxophone in the band.

After a series of successful performances at state institutions, Whitley's band received requests from around the state, country music venues, festivals, civic functions, and nursing homes. But as the short-timer musicians were released, Warden Whitley recognized a problem. Rapid turnover (though good for the prisoners going home) was hurting the band. The inconsistent lineup and a flood of performance requests meant that the Big River Band could only pull off relatively easy cover songs. But as Whitley felt more comfortable with the risk, he gradually replaced outgoing members with long-term prisoners, increasing the quality of the musicians each time. Every musician wanted the opportunity to travel, and he could assign trusty status to make that happen.

It wasn't long before he heard about Myron Hodges's guitar playing. Whitley called for him late one night. Upon meeting Hodges, Whitley sized him up with a challenge, betting he couldn't play "When the Levee Breaks," a classic Led Zeppelin track from their untitled fourth album. Hodges said, "Warden, you don't want to make that bet." (He had been playing rock since he was a kid, serenading his grade school friends out his window.) Whitley set his wager: "I'll make you a Class A trusty. I'll put you in a traveling band and send you around the state on a big blue bus." "Yeah?" Hodges said. "Warden, you better get that bus fueled up because you're gonna lose that bet."[76]

After "When the Levee Breaks," Hodges ran through snippets of other songs. Seeing that Hodges could play any style on the guitar and sensing that he could handle a crowd, Whitley gave Hodges trusty status and put him in the Big River Band.[77] Hodges soon brought in Robin Polk and Larry Wilkerson, essentially turning Megasound into a band licensed to travel. As the warden's band, they had access to better equipment, more time to rehearse and write, and life on the road, playing for free audiences.

According to Hodges, he adapted the band's rhetoric to meet the needs of prisoners and the new warden.

> When this new warden came in, it was like, "Look, man, let us give this prison a facelift." We have a reputation for being the bloodiest prison in the nation, and perhaps that was true at that time. But everybody here is not a monster. I mean, I'm not. I'm just a guy caught up in a bad situation. So how we going to do that? "Let's do it with a band. Send us out, man. Let us play music for people, make them happy and stuff, make them see us in a different light." And he pretty much was with that.[78]

In public interviews, Warden Whitley emphasized the voluntary nature of the band.[79] Casting musicians as volunteers rather than recipients of an institutional program presents rehabilitation as a self-driven project. The bargain between warden and prisoner was one in which prisoners could redefine themselves, and the warden could point to evidence of natural rehabilitation without expensive state programs.

The racial diversity of the group was also a signal of a well-run prison (whether or not it was based in reality). Their diverse repertoire crossed the color line, which not only made for good public relations, it got them lots of gigs. They could take whatever was thrown their way and appeal to a wide range of audiences. But with outside shows, they also inherited certain expectations for original songs left in the wake of the Westernaires—songs that seemed to authentically represent the experience of imprisonment.

To name a few, the Big River Band played the Strawberry Festival in Ponchatoula, the Blues Festival in Baton Rouge, the State Fair in Shreveport, the Frog Legs Festival in Rayne, the Cotton Festival in Bastrop, the Alligator Festival in St. Charles Parish, and the City of Lights Christmas Festival in Natchitoches. It soon became routine to load gear into the big blue bus and bring their mixed fare of covers and originals to eager audiences.

Infrastructure, procedures, and precedent were already in place. Players with Class-A trusty status could be outfitted with instruments with help from the Inmate Lending Fund. Performance fees also made a profit for the Inmate Lending Fund, making them an extension of strengthened voluntary associations. Administrative support from personnel director Ebba Wilson helped manage security and coordinate requests from outside. Like many of its predecessors, the Big River Band became in demand throughout the state.

Warden Whitley helped produce a CD as a demo and a way of fundraising for the group. On the recording, their eclecticism is on display. As a prison band, however, the uses of styles are rhetorical. Like using the spoken voice to signal racial, geographic, and cultural differences, the four tracks on the CD use genre to signal cultural differences—adapting Megasound's audiotopic sets designed for the yard.[80] Now playing to an outside audience, they shifted styles to cater to the public imagination. A close listen to these original songs reveals how the Big River Band's musical inflections expanded public images of the prisoner while also conforming to expectations.

In "This Is Your Life," elements of funk, soul, rap, R&B, and rock and roll intermingle. The song structure varies to accommodate multiple genre signals: a strong back beat, slap bass, overdriven lead guitar, and synth horns. The most notable genre shifts are to the rapped sections, which take on a register of a second-person addressee, seemingly inspired by *Scared Straight* programs initiated in the late 1970s. While the incorporation of rap is typical of R&B of its time, "This Is Your Life" was not innovative, or even current, in its style or approach. But that wasn't the point. In popular music, a rap interlude was an adult nod to new youth musical tastes. Here, rap added a register shift. It was a brief performance of *addressing* young people.

> The FBI, the IRS, and the DEA are gonna put you away
> Your mama's working hard tryna make ends meet
> And you're out there hanging in the streets
> Associating with the criminal elements
> Before you know it, you turn state's evidence
> You take a fall, and you're in the pen
> You watch your homeboys going in and again
> Round and round the revolving door
> Till you get too old and you die too poor
> Don't even get a decent burial
> A pine box and a jailhouse funeral
> No home, no wife, no kids, no car
> Is that what you want?
> Well, you better get your mind right
> 'Cause this is your life

"Wings of Another" bridges the gap between a 1980s power ballad and R&B with prominent synthesizer piano strings and meandering saxophone solos, scoring the regret and perhaps revealing scars through the metaphor of unfulfilled promises of love. The music augments this. Harmonically, it moves a D major to an E major, with the bass still in the tonic. The altered second chord creates a floating feel within an ambiguous tonal space. Next, a G major (IV chord) shifts to a minor, further pulling from standard diatonic expectations, offering movement outside of a rigid key. The harmonic motion matches the lyrics: "I've been drifting, often lonely..."

The chorus, however, introduces a determined cadence, changing registers by borrowing ♭VI (B♭ major) and ♭VII (C major) chords, driving the harmony with a sense of purpose to the tonic D chord. The drum parts match the change, shifting from spare ornamentation, becoming denser and more regular, joining precomposed rhythmic flourishes made by the whole band. The eventual musical insistence matches Larry Wilkerson's forceful vocals, following each male chorus imperative:

> *Run away*... and get lost in the wings of another
> *Fly away*... along the way, you were bound to discover

Another man . . . you're gonna need to be your lover
I understand . . .

In a radical style shift, the third track, "If My Body Could Follow My Mind," features Myron Hodges trading off impressive country guitar licks with a fiddle player while a simple walking bass rhythm moves through predictable dominant cadences. It's the most consistent genre-wise, and the lyrics play on a sense of regret: "Fast living and whiskey were my closest friends. I never thought that I'd get caught, wind up in the pen." It lacks the complex storytelling of Bud Wilkerson's Westernaires songs. Nevertheless, its goal is different, referencing a country-ness through superficial elements— instrumentation, twangy vocals and guitars, nostalgic rural imagery of jukeboxes, and obligatory mention of pickup trucks.

Finally, "Stay with Me" is a party song, upbeat syncopated R&B with hints of funk, contemporary gospel, and an old-school rap bridge that gives way to an in-the-pocket jazz fusion guitar solo. It's the kind of song that may have been good for escape on the yard: "Baby, won't you stay with me, tonight," punctuated with romantic promises. To an outside audience, it may have simply given relief to the songs that referenced prison, a break from the weight of incarceration, a song that simply got a crowd together, dancing to repeated pleas: "Stay with me. Stay with me. Stay with me."

The four songs represent radical versatility within the bounds of pop music styles. As an album, it genre hops so much that genre shifting becomes its main feature: marked by stylistic unexpectedness and abrupt register shifts. If you bought the CD at any number of festivals in 1992, you probably didn't put it on as background music. But you might have listened to it *as evidence* of a diverse group of prisoners reflecting and acting towards moral betterment, pausing to reflect on the realities of prison life and the humanity of prisoners. Through inflection, the group shifts groove, timbre, and lyrical imagery to widen audience expectations of what a prisoner is.

Prison, increasingly viewed as violent in the 1990s, was the "just deserts" for criminal acts. This same attitude led to the Violent Crime Control and Law Enforcement Act of 1994, signed into law by President Bill Clinton.[81] The public developed an increased appetite for punishment and a distaste for expensive programs. Cheap juvenile delinquency avoidance programs like *Scared Straight* amplified images of violent convicts even though violence at Angola was dropping after limited prisoners' rights reforms. Big River Band balanced musical essentialisms and stereotypical outlaw images only to subvert them through their sets. Eclecticism also did the work for Warden Whitley. The band members performed *choice* with each inflection, deliberately moving through unexpected musical styles. Choice had a new symbolic resonance with the public. It represented evidence that prisoners might choose a civic life over a criminal life.

The Big River Band managed a run of a few years representing 1990s Angola musically. Warden Whitley disbanded the group when a fight with drunk members broke out.[82] "There was a great band scandal," Hodges remembered. "This band got shut down. [The administration] were peeved. Administration was saying, 'Look, there will never be another traveling band at Angola. You all had your chance. You had an opportunity to make a difference, and you failed.'" Focused on the consequence of one rash episode instead of the years of changing public perception of prisoners, the Big River Band was the last secular group to tour. Since then, the only music to tour outside the gates has been gospel.

Gospel Melodies

Secular bands of the late 1970s and 1980s may have been stylistically omnivorous, but they couldn't compete with gospel acts—not because they weren't as good, but because gospel singers were expected to bring a spiritual authenticity to the stage. Instrumentalists at Angola could play in both R&B and gospel groups, but singers generally had to commit to one or the other. Many free-world singers experience this sacred/secular bind today.[83] Instrumentalists can be excused for taking any and all performance opportunities because they are understood to be hired professionals—dependent on performances to support themselves. They also play on the sidelines of the stage while singers command attention. Singers, front and center, may be judged on their authenticity, their words heard as messages, conspicuous, and uncomfortable with singing about God one night and about parties the other. Because of these dynamics, gospel developed differently at Angola.

Sacred singing practices go back to the nineteenth-century plantation. Accounts run through every decade of the prison. Folklorist John Lomax avoided recording the sacred singing in his 1933 and 1934 visits, considering it too influenced by White traditions.[84] Harry Oster recorded spirituals in the late 1950s.[85] Angola's gospel singing grew in the 1970s and 1980s because gospel themes were existential in a way that secular music was not.

More and more prisoners were staring down the possibility of spending the rest of their lives in prison. The hammer of incarceration was in full swing. From 1977 to 1995, national carceral expenditures rose 823 percent. The Black prison population increased dramatically (despite similar crime rates between White and Black populations). Increasingly abandoned, Black prisoners formed their own spiritual collectives in Angola's associations.

In the mid-1980s, Black congregations increasingly focused on growing problems in city neighborhoods. As a result, outside church presence at Angola began to diminish. Prisoner gospel practices filled the gap. The increased support for Black associations in the late 1970s led to what many prisoners considered a gospel renaissance. The central figure was John Henry Taylor Jr., who, like many musicians, moved from the field to stage in a matter of years. He provided the material—older songs from rural Black traditions that he had learned as a child.

Taylor arrived in 1970. He spent his first year at Camp A, assigned to work in the fields.[86] These were the days marked by outlawry that Charles Neville and others described in chapter 3—violent and unpredictable. "When I came here," he told me, "I was surprised when I looked at the scene, how the prison was being run by inmate guards. I was kind of shocked. I couldn't believe that an inmate that had a number like me, doing time like me, had a shotgun."[87] Danger lurked everywhere. As he described, "Treacherous. Madness. They was men lookin' like they was uncivilized. Just take advantage of people that didn't have no defense for themselves."[88] Taylor described outlawry everywhere he went:

> When you got a bunch of inmates in there and everybody on their own. And guys getting forces and using drugs, doing this and doing that. Came into the TV room. Someone there in the TV room say, "Don't change that dial," or "Leave that like it is. Anybody change it, come see me!" and all that kind of crazy stuff. So, I had already made my mind up and said, "I don't need to watch TV." I did get me a radio and stay by myself most of the time or read my Bible.[89]

Taylor was from a small town and didn't have the benefit of falling in with a New Orleans or Baton Rouge clique. So, he kept his head down and avoided trouble. "I stayed in prayer most of the time. I ran alone most of the time. I never did become friendship with none of these guys here because I couldn't trust neither one of them."[90] In the church, his place of refuge, he found the only group activity for which he was suited: the choir.[91] Most of the days, though, he labored in the fields. He soon made it to the main prison but still worked the same crops daily.

Eventually, as he described, musical collaboration found him when he met Willie Server:

> A year passed by, and I was working in the field. I was singing out in the field on a warm, hot day. . . .[92] I was cutting cane. I was singing pretty loud that day. A guy left all the way out of his line, come all the way through the cane over there where he heard my voice. He said, "Hey, man. Are you a gospel singer?"
>
> I said, "Yes, I am."[93] I really wasn't singing no gospel songs at that time. I was singing a blues number. . . .
>
> "I heard you *way over there*. I'm in Line 3. You're over here in Line 7," he said, "You sing gospel?"
>
> "Yeah, I sing gospel."
>
> "I could tell through your voice how you're singing that blues that you had a little gospel sound in you.[94] . . . I'm gonna be around Oak [Dormitory]. I want you to come back there after chow, the last meal. I got a three-man group I want you to meet."[95] "I need one more man, which is the baritone singer."
>
> I said, "Well, I'm that man. Baritone singer."[96]

Not only did Taylor have the style, but he also developed a voice that could carry without help from a microphone. Because Taylor's gospel-inflected voice made it all the way to Server's attention, Server knew he had not only a potential fourth member for his new gospel group but a strong singer with an authentic gospel approach. "I was surprised when he asked me," Taylor admitted, "because I didn't really think they had no gospel group here at that time."[97] Server was the lead singer and a fifth tenor.[98]

He introduced Taylor to the other members when they met behind the dormitory that evening. They were fortunate to have one trusty-status member who could get through the facility to meet them on the Big Stripe yard.[99] Musically, Taylor knew his way around all the vocal parts and had an encyclopedic knowledge of gospel repertoire.[100]

> So, they started asking me what songs did I know. I asked them, "What songs do y'all sing?" So, they was naming the songs that they sing, and I said, "I do all those songs."

They say, "Well, if you know all that, we can get started now."

So, we got started behind the building a cappella. When we did get started, they said, "Oh yeah! This is what we looking for." When they heard me blending in with them.[101]

While secular bands like Time Factor and Megasound offered audiotopia (a musical imagination of social heterogeneity), Taylor's singing offered harmony.

Musical exchange, of course, goes both ways. Taylor sized them up, noting how they responded to his singing as they tried out a few songs. "I began to put forth effort," he said, "when I felt how they was responding in the songs that we was singing."[102] There was enough reciprocity that each night, Taylor returned to the back of Oak Dormitory after his days in the fields to sing a cappella with his newfound group.

Over time, they gained a following. At one point, the crowd grew to nearly seventy people, and the spectacle caused alarm for a captain on duty. (This was around the time that the Black Panthers had been eradicated after the 1972 uprising.) "When you got a crowd of people comin' round like that," Taylor explained, "they don't know what's going on around there. . . . Got all these inmates comin' around the building from different dormitories."[103] When the captain followed the voice to the center, he said, "Oh, *this* is what's going on back here. [We] have to put y'all in a band room. 'Cause, y'all singin' too good out here!"[104] At that moment, Taylor envisioned his group in the busy back rooms in the recreation building and thought to himself, "What effect would take on the men if we was playing and we had music behind us?"[105]

It was the early 1970s, and the band room was a refuge from violence. Many musicians were eager to join in whatever projects came through the door. "The musicians came from nowhere out there, wanting to play automatic," Taylor remembered. "They wanted to play with the group that had experience under their belts at that time. So, they came in. They had a drummer, bass guitar, and the rhythm and lead man. So, we was on our way."[106] With space, musicians, and security, Taylor and Server took gospel to a new level.

Spiritual singing has been part of Angola's ministry since the nineteenth century. But the churches had been run by White free staff. It was more an administrative than associational practice. Generally, sacred music was restricted to accompanying church services. After desegregation, however, associations like the Methodist Men's Club gained relative independence and began hiring the Mighty Harmonizers, as Taylor called their group, for banquets.[107]

After a few years, members started going home. Taylor's life sentence passed through the change in sentencing practices, and he became one of the Ten-Sixers, facing natural life at Angola. He decided to build gospel back up with people likely to be at Angola for the rest of their lives. "I waited about a year or so," Taylor explained, "and I was able to get around and pick guys that wanted to learn how to sing."[108] He had to train them—mostly R&B singers who maybe had nostalgia for their families or for the moments of their youth when they went to church.

Taylor's concerts with the Mighty Harmonizers identified him as the authority.[109] Singers frequently approached him for singing advice, searching for that elusive style of gospel harmony. Eventually, he identified a few singers with enough confidence in popular music that he could train. "All they needed was a little brushing up, somebody to kind of push them, to bring it out of them," he explained.[110] Jewell Spotville was one of those singers, arriving in 1973 and seeking music opportunities in the band room. "I thought I could sing at the time," Spotville admitted. "I didn't know no harmony, but I could sing solo. So, I met [Taylor], and he taught me how to sing. He really gave me what I know now as far as harmonizing."[111]

Taylor developed his new group, the Gospel Melodies for three years with a core of dedicated singers. He strategically cultivated new singers in anticipation of change. As he explained,

> When you plant one good seed, another good seed come along. This seed here? One. This fella here? He's getting ready to go home, so we got one getting ready to be placed, the one that is leaving, and we keep it going. We kept it going for so long until we became something like, people would say, "Y'all fantastic, y'all good. There ain't nothin' like y'all here."[112]

Getting good required mentorship—picking up on nuance, learning to collectively and individually inflect the voice in service of the music, to account for each other. That's very hard to do by simply listening to a recording but possible when singing in each others' presence.

Plenty of Angola's top gospel singers told me that Taylor gave them an "old-school flavor."[113] That was especially valuable because gospel style also signified family and community. The sound itself created nostalgia for a time in many prisoners' lives, one rooted in family and community before the challenges of adulthood and alienation set in. Ray Jones, who came in the 1980s, first heard Taylor sing with the Gospel Melodies at the rodeo:

> When I heard this old man singing, I was singing rhythm & blues and all that kind of stuff, and I saw him. . . . I saw that old man singing, and it seemed like it just took me all the way back to my mother, my grandmother and in the time of the music and stuff. I'm looking at him. I say, "That's what I want to do. I want to sing the gospel."[114]

Once he began learning from Taylor, Jones noticed small but significant details. "I watched him close," he remembered and illustrated a difference. "I said, 'Lord.' He said, 'Lord-*ee*.'"[115]

The tiny vocal inflections were not only for style, they were part of a complex system of singing together. "It took a while," Taylor explained. "It wasn't no overnight thing, working with these guys. You had to go in the yard, go way off from everybody."[116] Prentice Robinson remembered singing with purpose constantly:

> All the days behind the building, in corners singing, and in the gym. . . . Everywhere we met—whether it was to sing, just to go to church, or whether it was just on the job—we got together and we would practice harmony. We would practice different turns, and we would practice different sounds, and it gave the group the Gospel Melodies a very unique sound.[117]

Albert Patterson remembered the intense practice it took to shift his R&B singing to gospel singing, which required knowing how every single sound fit together.

> Over and over and over again, he taught me. He said, look, in order for you to do the lead solo, you've got to sing all areas of the background. So, he taught me this one and that one and that one and constant drilling. And we all started getting back there in the wintertime. We was shaking, but we did. Big John showed a bunch of us.[118]

In time, they developed musical instincts particular to their way of singing gospel. Ray Jones described it as listening with an instinctive knowledge of the laws of harmony. "If I hear it, I can move right in there and get it," he explained, "Or I can hear that missing voice and go right in there and pick it up. . . . You just can't do it unless you can hear it. And so, he taught me all that: to listen, to hear. My first teaching was to sit down and listen."[119] Taylor had cultivated what he brought when he had arrived, planting one of the only seeds he had to plant: gospel music.

Part of what made the Gospel Melodies' singing distinctive was that it was particular to Taylor's upbringing—a practice that originated from listening to his mother at a very young age. Taylor's mother constantly sang songs like "Amazing Grace," "What a Friend We Have in Jesus," and "Just a Closer Walk with Thee," and he couldn't help but sing along.[120] "She'd be hitting songs at high notes when I was young," he remembered.

> I hit the same note that she hit, high ones. Young as I was, I had a soprano voice myself, and I could go way up there where she was.
> And she used to tell me, "What you trying to do, boy? Me?"
> "No, Mom, I figured I'd sing that song like you sing it."
> We kept on until me and her got used to singing behind each other. So, the time came when I got in the choir, and the choir wanted me in their section, soprano.[121]

As his voice deepened, he moved into other parts, eventually landing in the baritone section of a men's group at age thirteen.[122] This pathway through harmony parts was typical of a specific era of Black sacred music. But Black church singing practices were changing to more presentational forms in the 1980s, so his experience was becoming increasingly rare.

Taylor's rural church housed lifelong intergenerational congregations that had learned to sing together in several configurations—large choirs, quartets, men's choruses, and interactive worship services. Getting a feel for how parts worked together in church choirs, he built his harmonic knowledge on top of his mother's melodic inflections. "They were teaching me all of this," he said, "the tone of whatever they was playing. And sure, I advanced a whole lot. I learned how to be able to sing first tenor, second tenor, baritone, lead."[123] It wasn't only the conscious knowledge that Taylor brought to Angola—songs and melodic parts. It was his embodied knowledge and his ability to teach others through practice—a way of singing together. Teaching in prison, however, can be uniquely challenging.

Many musicians in many different prisons have told me that a significant challenge to teaching music in prison is that prisoners often don't take criticism well. In addition, music transmission is always multimodal, reliant on gestures, eye contact, observed rhythm, and pointed inflections in the flow of playing together.[124] Taylor relied on these techniques to such a degree that he didn't need words to teach. Sometimes the singers didn't realize that they were being taught. "They didn't know it at first," he said. "After time rolled on, they began to pick up. They'd begin to open up, and then the thing that was hidden in them. . . . I knew how to put certain moves and certain runs to make him come out more, more so. You know, like hitting certain notes, making certain sounds to what he's doing, giving it a little bit more energy."[125] Taylor gave me an example of how his ability to move his voice through all the parts and make pointed vocal inflections were part of his teaching:

> Some guy wanted to learn how to sing, how to be a tenor singer. I was able to leave my regular tone and go into a tenor voice to show him how to blend in. As the time go by, he began to learn how to use the voice. Then I would fall back into my baritone voice and pick a certain song and sing it, then fall back in the background, then show him how to make his voice blend into what I had just brought before him in tone. It was pretty hard, but they finally learned.[126]

Moving to the background was an indispensable pedagogical technique, but it was also a basis for group singing that turned many voices into a singular, layered voice.

> I'd get back in the background. I'll sing it, and then [put] my voice right in the background where his voice was, then make the other two hear how the song [works]. What I was doing, I was showing them if I make a [sings a melodic phrase] or, I show them [sings another phrase], they know how they get in, to blend in. . . . You know, like this song got a I-IV-V change. Well, when a I come, . . . I just show them how to run with the turnaround. When they get to the turnaround, I make it like, [sings a melodic phrase]. "Did you know I'm going home?" [sings a different phrase] "Oh, yeah!" Then they come back down, showing them how to come back home, how they come back home. I stay out there with them, helping them out, several guys like that, trying to teach them.[127]

I heard his method once in a reunion we managed to put together for my film—his timbre and melody gently nudging the other three supporting voices. Taylor influenced the others by changing from closed to open sounds.

His lips did the work that an equalizer (or more specifically, a low pass filter) does for a studio engineer's mix, bringing sounds forward or burying them by controlling brightness. It was surprisingly dynamic. His use of timbre was a technique lost in recording studios in the 1950s when recording engineers instructed Black musicians to be more consistent with their voices.

Changes in timbre helped Taylor conduct the group. Enunciation took a backseat to modulation—moving his voice in and out of the foreground. As I watched him close his lips to tuck his voice into the background, I understood what he had told me about the importance of the background: "I can show them through the runs and changes and how you make a lead singer stand out. So that's what I was all about—making a group stand out. . . . Showing the individual how to blend in. How to make a lead singer, how to dress him up, how to make him look good."[128] After we filmed the singing, Albert Patterson told me, "One thing about him, when he's enjoying a song, he will ride way backward. And once he come out of that . . . I don't know what you call it, but he ready to roll! You got to be ready to background him there, 'cause he wide open now."[129] All the drilling, steeping in harmony to develop a distinctive flavor, meant they knew each other musically. "I mean, we're familiar in singing," Taylor clarified. "He becomes familiar with me, and, like a family, we know that he could be standing on the side. He may hit a note or something, and I'm over here, and something will make me blend into what he's doing."[130]

By the 1980s, they could anticipate each other's every musical move. As they learned, Taylor learned. He made up for the absence of educational and sacred music programs by creating his own site for discovery. His ability to move to the background allowed him to listen to others for new approaches. He was training his students to teach him. "I didn't just want to be in the front the whole time," he explained. "I learn something from the other lead singers. They give me insight on certain things: how they use their words, how they make turns, how they make their note blend in."[131] Impressive as it was, Taylor wasn't in it for the show. Music gave him control over being in population.

Knowing each other musically gave Taylor a way of being private and social simultaneously. Spotville made the point this way: "Real private person. Ain't want nobody to know about his kids until he opened up one day. That kinda amazed me. 'You been around here all this time, and you ain't mentioned your kids?!'"[132] Taylor explained the importance of music as a narrow but crucial part of being known. "I express most of myself through song," he said.

"In so many ways, you can express yourself—in action, through your work. It don't necessarily have to be expressing yourself with your mouth all the time. You can express yourself through motion. People can read from your outer appearance the type of person that you are."[133] Music was an intentional way of being social, something outside of the rehabilitation-focused penitentiary logic of individual reflection. Singing created a dignified environment— professional and upstanding. "That brought in a different scenery," he said. "It kind of changed me around. Kind of gave me a little room."[134] As a form of uplift, gospel was transformative. He told me:

> It keeps your mind out of the gutter, keeps your mind from wandering off into things that it's not good for man to look upon, in, within himself. . . . It keeps the mind floating always on something positive. Not on anything negative most of the time. . . . So when I'm around people that talking corruptly, I move out. I say, "Excuse me, gentlemen. You all carry on." And I get out of the way. I find me a spot somewhere where I don't have to listen to that or hear all that.[135]

Creating the Gospel Melodies was a matter of moving to another spot, away from violence, self-aggrandizement, and tragedy. As Angola shifted from violence and turnover to aging men with terminal life sentences, gospel fixed Taylor's mind off the unfathomable possibility of dying at Angola. One of the songs he became known for was "I'll Keep On Living, After I Die." It suited occasions that required more gravity than what Megasound or the Big River Band could handle. Gospel provided testimony.[136]

The Gospel Melodies became a premier traveling gospel band once Warden Whitley reintroduced travel, offering members a taste of freedom, albeit limited.[137] "It felt nice," Taylor remembered. "I felt like I was free in the way that I was being treated, but it was not like the real freedom, being free, as in out in society. It wasn't that type of freedom. It made me feel free to get away from a lot of stuff that was taking place here."[138]

Like with the Big River Band and many others before, the beginning of the end came with a simple transgression. Taylor was too dignified to give me the details, only that someone used the band room for unsavory purposes.[139] Taylor was held responsible because he led the group. Transferred to Camp H, he took on new responsibilities, cleaning rooms and mopping hallways (a story I will pick up in the next chapter). The Gospel Melodies never recovered though its members linger and form the pillars of Angola's now active gospel scene. As a pioneer, Taylor was a living inflection point, adapting his musical skills to collaborate on his own terms.

Conclusion

While this book has been about associations, consider the important role of individuals who help inflect a new direction in musical collaboration. Consider prisoners' resources for riding out the consequences of laws, policies, and administrative turnover. As individuals, the contrast between John Taylor of the Mighty Harmonizers and the Gospel Melodies and Myron Hodges of Megasound and the Big River Band is a study in difference. Taylor's humility and Hodges's hubris are evident contrasts. Taylor was from a small town and older. His upbringing was marked by lifelong church involvement, which gave him musical resources to get through prison on his own, ironically, by being together. On the other hand, Hodges was hit in the first wave of desperation that swept through 1980s New Orleans. His resources came from a sense of confidence, a promise of post–civil rights entitlement.

The two men, however, share an unapologetic stance. Consummate and curious in both their respective practices, they held their ground and learned how to use musical inflection as a resource. Subtle but deliberate changes (in voice and guitar, respectively) made them adaptable to new performance opportunities, continuing musical practices that the prison could have snuffed out. Inflection gave them access to registers that they could use to address changes on the yard and changes in public perception through the post–prisoners' rights era, and up until the idea of rights seemed a thing of the past.

In 1996, President Bill Clinton signed the Prison Litigation Reform Act, a tool intended to end "frivolous" lawsuits by prisoners. The law made it easier for courts to dismiss cases before hearing them. It ratcheted up legal fees and limited the courts' ability to force changes in prison policies. The restrictive legislation aligned with the Supreme Court's abandonment of prisoners' rights. The gains of reducing outlawry and improving the conditions of stoop labor remained. But these gains weren't simply the power of successful policy. They were largely because Angola's prisoners got older, serving unending sentences. Gradually the men relied less on violence. Angola's shift to a more measured, predictable, and safe place has a lot to do with how men change as they age. In this sense, a shift from popular music to Black sacred music is part of that aging population's sound that shifted in the mid-1990s. It is partially the sound of truth-in-sentencing laws.

Moving into the 1990s, musicians would find support from a shrinking set of outside White evangelical organizations and a tourism industry. The musical sound of the prison eventually tipped in favor of John Henry Taylor Jr.'s earlier gospel efforts, although, as we will see in the next chapter, he would find that the pressures and expectations of gospel music at Angola were too much for him to bear. Angola's population grew older and many looked for spiritual redemption while still working toward actual release through legal means.

After Whitley, the prison changed under new leadership, legislation, and a new population joining the aging lifers. Musicians continued to associate within existing practices—refurbishing instruments, creating new bands, securing rehearsal spaces, and establishing new relationships with outsiders. When I visited for the first time in 2008, I stepped into a continuation of a century of musical activity.

6
Recapitulation

There was a sense of not needing a historical perspective when I first arrived at Angola. It was provided for. Like in a city's historic district, heritage was all over the place and easily digestible. With rolling fields and grazing livestock, the prison was nothing like the dozen California prisons I had visited already. Most of those felt cold and institutional, whereas Angola offered a sense of historical gravity. Heritage is a strange thing to combine with real guard towers, fences, and life sentences. For some, that combination is alluring. For others, it is an indictment of instituted state violence.[1] Regardless, Angola has become a focal point as the nation's largest and most historic active state prison.

I drove up to the gate and past the museum in my rented car, then knowing Angola mostly through Lead Belly's songs and Harry Oster's book. In my mind, folklore collapsed the prison into one space, lost in time. I knew nothing of the stories of musicians and practices that have made up the bulk of this book. Folk songs begged to be a soundtrack for my visit. A museum provided historical objects, including Lead Belly's prison records and a looped video of the rodeo from a documentary. Much of the narrative strewn through the museum championed the progress of the prison, something I have tried to complicate in this book by offering a very long-scale musical perspective. But when I first arrived, there seemed no need to bring anything but interest and questions.

Warden Burl Cain initiated the museum in 1998, converting a former bank building just outside the gates. He had come from American Farm Bureau Federation via Dixon Correctional Institution to become warden from 1995 to 2016. A sign at the front of the museum reads, "This is to remind us of the past that we don't want to go back to."

Any museum founded by a warden is sure to raise eyebrows. The museum has attracted critical attention among scholars who see it not as a museum but as an instrument of the administration.[2] As musicologist Velia Ivanova notes, the state exerts an eerily similar power in imprisonment and archiving—the ability to house, classify, and explain away.[3] It's no surprise that a prison would curate an archive. Making it public is simply the outward-facing part of state power and an attempt to fund an array of objectives through the tourism industry that has become an anchor to Louisiana's economy.

Angola's history has been memorialized in many ways. A guard tower and a cell now stand in the National Museum of African American History and Culture in Washington, DC. The Red Hat Cell Block (that I described in chapter 2) was added to the National Register of Historic Places in March 2003. The problem is that historicizing things can suggest that they have been decommissioned, that the powers that created and maintained them no longer operate. The museum contains many seemingly decommissioned objects—an electric chair, a prisoner-made knife, and a cell. And yet, capital punishment, violence, and mass warehousing still exist. My extended visits to the prison afforded me complex perspectives on the museum—a sense of its many missions and the polyphony of its stakeholders. I came to understand the museum as one of many institutions still entangled in the untold stories I recorded during interviews and read about in my *Angolite* research. In this last chapter, I hope to show that the history of Angola's music is still alive and complex and that it is still actively connected to the prison.

In musical composition, bringing back themes at the end is called a recapitulation. Best known in sonata form, it is a restatement of a melody, harmonic progression, or musical themes. As opposed to the closure that a sonata recapitulation offers at the end of an orchestral performance, I will keep expectations open when recapitulating the themes of each earlier chapter in reverse: *inflection, surfaces, politics, association,* and *astonishment.* I do this to show that history persists, practices adapt, and that legacies are alive.

This final chapter springs from my encounter with music at the prison as I produced my film there and then continued, after completing the film, following up on provocative aspects of contemporary music-making. When I was there, I found myself on a particular surface within the prison (though I wouldn't have called it by that term then). Others like me, such as Joseph Mouledous in the 1950s, mentioned in chapter 2, have taken prison jobs to do research. My own insight grew from my initial project of making a feature-length documentary film about musicians at Angola and developed when I returned with new questions.

When I brought my film crew, I saw the prison through images cinematographer John Slattery planned and collected. I listened to sound recordist Chauncy Godwin's carefully planned recordings, learning through his technical comments on placing microphones near so many hard cinderblock walls and constantly humming machines, how the human voice radiates in space, and spotting the jerry-rigged audio systems the prisoners maintained. We talked over the shoot with the prisoners and administration. When we weren't filming, Godwin, Slattery, and I constantly discussed the strangeness of prison through details of image and sound.

My relationship with the institution grew with my continued presence. Prisoners and administrators began to know me as a professor of music, a historian of the musical legacy there. I was also a regularly returning outsider who might advocate for prisoners and administrators alike—perhaps clearing up misunderstandings, setting some records straight, and even being a point of contact. I spent long days in the band rooms, the chapels, the rodeo grounds, the walk, the recreation yards, in cars with administrators, and to a degree, the housing units. I followed the networks of the bands, which kept me nearby the voluntary associations.

Music exists in plenty of other spaces—rap and solo singing in the cafeteria, the fields, the recreation yards, and the dormitories. And while that might seem closer to the solo singing that folklorists looked for, I found the professional activity at the prison most distinctive. The fact that prisoners, with minimal support from free-world staff, could build a formidable musical scene fascinated me. Music wasn't part of an outside-managed rehabilitation program, like it is in many other prisons. And the persistent volunteerism brought up questions that John Lomax had never asked. Perhaps most important, the complex ways of association stood in stark contrast to the picture of individual versus state (or David versus Goliath) that frames most scholarship and media portrayals of prison. Musicians struggled together to be musicians.

As I continued to return, I had to negotiate my role, making clear to everyone that I understood that my status as a guest was conditional on having a low and predictable impact. At the same time, I saw a story about musical freedom that might have a different impact. I developed my agenda based on who I was to them at first: White scholar/musician with a professional interracial film crew from Los Angeles. That offered me a degree of trust from the administration and the potential to represent prisoners more comprehensively (see figure 6.1). I did not know it then, but I was following a decades-long media engagement with the prison.

My upbringing in Tennessee gave me little credibility with Louisianans, but having done four years of work in California prisons (including making a short film and building an arts archive) made for meaningful comparative

Figure 6.1. Filming *Follow Me Down* with the Pure Heart Messengers, 2009 (photograph by Jeffrey Hilburn).

discussions. That experience also helped me with my approach. I took to heart two pieces of advice that a California Department of Corrections public information officer had told me: first, to be transparent about intentions because prison officials are in the business of identifying investigative "gotcha" journalists, and second, that when prisoners present themselves, they often deliver their best selves, just as we all do. These observations guided me, helping me orient to truth and transparency. They also guarded me against being tossed out of the prison. I stayed focused on music and, like ethnomusicologists often do, let issues of security, economy, race, and policies spring from music-centered discussions.

It suits my personality to find mutual understanding first rather than to provoke. This did not have to mean that I accepted the institution as it was. It gave me a different way to critique it. Initially, I found that I could ask this question to anyone: "What do most people get wrong about prison?" Then, I kept conversations loose and learned to listen to everyone. I found that some officers and administrators were also disturbed by mass incarceration. One officer, waiting with the Pure Heart Messengers and me as my film crew packed up, remarked at how long he'd known the men in the quartet. The Messengers joined in, ribbing the White officer for being naive when he had started as a wide-eyed eighteen-year-old. The officer turned to me and said, "I've known these guys for over half my life. I'd trust them as my neighbor. It's a shame I can't be on the parole board to let them out." Along with the camaraderie of that moment, I saw an insidious metaphor: a racial power inequity made tragic through ineffective sympathy. It was a dramatization of structural racism.

My status at the prison gave me insight into the complexity of the place and the relationships there. As I went from film documentarian to oral historian to professor, I found myself enmeshed in relationships that gave me insight into the many people in radically different situations of power. The film is a good example of my experience in Louisiana prisons at that time, conveying a sense of confusion and noise inherent to prison, an experience made sensible in moments through music. This chapter, however, develops what I learned by being there, written in order to situate those conditions and calculations within the Burl Cain era (1995–2016), one marked by performed reform, tourism, austerity, neoliberalism, and religiosity. When I was there, secular music was declining, but many older musicians held on to the institutions that had driven music-making for decades.

While it had been shifting since the 1970s, agribusiness slowed dramatically in the 2000s. Most prisoners couldn't handle the work. Prisoners were older than they ever had been before. With the 1970s truth-in-sentencing laws keeping people in prison for natural life and the increasing criminal prosecutions and higher sentencing, Angola's demographics had shifted. Young people still worked the fields, but many of the younger people sentenced in Louisiana would end up at one of the other seven facilities for men. These days, out of the nine hundred men who can endure work in the field, there are rarely more than three hundred in the fields at any given time. Some harvests even enlist prisoners from other institutions.

In many respects, Angola is like a nightmarish retirement community, now distinguished by its hospice program. The songs that were once alive on the fields are mostly memories that live in the men who have spent decades incarcerated there. But that does not mean the musical story is over. Music still serves as an organizing force for associations, a sound of solidarity, and a public relations tool. And as the terms of voluntary association have changed, so has the music. The primary shifts that affected the Burl Cain era are the prisoner age, religiosity, neoliberal profiteering, and tourism.

In a way, bands became less flexible in styles. As Samuel Stark told me, offering his personal history of the bands starting with his 1965 incarceration,

"There has been bands here that did play all types of music, whether it was blues, country and western, gospel, or whatever. They could play it all. Lately, that is not happening . . . not now."[4] The shift toward major public events and church activities created new musical needs. Many secular musicians still play but operate in narrower stylistic confines. Unable and unwilling to adapt to newer styles with younger musicians, they have been left with outdated media and musical technologies, and the pressures of public performance have narrowed the genres to popular (R&B, rock, and country) and, to a greater extent, Christian bands.[5] Christian popular music is stylistically diverse, but music for tourists in a prison tends to be safe, making visitors comfortable in a setting. The musicians are top-notch players. They enjoy reputations of being "professional" among musicians incarcerated in all the other Louisiana prisons. And so, it is worth examining why musicians who can play everything would narrow the styles they play.

Rap exists at Angola, but primarily in the fields and the cafeteria. In a way, the music akin to the old work songs is rap, alleviating prison labor-related problems by passing the time, establishing solidarity, occupying the mind with something meaningful, voicing discontent, and making connections to an imagined outside. But without the kind of club partnerships that now support the older generation's music, rap has less visibility and less connection to the legacy of music at Angola. Rappers do not entertain visiting church groups, are not featured at the rodeo, have only minor roles at the banquets, and have few resources given in the recreation department. Moreover, the clubs are dominated by older prisoners whose tastes skew older. In short, rappers are less aligned with the structures that grant liberties to club members. It exists out-of-law.

As I show how music in prison is still active, I will move from surfaces to the center of the prison for musicians: the band room. I will highlight connections to the earlier chapters to avoid a story of "progress" and be wary of how historicizing things (like slavery or colonialism) can hide their continued influence. Sensing history, rather than explaining it, we can see the continued flow of three tributaries: outlawry, slavery, and penance.

Inflection by Statute

Turning off the prison road from the B-Line, just past the cemetery, I drove through a white fence and parked right next to the Ranch House. In front, just off the steps of a porch lined with a dozen wooden rocking chairs, folding tables with white tablecloths awaited guests for a buffet lunch. I had been to the Ranch House several times. It always made me a little uncomfortable. It had an air of unapologetic plantation heritage, a remake of Angola's nineteenth-century Big House.

The Ranch House was a refuge for special guests and an occasional command center for Warden Cain. It felt more like a hunting lodge with its wood panels and mounted deer heads, except it was immaculate. Trusty prisoners cleaned and cooked there, deferential to anyone who sat at the long wooden table overlooking Angola's fields. Big Lou, the main White cook, humbly accepted praise for his cooking and was notably frank with strangers.

I once was introduced as the prison's music historian at that table, as small plates of pecan pie made their way around the table. The history of work songs, jazz, gospel, and country music kept the interest of a women's Christian group important enough to lunch there. White evangelical groups had been regulars since 1999 when state legislation privileged faith-based organizations for prison programming in the name of "moral rehabilitation."[6]

On this occasion, the Ranch House was crowded enough to spill the hospitality out to the front of the building. It was the closing day of the Arts and Crafts Festival, and a few dozen of us were invited to eat barbecue, beans, and rice. I managed polite conversations with local officials, church members, friends of the warden, and St. Francisville business owners, waiting for the band to finish their set so we could eat together and talk more about music. It took longer than I anticipated because my presence turned the stage into a musical reunion show. Myron Hodges led musical entertainment that was the equivalent of Big Lou's cooking—entertainment by the best trusty musicians the farm had to offer. An older couple took the opportunity to slow-dance, but for the most part, people waited in line for the buffet and talked as the band played. Larry Wilkerson happened to be on the cook staff. When I greeted him, he leaned in and said quietly, "Hey, you ask Myron to let me play." Knowing how much he and Wilkerson had told me about Megasound and the Big River Band, Wilkerson wanted me to hear it.

Like many other older members of Angola's music scene, Wilkerson had resigned from secular music and committed himself to singing gospel. Hodges waved Wilkerson into the square where the band was corralled. Conspicuous in his white cook-staff outfit, his singing turned heads. Together, Wilkerson and Hodges retraced grooves that had astonished countless festival audiences twenty years earlier (see figure 6.2).

Figure 6.2. Larry Wilkerson and Myron Hodges perform outside the Ranch House, 2013 (photograph by author).

After the performance, A. J. Freeman, Thomas "Fuzzy" Oliver, Calvin Lewis, Johnny Jones, Hodges, and I sat at a table that had been just cleared, and we dug into our lunches. I carefully distributed questions to give everyone ample time to eat. I asked about Wilkerson, who was busy with the cleanup. "He went all gospel on me," said Hodges, "and usually when guys turn gospel at Angola, for some reason they don't want to step outside of that.... I tried to get him to cross over, and he says, 'Nah, I can't do it.'"[7]

In a way, it was a smart move on Wilkerson's part. The influx of well-financed White evangelical groups and Warden Cain's reliance on Christian programming established a plethora of faith-based musical opportunities. The chapel made for an excellent stage. Equipment donations from church groups for services kept instruments updated. The new traveling gospel band now showcased the religious conversion that Cain, a Southern Baptist, championed. Shifts toward the church began in the mid-1990s.

In 1994, President Bill Clinton signed the Violent Crime Control and Law Enforcement Act, which included a provision that denied prisoners access to Pell Grant funding. At Angola, outside church groups filled that vacuum. When Warden Cain arrived in 1995, the New Orleans Baptist Theological Seminary (known as the Bible College) established an undergraduate degree at Angola—the only one attainable.[8] Cain initiated an Inmate Minister Program tied to the Bible College, which paid twenty cents per hour, the highest pay offered to any prisoner. Related, the Inmate Missionary Transfer Program transferred qualified Bible College graduates to other state prisons. The Louisiana Prison Chapel Foundation, a nonprofit organization, developed with a mission to build chapels at Louisiana prisons. To date, private donations and prisoner labor have given rise to five chapels at Angola that also make space for Muslim and Jewish services. Religiosity swept through the prisoner institutions. WLSP, the station that once broadcast Leotha Brown's *Jazz on the River* program, shifted to prerecorded programming from the Moody Bible Institute. Meanwhile, Cain became a regular speaker at megachurches and built elaborate relationships with burgeoning White evangelical groups.[9]

Warden Cain's initiative was a shot in the arm for Angola's prisoner-led spiritual associations. The Full Gospel Businessmen Fellowship, Church of God in Christ, Jehovah's Witnesses, Students of Islam, and United Methodist Men Fellowship moved from self-help clubs to powerful voluntary associations, just as the Lifers' Association had done in the 1970s with Warden Henderson's support and collaboration with outside organizations fighting for prisoners' legal rights.

Then, a 1999 set of statutes and a subsequent revision of the Department of Corrections policy furthered a shift—a new inflection—toward church projects.[10] The statutes made an active tie to religious programming in the name of Louisiana's penitentiary mission:

[T]he department shall direct efforts toward the rehabilitation of [inmates] in order to effect their return to the community as promptly as practicable. In order to accomplish this purpose, the secretary of the Department of Public Safety and Corrections shall establish programs of classification and diagnosis, education... and religious services."[11]

Associationalism, state power flowing through voluntary associations, was still in operation. But state-mandated rehabilitation efforts favored outside and (consequently) inside Christian associations. In another section of the statutes, the door opens for faith-based volunteer groups:

The legislature finds and declares that faith-based programs offered in state and private correctional institutions and facilities have the potential to facilitate inmate institutional adjustment, to help inmates assume personal responsibility, and to reduce recidivism. It is the intent of the legislature that the Department of Public Safety and Corrections and private vendors operating private correctional facilities work toward ensuring the availability and development of such programs at the correctional institutions and facilities of this state and shall continuously:

(1) Measure recidivism rates for all inmates participating in faith-based or religious programs.

(2) Work toward increasing the number of volunteers ministering to inmates from various faith-based institutions in the state.

(3) Develop community linkages with churches, synagogues, mosques, and other faith-based institutions to assist in the release of participants back into the community.[12]

Voluntarism is often touted as the driver of rehabilitative work, but behind the seeming spontaneity is legal access to Angola's operations. Tie that to the still-active trusty system (in this case, harnessing prison labor for event coordination), and the structures of Angola's religiosity become more clear. In a way, goals initiated under the penitentiary model—reduced recidivism and rehabilitation—come full circle to a Christian concept of penance instrumentalized on a former plantation.

The particular mix of Warden Cain's evangelical zeal, prisoners' inability to access Pell Grant funding, and the 1999 statutes greatly inflected Angola's musical sound. The opportunity to fund prisoner events through church organizations provided a windfall, but it also pushed secular music out of the club banquets. Bands chosen for the banquets now supported gospel—a style that had been active for decades but never central. Singers who committed to sacred music, like Larry Wilkerson, generally left the secular bands. Major events involving faith-based institutions (now legally tied to Angola's mission) replaced all-prison holiday events like the Fourth of July festival. For instance, Operation Starting Line, a national coalition of more than twenty faith-based groups founded in 2000, sponsored a major 2002 Easter Sunday concert featuring Aaron Neville and Charlie Daniels, drawing prisoners and wide media attention. The established secular musicians, looking for performance opportunities, all went to the rodeo.

Myron Hodges was able to continue playing secular music styles because he was versatile and dependable. But with narrower opportunities for rock, R&B, and country, Hodges inevitably crowded out other musicians playing and taking administrative roles. The day we ate lunch after the Arts and Crafts Festival, he was a guitarist in the Guts and Glory Band in the crow's nest for rodeo events and with the all-star group at the Ranch House buffet. Paperwork, communication, contingency plans, and drafting security clearances put him in touch with the administration and other midlevel voluntary associations. "I manage the affairs of all the groups of the main prison," he explained, "except for your gospel groups, your chapel groups, and all that. I manage about seven, eight groups that practice in the same music room."[13] It's a big job, managing the room where secular musicians rehearse, a space that they built for themselves.

After sacred groups had moved to newly-built prison chapels and other dedicated rehearsal spaces, secular musicians made a request for about $5,000 and lobbied to use leftover building supplies to build the band room they now occupy. Musicians and a few volunteer prisoners already assigned to construction jobs built the space just outside the recreation department, also paying for twenty-four-hour security stakeouts as they worked. They worked around the clock to convert a shakedown post (where prisoners are searched for contraband) into a relatively soundproofed space. It would have been even more soundproofed, but realizing it would be impossible to get a vacuum cleaner, they scrapped plans to carpet the room.[14] The band room is best understood as part of a larger shift in the prison, in fact, part of a larger shift in the country.

Economic geographer David Harvey argues that the late-twentieth-century US move toward free-market principles relied on evangelicalism.[15] Enabling religious organizations offered an anchor of social stability within neoliberalism, a theory that champions individual risk in expanded free markets. In other words, if markets became riskier, churches could provide salvation. In this view, religion offsets the social dismantling inherent to neoliberalism—the elimination of social services, the elimination of labor organizations, and the elimination of public welfare. This thinking had an effect on Angola's music. The active White evangelical presence, in the name of rehabilitation, created new spaces for some musicians, but importantly, it also impacted where the secular bands could perform, pushing them farther into the marketplace. Evangelical support moved into the prison at the same time corporate sponsorship increased for the rodeo. When I went, Coca-Cola, a local car dealership, and local political candidates vied for advertising attention amidst the spectacle initially designed to draw money into the Inmate Welfare Fund.

Strapped Rodeo Surfaces

The rodeo has a little something for everyone—if you count titillation and outrage. I was already a newly dubbed music historian of the prison when I first attended in 2013. Three main sites drew me: the rodeo arena, the music stages outside the arena, and the hobby craft section where prisoners sold handmade musical instruments among other things. There, I saw many of the musicians I had known for five years and some I had never met.

The day of the rodeo started early. Myron Hodges had risen before dawn on that crisp Sunday morning. All band equipment was already on the three performance stages at the rodeo. Busy in preparation, dozens of musicians had secured releases and allowed time to go through security, now reviewing playlists, tuning up, and getting ready for a full day of music. Hodges was wearing many hats that day. He was playing guitar for the Guts and Glory events band, filling in for a few of the bands on the side stage, and directing the sound reinforcement crew. He knew everyone involved because he had prepared the paperwork for each person two weeks earlier—double-checking names, residence units, and purpose for the movement through security for each musician and sound technician. He knew each prisoner's status well enough to ensure that the documents would move fluidly through the institution, collecting the necessary signatures from assistant wardens and officers without getting stuck for any concern.

Security staff were also up early. They drove Hodges's team to the rodeo site, conducted pat-downs, and relayed the motion to the administration via walkie-talkie. I asked Major Wilfred Cazelot his thoughts on the operation, and he offered plain appreciation. "The main feature of the rodeo is the bulls," he admitted. "But what takes you for the rest of the day are the different bands. If we didn't have inmate bands, look at the money the expense we'd have at hiring a band or three bands to come in and perform."[16] Cazelot's known penchant for country music is a boon for some musicians, opening the door for requests for internet research on new country songs they hear on the radio. Cazelot obliges by printing out lyrics and doing basic research on the performers the prisoners hear on the radio. Having security staff appreciate music helps make performance possible within such a restricted environment.

After hours of soundcheck, Hodges took his seat in front of eight well-used guitar effect pedals and silently checked the tuning on his Stratocaster. He wore a black T-shirt with a logo that identified his primary association. Three small crosses fit between a drawing of a steer skull and an American flag with the words, "Angola Rodeo Guts and Glory Band." He clipped a ballpoint pen to his collar, ready to take notes as he managed many components of the day's production and performed himself.

In the crow's nest, a space marked out high in the rodeo bleachers, Hodges and a few of Angola's top players worked through two hours of semi-improvised songs and themes. They watched the ring with stoicism and vigilance, ready to turn to a new song at any moment to match the action (see figure 6.3). They knew the entire program well, able to create transitions between events, yield to the announcer's voice, and lay into a well-known country, rock, or R&B song as filler during an injury or technical problem in the ring. Occasionally, Hodges took two steps toward the drummer to communicate a revision to the plan.

The event itself dramatizes individual risk. Snippets of "Barracuda" and "Another One Bites the Dust" provided commentary on the action, patriotic music scored the presentation of the American flag, and circus music accompanied the clowns. The music helped structure the long event and at times, without most people noticing it, took the burden off waiting for action in the ring.

I couldn't help noticing a difference in skills between the musicians and the inexperienced participants in the ring. There is a two-week limit for any training for prisoners who volunteer for rodeo events like "Convict Poker," where four sit at a table in the ring and compete to be the last one touching

Figure 6.3. Guts and Glory Band performing in the crow's nest, 2013 (photograph by author).

the table as a wild bull charges them. The rodeo spotlights young prisoners with violent offenses. (If the contestants were drug offenders, the public reaction might not be the same.) Young contestants draw attention, but the associations (bands, clubs, and councils) drive the production. In other words, the professionalism of the band was not scene-stealing. It enabled the spectacle in the ring.

During "Convict Poker," music brought the audience together to watch danger presented as sport. The rhythm invited us to share time with the four men at the table. Like in some dance music, the quick tempo made that sense of time more fine-grained, like the high frame rates of sportscasts. The feel of the music, the familiar melodies, and expected chord changes offered an emotional pole and promise of resolution, as does music that scores a dramatic scene of the film. It is horizontal music (the kind that George Russell introduced Charles Neville to in chapter 3), in this case assuring viewers that eventually one of these men will win the five-hundred-dollar prize for the bravery of not flinching and the luck of not being in the bull's path. Without music, each audience member would have been on their own to make sense of the moment.

The rodeo continues to be important for voluntary associations, and individuals get support through this complex structure of spectacle. The rodeo raises money for the Inmate Welfare Fund by exaggerating differences between prisoners and free people.[17] The scars of incarceration are necessarily obscured, masked by a caricature of prisoners dressed in throwback striped outfits, scars made invisible by the dramatic music scoring the event. In her book *Wounds of Returning*, about current tourism of slave plantations and prisons, Jessica Adams suggests that Angola's rodeo revolves around the "phobias about unstable social boundaries," that "tourists do not have to put much thought into what they are doing, and that is the point."[18] Adams is right, showing how the rodeo plays on discomfort while not actually challenging the audience. In this way, the surface of Angola is different than it was in the 1960s. The Goffmanian ritual (that I adapted into the concept of "surfacework" in chapter 4 to show the social interplay of a Westernaires show) has given way to a different exchange: consumer-driven financial support for titillation. Music, no longer front and center but still played by skilled prisoners, organizes and normalizes the rodeo. It chases away feelings, overheard remarks, and anything else that may distract from the drama of individual risk and sheer guts. Thankfully, there were other places where music played a different role.

Transposed Secular Banquet Surface

Outside the rodeo ring, I walked underneath red, white, and blue plastic pennant banners and past a Coca-Cola semitrailer. Dozens of clubs ran concession stalls. Conventional fare like hamburgers, sausages, loaded baked potatoes, and more unique offerings, like fried Coca-Cola, brought money to prisoners through the associations. On the surface, it was typical for a small fair: people digging for single bills to trade for food in paper containers that would pile up in plastic-lined fifty-five-gallon drums.

Beyond the food stalls, trusty prisoners, dressed in clean white outfits, stationed themselves in stalls and at tables to haggle with wandering shoppers. The routines of an open-air craft market shifted social relationships between free people and prisoners to more ordinary ones, to buyers and sellers. A couple who had driven to the rodeo from Texas loaded a hand-built rocking chair into their truck. A large airbrush painting of a tiger's eyes hung on display for savvy buyers. Dozens of prisoners without trusty status sold wares from within a large cage to the left. Moving back and forth along the outside of the chain-link fence, a trusty brokered the exchange of money and small handicraft goods that would fit through. I bought a duck call to see what the exchange would be like. It felt more like small-time capitalism, in fact. In the distance, a trusty stall with custom-built mandolins beckoned me. But as I walked over, I heard a familiar voice over a microphone.

I followed the sound to a makeshift performance stage underneath a slanted corrugated metal roof. Robin Polk, the bass player formerly of Time Factor and the Big River Band, was introducing his Camp F trusty band, Little Country. James Marsh (who spoke about being one of the few White field workers in chapter 5) was on drums. A banner hung behind him on a chain-link and barbed-wire fence. On it, underneath the band logo, an old joke read, "We play both kinds of music: country & western." Officers on a nearby watchtower listened as Little Country started to play.

Polk smiled when he saw me walk up. We had spent hours over the years talking about his music experiences from 1982 on. Now he had a chance to show me what he and Marsh do now. I wasn't the only familiar face. Friends and relatives milled about underneath. Some sat on camping chairs, eating lunch they just bought from the concession stands. A trusty rodeo worker carried his granddaughter to the keyboard player so she could get close to the music. The keyboard player was far enough to the side that later, his adult daughter managed to walk up and kiss him on the cheek.

Music didn't just provide nostalgia. Music was a presentation of their best selves, perhaps an astonishing one. Family members smiled through the set and saved a seat for their loved one in order to talk once the set was done. The audience was small and intimate. Most people who didn't know the band only paused. As I watched Marsh on drums, I thought of what he had said to me years earlier about playing the bigger stage of the rodeo arena: "You got to understand, my mom's seen me play in little bars. She never imagined at the time that it was five to six thousand people sitting there in this old arena.... It was like sitting in an auditorium and your child is up there doing a play, and you're like 'That's my boy!' It gives you more confidence, makes you want to keep doing what you're doing.... To her, you're a rock star, overnight."[19] His mother had passed, but the performance continued to offer family connections to others.

Many musicians spoke of family connections as central to their performance opportunities. Darren Green of Angola's Most Wanted Band told me:

> I have three kids. My oldest, she just turned nineteen. I have a son. He'll be eighteen in October. My youngest daughter, she'll be fifteen soon. This [Most Wanted Band] is like their family. This is their favorite band. They wish that we could produce CDs and tapes, something that they could listen to all the time. The last Sunday in October, they're telling me, "Dad, I can't wait to come back and see y'all in April." They just love coming to see this band play. They give all the guys a hug 'cause, like I said, it's like part of their family. My kids just love these guys.[20]

I stayed through a few songs, knowing enough not to intrude too much on family time, and made my way to the old rodeo ring, which now featured other bands throughout the day. I wanted to be sure to catch the Jazzmen and the Pure Heart Messengers. They had performed for my film, but I had never seen them play for a free-world audience.

I made my way back through the maze of hobby craft stalls to the old arena, a bit late to the set. "Here we go! Here we go" rang out from the side stage, the word "go" landing strongly on the downbeat. Ray Jones from the Pure Heart Messengers danced with a girlfriend he had made postincarceration. The Jazzmen broke into a New Orleans funk free-jam, inviting a keyboardist and a drummer from the audience to the stage. Both men had played with Jazzmen keyboardist Johnny Jones decades ago. They were there to see him.

"That drummer was awesome," Jones told me later about Rodney Rollins, "I've been knowing him for a long time. . . . We got plenty of buddies that come up here and get up and jam with us. That was like old times. You get a bunch of New Orleans musicians together, and they just go berserk on stage. I felt that old-time, back in 1970–80. Yeah, 80s."[21] Rollins held down the distinctive swung adaptation of the tresillo pattern of second-line music, filled with syncopated snare work. The regular drummer from the Jazzmen, now in the crowd, broke into a second-line dance, taken by the music. Trustys and free people alike danced, talked, and recorded video with their phones (see figure 6.4).

Rollins hopped off the stage after having obliged the Jazzmen's request. "Yeah, man, I appreciate you so much," he heard over the mic from behind him. "Thank you, brother!" I asked one of the Jazzmen what he thought about the impromptu jam. "Man, it was excellent," he replied. "We always enjoy somebody from the free world coming to play because we get so much experience from them. . . . I was amazed. He done made my day. I don't even have to play no more today." Calvin Lewis, president of the Jazzmen association, jumped on the drum kit and attempted to rein the audience back in. "All right! How's everybody out there?" A few drum hits briefly overpowered the

Figure 6.4. Dancing to the Jazzmen at the music stage outside the rodeo ring, 2013 (photograph by author).

crowd noise, spread across the old rodeo field that now lay in the shadow of the new 10,000-seat rodeo arena.

After introducing myself, I asked Rollins what it was like to play with the Jazzmen. It turned out that he was the drummer for the Humphrey Davis Band and Bourbon Street stalwart Big Al Carson. Over the sound of instruments tuning through the PA, recalibrating for the upcoming Jazzmen number, he burst into a smile. "Oh man, it was wonderful. It's a pleasure. It was wonderful to play with them guys. The joy, and sharing the love of the music industry. And we've all been doing it a long time."[22] It was the answer you get from someone playing a reunion show or a special tribute event for an end-of-career musician. In a way, it's just like that. The Jazzmen are the musicians missing from New Orleans, like the Nic Nacs before them, tied up 135 miles north. "It's an honor for me to play with those cats," he said of being invited to play with what was essentially the house band. "It felt the same, just like if we was doing a gig in a nightclub and stuff like that. It's the same feeling. It's no different. We all are human, you know."

I stayed for the rest of the set and later introduced myself to a new member of the Jazzmen, Andre Williams, a young keyboard player beginning his sixty years for armed robbery. He had worked hard to get it reduced from seventy years. Williams first joined a church choir, hoping to be part of something positive, something connected to his upbringing. "The thing about penitentiary is," he explained, "you're either going to find religion, or you're going to find sin. There's no 'in the middle.'" A few members of the Jazzmen had heard him in the choir and noticed his potential. For Williams, the elite association of the Jazzmen promised refuge. "I feel like I stick out. I wear glasses. I went to college. I don't believe in a lot of the habits around here." I asked him to clarify what he meant by "habits." "You know, penitentiary living: homosexuality, gambling, fighting, masculinity, you know. Everybody wants to run something, and we're all in prison. I don't get that at all. Nobody wants to come together and try to find everybody a way out. They just want to step on everybody, like crabs in a bucket."[23] Williams found meaning, focus, development, and camaraderie in association. He told me about writing music for and singing in musical theater productions, giving purpose to his constant songwriting, which he does alone when he can't get in front of a keyboard.

Playing club events with the Jazzmen gave him access to food and tobacco, putting him into the bartering economy of the prison. He explained, "Whatever you need, you have to have cigarettes. That's the currency around here—tobacco and food." Playing for cigarettes and food clarified his relationships with others. He didn't receive favors. He participated in clear economic exchange. "Say you need some shoes," he illustrated:

> Nobody [takes] your money. You pay them in cigarettes to get your shoes. It's illegal, all around the board. You ain't supposed to do it, and the rules and regulations says one inmate is not supposed to give another inmate anything, but it's strange how the rules bend when they don't want to give anything to help you do anything. You have to be here three years before you can even get incentive pay. I just made three years. That gives me two cents an hour. I mean, come on, are you serious?! But you know, anyway, what can I do? But my singing helps me out. Everybody wants somebody to come sing at their clubs. They do favors for you. They sell you trades.[24]

Angola continues to substitute an economy driven by volunteerism for state allocations to support its incarcerated citizens. That economy has continued to shift to tourism.

Hostile Takeover

Across the decades, rodeo revenues grew and state budgets for prison operations shrank. In 2000, the administration dissolved the Inmate Welfare Fund (formerly known as the Inmate Lending Fund) by replacing the prisoner members of the committee. They took control of rodeo finances that prisoner associations had managed for decades. Call it a hostile takeover. A newly created Inmate Rodeo Committee was tasked with planning the event, but with limited power. Administrators courted local businesses in nearby St. Francisville, building a new revenue stream through advertising that added to high-ticket sales. Myron Hodges had explained the impact of the takeover to me well before I attended the rodeo. It reduced musicians' access to financial power by fracturing the associations' official banking system. Afterward, the clubs that held the biggest pieces of the remaining financial system were the religious ones. Hodges explains:

> Before, when a band wanted to purchase band equipment, they would go to the Inmate Welfare Fund to get the money for that. So now the Inmate Welfare Fund is no more, so the bands don't have nowhere to go to get their band equipment. So now everybody have to latch on to a club who would

perhaps sponsor them. The money that's generated by clubs isn't nearly as great as the money that [was] generated by the Inmate Welfare Fund as a whole.

With the Bible College, NOTBS, when that came in, that started a whole of faith-based movement in the prison. And then there was some legislation that was pretty much saying, "Hey, look, we're not going to make it a law, but we going to say, 'Hey, you know, it's okay for the Department of Corrections or the institutions if they want to expand their faith-based arena in institutions. We condone that.'" It just became a movement. So, people now who get these degrees, when they become associated with clubs or propose a club charter to the DOC, usually it's predicated upon something faith-based. Because now they're feeling like, "Okay, we're going to benefit from this as individuals, just because this is something that can perhaps get me out of prison or help me make a better impression upon some part of the board—the review board, or something like that.

So, everybody kind of jumped on that bandwagon, you know, like "I can get this free college education here and I can go somewhere with it. Perhaps it's going to help get me out of prison, or help me be a better person, or help me become a preacher," you know what I'm saying? Helping to start a church. And people just got on that bandwagon. So now, the same people that used to come and ask me for my rock band or for my R&B band or for my Megasound band, . . . now they come and say, "Hey, look, man, I got a worship and praise team up here. Would you come help me arrange some music for them?" Or "We're putting together a new gospel band," or, "My gospel band is playing at the rodeo, man. Would you please come and sit in with us?"[25]

As a result, the faith-based associations became the financial backbone. During the same time, the growth of the rodeo created more performance opportunities for musicians. Hodges again explains:

At one time, if you wasn't playing country music, you couldn't play a rodeo. When that started changing, it was like, "Look, man, we going to expand this rodeo. We going to make as much money as we can at the rodeo, and the best way to do that is to expand everything, including our music. We're not going to just have country because everybody that come to the rodeo don't want to hear country. We're going to have as much as we can, so we going to have some gospel bands out there." Who ever heard of *gospel* at a rodeo?! "But we're going to have that in Angola. We're going to have gospel at this rodeo. Yeah, we're going to keep our country. We want country at our rodeo. Oh yeah, some R&B—yeah, we want that. A rock band? We're going to do some rock."

So, they just took the stage that was in the old rodeo arena, and they just kind of boxed it in, and they said, "Look, this stage is going to house any band that want to play out here at the rodeo grounds. It doesn't matter what you are—gospel, R&B, blah, blah, blah." But what that did it made it impossible for a band to get paid for playing a rodeo because there's no Inmate Welfare Fund, and no rodeo fund or general fund is going to pay thirty-something musicians, forty-something musicians for playing a rodeo.[26]

Gone are the days when musicians could earn twenty dollars for a rodeo performance to reinvest in the band or to request funds from the Inmate Welfare Fund. Except for the band in the crow's nest, musicians play the rodeo to see family and old friends, to meet new people, and to step outside themselves for the day.

Associated musicians at Angola have lost their institutions—primarily banking and education. They shifted to a tourism economy and church patronage. Competing for gigs, the bands continue to leverage flexible skills to reinvent themselves as work opportunities become more dynamic and unpredictable. And, like many musicians today, they are told that they will get exposure even though they are not paid. In the case of Angola, however, that speculative labor overlaps with the hope of getting out, which for many means securing release from a life sentence. Playing in a band can attract the attention of supporters for their cases, recommendations for parole, or documentation of productive activity while incarcerated. Without many institutions, music-making is now more than ever an individual speculative endeavor. Pockets of the interassociational banquet activism and prisoner sublime remain from the 1970s (described in chapter 4), though organizations like the ACLU or the Sentencing Project are unlikely to take a trip to the rodeo to have a meeting.

Banjo Scars

At the end of the day, I left the rodeo without making it over to the instrument makers. Part of me was more committed to seeing the performances of musicians I knew—a lingering sense of obligation I've developed from being a performer myself. Another part of me wanted to avoid the possibility of playing a subpar instrument. I'm pretty transparent when assessing stringed instruments. I grew up with poorly constructed instruments my family displayed on the living room wall, bought from vendors in Africa and Asia while on vacation. I was worried I'd find that what was for sale was just the aura of a prisoner-made artifact.[27]

A few days later, I roamed the main prison, following up on a few interviews. That's when I met William Hall, known as "Red," an amateur string player who had carved out a niche in the recreation department making banjos (see figure 6.5). I might have run across his stall near the rodeo arena. A middle-aged White man with a gentle demeanor, Hall explained how he made his four- and five-string banjos and their cases.

Initially, we focused on materials and his resourcefulness. Due to limitations, he makes frets out of hardwood. The original plans are from a March 1985 issue of a woodworkers' magazine. Hall sold his first banjo to another prisoner who could afford the high cost of the materials, a prominent member of the Bible College who gave it to his daughter for her sixteenth birthday.

Figure 6.5. William Hall in his woodshop in the recreation building, 2013 (photograph by author).

RECAPITULATION 255

When I asked about the backstory to his banjo-making, he slipped into a monologue that warrants a quote in length. It started with him as a child in Georgia with divorced parents, being raised by his mother and estranged from his father.

> I hadn't seen him in a long time—about ten years. Mom used to always threaten me because she had money, and he didn't. "I'm going to send you to your daddy!" I reached my teen years and said, "Well, send me to my daddy!" My dad was smarter than most, and he said, "Well, look. We'll give it a two-week trial run, see if we like each other or we want to kill each other. We'll decide then."
>
> He had a banjo hanging on his wall. He said, "Here's a little father-son project we could do, spend some time together, get to know each other. We'll build *you* a banjo." I was more interested in the woodworking than the banjo playing at the time or just spending time with him. I had a lot of hero worship for him. So, we spent the time together. We built a banjo, and that was really cool. The banjo I built, the only difference was [mine] had metal frets, and he had wooden frets.
>
> So, we decided I was going to stay, and this time, he wanted custody so he wouldn't have to repeat past mistakes. So, with custody, we had to get an attorney. The attorney wanted money. We didn't have money. So, we took the banjos down to the music store to get them appraised. This would have been 1985. The man behind the counter said, "I'll give you five hundred dollars apiece for them right now." So, we took the banjos to the attorney, let him decide which one he wanted, and he picked mine. So, I didn't have the banjo but a couple of weeks. I was just getting a feel for just holding it, much less playing it, when I lost it.[28]

Hall abruptly cut forward to the early 1990s, just after his incarceration.

> When I really started getting settled in the prison, in population, I had an opportunity to do a few things strictly for me. Dad's getting old. His health is failing. I got his banjo. I got something I can hold on to of his.... I started building the banjos again as a way to reconnect and spend time with Dad.... I got him to send me the plans, and I built one. Then I built two...[29]

Without my asking, he shifted to how the process of building banjos became meaningful in prison.

[Dad's] a woodworker, so anything I do with wood, I learned it all from him. In my heart and in my mind, I'm spending time with him. . . . I don't get to talk to him every day, but I can work with wood every day. I remember all his little safety tips, all his little quality tips, and talking about the different woods.

I've got tons of books on how to play different musical instruments. I don't have a single woodworking book in here. He taught me all that. He sat me down, showed me, walked me through it. So, whenever I do it, I'm still spending time with him. . . . It's almost like prayer time with God. You don't always have to verbalize. You just have to acknowledge the presence. . . . That's some quality time. Keep you sane. Gives you a little escape hatch from the penitentiary.[30]

I'm tempted to draw in theories of embodied knowledge, marshal poststructural French terms like "habitus" and recent ideas in ethnomusicology about the "paramparic body," unspoken knowledge carried socially through our bodies.[31] But it's not what he said, it's Hall's *use of testimony* that has a legacy at Angola.

Before I had hit "record," Hall looked at me over his glasses and asked, "You want to do this?" He asked for consent to move into the register of what I called "surfacework" in chapter 4. I understood his caveat better after his story, when he elicited the same compassion I felt for Jewell Spotville when he had cried about singing for his mother at the rodeo. Showing his scars, Hall simultaneously presented me with his truth and a performance of his truth. It made me a into surface by sympathetically and momentarily placing some of the burden of incarceration on me. Had I bought his banjo, his scars would be the aura of a banjo made in prison, a story for me to deploy whenever a guest asked me about the banjo with the wooden head and frets.

I wonder if Hall's story is like creative nonfiction, or even something closer to music. Isn't music understood to be just this: a performance connected to authentic expression but not necessarily dependent on a real feeling of the moment? At Angola, this practice is tied to the history of outward-facing musical performance—a decades-long development of surfaces. It also is structured by an administration that gives outsiders access, selects prisoners to engage with, and monitors the conversation. But rather than making these stories less truthful, I believe it complicates the truth by adding palpable layers of power, surveillance, and emotion.

Playing Politics

During the time I visited Angola, sacred music predominated. Laird Veillon told me as much in an early interview, comparing the scene in 2008 to when he arrived in the mid-1980s: "Back then, there were more secular groups and fewer gospel groups. Now there's like two secular bands.... Everything else is gospel band. It's all geared around that."[32] Indeed, when I first arrived, the administration referred me to the Pure Heart Messengers, the Main Prison Gospel Band, and Resurrection (a Christian rock group). Robin Polk explained, "You got *rap* gospel, they do *country* gospel, *soul* gospel, it's all mixed."[33]

In my early discussions, many musicians in religious bands offered me versions of religious conversion stories (scripts familiar to many born-again Christians) when telling me about the importance of music in their lives. These stories resonate with evangelicals, who can point to the very hour when God broke into their own lives as proof of their spiritual commitment.[34] Ray Jones, front man for the Pure Heart Messengers, built on Veillon's assessment of the gospel-centric music scene with evangelical polish:

> God has taken a land. I used to sing R&B, and I was good at it. When I come to Angola, I did it. Like I said, I was converted. I got into the gospel, and I love the life that I live in Christ. It's a great experience. It's just a forever wonderment for me to experience all the change that begins with the individuals themself.... We must focus upon discipline in ourself and to the things that we're doing.[35]

Many prisoners adopt self-discipline in response to incarceration through a vigilant moral commitment and the project of the self.[36] The themes of conversion told by imprisoned musicians are attractive because of the overlap between spiritual notions of rehabilitation and musical commitment, and they resonate with Angola's new visitors.

Gospel performance is another way of showing scars, a moral exchange that trades unveiling the pains of incarceration for sympathy and aid. Examples of musical scars include the added context to the Dixie Hummingbirds' classic song "I'll Keep on Living After I Die" when the singer himself is likely to die at Angola serving a life sentence. Or consider the power of song and testimony in my film, when the Pure Heart Messengers sing, "There's a blessing store for me," and Jewell Spotville says afterward, "I've been locked up here thirty-five, thirty-six years. I'm waiting on my blessing. I believe by faith, God going to deliver me out of this place."[37] This presentation of prison scars, rooted in implausible hope for release, prompts the kind of offerings that evangelicals are prepared to bring—monetary donations, group prayer, correspondence, and advocacy. But there are many more agendas at play.

Black men convicted of violent crimes, now singing about God, make for easy public relations for the prison.[38] No doubt, the Pure Heart Messengers are sincere in their faith. But the deep resonance of spiritual personal testimony, couched in Blackness and a criminal record, leads audiences to believe that prison has done well to pacify and restore order. The *prison's* performance, using gospel singers as a proxy, involves a sleight-of-hand, drawing attention to individuals and away from structural changes to the prison. In fact, Angola is more peaceful because most have aged out of violent tendencies.[39] Many of the results of prisoner activism in the 1970s led to structural changes that reduced violence. The convictions that predominate at Angola today also tend to be for nonhabitual crimes.

For instance, many studies show that murder tends to be a once-in-a-lifetime mistake. Samuel L. James, the nineteenth-century overseer of the plantation, knew this. The prototype of the trusty system he initiated placed men and women with the same convictions that the Pure Heart Messengers had—murder—in the big house as servants. He knew from experience that they could be trusted over those with nonviolent habitual convictions like robbery.[40] As the new iteration of trusty prisoners, gospel singers gain value by astonishing evangelical visitors.

There was always religious singing at Angola, from the "Véxilla Regis" sung by French colonists by Sugar Lake in 1699 to the church services that Isaac Franklin established on his plantation in the 1840s to the prisoner funeral that Stella Johns witnessed in the early 1900s to the singers that John Lomax passed on when scouting for "sinful tunes" in 1934 to John Henry Taylor Jr.'s Gospel Melodies in the 1980s. So why then, at the apex of spiritual activity at the prison and with the most substantial legal support for religious voluntary associations, did John Henry Taylor Jr., featured in chapter 5, quit the Gospel Melodies? I continue to ask this question. I wrote about it in my dissertation.[41] I published an article about it.[42] I featured his explanation in my film.[43] I find it helpful to learn about music by listening to its disappearance.

In person, Taylor was a compelling figure, dignified and stubborn. His baritone voice was strong, his vibrato distinctive, and his command over a gospel quartet formidable. Yet, when I met him, he was a solitary figure. Members of the Pure Heart Messengers had pointed me to him as the "father of the gospel scene."[44] Taylor was part of their conversion stories. By their accounts, he led them from singing R&B to knowing the ins and outs of gospel harmony. Early on, they dramatized my search for the roots of Angola's gospel renaissance. Albert Patterson suggested including him in my film. "I think that he would be quite an addition if he would come back at his age now," he said. "I've been talking to him about church, but you know, it's going to be hard to convince him."[45] Indeed, Taylor was elusive and at times, obstinate.

Taylor was known as "The Road-Walker," because he had the coveted job of picking up trash on the road circling the main prison by himself. "I walk around sometimes twice a day and once a day," he explained plainly. "After that, I come in. I don't have very much to do. I just do a little walking and talking, praying and singing."[46]

Taylor chose the perimeter of the main prison over the surfaces of the prison he once dominated as an in-demand gospel singer. His new job gave him freedom *from* association, freedom to walk alone and sing. He let me follow him with my film crew on two separate occasions (see figure 6.6).

Each time, he donned a reflective vest and walked out of the main prison with a long trash picker pin in one hand and a white plastic bucket in the other. He explained the importance of the vest to me: "This protects me on the road, shows that I'm a trusty. Without this, they might think that I'm

Figure 6.6. John Henry Taylor singing on the perimeter of the main prison, 2009 (still from *Follow Me Down*).

trying to escape."[47] Once he got to the perimeter road, he sang to himself. His singing gave him freedom away from others. It was as close to a field holler as I ever recorded:

> Savior, Savior,
> Hear my humble cry;
> While on others Thou art calling,
> Do not pass me by.

It's a well-known song. "Pass Me Not, O Gentle Savior" had been recorded by Bob Dylan, M. C. Hammer, and many others. A few cars drove past as he picked up litter, walking the gravelly edge of the road.

I interviewed him at length about why he quit singing with groups, adding to what I learned from other musicians. He wasn't one to spill stories. His sense of uprightness kept him from speaking poorly about anyone. (Or maybe it was an old habit of guarding your words amidst a fiery rumor mill.) Eventually, I put together enough of his story and edited it together for my film. Here's the part after he describes building up a new group, replacing released members of the Gospel Melodies. After all that work, he was moved to one of the camps:

> I got transferred and went to Camp H. When I came back over, the group was in another man's hands. And he started giving the group some *by-laws*. That's something we didn't need. And I told them, I said, this group here has never been run by by-laws. We are all men. We all come together in agreement.
>
> Laws were made for people that do wrong. That's why they have to have laws, for people that do wrong. If you ain't going to do right, we don't even need you in the group. 'Cause I don't put no law on no man to force no man to do nothing. That's why I had the group like I had it. So, I said, "Well, I ain't going to do this. I'm going to let them learn for theyselves."[48]

When I first heard John Taylor complain about by-laws, I thought it was strange. The idea that imprisoned musicians would establish by-laws strayed from the idea that art could create a niche or sanctuary, metaphors that many scholars use to describe semisovereign spaces that prisoners create in prison.[49] I later wrote about Taylor's complaint about by-laws as evidence of disenfranchisement, that he returned to the Gospel Melodies only to find it more similar to a prison bureaucracy than a voluntary fellowship.[50] When I screened *Follow Me Down* throughout the country, I could count on audiences chuckling at the mention of "by-laws," whether screening inside or outside of prisons.

In my sense of things, Taylor's story epitomized the ethical debate about doing art for the "right" reasons. The idea of by-laws being part of the spontaneous collaboration of harmony singing seemed ridiculous. Little did I know that by-laws were at the heart of Angola's associations, the very places where individuals could find limited freedom in sanctioned collaboration. The by-laws of the gospel groups were private laws restricted to the association's domain. They have been part of the fabric of freedom woven into the unfreedom of Angola for decades. By-laws came with suretyship and the deliverable public good that the association provided. But after Warden Cain's arrival in 1997, associationalism became a more integral part of religious practice.

Following the 1999 revised Louisiana statutes that opened Angola's door to evangelical groups, the spiritual and penitentiary missions blurred into the organizational space that existed between the administration and the individual prisoner. (Recall Joseph Mouledous's concept of "interstitiality" in chapter 2 used to describe the gradients of power from warden to "inmate guard-trusties" to "gunmen.")[51] No doubt, the heightened religious club activity made the prison safer and many prisoners more solvent, but recognize that *any kind* of associational activity granting administrative power to prisoner clubs can ward off outlawry because it provides meaningful social structure.

With a legal mandate to include religious organizations in rehabilitation efforts and an infrastructure of prisoner clubs, Angola became a beacon for evangelical groups. That changed Taylor's relationship to group singing. Religiosity grew in the associations and the associations began to organize religiosity. Increasingly, Taylor found himself in a crowded field amidst other singers who negotiated the many agendas found on Angola's surfaces. With an aging population, desperation to get out of Angola grew, drawing more into a gospel scene supported by new outside church groups. Taylor's resignation from gospel says less about the administration's encroachment than it does about how the 1999 statutes changed the nature of volunteerism in twenty-first-century Angola.

As with today's concerns over increasing corporate sponsorship in free-world arts presentations, support from White evangelical groups presents

262 INSTRUMENT OF THE STATE

contrasting systems of value.[52] For Taylor, the shift was so significant that he saw current practices as categorically different. "They got a group," he said of the sacred musical fare that the administration supported when I interviewed him, but "the only group that I can tell you that is trying to get solid is the one at Camp F. These over here [the main prison], they're not solid. They're more like politicians. They accept glory. They're lookin' for prestige. They love to go outside, but they're not really real. If they were real, I would be there."[53] The emergence of virtuosic gospel singing, onstage, microphone in hand, enabled by myriad White evangelical tourists, is a shade of difference from Taylor's earlier gospel practice, one rooted in unspoken principles of harmony. For him, politics got in the way of practice when gospel moved to the evangelical surface of the prison.

Association for Rights

For Angola's incarcerated musicians, the band room is the center of the prison. It's a distinctive space that preserves the small but significant freedoms developed by musicians for decades, a place away from ordinary prison life for rehearsing, planning, learning, and creating together. A close read of the details of the room brings out these important, yet precarious freedoms based on an American sense of rights.

The first thing I noticed about the plywood door, the only door to the small band room, was its doorknob, the kind with a centered twist lock. It's not the kind that opens with the large keys that guards use for the gates, but one that anyone can twist once they are inside, also called a "privacy lock." These are more often used in administrative offices than in the spaces that prisoners use. The more I thought about that knob, I saw it as part of a more elaborate system that offered privacy to musicians granted access to the room.

Getting to the band room took getting through at least three sallyports and a few locked gates, down a set of steps to a rectangular patch of grass, and then up a half-dozen steps. Once inside, the world was filled with instrument cases, a mixing board, a PA system, a mustard-yellow watercooler, and a drum kit, illuminated by the fluorescent overhead light, muted only by the off-white paint on the cinderblock walls (see figure 6.7).

Privacy there was unusual for a prisoner. So was the relative quietness of the space. Even for me, it was striking to arrest the constant noise of the prison. The windowless twenty-by-twenty-foot room was a refuge from a

Figure 6.7. Mickey Lanerie and Laird Veillon in the band room at the main prison, 2008 (photograph by author).

soundscape filled with men's constant chatter and sporadic metallic clanks. Soundproofing material behind the walls also kept sounds from getting outside. Musicians could be loud and unrehearsed. They could also keep inevitable arguments out of earshot, keeping up the impression that musicians all got along, that music magically brought people together.

Considering it as a musician, the space filled my imagination. How would I value this if I were here? I found easy answers from the musicians I met there. "I wish I could stay in the band room. I wish I could move my bunk in the band room. It's like a freedom zone for me," said Laird Veillon.[54] "It's basically like a hobby shop except the people in the hobby shop make money, and we don't," cracked Calvin Lewis. He then continued more seriously, "Basically, that's what it is. It's something where you can go to be at peace."[55] Guitarist Russell Joe Beyer followed with, "It's one of the few things that I guess still bring you happiness in here, 'cause you don't have much."[56] Their attitudes certainly reflect senses of sanctuary, niche, or haven.

To outside audiences, individual privacy and artistic production in the austere prison setting are often meaningfully linked. They affirm broader values of rugged individualism and liberal concerns over the pain of incarceration. These different but related understandings of so-called outsider art stress different components of a shared equation: *talent + constriction = prison art*. Rugged individualists see talent defeating the constriction. Liberal audiences see the humanity of talent within the inhumanity of incarceration. Both perspectives, however, hinge on an American sense of constitutional rights that bear on privacy: maintaining personal beliefs (First Amendment), to be secure in person and possessions (Fourth Amendment), and liberty (Fourteenth Amendment) against all odds.

Left out of this symbolic equation of "prison art" is collaboration and how prisoners gain rights (or something at least close to rights) to make art. Sanctuary provides freedom *from*. But charter, a fundamental part of associations at Angola, offers freedom *to*. Back to the twist-lock on the band room door: there are two essential aspects of freedom in the band room—the security it enables (freedom *from* ordinary prison) and the ability to twist it in either direction (freedom *to* be musicians). Music brings out the latter freedom, and many of these freedoms in the United States are based on a constellation of legal rights.

Many prisoners' rights efforts in the United States center on the Eighth Amendment—freedom from "cruel and unusual punishments inflicted." Many of the daily freedoms that musicians describe, however, are permissions, which like permits, are ways the state grants individuals liberty to use state resources. If you've been to a state park in the United States, gone fishing or hunting there, or reserved a picnic table at a municipal park, you have received a permit. This formal process dampens your sense of entitlement but still allows you a sense of freedom. Land and resources are still public but managed by the state. In this way, your right passes through state management.

The distinction between rights and privileges characterizes the band room and its equipment. While the band room may give prisoners a sense of liberty, that liberty is, in fact, curtailed by the state's power over the prisoners granted by the Thirteenth Amendment.[57] There is a difference between liberty and privileges. Needing permission discourages the notion that any prisoner is entitled to musical instruments, just as needing to get a fishing license discourages the notion that a catfish belongs to anyone who can catch it. But there are three crucial differences between band room privileges and actual liberty: Imagine needing to go through a state agency to walk down a sidewalk. Imagine that the permitting agency is highly unreliable. And imagine that everything—including you and each one of your associates—is state property. Those conditions reflect "liberty" within prison. The state retains authority over the distribution of privileges.

Most literature on art and education programs in US prisons focuses on incentive systems.[58] That goal-oriented view is no stranger to Angola. Gary Frank, the free-staff director of the recreation department, told me about the importance of instituting musical privileges:

> They don't want to lose that [privilege]. Warden Cain is really straight on that. He says, "I don't take these things from you. You take them from you." If a guy messes up in the band room, he tells them.... They kind of police each other pretty good. When I first got here, I wondered how that worked. I said, "How does that work with all these instruments in there as potential weapons?" But there's never any trouble in there. Never. Never a fight or anything like that.[59]

Keep in mind, Frank worked primarily with individuals wanting to check out a guitar, for instance, to play in the corner of the gym. The added layer of rights-through-permit at Angola is something different. It is the legacy of associations. The band room has given musicians more autonomy from the recreation department because bands are chartered voluntary groups. If state resources are managed through the prison administration, associational activity passes the state's power to the network of chartered bands with official membership, by-laws, and surety. And although that power is precarious and conditional, it is part of an exchange: volunteering to play in an unpaid, in-house band for any event that the administration may need and, in return, securing the rights through permission.

In the first year of my talking to musicians at Angola, it always seemed odd that bands all had unique origin stories tied to specific institutional needs. I am used to origin stories of famous bands that center on a creative idea, a gregarious artistic personality, or an unwavering desire for success. My own experience forming bands failed to acknowledge simpler things like my access to space—a garage or basement or university rehearsal room—that depended on property rights my community had. Jazz origin stories—especially those among musicians experiencing less private privilege—often gloss over how musicians first got access through public school programs or churches and how they used venues after working hours for rehearsal spaces. The incarcerated musicians at Angola were always cognizant of the rationale behind musical groups. It was a way of guarding their claim to state resources.

Most secular band origin stories at Angola sprang from a rodeo need. Member Mickey Lanerie explained how the country band Angola's Most Wanted began.

> The band was originally started for the rodeo. You had Warden [Captain] Mike Roberts that came here, and he wanted to kick off a country and western band. That's why on the logo it says, "Angola's Most Wanted, Country and Western Band." Through the years, they kind of changed up with a little old rock 'cause a lot of people like hearing that, they enjoy it. But it actually originally started to be a rodeo country band. It's been torn down, pieced back together, torn down, pieced back together. We've been around since about 2000, 2001, something like that.[60]

Similarly, when band room orderly Matthew Trent brought me to the Pure Heart Messengers, he said, by introduction, "They were created to bring about a new and better sound out in the rodeo arena for the rodeo."[61] The Jazzmen, now the longest-running active band at Angola, were chartered to provide R&B to the rodeo. But they also preserve some of the jazz traditions in jam sessions in the band room. Myron Hodges and Matthew Morgan got sponsorship from Assistant Warden Mike Roberts to exclusively entertain parties at the Ranch House with country music.[62]

Being a chartered member of one of these groups brings privileges of using and securing property, assembly, and a greater freedom of movement about the prison. My description of gaining rights through permissions is not a legal analysis but rather an investigation into how musical associations grant power to individual members. In the US, constitutional rights are embedded into daily life. They radiate out into seemingly small actions and beliefs. They are the reason you might not think twice about walking on a sidewalk, speaking your mind, or turning away a door-to-door solicitor. Life in prison requires a rethinking of rights and the ability to find rights in privileges.

Property

Private property rights are central to the US Constitution and a fundamental aspect of American exceptionalism.[63] The Fourth Amendment guarantees that the "right of the people to be secure in their persons, houses, papers, and effects, against unreasonable searches and seizures, shall not be violated."[64]

In prison, many musicians complain about the lack of storage and security for their instruments. Some instruments are sent to them by family members, some purchased from other prisoners, some given as gifts, and some purchased by the state. Keeping them safe is a significant challenge. A small metal box for personal effects in the dorms provides too small a space to hold instruments. Even if it did, searches and seizures often disrupt personal property. All are affected by the searches that follow the discovery of drugs or cellphones, even those who follow rules. Belongings are often disrupted, damaged, or taken by careless and unpredictable searches. Having a band room, however, meant more than just safer instruments.

The transformation of a shakedown shack into a band room was highly symbolic for the musicians. In prison, sleeping, showering, and defecating—in fact, any daily activity—is always in the open. More dramatically, strip searches and pat-downs are institutional invasions of privacy that constantly humiliate prisoners. As a shakedown shack right off the recreation department, the small building was a reminder that you were untrustworthy, always suspect of walking back to the dorms with something from the recreation department. Converted to a band room, that same space became an emblem of privacy. The lock on the door and its independence from the recreation department changed the building's function. It provided privacy—the Fourth Amendment right otherwise lost in prison. There were practical gains with the conversion as well.

If it weren't for the band room, music at Angola might have revolved around what ethnomusicologist Gavin Steingo calls the "aesthetics of propinquity" or put more simply, what you can make by whatever you can have within arm's reach, whatever you can guard against being stolen or broken.[65] Gaining the right to secure musical equipment is not as simple as twisting a door lock. Rather, being a member of a chartered band brings security, a way of using the constant surveillance and security of prison to your advantage, to be able to walk away from a room full of expensive equipment knowing that it was safe.

Property scholar Craig Anthony Arnold describes property as a "web of interests," which he defines as "a set of interconnections among persons, groups, and entities each with some stake in an identifiable . . . object, which is at the center of the web."[66] Angola's trusty system and interlinked associations work to guarantee the resources of the room, as best as possible. Securing an instrument in the band room by marshaling help from prisoners, administration, and guards hews close to Arnold's definition of property and Fourth Amendment rights in prison: a web of interests.

Matthew Trent's job as band room orderly is to broker among musicians who always want new equipment, an administration reluctant to spend money on gear, and audiences who expect an event to proceed without a technical glitch. "We have a lot of people come in here, and we need to be as professional as possible. So, I take the job serious," he told me.[67] Through use and a clear justification, instruments gain more than monetary value. They gain what philosopher Walter Benjamin called "cult value," the value given to objects controlled and then revealed as part of ritual or participation in an event.[68] In the privacy of the band room, musicians lay claim to instruments that only they can use, by virtue of their collective talent, to draw audiences to the rodeo and entertain visitors. They claim rights to securing property by being useful musicians within a complex web of interests.

Assembly

Custody, a central mission of the vast majority of prisons, impinges on the freedom to assemble, a right guaranteed by the First Amendment of the US Constitution: "the right of the people peaceably to assemble, and to petition the Government for a redress of grievances." In prison, assignment through a classification office usually determines those with whom you live, those next to whom you sleep, and those with whom you work, making it hard to assemble with people of your choice. Cliques have always formed at Angola, but since they are technically uncharted by the administration, they lack many of the resources that sponsored associations have. Clubs rooted in prison enterprise secure entitlement of classification, of choosing who is in the group. In other words, by being a member, you gain more power to assemble.

The band room, supporting the prison's many events directly, has more autonomy from the recreation or education departments. Musicians there gain some freedom in being able to choose bandmates. Frederick Jones, who had completed thirty-three years at Angola, appreciated the predictability of being in the company of the Jazzmen behind closed doors, even though it never guaranteed agreement:

> You're dealing with stable people. We kind of form a little union with each other. Because in here, we argue amongst ourselves all the time, but there's still a peace within the argument because we basically know where we stand with everybody....

RECAPITULATION 269

> We try not to allow anybody in here that's gonna be what we call disruptive—that's gonna change the atmosphere that we have in here. Like I said, although sometimes we argue amongst ourselves, we never look at it. It's nothing serious. 'Cause if you've been in a band, you know that sometimes, within the musicians, you see things differently, you feel things differently, and it takes a while to agree, ... to get everybody on the same page. But this is home. This is home to some people to get away from all the other things—to get away from everything. Just get this room and close that little door, we be okay.[69]

Separately, Jesse Lee of Angola's Most Wanted told me about how arguments can threaten the right for musicians to assemble. When considering new members, they look carefully at how well the prospective member might fit in.

> See, the situation that we're in, we can't afford to bring someone in here, get them to start learning these parts, build songs with the band, and then tomorrow, he gets locked up 'cause he got caught getting high or whatever. That leaves us in a tight position. Could also get us in trouble because he was in the band. So, we try to avoid all that. Before we put anyone in here, we look at their day-to-day lives, how they conduct themselves within the penitentiary as well as how they conduct themselves in here.[70]

Donald Thomas, also of Most Wanted, made it personal and intersubjective: "I want nobody coming in here that's gonna jeopardize my opportunity for a little release. That's just the way I am. I'm with the group. We do everything as a group when we're in here."[71] In prison, when arguments always risk leading to violence, having a predictable group with whom to argue is valuable.

When playing music in the band room, the locked door, lack of windows, soundproofing, and the awkwardness of interrupting rehearsal all become tools for maintaining the freedom to assemble, secure in the flow of the song, in a place where there is little relief from people. In music, assembly is the act of sharing time, attending to the same downbeat, occupying a subdivision, or cadentially signaling a move toward the next part of a song.

Specialty knowledge, good musicianship, and permission to use the space help guarantee the right to assembly. Matthew Trent described how he qualified for the position of band room orderly and continued to hold on to the position as his primary job assignment.

> I learned this here in this prison.... I used to work for recreation. Recreation was over all of this, and they changed it up a little bit. The guy that trained me actually works for Warden Cain up there repairing stuff, but he trained me. He's a certified electronic technician. I just took care of the softball fields and all that, and one day he told me, "You need to learn this." And he started training me. That's how I got into it. Outside of that, I'd never really involved myself in sound equipment. That happened in 1999, and I've been doing it ever since.[72]

Trent's job assignment shift was the same year Louisiana statutes opened the door to faith-based groups. He was in demand because Angola needed audio technicians to support the influx of outside evangelical group events.

When I arrived nine years later, in 2008, the room was tightly scheduled with five bands, a few classes, and private lessons.[73] The secular bands shared the space with religious groups except for the Main Prison Gospel Band, the most active of all the bands. They had their own space. The logic of musical need, which is always also interpersonal, governs the equitable use of the space just like a town's civic center makes meeting space available to various community groups in the name of First Amendment rights.

Membership of the groups often shifts, but importantly, the ability to assemble under a chartered band continues. Every time I met the Jazzmen or Angola's Most Wanted, they had a slightly different lineup. Some of this was the natural evolution of the groups. Since most have long sentences, it was rare that an absent member had gone home. But some members got transferred to other facilities or relocated to the satellite out-camps. Some quit, and some lost privileges due to infractions. Mickey Lanerie of Most Wanted explained the nature of change to me when I asked about the turnover: "A few of the old members had—I hate to say it like that—but we're kind of ego-tripping. This group here, the new group that we have now which hasn't been together . . ." Jesse Lee jumped in, "A month or two." Lanerie continued, "Not very long at all. I like the chemistry. Overall, we're able to play freely."[74] Keeping the chemistry of assembly was important, but so was maintaining the band name, a claim of right-through-permit. Since 1998, they had kept the band alive. At Angola, a band is more a flexible manifestation of the right to assemble than it is an original lineup of the group.

Mobility

Thinking about the counterclockwise twist of the lock (the ability to unlock) forced me to revise my fundamental understanding of the band room as a sanctuary. I expected that the band room would be only an insular refuge (in many prisons, it is). Major Wilfred Cazelot, however, described the opposite, noting the erroneous media image that might lead you to think of music as an unconnected, solitary activity:

> You see it in the movies: an inmate sitting on a bunk in a dark cell and the faucet leaking, and he's playing a harmonica.... [Instead], you find music entangled into *everything* that we do, whether it would be in the visiting shed or some type of function at night, whether it would be a church service or just a club gathering, most of the time there's music there.[75]

I began to think about the band room as a node in a network of possibility, following musicians through gates, wandering with purpose, anything but alone. The band room is right in the middle of the main prison, near where the cafeteria had been in the original plans.

As an incidental consequence of the recreation department taking over the cafeteria space and the band room later gaining autonomy from the recreation department, musicians gained the ability to move about the whole compound because of the band room's central location. What made geographic sense for getting dozens of dormitories to eat all together, fifty years later gave musicians an easier time getting anywhere on the compound.

The mission of musical associations granted Matthew Trent mobility. "I spend about seven days a week doing sound," he explained to me in the band room after a tour of all the prison's musical spaces. "I'm either doing something in this room, or I'm down in the chapel or somewhere out on this farm doing something."[76] While he didn't play music, he was integral to the music scene, twenty-two years into his life sentence for aggravated rape. The music scene was essential to his mobility. His trusty-status position kept him busy setting up, repairing things, hauling equipment, and teaching others when he wasn't engineering sound for music events around the prison.

Angola's band room is best understood not just as a physical building but as a *use* of architecture. Its use has limits. While all these gains of rights-through-permit claimed through using the band room make a world of difference in the daily lives of prisoners and in Angola's professional musical sound, prison inevitably interrupts music. The count, a periodic inventorying of bodies, can pause a song or restrict movement, for instance when hauling speakers and audio cables from the chapel. Regular work assignments, "day jobs," as the musicians call them, take precedence over volunteer work playing in bands. The penitentiary focus on the individual emphasizes the "I" of being a prisoner over the "we" of music-making. But in moments, through associationalism, musicians secure the rights of property, assembly, and mobility, moving throughout the prison together with purpose.

Astonishing Call of the Canaries

As I walked up to the chapel on my very first visit to Angola, prisoners nodded at me, holding Styrofoam cups of coffee. A trusty in a white uniform immediately offered me a cup once I entered through the glass door. I took a seat in the pews and talked with a few of the musicians. Most were singers in gospel groups. Matthew Trent adjusted levels on the mixing board as instrumentalists tuned up onstage.

I was astonished when I heard music for the first time in Angola. The musicians were outstanding. I could hear their prowess even in styles that I don't particularly follow. I should have been prepared for that. At Elayn Hunt Correctional Center the day before, a prisoner told me that the "real professionals" were at Angola. That may have been a strange thing for you to read if you hadn't nearly finished this book—that a prison could be an excellent place to listen to music, and that one prison might have better music than another. Had I known what I know now, I would have listened differently, tuned in to the legacy of musicians who wove jazz and popular music into an array of prisoner-run associations. I would have known that Angola had been in the business of playing for outsiders for a hundred years and would have heard "professionalism" as a legacy of conditional volunteerism, political efforts, claims to stages created for outside audiences, and attempts to maintain small freedoms gained through a long history of music-making.

I knew from my own experience as a musician that music can be as much a form of labor as it is a form of human expression, but I couldn't have predicted that some musicians would look bored while playing, like service workers saving their strength by not offering you the emotional labor of being friendly. Others were prepared to tell me how hard life in prison is, showing scars, engaging in another form of exchange. Some gave testimony to what lurked beneath the surface of the musical performance—the horror of facing the rest of your life in prison, the small moments of joy and hope, the anger at going to such great lengths to maintain basic human connections. What I heard as "prison music" wasn't an escape, it was a musical encounter of prison.

I walked away that first day with a reconsideration of how music astonishes and how it might astonish us more effectively. I'll conclude the book facing inward and then outward: beginning with the legacy of Lead Belly to Angola's current musicians and then closing with consideration of astonishment's value to those of us not experiencing prison.

Lead Belly Remembered

Lead Belly still prominently represents the Louisiana State Penitentiary. When I have described this project to people, I mention his name, and people nod in recognition. For a time, I asked incarcerated musicians what they thought about Lead Belly. I was trying to find a route toward understanding legacy and glean a sense of a musical continuum.

In the booth of WLSP, Robin Polk, formerly of Megasound, took a break with me as the Moody Bible Institute prerecorded program ran. We began talking about John Lomax, and Polk got animated. "I want to play a cut by Lead Belly, a recording that Lomax did, a guy from Texas," he said. "It's called the 'Midnight Special.' You know, he was right here at Angola, Camp A, I believe it was. . . . He did get out and went on."[77] I was surprised how much he knew of the seventy-five-year-old recordings.

In the Camp F band room, I brought recordings to play for former Nic Nacs saxophonist Leotha Brown. "Lead Belly," Brown acknowledged, letting out a knowing laugh as soon as he heard the 1934 recording. "His style is fascinating. . . . His lyrics are down to earth, something he has actually experienced or thought of. When he says, 'Let the Midnight Special shine on me,' first thing came to my mind is that 'This guy ready to go.'" Brown reflected on the meaning of the lyrics and then pivoted to Lead Belly's story. "This has something to do with the Midnight Special helping him to get out of here. And he actually got out. He got out, and he had a pretty good musical career during that time." And then Brown offered Lead Belly's biography. As I listened, I knew that the details of it were wrong. But soon I realized that Brown was actually describing himself instead.

Lead Belly, when he came here, I think he was a young, young man. He got in trouble, I think in a barroom, in a barroom with something. I think he had to kill a man or something of that nature.

When he came here, [prisoners] gravitated toward him because of his musical ability. He would sing for the guys and stuff like that. . . . A lot of times in prison when I came here, the lights would go out, the first thing they used to do was sit on the bed and beat on the bunks, and they start singing in the dark.

Lead Belly caught the interest of some music producer. Some say that some of them were part of the administration or the administration knew these people who were in music. I think they saw the opportunity of saying, "Hey, we can cash in on this guy's talent." And he had it. There was nothing wrong with it because when he had it here, he wasn't getting anything out of it except maybe the pleasure itself. But, by him using his talent and not letting his talent laid to waste, he put himself in a position where people who could help him helped him get out.[78]

The blended biography speaks to the hope that Lead Belly offered Brown. Again, he shifted, separating himself from Lead Belly while still showing the relationship between himself and the legend.

I'd like the Midnight Special to shine on me! They have a thing called a "12:01." That's when you leave prison. You can leave out of here one minute after midnight. That's what went through my mind. Like the "don't get in trouble with the man, don't squabble, don't fight," these could stop you from getting to that Midnight Special. . . .

He set a precedent in a sense. Maybe it was set before him, but by the popularity he achieved in prison, I think his music had a lot to do with his release. . . . He was a forerunner. That's the way I look at Lead Belly. He was a forerunner.[79]

In the main prison band room, Frederick Jones of Angola's Most Wanted also saw achievable hope in Lead Belly's professional accomplishments. Jones tied musical legacy to the strong possibility that he might die at Angola. "We are trying to become legends in our own way even—and I don't want you to misinterpret how I'm saying this . . . if we don't get what Lead Belly got [release from Angola], we wanna just set the standards for ourselves as a band."[80]

Musicians at Angola had all kinds of reasons to preserve Lead Belly's legacy. Gary Jameson of the Jazzmen felt like Lead Belly's legacy in Angola was at risk of disappearing. He said:

> There's a generation here now that probably never heard of him, and if they heard of him, they wouldn't care. As musicians at Angola, we know of him, we know of the legend, we know of the story of Lead Belly. We're grateful for that story. However, that was a whole other era. We don't really believe that we can play our way out of prison like Lead Belly did. It would be nice—and some of us are gifted enough to do that. However, it is what is, as they say. Lead Belly, may he rest in peace."[81]

Jameson's statement leaves the question open: What is the relevance of a 1930s prisoner to a twenty-first-century one?

A Radical Revision of an Old Metaphor

Recently, I received a letter from Angola. "NOT CENSORED," a stamp on the back read, along with the date and "LA. STATE PEN. AN ALL MALE PENAL INSTITUTE" underneath. It was from Calvin Lewis, known as Tex, the leader of the Jazzmen (now one of the most prominent and venerable musical groups at Angola) and president of the Angola Drama Club. The letter began, "I hope you remember me . . ." I was reminded how prisoners are always forgotten, that they tend to assume that their victims are the only ones who remember them.

Lewis was one of the many musicians who led me through the music scene at Angola, though I had not seen him since Charles Neville and I came to the prison for a symposium organized by the prison museum in 2016. (He and Myron Hodges would later write forewords to this book after reading a draft manuscript I mailed to them.)

Lewis's letter invited me back to give a lecture on the history of music at the prison, augmenting classes he continues to run from the band room. Participating in the research for this book, Lewis and the other musicians found value in preserving the history of music in a place filled with horror, that has held him for decades, a place he would leave in an instant if given the chance. His interest in Angola's history of music raises important questions.

How should we remember the musicians that populate this book? How might we exercise caution in our own astonishment?

As I warned in the introduction to the book, both prison and music are strong metaphors. Featured in countless poems, scenes in movies, and folk songs, the music of imprisonment pits freedom against constraint. It's an ancient metaphor. In the mythology of prison, confinement prepares the prisoner for existential illumination. The tension inherent in the phrase "prison music" recalls Prometheus, imprisoned by the Greek gods for his cunning theft of fire from Zeus. While Prometheus was chained to a rock by the sea for his crime, the sea said to him, "Know thyself." Here is the root of the myth of prison as a site for epiphany.[82] People, by contrast, are not metaphors.

I hesitate in finding silver linings in prisons, in congratulating each other for our compassion toward the incarcerated, and finding our own hopes on the backs of those who have suffered violence in the name of public safety, profit, and revenge. I am tempted just to stop writing here, to offer an ellipsis instead of closure, to deny the idea that there is an end in sight for people who wake up each day in prison with life sentences. If I just stopped writing, the unexpected break might pass the momentum of thinking musically about incarceration to you. Instead, I'll offer a more graceful handoff while leaving the people that populate this book intact as whole human beings.

The caged bird is one of the most potent images in prison art—nearing the point of cliché. It's also quite old. Chris Franklin, formerly enslaved, described a social dance in Louisiana based on the ancient metaphor. "One thing dey calls, 'Bird in de Cage.'" he explains. "Three join hands round de gal in de middle, and dance round her, and den she git out and her pardner git in the center and dey dance awhile."[83] The caged bird metaphor reaches back before prison swept into the lives of the descendants of these dancers.

I hope this book generates new questions about the nature of cages: *Where, exactly, is the cage in its extended sense, and how did it get there?* I hope that we don't miss the flock for the bird: *What are the birds doing together?* And finally, I hope we consider ourselves responsive listeners: *Why are we listening to the calls? How best might we respond?* It should be clear that I believe there is a value to music made in prison, but to conclude the book, I'll tie some value to a radical revision of the caged bird image, expanded through the questions above.

Imagine that the birds are in a coal mine, the kind where British miners used canaries as warning signals before electronic carbon monoxide detectors existed. A canary's higher breathing rate and metabolism meant they would succumb to carbon monoxide poisoning before the coal miners. As an instrument used by the mining company, the canary provided a signal. Miners listened for silence to judge their own safety. Now imagine the coal mine without humans and then, if you can, adopt the perspective of the canaries, trapped in cages that are themselves trapped in a coal mine. From that perspective, we might listen differently. What if a few of us were farther down the mine, out of sight, sounding out in distress? If we were all canaries, we'd hear more subtle warnings, concerted efforts to flee, the flagging inflections of canary song that sound out as poison sets into the bloodstream.

Prison music, heard as a musical encounter of prison, may provide instruction for other forms of constriction that we will undoubtedly face in the future. There are radical changes to our world: the advance of the Anthropocene (the era when humans began to profoundly affect the Earth's environment), the rise of global authoritarianism, outlawry in growing refugee camps, and economic disruptions due to shifting arrangements of global power. In the face of these realities, we might know human resourcefulness better if we learn to listen to musicians who associate in the harshest conditions. Attuning ourselves to prison music, we can listen like canaries distributed throughout the mines, not so we can contemplate individual freedom, but to remember how to marshal resources for associational enterprise when things begin to go wrong.

Notes

Introduction

1. Russel Joe Beyer, interview with author, Louisiana State Penitentiary, Angola, LA, December 17, 2008.
2. Leotha Brown, interview with author, Louisiana State Penitentiary, Angola, LA, July 13, 2009.
3. Brown, interview, December 16, 2008.
4. Wilfred Cazelot, interview with author, Louisiana State Penitentiary, Angola, LA, October 19, 2009.
5. Kai Fikentscher, *"You Better Work!" Underground Dance Music in New York*, Music/Culture (Hanover, NH: University Press of New England, 2000), 40–41.
6. Anthony Seeger, *Why Suyá Sing: A Musical Anthropology of an Amazonian People* (Urbana: University of Illinois Press, 2004), 70–74.
7. Benjamin J. Harbert, "Doing Time: The Work of Music in Louisiana Prisons" (PhD diss., University of California, Los Angeles, 2010); *Follow Me Down: Portraits of Louisiana Prison Musicians*, directed by Benjamin J. Harbert (New York: Films for the Humanities & Sciences, 2012), DVD.
8. Benjamin J. Harbert, "Only Time: Musical Means to the Personal, the Private and the Polis at the Louisiana Correctional Institute for Women," in "Women's Prison Music," special issue, *American Music* 30, no. 2 (Summer 2012): 203–240.
9. See Leonidas Cheliotis, "Decorative Justice: Deconstructing the Relationship between the Arts and Imprisonment," *International Journal for Crime, Justice and Social Democracy* 3, no. 1 (April 2014): 16–34; Leonidas Cheliotis and Aleksandra Jordanoska, "The Arts of Desistance: Assessing the Role of Arts-based Programmes in Reducing Reoffending," *Howard Journal* 55, no. 1–2 (May 2016): 25–41.
10. Benjamin J. Harbert, "Prometheus Sings: The Mythology of Prison Music" (master's thesis, University of California, Los Angeles, 2007); for an overview of the archives I compiled at UCLA, see Maureen Russell, "Highlights from the Ethnomusicology Archive: California-Arts-in-Corrections," *Ethnomusicology Review* (December 2015).
11. For work highlighting noninstrumental arts programs and examples of prison art-making outside of rehabilitative aims, see Nicole Fleetwood, *Marking Time* (Cambridge, MA: Harvard University Press, 2020); Andy McGraw, "Musical Sanctuary in the Richmond City Jail," *Tacet: Sound in the Arts* 4 (2016); William Cleveland, *Art in Other Places: Artists at Work in America's Community and Social Institutions* (New York: Praeger, 1992); Maria Mendonça, "Gamelan in Prisons in England and Scotland: Narratives of Transformation and the 'Good Vibrations' of Educational Rhetoric," *Ethnomusicology* 54, no. 3 (Fall 2010): 369–394.

12. Mantle Hood, "The Challenge of 'Bi-Musicality,'" *Ethnomusicology* 4, no. 2 (May 1960): 55–59.
13. I am deeply indebted to Marianne Fisher-Giorlando and the staff at *The Angolite* for help locating, digitizing, and combing through decades of the publication and the records that remain in the office.
14. State of Louisiana, *Board of Control, State Penitentiary Annual Report—Calendar Year 1901* (New Orleans, 1902), 51.
15. Louisiana Department of Public Safety and Corrections, "Demographic Dashboard: Population Count," December 31, 2021, https://doc.louisiana.gov/demographic-dashboard/.
16. The Sentencing Project, "State-by-State Data: State Imprisonment Rate: Louisiana," US Bureau of Justice Statistics Data, 2019, https://www.sentencingproject.org/the-facts/#map.
17. US Census Bureau, "Quick Facts: Louisiana," July 1, 2019, https://www.census.gov/quickfacts/LA.
18. As for convictions, 40.05 percent have been convicted of violent crimes, 18.77 percent of drug crimes, 17.1 percent of property crimes, and 23.04 percent of other crimes.
19. Ashley Nellis, *No End in Sight: America's Enduring Reliance on Life Imprisonment*, The Sentencing Project, 2021, 10, https://www.sentencingproject.org/wp-content/uploads/2021/02/No-End-in-Sight-Americas-Enduring-Reliance-on-Life-Imprisonment.pdf.
20. John Simerman, "'The Only Way We Get Out of There Is in a Pine Box,'" *The Marshall Project*, December 14, 2021, https://www.themarshallproject.org/2021/12/17/the-only-way-we-get-out-of-there-is-in-a-pine-box.

Chapter 1

1. Laird Veillon, interview with author, Louisiana State Penitentiary, Angola, LA, April 11, 2008.
2. Clare D'Artois Leeper, *Louisiana Place Names: Popular, Unusual, and Forgotten Stories of Towns, Cities, Plantations, Bayous, and Even Some Cemeteries* (Baton Rouge: Louisiana State University Press, 2012), 18.
3. Texas, Mississippi, and Arkansas share history and structural characteristics with Angola and each has prisons that many historians have categorized as "plantation prisons." For an overview, see Marianne Fisher-Giorlando, "Plantation Prisons," in *Encyclopedia of Prisons & Correctional Facilities*, ed. Mary Bosworth (Thousand Oaks, CA: SAGE Publications, 2005), 702–705. For Texas, see Robert Perkinson, *Texas Tough: the Rise of America's Prison Empire* (New York: Metropolitan Books, 2010). For Mississippi, see David M. Oshinsky, *"Worse Than Slavery": Parchman Farm and the Ordeal of Jim Crow Justice* (New York: Simon & Schuster, 1997). For Arkansas, see Bruce Jackson, *Inside the Wire: Photographs from Texas and Arkansas Prisons* (Chicago: University of Chicago Press, 2013). For an updated overview of plantation

prisons, see Maurice Chammah, "Prison Plantations," The Marshall Project, May 1, 2015, https://www.themarshallproject.org/2015/05/01/prison-plantations.
4. George Rusche and Otto Kirchheimer, *Punishment and Social Structure* (New Brunswick, NJ: Transaction Publishers, 2003), 5.
5. Caleb Smith, *The Prison and the American Imagination* (New Haven, CT: Yale University Press, 2009), 136.
6. Although the bill of sale called the property "Angola," after one of the plantations, the state bought four plantations including Loango, Bellevue, and Kilarney plantations. See Stephanie L. Perrault, Charles E. Pearson, Carey L. Coxe, Sara A. Hahn, Thurston H. G. Hahn III, Dayna Lee, Katherine M. Roberts, and Joanne Ryan, *Archaeological Data Recovery at Angola Plantation 16WF121 and 16WF122, West Feliciana Parish, Louisiana* (Baton Rouge: Coastal Environments, 2006), 40.
7. For a classic study on the European roots of romanticized outlaws, see Eric Hobsbawm, *Bandits* (New York: New Press, 2000). For consideration of American fascination, see Richard E. Meyer, "The Outlaw: A Distinctive American Folktype," *Journal of the Folklore Institute* 17, no. 2/3 (May–December 1980): 94–124. The endurance of the practice into the twenty-first century is evident in Ta-Nehisi Coates, "Outlaw Culture," *Atlantic*, April 13, 2012.
8. Mary R. Grestein, "Germanic Warg: The Outlaw as Werwolf," in *Myth in Indo-European Antiquity*, ed. Gerald James Larson, C. Scott Littleton, and Jaan Puhvel (Berkeley: University of California Press, 1974), 141–144.
9. Mary J. Bunch, "Outlawry and the Experience of the (Im)possible: Deconstructing Biopolitics" (PhD diss., University of Western Ontario, 2010), 1.
10. See Caroline Elkins, *Legacy of Violence: A History of the British Empire* (New York: Alfred A. Knopf, 2022), 52.
11. Gerald L. Neuman, "The Lost Century of American Immigration Law (1776–1875)," *Columbia Law Review* 93, no. 8 (December 1993): 1844–1845.
12. Smith, *The Prison and the American Imagination*, 136. For the historical development of using architecture as a means to solve social problems like criminality, see David J. Rothman, *The Discovery of the Asylum: Social Order and Disorder in the New Republic* (Boston: Little, Brown, 1971), 79–108. For wider examples of a separate Southern development of convict-leasing, see Perkinson, *Texas Tough*, 124–125; Marie Gottschalk, *The Prison and the Gallows: The Politics of Mass Incarceration* (New York: Cambridge University Press, 2006), 47–50; Christopher R. Adamson, "Punishment After Slavery: Southern State Penal Systems, 1865–1890," *Social Problems* 30, no. 5 (June 1983): 555–569.
13. For an overview of the antebellum use of outlawry, see Deborah A. Rosen, "Slavery, Race, and Outlawry: The Concept of the Outlaw in Nineteenth-Century Abolitionist Rhetoric," *American Journal of Legal History* 58, no. 1 (March 2018): 127–130.
14. A third of Louisiana's antebellum penitentiary was Black. For more on the history of Louisiana State Penitentiary before the Civil War, see Marianne Fisher-Giorlando, "Women in the Walls: The Imprisonment of Women at the Baton Rouge Penitentiary, 1835–1862," in *The Wall Is Strong: Corrections in Louisiana*, 4th ed., ed. Burk Foster, Wilbert Rideau, and Douglas Dennis (Lafayette: University of Louisiana Press, 2014),

16-25, and Jeff Forret, "Before Angola: Enslaved Prisoners in the Louisiana State Penitentiary," *Louisiana History* 54, no. 2 (Spring 2013): 133-171.
15. Gilles Vandal, "Regulating Louisiana's Rural Areas: The Functions of Parish Jails, 1840-1885," *Louisiana History: The Journal of the Louisiana Historical Association* 42, no. 1 (Winter 2001): 64-65.
16. Johan Thorsten Sellen, *Slavery and the Penal System* (New York: Elsevier, 1976), 140.
17. Vandal, "Regulating Louisiana's Rural Areas," 68-73.
18. Paul Gowder, *The Rule of Law in the United States: An Unfinished Project of Black Liberation* (Oxford: Hart, 2021), 162.
19. Cecilia Menjívar, "Liminal Legality: Salvadoran and Guatemalan Immigrants' Lives in the United States," *American Journal of Sociology* 111, no. 4 (January 2006): 1007.
20. Jeremy Travis, "Invisible Punishment: An Instrument of Social Exclusion," in *Invisible Punishment: The Collateral Consequences of Mass Imprisonment*, ed. Marc Mauer and Meda Chesney-Lind (New York: The New Press, 2002), 17-18. For a study of increasing use of denial-of-rights see Velmer S. Burton, Francis T. Cullen, and Lawrence F. Travis III, "Collateral Consequences of a Felony Conviction: A National Study of State Statutes," *Federal Probation* 51, no. 3 (September 1987): 52-60.
21. C. Fred Alford, "What Would It Matter If Everything Foucault Said About Prison Were Wrong? 'Discipline and Punish' after Twenty Years," *Theory and Society* 29, no. 1 (February 2000): 127.
22. Smith, *Prison and the American Imagination*, 38-41.
23. David J. Rothman, "Perfecting the Prison: United States 1789-1865," in *The Oxford History of the Prison: The Practice of Punishment in Western Society* ed. David J. Rothman and Norval Morris (New York: Oxford University Press, 1998), 103; Gottschalk, *The Prison and the Gallows*, 46.
24. In Louisiana, the local parish institution is called a "prison" rather than a jail, but, in effect, it fills the same role as would a county jail in other parts of the United States.
25. George Wilson Pierson, *Tocqueville in America* (Garden City, NY: Doubleday, 1996), 622.
26. Rothman, "Perfecting the Prison," 105-107; Lawrence M. Friedman, *Crime and Punishment in American History* (New York: Basic Books, 1993), 80.
27. Mark T. Carleton, *Politics and Punishment: The History of the Louisiana State Penal System* (Baton Rouge: Louisiana State University Press, 1971), 3.
28. For details on the demographics and convictions, including enslaved prisoners, at the Louisiana State Penitentiary, see Kelly Birch, "Slavery and the Origins of Louisiana's Prison Industry, 1803-1861" (PhD diss., University of Adelaide, 2017), 106-107.
29. Brett Josef Derbes, "'Secret Horrors': Enslaved Women and Children in the Louisiana State Penitentiary, 1833-1862," *Journal of African American History* 98, no. 2 (Spring 2013): 279.
30. Rothman, "Perfecting the Prison," 106.
31. Marianne Fisher-Giorlando, "The Walls," *64 Parishes* (Winter 2019), https://64parishes.org/the-walls.
32. Gary W. Bowman, Simon Hakim, and Paul Seidenstat, *Privatizing Correctional Institutions* (New Brunswick, NJ: Transaction Publishers, 1993), 36.

33. Carleton, *Politics and Punishment*, 21.
34. Theo Hester to his parents, Baton Rouge, July 30, 1893, in O'Bryan (Robert P.) and Family Papers, W-33, Folder #7 (Baton Rouge: Louisiana and Lower Mississippi Valley Collections, LSU Libraries).
35. Richard Follett, "Slavery and Technology in Louisiana's Sugar Bowl," in *Technology, Innovation, and Southern Industrialization: from the Antebellum Era to the Computer Age*, ed. Susanna Delfino and Michele Gillespie (Columbia: University of Missouri Press, 2008), 68–95.
36. Follett, "Slavery and Technology in Louisiana's Sugar Bowl," 86.
37. Rothman, "Perfecting the Prison," 304–305.
38. Rothman, "Perfecting the Prison," 328–329.
39. Edward E. Baptist, *The Half Has Never Been Told: Slavery and the Making of American Capitalism* (Boulder, CO: Basic Books, 2014), 360–361.
40. Shane White, *The Sounds of Slavery: Discovering African American History through Songs, Sermons, and Speech* (Boston: Beacon 2005), 41–42, 47.
41. Follett, "Slavery and Technology in Louisiana's Sugar Bowl," 83.
42. Joshua Rothman, email correspondence with author, July 19, 2021.
43. R. Murray Schafer, *The Soundscape: Our Sonic Environment and the Tuning of the World*, 2nd ed. (New York: Simon & Schuster, 1993), 215.
44. Perrault et al., *Archaeological Data Recovery at Angola Plantation*, 78–79.
45. Perrault et al., *Archaeological Data Recovery at Angola Plantation*, 242.
46. William Francis Allen, Charles Pickard Ware, and Lucy McKim Garrison, *Slave Songs of the United States* (New York: A. Simpson, 1867).
47. J. Vincenza Scarpaci, "Labor for Louisiana's Sugar Cane Fields: An Experiment in Immigrant Recruitment," *Italian Americana* 7, no. 1 (Fall/Winter 1981): 22–25.
48. *Acts Passed at the Second Session of the Fifteenth Legislature of the State of Louisiana, Begun and Held in the City of New Orleans, December 13, 1841* (New Orleans: J. C. De St. Romes, 1842), 518–520; *Annual Report of the Chief Engineer of the Board of Public Works, for the year ending December 31, 1860, to the Legislature of the State of Louisiana* (Baton Rouge: J. M. Taylor, State Printer, 1861).
49. The practice of putting prisoners to work outside the prisons developed after the Civil War. Before then, and only for about a year, free men of color were put to work on the local roads with local government approval. Coordinating outside labor, however, proved to be too expensive. Prisoners returned where they were segregated and given various jobs in the Baton Rouge Penitentiary. For more on convict leasing, see Nathan Cardon, "'Less Than Mayhem': Louisiana's Convict Lease, 1865-1901," *Louisiana History* (Fall 2017): 419; Carleton, *Politics and Punishment*, 22–24; Matthew J. Mancini, *One Dies, Get Another: Convict Leasing in the American South, 1866-1928*, Columbia: University of South Carolina Press, 1996, 144; Alex Lichtenstein, *Twice the Work of Free Labor: The Political Economy of Convict Labor in the New South* (New York: Verso, 1996), 166; Sarah Haley, "Convict Leasing, (Re)Production, and Gendered Racial Terror," in *No Mercy Here* (Chapel Hill: University of North Carolina Press, 2016), 58–118.

50. Joshua D. Rothman, *The Ledger and the Chain: How Domestic Slave Traders Shaped America* (New York: Basic Books, 2021), 361.
51. Mancini, *One Dies, Get Another*, 31.
52. Carleton, *Politics and Punishment*, 36.
53. Oshinsky, *"Worse Than Slavery,"* 136.
54. In Carleton, *Politics and Punishment*, 37.
55. In Sellen, *Slavery and the Penal System*, 149.
56. For an account of how work songs became racialized folklore, see Karl Hagstrom Miller, *Segregating Sound: Inventing Folk and Pop Music in the Age of Jim Crow* (Durham, NC: Duke University Press, 2010), 5. For examples of early folk songs collections of convict labor songs see Howard W. Odum and Guy B. Johnson, *The Negro and His Songs: A Study of Typical Negro Songs in the South* (Chapel Hill: University of North Carolina Press, 1925); Howard W. Odum and Guy Benton Johnson, *Negro Workaday Songs* (Chapel Hill: University of North Carolina Press, 1926); Lawrence Gellert, *Negro Songs of Protest* (New York: American Music League, 1936); Alan Lomax and John Avery Lomax, *American Ballads and Folk Songs* (New York: Dover, 1994), 58–88; John A. Lomax, Alan Lomax, Ruth Crawford Seeger, and Harold William Thompson, *Our Singing Country: A Second Volume of American Ballads and Folk Songs* (New York: Dover, 2000), 380–404.
57. See, for instance, Allen et al., *Slave Songs of the United States*; Fisk Jubilee Singers and Theodore F. Seward, *Jubilee Songs: As Sung by the Jubilee Singers of Fisk University* (New York: Biglow & Main, 1872).
58. Saidiya V. Hartman, *Scenes of Subjection: Terror, Slavery, and Self-Making in Nineteenth-Century America* (New York: Oxford University Press, 1997), 25.
59. Matthew J. Schott, *Louisiana Politics and the Paradoxes of Reaction and Reform 1877–1928* (Lafayette: University of Louisiana Press, 2000), 132.
60. Mark T. Carleton, "The Politics of the Convict Lease System in Louisiana: 1868–1901," *Louisiana History* 8, no. 1 (Winter 1967): 22–23.
61. Friedman, *Crime and Punishment in American History*, 74.
62. US Const. amend. XIII, § 1.
63. For a full account of the political quandary toward the end of the lease system, see Carleton, *Politics and Punishment*, 59–84.
64. Carleton, *Politics and Punishment*, 23.
65. Carleton, *Politics and Punishment*, 43.
66. For a general discussion of how prison labor adapted and transformed agricultural labor, see Mancini, *One Dies, Get Another*, 43–44.
67. Perrault et al., *Archaeological Data Recovery at Angola Plantation*, 100.
68. Joseph C. Mouledous, "Pioneers in Criminology: Edward Livingston (1764–1836)," *Journal of Criminal Law and Criminology* 54. no. 3 (September 1963): 284.
69. Anne Butler and C. Murray Henderson, *Angola, Louisiana State Penitentiary: A Half-Century of Rage and Reform* (Lafayette: Center for Louisiana Studies, University of Southwestern Louisiana, 1990), 31.
70. Perrault et al., *Archaeological Data Recovery at Angola Plantation*, 100.

NOTES TO PAGES 28–37   285

71. Matthew J. Mancini, "Convict Leasing," *64 Parishes,* May 27, 2011, https://64paris hes.org/entry/convict-leasing.
72. Lichtenstein, *Twice the Work of Free Labor,* 160.
73. "History and description of the Angola State Prison farms in 1901," *Daily States,* July 14, 1901, 18.
74. "Convict Farmers of Louisiana," *Daily States,* July 14, 1901, 18.
75. "Convict Farmers of Louisiana," 18.
76. See Harry Braverman, *Labor and Monopoly Capital: The Degradation of Work in the Twentieth Century,* 25th anniversary ed. (New York: Monthly Review Press, 1998), 86. For the original writing, see Frederick Winslow Taylor, *The Principles of Scientific Management* (New York: Harper, 1911).
77. Personal communication with Anna Lomax Wood, phone, November 29, 2012.
78. "Convict Farmers of Louisiana," 18; see also Alcée Fortier, *Louisiana: comprising sketches of parishes, towns, events, institutions, and persons, arranged in cyclopedic form,* Vol. 1 (Madison, WI: Century Historical Association, 1914), 199.
79. Butler and Henderson, *Angola, Louisiana State Penitentiary,* 9.
80. "Convict Farmers of Louisiana," 18.
81. J. Martin Daughtry, *Listening to War: Sound, Music, Trauma, and Survival in Wartime Iraq* (New York: Oxford University Press, 2015), 98.
82. Daughtry, *Listening to War,* 79.
83. "History and description of the Angola State Prison farms in 1901," 9–10.
84. Miller, *Segregating Sound,* 6.
85. "The Buzzard Lope: A New Dance Step That Has Captured All of Georgia," *Morning Oregonian Newspaper,* April 17, 1890, 12.
86. "History and description of the Angola State Prison farms in 1901," 10.
87. "History and description of the Angola State Prison farms in 1901," 10.
88. "Detailed description of song and dance at Angola," *Times Picayune* (New Orleans), July 14, 1901, 30.
89. "Figures Showing What Has Been Accomplished by the Board of Control—Value of the Property," *Times Picayune* (New Orleans), April 15, 1906, 23.
90. Dennis Childs, *Slaves of the State: Black Incarceration from the Chain Gang to the Penitentiary* (Minneapolis: University of Minnesota Press, 2015), 122.
91. "Need for organs, banjos, and guitars," *Times Picayune* (New Orleans), July 14, 1901, 6.
92. Typed personal account by Stella B. Johns, ca. 1950, Folder "Johns. Rev. J.S., Chaplain at Angola for 20 Years," Reverend Henry S. Johns' Collection, Angola Prison Museum, Angola, Louisiana.
93. "Mrs. Booth Visits Penitentiary and Several of State Convict Camps," *Daily Picayune* (New Orleans), February 9, 1912, 9.
94. Carleton, *Politics and Punishment,* 116.
95. Michael P. Roth, *Prisons and Prison Systems: A Global Encyclopedia* (Westport, CT: Greenwood Press, 2006), 56–57. To northerners, the sight may have been a horrific (or nostalgic) return to bondage. But to southerners, the chain gang was a modern and humane innovation developed by early-twentieth-century southern

reformers, a stark contrast with the convict-lease system still active in other parts of the South, see Gottschalk, *The Prison and the Gallows*, 51–52.

96. Edward W. Stagg and John Lear, "America's Worst Prison," *Collier's Weekly*, November 22, 1952, 14.
97. "Angola Band at Christmas Party," *State Times Advocate* (Baton Rouge, LA), December 14, 1925, 10.
98. "140 Members of Local Service Clubs Guests of State Penitentiary," *Morning Advocate* (Baton Rouge, LA), July 20, 1933, 1–2; "Employee of State Department Describes Thanksgiving Visit to Penitentiary at Angola," *Morning Advocate* (Baton Rouge, LA), November 25, 1940, 1, 6.
99. John Avery Lomax et al., *Negro Folk Songs as Sung by Lead Belly "King of the Twelve-String Guitar Players of the World," Long-Time Convict in the Penitentiaries of Texas and Louisiana* (New York: Macmillan, 1936), ix.
100. Roger D. Abrahams, "Mr. Lomax Meets Professor Kittredge," *Journal of Folklore Research* 37, no. 2–3 (May–December 2000): 112.
101. John Cowley, "'Take a whiff on me': Leadbelly's Library of Congress recordings 1933–1942. An assessment," *Blues and Rhythm* 59 (March/April 1991): 3.
102. Nicole Brittingham Furlonge, *Race Sounds: The Art of Listening in African American Literature* (Iowa City: University of Iowa Press, 2018): 29, 109.
103. Furlonge, *Race Sounds*, 108–109.
104. Scott Christianson, "Prisons: History," in *Encyclopedia of Crime and Justice* 3, ed. Joshua Dressler (New York: Macmillan, 2002): 1168–1175.
105. *The Angolite*, June 20, 1953.
106. In Carleton, *Politics and Punishment*, 112.
107. William Ivy Hair, *The Kingfish and His Realm: The Life and Times of Huey P. Long* (Baton Rouge: Louisiana State University Press, 1997), 230.
108. Carleton, *Politics and Punishment*, 112.
109. Carleton, *Politics and Punishment*, 132.
110. Carleton, *Politics and Punishment*, 131.
111. Charles K. Wolfe and Kip Lornell, *The Life and Legend of Leadbelly* (New York: Da Capo Press, 1999), 103.
112. Wolfe and Lornell, *The Life and Legend of Leadbelly*, 103; Lomax et al., *Negro Folk Songs as Sung by Lead Belly*, 24.
113. Lomax et al., *Negro Folk Songs as Sung by Lead Belly*, ix.
114. Richard Slotkin, *Gunfighter Nation: The Myth of the Frontier in Twentieth-Century America* (New York: Atheneum, 1992), ix.
115. John A. Lomax, "'Sinful Songs' of the Southern Negro," *Musical Quarterly*, no. 2 (1934): 183; Benjamin Filene, "'Our Singing Country': John and Alan Lomax, Leadbelly, and the Construction of an American Past," *American Quarterly* 43, no. 4 (December 1991): ix; Jerrold Hirsch, "Modernity, Nostalgia, and Southern Folklore Studies: The Case of John Lomax," *Journal of American Folklore* 105, no. 416 (Spring 1992): 188.
116. John Szwed, *Alan Lomax: The Man Who Recorded the World* (New York: Viking Penguin, 2010): 37.

117. Cowley, "'Take a whiff on me,'" 2.
118. Hirsch, "Modernity, Nostalgia, and Southern Folklore Studies," 194; Patrick B. Mullen, "The Dilemma of Representation in Folklore Studies: The Case of Henry Truvillion and John Lomax," *Journal of Folklore Research* 37, no. 2-3 (May–December 2000): 157.
119. Lomax et al., *Negro Folk Songs as Sung by Lead Belly*, 24.
120. Mark Allan Jackson, *Jail House Bound: John Lomax's First Southern Prison Sojourn, 1933* (Morgantown: West Virginia University Press, 2012).
121. Alan Lomax and Gage Averill, *Alan Lomax: Selected Writings, 1934–1997*, ed. Ronald D. Cohen (New York: Routledge, 1997), 26.
122. Wolfe and Lornell, *The Life and Legend of Leadbelly*, 115.
123. Alan Lomax, *The Land Where the Blues Began* (New York: Pantheon, 1993), 181.
124. You might argue that a shallow depth-of-field in photography provides something akin to the less discernible audibility of a recording. But still, there is an evident unknown both beyond-the-frame and out-of-focus.
125. For a rich discussion comparing photographs and sound recordings, see Peter Doyle, *Echo and Reverb: Fabricating Space in Popular Music, 1900–1960* (Middletown, CT: Wesleyan University Press, 2005) 39.
126. Lomax and Lomax, *American Ballads and Folk Songs*, xxxv.
127. Filene, "'Our Singing Country,'" 617; Dominic Strinati, *An Introduction to Theories of Popular Culture*, 2nd ed. (New York: Routledge, 2004), 5.
128. Lomax, "'Sinful Songs' of the Southern Negro," 181.
129. Jonathan Sterne, *The Audible Past: Cultural Origins of Sound Reproduction* (Durham, NC: Duke University Press, 2003), 24.
130. Personal communication with Anna Lomax Wood, phone, November 29, 2012.
131. Library of Congress, *Report of the Librarian of Congress for the Fiscal Year Ending June 30, 1934* (Washington, DC: US Government Printing Office, 1934), 124–128.
132. Lomax et al., *Negro Folk Songs as Sung by Lead Belly*, xiii.
133. Lomax et al., *Negro Folk Songs as Sung by Lead Belly*, xiii.
134. Lomax et al., *Negro Folk Songs as Sung by Lead Belly*, xi.
135. Both Lomax and Lead Belly supported their work by presenting to audiences. Early folklorists did not have access to research grants like we do today. Lomax's supporting revenue came from publication revenues.
136. Filene, "'Our Singing Country,'" 609; Lomax et al., *Negro Folk Songs as Sung by Lead Belly*, 8–9.
137. Bruce Crowther, *Captured on Film: The Prison Movie* (London: B. T. Batsford, 1989), 4.
138. David Gonthier, *American Prison Film Since 1930: From The Big House to The Shawshank Redemption* (Lewiston, NY: Edwin Mellen Press, 2006): 19.
139. Gonthier, *American Prison Film Since 1930*, 24.
140. Gonthier, *American Prison Film Since 1930*, 25.
141. Ethan Blue, *Doing Time in the Depression: Everyday Life in Texas and California Prisons* (New York: New York University Press, 2012): 136.

142. John Dougan, "The Mistakes of Yesterday, the Hopes of Tomorrow: Prison, Pop Music, and the Prisonaires," *American Music* 17, no. 4 (Winter 1999): 455.
143. Blue, *Doing Time in the Depression*, 137.
144. "Radio: Hoosegow Harmony," *Time*, February 7, 1944.
145. See Michael Hicks, "The Imprisonment of Henry Cowell," *Journal of the American Musicological Society* 44, no. 1 (Spring 1991): 92–119.
146. Correspondence, John A. Lomax, October 1934, American Folklife Center, Library of Congress, John A. Lomax and Alan Lomax papers, 1932–1968 (AFC 1933/001), Box 1, Folder 22.
147. Velia Ivanova, "The Musical Heritage of Incarceration: The Curation, Dissemination, and Management of the Lomax Collection Prison Songs" (PhD diss., Columbia University, 2021), 30.
148. H. Bruce Franklin, "Songs of an Imprisoned People," *Melus* 6, no. 1 (1979): 12–13.
149. Erich Nunn, *Sounding the Color Line: Music and Race in the Southern Imagination*, The New Southern Studies (Athens: University of Georgia Press, 2015), 82.
150. Nunn, *Sounding the Color Line*, 83.
151. Hirsch, "Modernity, Nostalgia, and Southern Folklore Studies," 192–193.
152. Lomax, "'Sinful Songs' of the Southern Negro," 181.
153. Nolan Porterfield, *Last Cavalier: The Life and Times of John A. Lomax, 1867–1948*, Folklore and Society (Urbana: University of Illinois Press, 2001), 330–333.
154. Lomax et al., *Negro Folk Songs as Sung by Lead Belly*, 25.
155. Filene, "'Our Singing Country,'" 611–613; Lomax et al., *Negro Folk Songs as Sung by Lead Belly*, 7–27.
156. Porterfield, *Last Cavalier*, 366–374; Filene, "'Our Singing Country,'" 610–611.
157. Carl Engel, "Views and Reviews," *Musical Quarterly* 23, no. 3 (July 1937): 390.
158. Engel, "Views and Reviews," 393.
159. *The Angolite*, November 12, 1976.
160. *The Angolite*, July 4, 1953, 3.
161. Butler and Henderson, *Angola, Louisiana State Penitentiary*, 44.
162. Vellion, interview.

Chapter 2

1. Dennis Childs, *Slaves of the State: Black Incarceration from the Chain Gang to the Penitentiary* (Minneapolis: University of Minnesota Press, 2015), 118.
2. Alexis de Tocqueville's primary task was to survey the penitentiary, a radically new institution particular to the United States. In 1833, Tocqueville and his close friend Gustave de Beaumont coauthored a report titled *On the Penitentiary System in the United States and Its Application to France* based on their visits to Cherry Hill Prison in Philadelphia and the Auburn Prison in New York. In contrast to French prisons that equally practiced punishment and abandonment, the penitentiary isolated each prisoner to prevent corruption, made work central to how prisoners were to serve

NOTES TO PAGES 54–61   289

   their sentence, and the goals of incarceration were rehabilitative. They saw enough evidence in the conditions of the prisons and the moral and spiritual changes in each individual. These innovative techniques were found in only some places in the United States, but they were astonished enough to define prisons by these new institutions.
3. Alexis de Tocqueville, Harvey Claflin Mansfield, and Delba Winthrop, *Democracy in America* (Chicago: University of Chicago Press, 2002), 180.
4. William J. Novak, "The American Law of Association: The Legal-Political Construction of Civil Society," *Studies in American Political Development* 15 (Fall 2001): 172.
5. Novak, "The American Law of Association," 175.
6. Brian Balogh, *The Associational State: American Governance in the Twentieth Century* (Philadelphia: University of Pennsylvania Press, 2015), 3.
7. Balogh, *The Associational State*, 10.
8. Eldon J. Eisenach, "Bookends: Seven Stories Excised from the Lost Promise of Progressivism," *Studies in American Political Development* 10, no. 1 (Spring 1996): 18.
9. Eisenach, "Bookends," 178.
10. Fatima Shaik, *Economy Hall: The Hidden History of a Free Black Brotherhood* (New Orleans: The Historic New Orleans Collection, 2021).
11. Rebecca M. McLennan, *The Crisis of Imprisonment: Protest, Politics, and the Making of the American Penal State, 1776–1941* (New York: Cambridge University Press, 2008), 194.
12. As Bill Cleveland, who once directed California's Arts in Corrections, the largest arts programs in US prisons, told me once, prisons are best understood as being in a state of constant truce between administration and prisoners.
13. W. B. Carnochan, "The Literature of Confinement," in *The Oxford History of the Prison: The Practice of Punishment in Western Society*, ed. N. Morris and D. J. Rothman (New York: Oxford University Press, 1995), 382.
14. See Michelle Alexander, *The New Jim Crow*, 2nd ed. (New York: Penguin, 2019); Ava DuVernay, dir., *13th* (Sherman Oaks, CA: Kandoo Films, 2016), DVD.
15. Harry Oster to Rae Korson, January 5, 1957, Harry Oster collection of Louisiana, Mississippi, and Iowa recordings, 1957–1966, American Folklife Center.
16. Ranko Vujosevic, "Dr. Harry Oster: His Life, Career and Field Recordings," *Blues Notes, Monthly Publication of the Johnson County Blues Society*, no. 9 (August 1995): 1–9.
17. Jeff Harris, "Angola Bound—The Blues of Harry Oster," *Big Road Blues Show*, WGMC Jazz 90.1 (Rochester, NY), November 8, 2009.
18. Harry Oster, *Southern Prison Blues*, liner notes and recording, recorded 1968 at Louisiana State Penitentiary, TR 2066-AB, LP.
19. Harry Oster, *Living Country Blues* (Detroit: Folklore Associates, 1969), 1–2.
20. Vujosevic, "Dr. Harry Oster."
21. Vujosevic, "Dr. Harry Oster."
22. Oster, *Southern Prison Blues*.

23. Harry Oster, *Angola Prisoners' Blues,* liner notes and recording, recorded 1952–1959 at Louisiana State Penitentiary, CD-419, reissued by Arhoolie in 1996, compact disc.
24. Oster, *Southern Prison Blues.*
25. "AFSC Hires a Communist," *Tocsin,* September 5, 1964.
26. Joseph C. Mouledous, "Sociological Perspectives on a Prison Social System" (master's thesis, Department of Sociology, Louisiana State University, Baton Rouge, 1962).
27. Joseph C. Mouledous, "Organizational Goals and Structural Change: A Study of the Organization of a Prison Social System," *Social Forces* 41, no. 3 (March 1963): 285.
28. Balogh, *The Associational State,* 10.
29. Mouledous, "Organizational Goals and Structural Change," 285.
30. It is convention at Angola to use "trustys" as the plural form of "trusty."
31. Mouledous, "Organizational Goals and Structural Change," 288.
32. Mouledous, "Sociological Perspectives on a Prison Social System," 85–86.
33. See Mark T. Carleton, *Politics and Punishment: The History of the Louisiana State Penal System* (Baton Rouge: Louisiana State University Press, 1971), 130–134; Mouledous, "Sociological Perspectives on a Prison Social System," 85–86.
34. Joshua A. Mitchell, "'All Those Little Spools and Lights': The Moving Image at Angola Prison," *Film History* 32, no. 2 (Summer 2020): 37.
35. Marianne Fisher-Giorlando and Kerry Meyers, "Bad Girls Convict Women, Part 3, 1950 to a home for their own," *The Angolite,* May/June 2012, 36.
36. There is very little mention of Oster's musicians in the pages of *The Angolite.* There are likely a few reasons for the omission. The musicians Oster recorded were older and thus less involved in the more current music scene, and they also tended to be from rural areas, unlike the newer urban prisoners. Most significantly, Oster recorded the forgotten gunmen of Camp A, the ones who had less social capital than those transferred to the new prison, which opened a few years before Oster came.
37. Kalen M. A. Churcher, "Journalism Behind Bars: The Louisiana State Penitentiary's Angolite Magazine," *Communication, Culture & Critique* 4, no. 4. (December 2011): 393.
38. Scott Whiddon, "'To Live Outside the Law, You Must Be Honest': Words, Walls, and the Rhetorical Practices of *the Angolite*," in *Agency in the Margins: Stories of Outsider Rhetoric,* ed. Anne Meade Stockdell-Giesler (Madison, NJ: Fairleigh Dickinson University Press, 2010), 170.
39. Mitchell, "'All Those Little Spools and Lights,'" 41.
40. "Angola Nurse Resigns Post," *State-Times* (Baton Rouge), April 3, 1951, 1.
41. Edward W. Stagg and John Lear, "America's Worst Prison." *Collier's,* November 22, 1952, 13–16.
42. Stagg and Lear, "America's Worst Prison," 13, 15.
43. Carleton, *Politics and Punishment,* 150.
44. For a brief history and discussion, see Alfred C. Schnur, "The New Penology: Fact or Fiction?" *Journal of Criminal Law & Criminology* 49, no. 4 (Fall 1959): 331–334.
45. Fisher-Giorlando and Meyers, "Bad Girls Convict Women, Part 3," 34.

NOTES TO PAGES 68–73   291

46. Larry Sullivan, *The Prison Reform Movement: Forlorn Hope* (Boston: Twayne, 1990), 61.
47. Edgardo Rotman, "The Failure of Reform: United States, 1865–1965," in *The Oxford History of the Prison: The Practice of Punishment in Western Society*, ed. N. Morris and D. J. Rothman (New York: Oxford University Press, 1995), 168.
48. Sharon Johnson Rion, *Beyond His Time: The Maurice Sigler Story* (Lanham, MD: American Correctional Association, 2001), 18.
49. "Bookkeeper Discloses $712.80 Now in Fund," *The Angolite*, January 8, 1955, 1.
50. "Editorial: A 'Prisoners' Fund," *The Angolite*, May 5, 1953, 5.
51. Childs, *Slaves of the State*, 99.
52. Archie Green, "Hillbilly Music: Source and Symbol," *Journal of American Folklore* 78, no. 309 (July–September 1965): 223; Anthony Harkins, *Hillbilly: A Cultural History of an American Icon* (New York: Oxford University Press, 2005), 72.
53. "Candidate for Hillbillies: Man Invents 'Coke-a-Phone,'" *The Angolite*, August 7, 1954, 3.
54. "Hillbilly Music Is a Disease," *The Angolite*, March 26, 1955, 4.
55. Carleton, *Politics and Punishment*, 164; Mouledous, "Sociological Perspectives on a Prison Social System," 134–135, 143; "Warden Lists LSP's Aims," *The Angolite*, May 30, 1953, 5.
56. Les Winslow, "Hitting the High Notes," *The Angolite*, February 1953, 6.
57. It is safe to assume that Sigler's championing of the bands was similar in agenda to Tennessee governor Edwards's relationship with the Prisonaires, a vocal group of prisoners from Tennessee State Penitentiary. As John Dougan argues, the progressive governor "saw their singing as a validation of his and [Warden] Clement's goal of instituting a new, progressive program of penal reform that emphasized rehabilitation and skills training rather than punishment." John M. Dougan, *The Mistakes of Yesterday, the Hopes of Tomorrow: The Story of the Prisonaires* (Amherst: University of Massachusetts Press, 2012), 51.
58. John M. Sloop, *The Cultural Prison: Discourse, Prisoners, and Punishment* (Tuscaloosa: University of Alabama Press, 1996), 32–33.
59. "Angola Shows Some Improvement in a Year," *State Times Advocate* (Baton Rouge), June 30, 1953, 1.
60. Jazz offered a similar metaphor to the later US State jazz ambassador program in which jazz musicians represented individualism in the Cold War cultural diplomacy. See Iain Anderson, *This Is Our Music: Free Jazz, the Sixties, and American Culture* (Philadelphia: University of Pennsylvania Press, 2007).
61. *The Weekly News* (Marksville, LA), October 17, 1953, 1; *The Town Talk* (Alexandria, LA), October 3, 1953, 11; *The Monroe News-Star* (Monroe, LA), May 22, 1953, 12.
62. Carleton, *Politics and Punishment*, 165.
63. For a contemporary account of the politics of music and the punitive public conception of prison, see Lily Hirsch's account in *Music in American Crime Prevention and Punishment* (Ann Arbor: University of Michigan Press, 2012), 85–109.
64. "Hillbilly Ork Here," *The Angolite*, October 3, 1953, 5.

65. "Angola's Band Trips Illegal, Officials Rule," *The Daily Advertiser* (Lafayette, LA), September 29, 1953, 21.
66. *The Town Talk* (Alexandria, LA), October 8, 1953, 10.
67. "And the Band Played!" *The Angolite*, June 13, 1953, 9.
68. "2 Bands to Play Thanksgiving Day," *The Angolite*, November 21, 1953, 8.
69. The Boggs Act of 1951 had a major impact on criminalizing and racializing the drug trade. For more on this, see Amund R. Tallaksen, "Junkies and Jim Crow: The Boggs Act of 1951 and the Racial Transformation of New Orleans' Heroin Market," *Journal of Urban History* 45, no. 2 (March 2019): 230–246.
70. "Armed Robbery Suspect Booked," Police Reports, *Times Picayune* (New Orleans), March 18, 1953, 5.
71. Kibby Ballam, The Mail Bag, *The Angolite*, November 21, 1953, 6.
72. "Jail Sonny Thompson Orchestra on Dope Charge," *Jet*, June 25, 1953, 59; "Sonny Thompson Bandmen Get 10 Years for Dope," *Jet*, July 9, 1953, 60.
73. "Musician to Roll," *The Angolite*, November 13, 1954, 9.
74. "Cavaliers to Play Outside on July 4," *The Angolite*, June 13, 1953, 3.
75. "Humbugs Absent as 2000 Observe July 4," *The Angolite*, July 11, 1953, 2.
76. "Fete Set Today at Camp E," *The Angolite*, July 4, 1953, 1, 8.
77. Local Briefs, *The Angolite*, August 15, 1953, 8.
78. "Everybody Had a Big Day," *The Angolite*, September 12, 1953, 2.
79. "Everybody Had a Big Day," 2.
80. "Show Premiere on Tonight at Camp Eye," *The Angolite*, March 14, 1954, 10; "Black and Tan Revue Scores Hit with Show," *The Angolite*, March 24, 1954, 7.
81. "Troupe Maps Show," *The Angolite*, February 20, 1954, 5.
82. "Cavaliers to Play Outside on July 4," 3.
83. "Love That Jive!" *The Angolite*, June 27, 1953, 4.
84. "Music Class Set," *The Angolite*, September 19, 1953, 2.
85. "Humbug Moves Band," *The Angolite*, August 14, 1954, 1.
86. "Jam Session at F," *The Angolite*, September 25, 1954, 9; "Jive for Effers," *The Angolite*, October 23, 1954, 7.
87. "Musician to Roll," *The Angolite*, November 13, 1954, 9; "Serenade Show Plan Fizzles," *The Angolite*, November 27, 1954, 9.
88. Maurice Sigler in Lane Nelson, "Looking Back: Those Were the Days," *The Angolite* 25, September/October 2000, 38.
89. "Let Us Lower the Bars," *The Angolite*, May 15, 1954, 4.
90. "Woman is freed, arrested anew," *Times Picayune* (New Orleans), March 23, 1953, 4.
91. Records of the Day, *Times Picayune* (New Orleans), March 21, 1953, 31.
92. Ballam, The Mail Bag, November 21, 1953, 6.
93. "2 Bands to Play Thanksgiving Day," *The Angolite*, November 21, 1953, 8.
94. Kibby Ballam, The Mail Bag, *The Angolite*, October 17, 1953, 5.
95. "Musicians May Ask Jam Session Okay," *The Angolite*, October 10, 1953, 6.
96. Ballam, The Mail Bag, October 17, 1953, 5.
97. Ballam, The Mail Bag, October 17, 1953, 5.
98. Ballam, The Mail Bag, October 17, 1953, 5.

NOTES TO PAGES 80–86   293

99. Ballam, The Mail Bag, November 21, 1953, 6.
100. Kibby Ballam, The Mail Bag, *The Angolite*, April 2, 1955, 6.
101. Ballam, The Mail Bag, *The Angolite*, November 21, 1953, 6.
102. Often it is hard to find reasons for administrative decisions. Leadership does not feel compelled to explain a rationale, and it speaks more to the condition of prison that the support structure is unpredictable.
103. Ballam, The Mail Bag, *The Angolite*, November 21, 1953, 6.
104. Ballam, The Mail Bag, *The Angolite*, November 21, 1953, 6.
105. Ballam, The Mail Bag, *The Angolite*, November 21, 1953, 6.
106. "Quartet Awaits Top Okay on Platter-Cutting Deal," *The Angolite*, January 30, 1954, 10.
107. "It's Official Now . . . Jam Session OK," *The Angolite*, February 13, 1954, 2.
108. "2700 Gals and Galluses All Set for Fete," *The Angolite*, July 3, 1954, 1; "Be-Bop, Stunts Slay Audience," *The Angolite*, July 10, 1954, 2.
109. "Be-Bop, Stunts Slay Audience," 2.
110. "Be-Bop, Stunts Slay Audience," 2.
111. "Has Free Leg," *The Angolite*, July 8, 1955, 12.
112. "Players to Rebuild Antique Piano," *The Angolite*, August 6, 1955, 7.
113. "Parolee Sought in Knife Slaying," *Times Picayune* (New Orleans), March 17, 1953, 1; "Parolee Booked in Fatal Knifing," *Times Picayune* (New Orleans), March 19, 1953, 31; "Cops Shakedown Story Given Jury," *Times Picayune* (New Orleans), April 9, 1953, 6.
114. Police Reports, *Times Picayune* (New Orleans), May 26, 1949, 27.
115. Carleton, *Politics and Punishment*, 161.
116. Lester Thompson, The Mail Bag, *The Angolite*, February 26, 1955, 10; Lester Thompson, The Mail Bag, *The Angolite*, April 9, 1955, 6.
117. Thompson, The Mail Bag, *The Angolite*, February 26, 1955, 10.
118. The Mail Bag, *The Angolite*, March 26, 1955, 6.
119. The Mail Bag, *The Angolite*, April 9, 1955, 6; "Musicians Seek Limelight Spot," *The Angolite*, April 9, 1955, 8; The Mail Bag, *The Angolite*, June 18, 1955, 5; The Mail Bag, *The Angolite*, July 9, 1955, 6.
120. "Music Program Bills 'Angolite Mambo' Theme," *The Angolite*, September 3, 1955, 10.
121. Childs, *Slaves of the State*, 116.
122. Ralph Ellison, *The Collected Essays of Ralph Ellison: Revised and Updated* (New York: Random House, 2011), 535.
123. For an investigation into the complexity of Bert Williams, see Louis Chude-Sokei, *The Last 'Darky': Bert Williams, Black-on-Black Minstrelsy, and the African Diaspora* (Durham, NC: Duke University Press, 2006).
124. The Mail Bag, June 18, 1955, 5.
125. "Gola 'PlayBoys' Wow Camp C," *The Angolite*, April 30, 1955, 6.
126. "Ballam's Music Hitting Solid Popularity Peak," *The Angolite*, May 7, 1955, 9.
127. David Dietz, "Long Night's Journey into Day," *Independent Journal, Marin County*, November 1, 1971, 17.

128. The Mail Bag, *The Angolite*, June 18, 1955, 5.
129. The Mail Bag, *The Angolite*, July 9, 1955, 5.
130. The Mail Bag, *The Angolite*, August 13, 1955, 6.
131. "Last Minute Labor Day Plans Ok'd by Committee," *The Angolite*, September 3, 1955, 1, 10.
132. "Push Holiday Plans," *The Angolite*, August 27, 1955, 1; "Music for All Slated," *The Angolite*, August 20, 1955, 13.
133. The Mail Bag, *The Angolite*, July 9, 1955, 5; The Mail Bag, *The Angolite*, August 13, 1955, 6.
134. "3 Combos in Act!" *The Angolite*, September 10, 1955, 8.
135. "One World—One People," *The Angolite*, November 19, 1955, 7.
136. "Press, Radio Men See New Prison Buildings on Tour," *The Angolite*, April 24, 1954, 2; "Lawmakers Visit 'Gola,'" *The Angolite*, May 29, 1954, 1–2; "A New Angola, A New Idea," *The Angolite*, September 25, 1954, 7; "Sportsmen to Seek League Integration at New Prison," *The Angolite*, August 20, 1955, 12.
137. Rion, *Beyond His Time*, 22.
138. "Music For All in Piped Radio Here!" *The Angolite*, April 7, 1954, 1, 4.
139. Cellblock Slants, *The Angolite*, November 17, 1956, 6.
140. "WLSP Gets Equipment," *The Angolite*, September 7, 1957, 1.
141. "TV Show Previewed Here," *The Angolite*, October 12, 1957, 1.
142. "New Records Given WLSP," *The Angolite*, October 12, 1957, 1.
143. Ethan Blue, *Doing Time in the Depression: Everyday Life in Texas and California Prisons* (New York: New York University Press, 2012), 138.
144. "WLSP Is Now on the Air," *The Angolite*, December 8, 1956, 1, 6.
145. "Something New," *The Angolite*, December 15, 1956, 3, 6.
146. "New Band Instruments Due?" *The Angolite*, November 5, 1955; "School Bells Ring," *The Angolite*, March 24, 1956, 1; "New Horns Due for Tooters," *The Angolite*, May 12, 1956, 10; "Music Classes Open at New Unit," *The Angolite*, May 19, 1956, 8.
147. "Seek Performers to Aid July 4 Fete Plans," *The Angolite*, April 28, 1956, 1; "Let 'Em Set Up Department, Then Blows," *The Angolite*, August 18, 1956, 1, 4.
148. The Mail Room, *The Angolite*, October 20, 1956, 3.
149. "Vieux Carre Pianist Given Three Years," *Times Picayune* (New Orleans), July 26, 1955, 5.
150. "Combo Ready; Why the Delay?" *The Angolite*, October 8, 1955, 9.
151. The Mail Bag, *The Angolite*, December 10, 1955, 7.
152. The Pines, *The Angolite*, October 5, 1957, 3.
153. "Musicians' Plea Nixed on Forming Combo at Camp 'A,'" *The Angolite*, November 5, 1955, 11.
154. The Pines, *The Angolite*, March 9, 1957, 7.
155. Lester Thompson, The Mail Box, *The Angolite*, March 30, 1957, 9, 12.
156. Lending Fund Minutes, *The Angolite*, March 16, 1957, 3.
157. Lester Thompson, The Mail Box, *The Angolite*, March 9, 1957, 2.
158. The Pines, *The Angolite*, March 9, 1957, 7.
159. "The Willows," *The Angolite*, May 18, 1957, 8.

160. "The Willows," 8.
161. "New Women's Unit," *The Angolite*, April 14, 1956, 4.
162. "Women's Council Holds Meeting," *The Angolite*, September 28, 1957, 1.
163. For an overview of considerations of music in women's prison, see Benjamin J. Harbert, "Guest Editor's Introduction," Special Issue on Women's Prison Music, *American Music* 31, no. 2 (Summer 2013): 127–133.
164. Sarah Haley, *No Mercy Here: Gender, Punishment, and the Making of Jim Crow Modernity* (Chapel Hill: University of North Carolina Press, 2016), 215.
165. Childs, *Slaves of the State*, 108.
166. "Women Get Church Organ," *The Angolite*, November 19, 1955, 3.
167. "Women's Council Holds Meeting," 1, 12.
168. "The Willows," *The Angolite*, June 22, 1957, 8; "Nic-Nacs Thrill Willows Again," *The Angolite*, July 20, 1957, 5.
169. "Women's Council Holds Meeting," 1, 12.
170. Hickory Nuts, *The Angolite*, October 12, 1957, 7.
171. Hickory Nuts, *The Angolite*, October 19, 1957, 6.
172. "The Cyprus Lowdown," *The Angolite*, September 21, 1957, 6.
173. Walnut Citizens, *The Angolite*, November 2, 1957, 7.
174. *The Angolite*, January 31, 1959, 8.
175. *The Angolite*, February 7, 1959, 1.
176. Lin Sharpe, email correspondence with the author, October 13, 2006.
177. For a sustained argument from this perspective of Angola's music as prison labor, see Childs, *Slaves of the State*, 117.
178. "Fourth Band in Talent Show," *The Angolite*, February 14, 1959, 1.
179. Theodore Jack, *The Angolite*, February 7, 1959, 10.
180. "Talent Show Shaping Up," *The Angolite*, February 21, 1959, 1.
181. Rion, *Beyond His Time*, 25.
182. Carleton, *Politics and Punishment*, 178.
183. Rumors into the 1960s claimed that she was pregnant. Charles Neville, interview with author, Georgetown University, Washington, DC, March 30, 2017.
184. Carleton, *Politics and Punishment*, 179.
185. "Prison Flogging," *Shreveport Times* (Shreveport, LA), March 20, 1961, 4.
186. Douglas Dennis in Lane Nelson, "Looking Back: Those Were the Days," *The Angolite* 25, September/October 2000, 38.
187. Intensive searching yielded no traces of these musicians postrelease (which speaks to how incarceration can decimate job prospects for returning citizens) save for Les Winslow and Louis "Fuzz" Surgent. Winslow started a small music school with two studios in West Monroe. He and his trio (accordion, violin, and bass) took regular gigs at members-only restaurants, clubs, and weddings. He kept his conviction and time at Angola to himself. Personal communication with James C. "Buddy" Moore, phone, July 19, 2013. After Surgent's release from Angola, he was later convicted and sentenced in California where he again became a leader in the music scene. Dietz, "Long Night's Journey into Day," 17.

188. Joachim-Ernst Berendt, *The Jazz Book: From Ragtime to Fusion and Beyond*, 7th ed. (Chicago: Chicago Review Press, 2009).
189. William Claxton and Joachim-Ernst Berndt, *Jazzlife: A Journey for Jazz Across America in 1960* (Cologne, Germany: Taschen, 2013), 27.
190. Claxton and Berndt, *Jazzlife*, 27.
191. John S. Wilson, "SWING, SWING: A German Visitor Finds Jazz All Over U.S.," *New York Times*, July 24, 1960, X9.
192. James Khoury, "Subculture at Angola: Jazz Music, Collaboration, and Experience." Final paper (MUSC 324: Music in U.S. Prisons), Department of Performing Arts, Georgetown University, 2017, 3–4.

Chapter 3

1. Leotha Brown, interview with author, Louisiana State Penitentiary, Angola, LA, December 16, 2008.
2. Matt Micucci and Brian Zimmerman, "Song of the Day: Cannonball Adderley Quintet, 'Work Song,'" *JAZZIZ* Magazine 25, November 2020.
3. Brown, interview, December 17, 2008.
4. Brown, interview, December 16, 2008.
5. Mark T. Carleton, *Politics and Punishment: The History of the Louisiana State Penal System* (Baton Rouge: Louisiana State University Press, 1971), 185.
6. Charles Neville, interview with author, Louisiana State Penitentiary, Angola, LA, March 11, 2016.
7. Albert Woodfox and Leslie George, *Solitary: Unbroken by Four Decades in Solitary Confinement. My Story of Transformation and Hope*, First Grove Atlantic Hardcover Edition (New York: Grove Press, 2019), 44.
8. Neville, interview.
9. Howard W. Odum and Guy B. Johnson, *The Negro and His Songs: A Study of Typical Negro Songs in the South* (Chapel Hill: University of North Carolina Press, 1925); Howard W. Odum and Guy Benton Johnson, *Negro Workaday Songs* (Chapel Hill: University of North Carolina Press, 1926); Lawrence Gellert, *Negro Songs of Protest* (New York: American Music League, 1936); H. Bruce Franklin, "Songs of an Imprisoned People," *MELUS* 6, no. 1 (Spring 1979): 6–22; Bruce Jackson, *Wake Up Dead Man: Hard Labor and Southern Blues* (Athens: University of Georgia Press, 1999).
10. Jackson, *Wake Up Dead Man*, xxv, 29.
11. I am referencing Michel de Certeau's idea that "space is a practiced place" or, in his more detailed explanation, "a place is the order (of whatever kind) in accord with which elements are distributed in relationships of coexistence ... an instantaneous configuration of positions. It implies an indication of stability." Michel de Certeau, *The Practice of Everyday Life*, trans. Steven F. Rendall (Berkeley: University of California Press, 2011), 117.
12. "Inside Angola: 'In the Field," *The Angolite*, September/October 1979, 55.

13. "Inside Angola," 53.
14. Neville, interview.
15. "Inside Angola," 55.
16. Neville, interview.
17. Neville, interview.
18. The stretches of desert along the US-Mexico border similarly serves as a technology of violence, intentionally left barren by the state. People die of thirst in the Rio Grande Valley.
19. Jerry Allison, Darryl Bowman, Herman Tausing, Clifford Hampton, Herbert Williams, and Walter Quinn, interview with author, Louisiana State Penitentiary, Angola, LA, April 22, 2013.
20. Allison et al., interview.
21. Neville, interview.
22. Neville, interview. I heard Neville perform a full version of "The Signifyin' Monkey" when I invited him to speak to prisoners at the Jessup Correctional Institution in Maryland in 2017. Filled with language that would ordinarily lead to an infraction among prisoners, Neville's rendition had prisoners, officers, and administrators laughing and hanging on to every word for at least a half-hour.
23. Samuel Stark, interview with author, Louisiana State Penitentiary, Angola, LA, April 22, 2013.
24. Allison et al., interview.
25. Allison et al., interview.
26. Brown, interview, July 13, 2009.
27. Jackson, *Wake Up Dead Man*, 32.
28. Neville, interview.
29. The concept of "affective labor" has been used more to understand professional and service work in a post-Fordist economy. For a primer on the concept, see Michael Hardt, "Affective Labor," *Boundary 2* 26, no. 2 (Summer 1999): 89. For other uses of using affective labor as a theoretical frame in ethnomusicological studies, see Ana Hofman, "Music (as) Labour: Professional Musicianship, Affective Labour and Gender in Socialist Yugoslavia," *Ethnomusicology Forum* 24, no. 1 (February 2015): 28–50 and Kelley Tatro, "The Hard Work of Screaming: Physical Exertion and Affective Labor Among Mexico City's Punk Vocalists," *Ethnomusicology* 58, no. 3 (Fall 2014): 431–453.
30. Larry Wilkerson, interview with author, Louisiana State Penitentiary, Angola, LA, April 23, 2013.
31. Wilbert Rideau, *In the Place of Justice: A Story of Punishment and Deliverance* (New York: Alfred A. Knopf, 2010), 96; Wilbert Rideau and Billy Sinclair, "Prisoner Litigation: How It Began in Louisiana," *Louisiana Law Review* 45, no. 5 (May 1985): 1067–1068.
32. Charles Vernardo, interview with author, Louisiana State Penitentiary, Angola, LA, April 22, 2013.
33. Neville, interview; Rideau, *In the Place of Justice*, 76; Woodfox, *Solitary*, 25–26.
34. "Music Room Sounds," *The Angolite*, March 7, 1964, 7.

35. "Sounds at Sundown," *The Angolite*, August 1, 1964, 8.
36. Carleton, *Politics and Punishment*, 185.
37. Neville, interview with author, Georgetown University, Washington, DC, March 30, 2017.
38. *The Angolite*, March 2, 1963, 3.
39. "Music Room Sounds," *The Angolite*, April 25, 1964, 7.
40. *The Angolite*, November 23, 1963.
41. *The Angolite*, November 6, 1963.
42. *The Angolite*, November 6, 1963.
43. Allison et al., interview.
44. Neville, interview with author, Louisiana State Penitentiary, March 11, 2016.
45. Art Neville, Aaron Neville, Charles Neville, and Cyril Neville, *Brothers: An Autobiography* (Cambridge, MA: Da Capo Press, 2001), 156.
46. Adam R. Rathge, "Mapping the Muggleheads: New Orleans and the Marijuana Menace, 1920–1930," *Southern Spaces*, October 23, 2018, https://southernspaces.org/2018/mapping-muggleheads-new-orleans-and-marijuana-menace-1920-1930/ (accessed June 2, 2021).
47. Neville, interview with author, Georgetown University, Washington, DC, March 30, 2017.
48. "Music Room Sounds," *The Angolite*, March 7, 1964, 7.
49. Dr. John and Jack Rummel, *Under a Hoodoo Moon: The Life of Dr. John the Night Tripper* (New York: St. Martin's Press, 1994), 51, 60–61, 145, 158.
50. Neville, interview with author, Louisiana State Penitentiary, March 11, 2016.
51. Paul Berliner, *Thinking in Jazz: The Infinite Art of Improvisation* (Chicago: University of Chicago Press, 1994), 16–17; Ingrid Monson, *Freedom Sounds: Civil Rights Call Out to Jazz and Africa* (New York: Oxford University Press, 2007), 84.
52. Berliner, *Thinking in Jazz*, 29.
53. Neville, interview with author, Louisiana State Penitentiary, March 11, 2016.
54. Charles Suhor, "Don Suhor: From Dixieland to Bopsieland," *The Jazz Archivist* 29 (2016): 7–8.
55. Charles Suhor, *Jazz in New Orleans: The Postwar Years Through 1970*, Studies in Jazz 38 (Lanham, MD: Scarecrow Press, 2001), 249.
56. There are several editions of Russell's work, each slightly different from the other. While Russell wrote it in 1953 and the copyright date is 1959, Neville had procured the 1964 edition: George Russell, *The Lydian Chromatic Concept of Tonal Organization for Improvisation* (Cambridge, MA: Concept Publishing Company, 1964).
57. Neville, interview with author, Louisiana State Penitentiary, March 11, 2016.
58. Neville et al., *Brothers*, 155.
59. Monson, *Freedom Sounds*, 14, 304.
60. Technically, the Lydian scale can be derived from a stack of fifths: C G D A E B F♯. The major scale is not. Because of this inherent stability of fifths, Russell argued, the notes in the Lydian scales are more resolved in relation to the tonic. Try playing a stack of fifths on a piano from C all the way to B. If you then play an F natural, it will likely feel unresolved.
61. Russell, *The Lydian Chromatic Concept of Tonal Organization for Improvisation*, xvi–xvii, C.

62. Monson, *Freedom Sounds*, 97.
63. Berliner, *Thinking in Jazz*, 118.
64. Nicole Brittingham Furlonge, *Race Sounds: The Art of Listening in African American Literature* (Iowa City: University of Iowa Press, 2018), 21.
65. Charles Neville, "Sounds of Music," *The Angolite*, June 17, 1966, 8.
66. Crism, "Sounds of Music," *The Angolite*, November 15, 1966, 17.
67. Crism, "Sounds of Music," 16.
68. I am referencing a conversation I had with Neville about Michel Foucault's notion of "subjugated knowledge," which he defines as "a whole set of knowledges that have been disqualified as inadequate to their task or insufficiently elaborated," and argues that it "is through the re-appearance of this knowledge . . . that criticism performs its work." See Michel Foucault, *Power/Knowledge: Selected Interviews and Other Writings, 1972–1977*, ed. Colin Gordon (New York: Pantheon Books, 1980), 82.
69. There are principles behind avoiding parallel fifths. Independent melodies can lose their distinction because the relationship of the fifth is very consonant. The problem with understanding this as a rule of music theory is that it is specific to a certain kind of polyphonic music in European tradition. Authors of European music theory texts rarely qualify them as stylistic but rather assume that they are universal rational theories.
70. Russell, *The Lydian Chromatic Concept of Tonal Organization for Improvisation*, 49.
71. "James Black," DRUMMERWORLD, https://www.drummerworld.com/drummers/James_Black.html (accessed May 9, 2020).
72. Riley Herlin and Johnny Vidacovich, *New Orleans Jazz and Second Line Drumming* (Van Nuys, CA: Alfred Publishing, 2006), 66–67.
73. Suhor, *Jazz in New Orleans*.
74. Neville, interview with author, Louisiana State Penitentiary, March 11, 2016.
75. Neville, "Sounds of Music," *The Angolite*, March 15, 1967, 12.
76. Neville, interview with author, Louisiana State Penitentiary, March 11, 2016.
77. Neville, interview with author, Louisiana State Penitentiary, March 11, 2016.
78. For more on America's history of associationism, see William J. Novak, *The People's Welfare: Law and Regulation in Nineteenth-Century America* (Chapel Hill: University of North Carolina Press, 1996).
79. Neville, interview with author, Louisiana State Penitentiary, March 11, 2016.
80. George Russell, *George Russell's Lydian Chromatic Concept of Tonal Organization*, 4th ed. (Brookline, MA: Concept Pub. Company, 2001), 171.
81. Russell, *George Russell's Lydian Chromatic Concept*, 64.
82. Alan Lomax, *The Land Where Blues Began* (New York: Pantheon, 1993), 273–277.
83. There are many other instances of thinking creative music while performing repetitive tasks, including the famous example of Berry Gordy thinking music on the automobile assembly lines in Detroit before founding Motown Records. See Mark Slobin, *Motor City Music: A Detroiter Looks Back* (New York: Oxford University Press), 2018, 163.
84. Ray B. Browne, "Some Notes on the Southern 'Holler,'" *Journal of American Folklore* 67, no. 263 (January–March, 1954): 73–77.
85. Lomax, *The Land Where Blues Began*, 269.
86. Neville, interview, Louisiana State Penitentiary, March 30, 2017.

87. Ethnomusicologist Tim Rice describes the importance of socially isolated space of the pasture, where Bulgarian bagpipe players learn while tending sheep (to the relief of tender ears back in the village). Free from audiences, learning musicians could think through ideas, explore intellectual dead-ends, or fail to solve a musical problem without the exigency of bandmates or audiences. Timothy Rice, *May It Fill Your Soul: Experiencing Bulgarian Music* (Chicago: University of Chicago Press, 1994), 44.
88. Neville, interview, Louisiana State Penitentiary, March 30, 2017.
89. Many musicians in Louisiana's prison fields today have told me that their heads get filled with musical ideas due to the boredom of the work. Clay Logan and Warren Scott, interview with author, Elayn Hunt Correctional Center, St. Gabriel, LA, April 12, 2012. Wider studies on the effects of mundane tasks have made links between boredom and creativity. In a clinical study, participants were asked to read from the telephone books for extended periods of time—arguably one of the more boring tasks. Afterward, they found that creative thinking improved. See Sandi Mann and Rebekah Cadman, "Does Being Bored Make Us More Creative?" *Creativity Research Journal* 26, no. 2 (2014): 165–173.
90. See Gellert, *Negro Songs of Protest*, 7; Lomax, *The Land Where the Blues Began*, 261; Jackson, *Wake Up Dead Man*, 11–12, 126, 177.
91. Charles Neville, "Sounds of Music," *The Angolite*, March 15, 1967, 13.
92. Ryan A. Brasseaux, "A Biographical Sketch: James Carrol Booker III," *Louisiana History* 39, no. 4 (Fall 1998): 480.
93. Jim Beckerman, "Musical Genius Getting His Due," *Herald News* (Woodland Park, NJ), July 28, 2013. Life Section, 2.
94. Brown, interview, December 17, 2008.
95. Brown, interview, December 17, 2008.
96. Neville, interview, March 11, 2016.
97. Russell, *The Lydian Chromatic Concept of Tonal Organization for Improvisation*, 49.
98. Neville et al., *Brothers*, 155.
99. Neville et al., *Brothers*, 156.
100. Neville, interview, Louisiana State Penitentiary, March 30, 2017.
101. Paraphrased in Neville, interview.
102. Brasseaux, "A Biographical Sketch," 480.
103. Rideau and Sinclair, "Prisoner Litigation," 1061.
104. Russell, *George Russell's Lydian Chromatic Concept of Tonal Organization*, 224.

Chapter 4

1. Warren Harris, Art Silvertone, Laird Veillon, Jewell Spotville, Ray Jones, and Johnny Jones, interview with author, Louisiana State Penitentiary, Angola, LA, April 10, 2008.
2. Michael Kleinsteuber, Head of Digital Solutions, Standard Chartered Bank, text message to author, June 20, 2022.

NOTES TO PAGES 145–151   301

3. Wilbert Rideau and Billy Sinclair, "Prisoner Litigation: How It Began in Louisiana," *Louisiana Law Review* 45, no. 5 (May 1985): 1061–1076.
4. Wilbert Rideau, *In the Place of Justice: A Story of Punishment and Deliverance* (New York: Alfred A. Knopf, 2010), 77.
5. For further critical reading on the Angola Rodeo, see Melissa R. Schrift, "The Wildest Show in the South: The Politics and Poetics of the Angola Prison Rodeo and Inmate Arts Festival," *Southern Cultures* 14, no. 1 (Spring 2008): 22–41; Dennis Childs, *Slaves of the State: Black Incarceration from the Chain Gang to the Penitentiary* (Minneapolis: University of Minnesota Press, 2015), 98–99; and Aviva Shen, "Angola prison rodeo offers risks and rewards for Louisiana's hard-knock lifers," *The Guardian*, October 29, 2016, https://www.theguardian.com/us-news/2016/oct/29/angola-prison-rodeo-louisiana.
6. *State Times Advocate* (Baton Rouge), September 11, 1970, 12-C.
7. "Rodeo: Wild and Wet!" *The Angolite*, November 15, 1966, 3–4.
8. "The Continentals to Play at Banquet—Norwood to Emcee," *The Angolite*, June 17, 1966, 6; *The Angolite*, December 25, 1966, 14.
9. "Rodeo," *The Angolite*, 4.
10. Anne Butler and C. Murray Henderson, *Angola, Louisiana State Penitentiary: A Half-Century of Rage and Reform* (Lafayette: Center for Louisiana Studies, University of Southwestern Louisiana, 1990), 87.
11. Butler and Henderson, *Angola*, 97.
12. Butler and Henderson, *Angola*, 87.
13. Jessica Adams, *Wounds of Returning: Race, Memory, and Property on the Postslavery Plantation* (Chapel Hill: University of North Carolina Press, 2007), 135–158; Melissa R. Schrift, "The Wildest Show in the South: The Politics and Poetics of the Angola Prison Rodeo and Inmate Arts Festival," *Southern Cultures* 14, no. 1 (Spring 2008): 22–41.
14. Michel Foucault, *Discipline and Punish: The Birth of the Prison*, 2nd ed. (New York: Vintage, 1991), 232–256. For an update of Foucault's notion of hidden carceral power, see C. Fred Alford, "What Would It Matter If Everything Foucault Said About Prison Were Wrong? 'Discipline and Punish' after Twenty Years," *Theory and Society* 29, no. 1 (February 2000): 125–146.
15. *The Angolite*, December 25, 1966, 13.
16. Nan Nadler, "Angola Cons Have Music, Will Travel to Perform," *Daily World* (Opelousas, LA), July 25, 1968, 12.
17. James B. Johnson Jr., "Prison Songs—Past and Present," *Louisiana Magazine*, 1968, 13. For an overview on the development of outlaw country, see Max Fraser, "Down in the Hole: Outlaw Country and Outlaw Culture," *Southern Cultures* 24, no. 3 (Fall 2018): 89–92.
18. "Angola Band Steals Old South Jamboree Show," *Times-Star* (Denham Springs), September 5, 1968, 3.
19. Charles Lussier, "Baton Rouge TV Star, Community Leader 'Buckskin Bill' Black Dies," *The Advocate*, January 12, 2018.
20. Johnson, "Prison Songs," 13; Nadler, "Angola Cons Have Music," 12.

21. "A Look Back at Buckskin Bill, an Icon Who Entertained Generations in EBR," *St. George Leader* (Baton Rouge), January 25, 2018.
22. Brian Balogh, *The Associational State: American Governance in the Twentieth Century* (Philadelphia: University of Pennsylvania Press, 2015), 28–30.
23. Balogh, *The Associational State*, 31.
24. For a contemporary analysis of what I am calling "astonishment," see Leonidas Cheliotis's writing on "decorative justice." Leonidas Cheliotis, "Decorative Justice: Deconstructing the Relationship between the Arts and Imprisonment," *International Journal for Crime, Justice and Social Democracy* 3, no. 1 (April 2014): 16–34; Leonidas Cheliotis and Aleksandra Jordanoska, "The Arts of Desistance: Assessing the Role of Arts-Based Programmes in Reducing Reoffending," *Howard Journal* 55, no. 1–2 (May 2016): 25–41.
25. John M. Sloop, *The Cultural Prison: Discourse, Prisoners, and Punishment* (Tuscaloosa: University of Alabama Press, 1996).
26. "'Tangipahoa on the Go' Fair Underway in Amite," *State Times* (Baton Rouge), October 1968.
27. Margaret Dixon, "Unique Inquisition Ready to Show Off," *Sunday Advocate* (Baton Rouge), October 20, 1968.
28. "Beauty Contest for Men Slated at Livonia," *The Morning Advocate* (Baton Rouge), May 7, 1969.
29. "Convicted Killer Returned to Angola After Capture," *Times Picayune* (New Orleans), May 9, 1969.
30. "Music Festival Set at Angola," *Morning Advocate* (Baton Rouge), May 24, 1969.
31. *State Times Advocate* (Baton Rouge), August 25, 1970, 11.
32. *State Times Advocate*, 11.
33. *Cooper v. Pate*, 378 U.S. 546, 1964.
34. Team of Inspectors Critical of La. Pen.," *Sunday Advocate* (Baton Rouge), March 21, 1974.
35. *Pat Terrell et al. v. Louis M. Sowers et al.* Civil No. 71-260, E.D.La., filed August 5, 1971.
36. Louisiana Advisory Committee to the United States Commission on Civil Rights, "A Study of Adult Corrections in Louisiana," May 1976, 20.
37. Louisiana Advisory Committee, "A Study of Adult Corrections in Louisiana," 89.
38. Jerry Allison, Darryl Bowman, Herman Tausing, Clifford Hampton, Herbert Williams, and Walter Quinn, interview with author, Louisiana State Penitentiary, Angola, LA, April 22, 2013.
39. Bud Wilkerson, interview with author, Louisiana State Penitentiary, Angola, LA, April 22. 2013.
40. Dora Rabelais, email to author, 2012.
41. Nadler, "Angola Cons Have Music, 12; "A Look Back at Buckskin Bill"; "Who is Buckskin Bill?" *WAFB9*, Baton Rouge, LA, October 11, 2006, https://www.wafb.com/story/5525752/who-is-buckskin-bill/ (accessed March 21, 2022).
42. "Villa Feliciana Art Exhibition Slated Sunday," *State Times* (Baton Rouge), October 3, 1972, 9.
43. *The Angolite*, March 4, 1979, 16, 21–22.

44. Albert Woodfox, *Solitary: Unbroken by Four Decades in Solitary Confinement. My Story of Transformation and Hope* (New York: Grove Press, 2019), 37.
45. Woodfox, *Solitary,* 109–110.
46. Erving Goffman, *Asylums: Essays on the Social Situation of Mental Patients and Other Inmates* (New Brunswick, NJ: Aldine Transaction, 2009).
47. Erving Goffman, *Interaction Ritual: Essays on Face-to-Face Behavior* (New York: Doubleday, 1967), 12.
48. Goffman, *Interaction Ritual,* 22.
49. Clarence Wilkerson, *Angola Tapes,* recorded at Louisiana State Penitentiary, Angola, LA, 1973. Personal collection.
50. Wilkerson, *Angola Tapes.*
51. Wilkerson, *Angola Tapes.*
52. Aaron A. Fox, *Real Country: Music and Language in Working-Class Culture* (Durham, NC: Duke University Press, 2004), 107.
53. Goffman, *Interaction Ritual,* 21–22.
54. Erving Goffman, *Stigma: Notes on the Management of Spoiled Identity* (New York: Simon & Schuster, 1963), 3.
55. Goffman, *Stigma,* 45.
56. One commonality I have seen in many years of watching prison musicians is the ways in which onstage posture walks the line between expressive posturing and deferential slouching. My film presents plenty of examples of this. Historical photos of the Westernaires also bear evidence of this prison-specific posture.
57. Goffman, *Stigma,* 2–31. The hypothetical concert here is informed by my conversations with Bud Wilkerson, other incarcerated musicians who played country music to outside audiences, and informal conversations with people who remember the band's performances. To my knowledge, there is no detailed account of a particular show.
58. Fox, *Real Country,* 108–109, 117.
59. Caleb Smith, "Editor's Introduction," in *The Life and the Adventures of a Haunted Convict* (New York: Random House, 2016), xl.
60. Sloop, *The Cultural Prison,* 108–110.
61. Wilkerson, *Angola Tapes.*
62. Wilkerson, *Angola Tapes.*
63. Fox, *Real Country,* 88.
64. Rachel A. Smith, "Segmenting an Audience into the Own, the Wise, and Normals: A Latent Class Analysis of Stigma-Related Categories," *Communication Research Reports* 29, no. 4 (October 2012): 257–265.
65. As music historian Karl Hagstrom Miller argues, popular music in the early twentieth century began to split into racialized narratives. He writes, "[T]he hillbilly ultimately told a story of commonality while the minstrel remained an exercise in difference." *Segregating Sound: Inventing Folk and Pop Music in the Age of Jim Crow* (Durham, NC: Duke University Press, 2010), 146.
66. Sloop, *The Cultural Prison,* 116–123.
67. *Zablocki v. Redhail,* No. 76-879, 434 U.S. 374, 1978.

68. "The Axe on Travel," *The Angolite*, March/April, 17–18.
69. "The Axe on Travel," 21.
70. Larry Bartlett, "Profile of a Prison," *Times-Picayune* (New Orleans), October 11, 1970, 8.
71. Bartlett, "Profile of a Prison," 6–8.
72. *State Times Advocate* (Baton Rouge), September 11, 1970, 11.
73. Leotha Brown, interview with author, Louisiana State Penitentiary, Angola, LA, December 17, 2008.
74. Michael Lindsay, interview with author, Louisiana State Penitentiary, Angola, LA, November 7, 2012.
75. Butler and Henderson, *Angola*, 52.
76. Butler and Henderson, *Angola*, 160.
77. Balogh, *The Associational State*, 28–30.
78. *The Angolite*, June 17, 1964.
79. Butler and Henderson, *Angola*, 4.
80. Burk Foster, Wilbert Rideau, and Douglas Dennis, *The Wall Is Strong: Corrections in Louisiana*, 4th ed. (Lafayette: University of Louisiana Press, 2014), 108.
81. Robert L. Harris, "Early Black Benevolent Societies, 1780–1830," *Massachusetts Review* 20, no. 3 (Fall 1979): 603–625; Michael P. Smith, "Behind the Lines: The Black Mardi Gras Indians and the New Orleans Second Line," *Black Music Research Journal* 14, no. 1 (Fall 1994): 43–73.
82. Harriet A. Jacobs, *Incidents in the Life of a Slave Girl* (New York: Oxford University Press, 1988), 32.
83. Foster et al., *The Wall Is Strong*, 107.
84. *The Angolite*, June 17, 1964.
85. 331 F. Supp. 1123 (E.D. La. 1971); Rideau and Sinclair, "Prisoner Litigation," 1066.
86. Foster et al., *The Wall Is Strong*, 109.
87. *The Angolite*, January 2, 1978, 43–44.
88. *The Angolite*, April 5, 1974, 27.
89. *The Angolite*, April 5, 1974, 15.
90. Thomas, "Twin" Wiltz, "Sound of Music," *The Angolite*, April 5, 1974, 4.
91. See Nicole Brittingham Furlonge, *Race Sounds: The Art of Listening in African American Literature* (Iowa City: University of Iowa Press, 2018), 41–58. For his collected writings on jazz, see Ralph Ellison, *Living with Music: Ralph Ellison's Jazz Writings*, ed. Robert G. O'Meally (New York: Modern Library, 2003).
92. Ralph Ellison, "The Art of Fiction: An Interview," in *The Collected Essays of Ralph Ellison* (New York: Modern Library, 1995), 216.
93. Ralph Ellison, "On Initiation Rites and Power: A Lecture at West Point," in *The Collected Essays of Ralph Ellison* (New York: Modern Library, 1995), 536.
94. W. E. B. Du Bois, *The Souls of Black Folk* (New York: Dover, 1994).
95. Rideau, *In the Place of Justice*, 85; Lydia Pelot-Hobbs, "Organizing for Freedom: The Angola Special Civics Project, 1987–1992" (master's thesis, University of New Orleans, 2011), 47.

96. Norval Morris, "The Contemporary Prison," in *The Oxford History of the Prison: The Practice of Punishment in Western Society*, ed. N. Morris and D. J. Rothman (New York: Oxford University Press, 1995), 216–218.
97. Ronald Gene Wikberg, *A Graphic & Illustrative History 1879 to 1979: Life Sentences in Louisiana* (Angola: Louisiana State Penitentiary, n.d.).
98. Tommy Mason, "The Lifers Association," *The Angolite*, September/October 1982.
99. Rideau, *In the Place of Justice*, 83; *The Lifer*, ed. Wilbert Rideau, Tommy Mason, Robert Jackson, and Kenneth Plaisance (West Feliciana Parish, LA: Documents and Published Materials-Published Works, National Museum of African American History and Culture, January/February/March 1974).
100. *The Advocate* (Baton Rouge), March 21, 1974, 52.
101. Wilbert Rideau, "Lifers of Angola," *The Angolite*, October, 1974, 21.
102. Edward Cook, phone interview with author, February 17, 2013.
103. Orissa Arend, "Black vs. Blue," *New Orleans Magazine*, October 1, 2015, https://www.myneworleans.com/black-vs-blue/.
104. *The Angolite*, October, 1974, 20.
105. Rideau, *In the Place of Justice*, 79.
106. Miller, *Segregating Sound*, 73–79.
107. Paul Gilroy, *The Black Atlantic: Modernity and Double Consciousness* (Cambridge, MA: Harvard University Press, 1993).
108. Gilroy, *The Black Atlantic*, 37.
109. *The Angolite*, October, 1974.
110. Wilbert Rideau, "Escape . . ." *The Angolite*, July 8, 1976, 25.
111. *The Angolite*, December 25, 1966, 14.
112. Charles Vernardo, interview with author. Louisiana State Penitentiary. Angola, LA, April 22, 2013.
113. Foster et al., *The Wall Is Strong*, 108.
114. Foster et al., *The Wall Is Strong*, 110.
115. Foster et al., *The Wall Is Strong*, 109.
116. Monica L. Bergeron, "Second Place Isn't Good Enough: Achieving True Reform Through Expanded Parole Eligibility," *Louisiana Law Review* 80, no. 1 (2020): 109–163, 124.
117. Harris et al., interview.
118. Benjamin Harbert, "Ethnomusicological Vérité: Filming Musicians in Louisiana and California State Prisons," paper presented at Society for Ethnomusicology Annual Meeting, Middletown, CT, 2008.
119. Benjamin Harbert, "Doing Time: The Work of Music in Louisiana Prisons" (PhD diss., University of California, Los Angeles, 2010).
120. Jewell Spotville and Emmanuel Lee, interview with author, Louisiana State Penitentiary, Angola, LA, April 13, 2012.
121. George Jackson, *Blood in My Eye* (Baltimore: Basic Classic Press, 1990).
122. Benjamin Harbert, dir., *Follow Me Down: Portraits of Louisiana Prison Musicians* (New York: Films for the Humanities & Sciences, 2012), DVD.

Chapter 5

1. Robert T. Chase, "We Are Not Slaves: Rethinking the Rise of Carceral States through the Lens of the Prisoners' Rights Movement," *Journal of American History* 102, no. 1 (June 2015): 76.
2. Rachel Breunlin and Helen A. Regis, "Putting the Ninth Ward on the Map: Race, Place, and Transformation in Desire, New Orleans," *American Anthropologist* 108, no. 4 (December 2006): 746.
3. John M. Sloop, *The Cultural Prison: Discourse, Prisoners, and Punishment* (Tuscaloosa: University of Alabama Press, 1996), 132–139.
4. The ruling found merit in the plaintiff's claim that not providing exercise to death row confinement and the trusty system itself violated protection against cruel and unusual punishment (Eighth Amendment) and that the arbitrary use of administrative segregation denied due process (Fourteenth Amendment) for disciplinary actions. *Sinclair v. Henderson*, 331 F. Supp. 1123 (E.D. La. 1971).
5. This ruling held that a litany of Angola's conditions constitutes violations of Eighth Amendment freedom from cruel and unusual punishment beyond *Sinclair v. Henderson. Williams v. Edwards*, Nos. 75-2792, 75-3883 (1977).
6. Here I borrow John Street's notion that music has political power when giving structure to certain feelings, representing history, dreams, community, and sentiment. See John Street, "Rock, Pop and Politics," in *The Cambridge Companion to Pop and Rock*, ed. Simon Frith, Will Straw, and John Street (New York: Cambridge University Press, 2000), 247.
7. *State v. Neal*, 275 So. 2d 765 (La. 1973).
8. *Williams v. McKeithen*, 495 F. Supp. 707 (M.D. La. 1980).
9. Wilbert Rideau, "Veterans Incarcerated," *Penthouse: The International Magazine for Men* 7, no. 8, April 1976, 166.
10. Bleu Evans, telephone interview with author, February 17, 2013.
11. "Boogie Down," *The Angolite*, March 4, 1978, 9.
12. Evans, interview.
13. "A Star Is Born?" *The Angolite*, July 8, 1978, 10.
14. "Boogie Down," 9.
15. "A Star Is Born?" 10.
16. "End of an Era," *The Angolite*, March 4, 1976, 1.
17. Chase, "We Are Not Slaves," 80–81.
18. *Elie v. Henderson*, US District Court for the Eastern District of Louisiana, 340 F. Supp. 958 (E.D. La. 1972). March 31, 1972, 963.
19. Gary Taubes and Cristin Kearns Couzens, "Big Sugar's Sweet Little Lies," *Mother Jones*, October 31, 2012.
20. "In the Field," *The Angolite*, September 10, 1979, 51–56.
21. John Henry Taylor Jr., interview with author, Louisiana State Penitentiary, Angola, LA, April 11, 2008.
22. Rideau, *In the Place of Justice*, 227.

NOTES TO PAGES 196–207   307

23. Michael Dyer and Calvin Lewis, interview with author, Louisiana State Penitentiary, Angola, LA, November 7, 2012.
24. Stanley Lindsay, interview with author, Louisiana State Penitentiary, Angola, LA, November 7, 2012.
25. Lindsay, interview.
26. Lindsay, interview.
27. Daniel Washington and Walter Quinn, interview with author, Louisiana State Penitentiary, Angola, LA, November 5, 2012.
28. Dyer and Lewis, interview.
29. Lindsay, interview.
30. James Marsh, interview with author, Louisiana State Penitentiary, Angola, LA, November 7, 2012.
31. Marsh, interview.
32. Marsh, interview. For similar but more colorful folkloric descriptions of a similar utility, see Alan Lomax and John Avery Lomax, *American Ballads and Folk Songs* (New York: Dover, 1994), 57; John A. Lomax, Alan Lomax, Ruth Crawford Seeger, and Harold William Thompson, *Our Singing Country: A Second Volume of American Ballads and Folk Songs* (New York: Dover, 2000), 379.
33. Marsh, interview.
34. Marsh, interview.
35. *The Angolite*, November 12, 1980.
36. Lindsay, interview.
37. Lindsay, interview.
38. Quinn and Washington, interview.
39. Robin Polk, interview with author, Louisiana State Penitentiary, Angola, LA, November 5, 2012.
40. Robin Polk, interview with author, Louisiana State Penitentiary, Angola, LA, July 13, 2009.
41. Polk, interview, November 5, 2012.
42. Polk, interview, July 13, 2009.
43. Polk, interview, November 5, 2012.
44. Polk, interview, July 13, 2009.
45. Quinn and Washington, interview.
46. Myron Hodges and Donald Thomas, interview with author, Louisiana State Penitentiary, Angola, LA, November 5, 2012.
47. Breunlin and Regis, "Putting the Ninth Ward on the Map," 746.
48. Matt Sakakeeny, *Roll with It: Brass Bands in the Streets of New Orleans* (Durham, NC: Duke University Press, 2013), 11.
49. Breunlin and Regis, "Putting the Ninth Ward on the Map," 744–764.
50. Tommy R. Mason, "Second Lining . . . On the River?" *The Angolite*, March 4, 1976, 43.
51. "A Time to Smile," *The Angolite*, January/February, 1977, 39.
52. Tracy Owens Patton and Sally M. Schedlock, "Let's Go, Let's Show, Let's Rodeo: African Americans and the History of Rodeo," *Journal of African American History* 96, no. 4 (Fall 2011): 503–521.

53. Lindsay, interview.
54. *The Angolite*, May 6, 1979, 8.
55. *Handbook on the Anti-Drug Abuse Act of 1986*. Washington, DC: US Dept. of Justice, Criminal Division, 1987, https://www.ojp.gov/pdffiles1/Photocopy/157817NCJRS.pdf.
56. Courtney Harper Turkington, "Louisiana's Addiction to Mass Incarceration by the Numbers," *Loyola Law Review* 63, no. 3 (Fall 2017): 566.
57. Maureen Mahon, *Right to Rock: The Black Rock Coalition and the Cultural Politics of Race* (Durham, NC: Duke University Press, 2004), 11. See also Bakari Kitwana, *The Hip Hop Generation: Young Blacks and the Crisis in African American Culture* (New York: Basic Civitas, 2002), 3–8.
58. Dyer and Lewis, interview.
59. Jewell Spotville, Warren Harris, Art Silvertone, Laird Veillon, Ray Jones, and Johnny Jones, interview with author, Louisiana State Penitentiary, Angola, LA, April 10, 2008.
60. Larry Wilkerson, interview with author, Louisiana State Penitentiary, Angola, LA, April 23, 2013.
61. Hodges and Thomas, interview.
62. Myron Hodges, email correspondence with author, April 7, 2022.
63. For more on prison's coerced knowledge of the self, see Michel Foucault, *Discipline and Punish: The Birth of the Prison*, 2nd ed. (New York: Vintage, 1991), 295–296.
64. Ashley Lucas, "When I Run in My Bare Feet: Music, Writing, and Theater in a North Carolina Women's Prison," *American Music* 30, no. 2 (Summer 2013): 134–162, 158–159; Maria Mendonça, "Gamelan in Prisons in England and Scotland: Narratives of Transformation and the 'Good Vibrations' of Educational Rhetoric," *Ethnomusicology* 54, no. 3 (Fall 2010): 369–394.
65. Sakakeeny, *Roll with It*, 109–110.
66. Kenneth Johnston, "They Did It Again," *The Angolite*, May/June 1977, 48–49.
67. Polk, interview, November 5, 2012.
68. Polk, interview, July 13, 2009.
69. This analysis comes from a critical reading of Joni Mitchell's use of androgyny and racial passing in Kevin Fellezs, "Gender, Race, and the Ma(s)king of Joni Mitchell," in *The Cambridge Companion to the Singer-Songwriter*, ed. Katherine Williams and Justin A. Williams (Cambridge, UK: Cambridge University Press, 2016), 201–214.
70. Hodges, email, April 7, 2022.
71. Myron Hodges, interview with author, Louisiana State Penitentiary, Angola, LA, November 7, 2012.
72. Hodges, email, April 7, 2022.
73. Josh Kun, *Audiotopia: Music, Race, and America* (Berkeley: University of California Press, 2005), 22–23.
74. James Minton, "'On the Road Again': Special to Angola," *State Times* (Baton Rouge), December 27, 1990, 1-B.
75. Minton, "'On the Road Again,'" 1-B.
76. Hodges, interview, April 21, 2013; Hodges, email, April 7, 2022.
77. *The Angolite*, March/April, 1992.

78. Hodges and Thomas, interview.
79. James Minton. "Louisiana State Penitentiary Has a Band on the Road Again," *The Advocate* (Baton Rouge), December 28, 1990, 3-B.
80. Kun, *Audiotopia*, 68; Jennifer Lynn Stoever, *The Sonic Color Line: Race and the Cultural Politics of Listening* (New York: New York University Press, 2016), 16–18.
81. Sloop, *The Cultural Prison*, 132–142.
82. *The Angolite*, March/April, 1993.
83. For more in-depth examinations of the complex tensions between sacred and secular practices in African American music, see Melvin L. Butler, *Island Gospel: Pentecostal Music and Identity in Jamaica and the United States* (Urbana: University of Illinois Press, 2019); Teresa L. Reed, *The Holy Profane: Religion in Black Popular Music* (Lexington: University Press of Kentucky, 2003); and Jon Michael Spencer, *Blues and Evil* (Knoxville: University of Tennessee Press, 1993).
84. John A. Lomax, "'Sinful Songs' of the Southern Negro," *Musical Quarterly* 20, no. 2 (April 1934): 186.
85. Harry Oster, *Angola Prison Spirituals*, Louisiana Folklore Society LFS A-6, 1959, LP.
86. Taylor, interview, December 16, 2008.
87. Taylor, interview, October 21, 2009.
88. Taylor, interview, December 16, 2008.
89. Taylor, interview, December 16, 2008.
90. Taylor, interview, December 16, 2008.
91. Taylor, interview, April 11, 2008.
92. Taylor, interview, October 21, 2009.
93. Taylor, interview, April 11, 2008.
94. Taylor, interview, October 21, 2009.
95. Taylor, interview, April 11, 2008.
96. Taylor, interview, December 16, 2008.
97. Taylor, interview, December 16, 2008.
98. Taylor, interview, October 21, 2009.
99. Taylor, interview, December 16, 2008.
100. Taylor, interview, December 16, 2008.
101. Taylor, interview, December 16, 2008.
102. Taylor, interview, December 16, 2008.
103. Taylor, interview, December 16, 2008.
104. Taylor, interview, December 16, 2008.
105. Taylor, interview, December 16, 2008.
106. Taylor, interview, December 16, 2008.
107. For a description of prisoner religious associations at Angola, see Michael Hallett, *The Angola Prison Seminar: Effects of Faith-Based Ministry on Identity Transformation, Desistance, and Rehabilitation* (New York: Routledge, 2017).
108. Taylor, interview, October 21, 2009.
109. Taylor, interview, April 11, 2008.
110. Taylor, interview, October 21, 2009.

310   NOTES TO PAGES 225–233

111. Ray Jones, Jewell Spotville, and Albert Patterson, interview with author, Louisiana State Penitentiary, Angola, LA, October 19, 2009.
112. Taylor, interview, December 16, 2008.
113. Ray Jones, Jewell Spotville, Emmanuel Lee, and Albert Patterson, interview with author, Louisiana State Penitentiary, Angola, LA, July 13, 2009; Jewell Spotville and Emmanuel Lee, interview with author, Louisiana State Penitentiary, Angola, LA, April 13, 2012.
114. Johnny Jones, Warren Harris, Art Silvertone, Laird Veillon, Jewell Spotville, and Ray Jones, interview with author, Louisiana State Penitentiary, Angola, LA, April 10, 2008.
115. Johnny Jones et al., interview.
116. Taylor, interview, April 11, 2008.
117. Prentice Robinson, interview with author, Louisiana State Penitentiary, Angola, LA, October 21, 2009.
118. Ray Jones et al., interview, October 19, 2009.
119. Ray Jones, interview with author, Louisiana State Penitentiary, Angola, LA, October 21, 2009.
120. Taylor, interview, October 21, 2009.
121. Taylor, interview, October 21, 2009.
122. Taylor, interview, October 21, 2009.
123. Taylor, interview, October 21, 2009.
124. Matthew Rahaim, *Musicking Bodies Gesture and Voice in Hindustani Music* (Middletown, CT: Wesleyan University Press, 2012); Timothy Rice, *May It Fill Your Soul: Experiencing Bulgarian Music* (Chicago: University of Chicago Press, 1994).
125. Taylor, interview, October 21, 2009.
126. Taylor, interview, December 16, 2008.
127. Taylor, interview, April 11, 2008.
128. Taylor, interview, October 19, 2009.
129. Ray Jones et al., interview.
130. Taylor, interview, October 21, 2009.
131. Taylor, interview, October 21, 2009.
132. Spotville and Lee, interview.
133. Taylor, interview, December 16, 2008.
134. Taylor, interview, December 16, 2008.
135. Taylor, interview, October 21, 2009.
136. Taylor, interview, December 16, 2008; Spotville and Lee, interview.
137. Taylor, interview, December 16, 2008; Ray Jones et al., interview.
138. Taylor, interview, December 16, 2008.
139. Taylor, interview, October 21, 2009.

Chapter 6

1. Dennis Childs, *Slaves of the State: Black Incarceration from the Chain Gang to the Penitentiary* (Minneapolis: University of Minnesota Press, 2015); Kathryn Gillespie, "Placing Angola: Racialization, Anthropocentrism, and Settler Colonialism at the

Louisiana State Penitentiary's Angola Rodeo," in *Colonialism and Animality: Anti-Colonial Perspectives in Critical Animal Studies*, ed. Kelly Struthers Montford and Chloë Taylor (New York: Routledge, 2020), 250–276; Clint Smith, *How the Word Is Passed: A Reckoning with the History of Slavery Across America* (New York: Little, Brown, 2021).

2. See Jessica Adams, *Wounds of Returning: Race, Memory, and Property on the Postslavery Plantation* (Chapel Hill: University of North Carolina Press, 2007), 135–158; Childs, *Slaves of the State*, 93–140; Smith, *How the Word Is Passed*, 85–117.

3. Velia Ivanova, "The Musical Heritage of Incarceration: The Curation, Dissemination, and Management of the Lomax Collection Prison Songs" (PhD diss., Columbia University, 2021), 19–26.

4. Samuel Stark, interview with author, Louisiana State Penitentiary, Angola, LA, April 22, 2013.

5. For a discussion of uses of residual media among prisoners who do not have access to digital media, see Christina L. Baade, "Incarcerated Music: Broadcasting and the Tactics of Music Listening in Prison," in *Music and the Broadcast Experience: Performance, Production, and Audiences*, ed. Christina L. Baade and James Andrew Deaville (New York: Oxford University Press, 2016), 310–324.

6. Rebecca Sager, *Faith, Politics, and Power: The Politics of Faith-Based Initiatives* (New York: Oxford University Press, 2010), 109; Louisiana Statutes of 1999, revised 2017. § 15:828.2, 2017.

7. A. J. Freeman, Thomas "Fuzzy" Oliver, Calvin Lewis, Johnny Jones, and Myron Hodges, interview with author, Louisiana State Penitentiary, Angola, LA, April 21, 2013.

8. For more on the undergraduate degree programs offered in Louisiana State Penitentiary, see "Prison Ministry Displays the Power of the Gospel," New Orleans Baptist Theological Seminary, NOBTS, https://www.nobts.edu/news/articles/2019/AngolaReflection.html (accessed September 24, 2021) and Erik Eckholm, "Bible College Helps Some at Louisiana Prison Find Peace," *New York Times*, October 5 2013, https://www.nytimes.com/2013/10/06/us/bible-college-helps-some-at-louisiana-prison-find-peace.html (accessed September 24, 2021).

9. See Daniel Bergner, *God of the Rodeo: The Search for Hope, Faith, and a Six-Second Ride in Louisiana's Angola Prison* (New York: Crown, 1998).

10. For a discussion of the legality of faith-based state programming in Louisiana prisons, see Roy L. Bergeron Jr., "Faith on the Farm: An Analysis of Angola Prison's Moral Rehabilitation Program Under the Establishment Clause," *Louisiana Law Review* 71, no. 4 (Summer 2011): 1221–1257.

11. Louisiana Revised Statutes Tit. 15, § 828, classification and treatment programs; qualified sex offender programs; reports; earned credits.

12. Louisiana Revised Statutes Tit. 15, § 828.2. Faith-based programs for inmates; development; monitoring.

13. Freeman et al., interview.

14. Laird Veillon, interview with author, Louisiana State Penitentiary, Angola, LA, December 16, 2008; Matthew Trent, interview with author, Louisiana State Penitentiary, Angola, LA, October 19, 2009.

15. David Harvey, *A Brief History of Neoliberalism* (New York: Oxford University Press, 2005), 84.

16. Wilfred Cazelot, interview with author, Louisiana State Penitentiary, Angola, LA, October 19, 2009.
17. The Inmate Welfare Fund became the new name for the Inmate Lending Fund described in chapter 2.
18. Adams, *Wounds of Returning*, 150.
19. James Marsh, interview with author, Louisiana State Penitentiary, Angola, LA, November 7, 2012.
20. Darren Green, interview with author, Louisiana State Penitentiary, Angola, LA, October 9, 2009.
21. Freeman et al., interview.
22. Rodney Rollins, interview with author, Louisiana State Penitentiary, Angola, LA, April 21, 2013.
23. Andre Williams, interview with author, Louisiana State Penitentiary, Angola, LA, April 21, 2013.
24. Williams, interview.
25. Myron Hodges and Donald Thomas, interview with author, Louisiana State Penitentiary, Angola, LA, November 5, 2012.
26. Hodges and Thomas, interview.
27. For an influential analysis of "aura" in art, see Walter Benjamin, "The Work of Art in the Age of Mechanical Reproduction," in *Illuminations* (New York: Schocken, 2007), 221.
28. William Hall, interview with author, Louisiana State Penitentiary, Angola, LA, April 23, 2013.
29. Hall, interview.
30. Hall, interview.
31. Pierre Bourdieu, *Outline of a Theory of Practice*, trans. Richard Nice (Cambridge: Cambridge University Press, 1977), 72–95; Matthew Rahaim, *Musicking Bodies: Gesture and Voice in Hindustani Music* (Middletown, CT: Wesleyan University Press, 2012), 107–134.
32. Warren Harris, Art Silvertone, Laird Veillon, Jewell Spotville, Ray Jones, and Johnny Jones, interview with author, Louisiana State Penitentiary, Angola, LA, April 10, 2008.
33. Robin Polk, interview with author, Louisiana State Penitentiary, Angola, LA, November 12, 2012.
34. For a longer history of religious conversion testimony, see D. Bruce Hindmarsh, *The Evangelical Conversion Narrative: Spiritual Autobiography in Early Modern England* (Oxford: Oxford University Press, 2007), 251–252.
35. Harris et al., interview.
36. Maintaining a particular hairstyle, exercising, and organizing personal belongings can become vital self-discipline practices in prison.
37. Benjamin Harbert, dir., *Follow Me Down: Portraits of Louisiana Prison Musicians* (New York: Films for the Humanities & Sciences, 2012), DVD, 4:53.
38. For a comprehensive analysis, see John M. Dougan, *The Mistakes of Yesterday, the Hopes of Tomorrow: The Story of the Prisonaires* (Amherst: University of Massachusetts Press, 2012), 53; Leonidas K. Cheliotis, "Our Violence and Theirs: Comparing Prison

Realities," *South Atlantic Quarterly* 113, no. 3 (Summer 2014): 443–446; Leonidas Cheliotis and Aleksandra Jordonoska, "The Arts of Desistance: Assessing the Role of Arts–Based Programmes in Reducing Reoffending," *Howard Journal of Crime and Justice* 55, no. 1–2 (2016): 25–41.

39. Rolf Loeber and Dale Hay, "Key Issues in the Development of Aggression and Violence from Childhood to Early Adulthood," *Annual Review of Psychology* 48, no. 1 (February 1997): 371–410; Triana Rego, "Male Antisocial Behavior and Psychological Development: 'Growing Up' and Its Impact on Aggressive Conduct," *Journal of Psychology and Clinical Psychiatry* 5, no. 1 (2016).

40. Stephanie L. Perrault et al., "Archaeological Data Recovery at Angola Plantation 16WF121 and 16WF122 West Feliciana Parish, Louisiana" (Coastal Environments, Inc., Baton Rouge, LA; US Army Corps of Engineers, New Orleans District, August 2006), 99.

41. Benjamin J. Harbert, "Doing Time: The Work of Music in Louisiana Prisons" (PhD diss., University of California, Los Angeles, 2010), 275–283.

42. Benjamin Harbert, "I'll Keep on Living After I Die: Musical Manipulation and Transcendence at Louisiana State Penitentiary," in *International Journal of Community Music* 3, no. 1 (2010): 72–74.

43. Harbert, dir., *Follow Me Down*, 20:20–28:26.

44. Albert Patterson, Ray Jones, Jewell Spotville, and Emmanuel Lee, interview with author, Louisiana State Penitentiary, Angola, LA, October 19, 2009.

45. Patterson et al., interview.

46. John Henry Taylor Jr., interview with author, Louisiana State Penitentiary, Angola, LA, July 13, 2009.

47. John Henry Taylor Jr., interview with author, Louisiana State Penitentiary, Angola, LA, December 16, 2008.

48. Harbert, dir., *Follow Me Down*, 22:20–23:53.

49. Hans Toch, *Living in Prison: The Ecology of Survival* (New York: Free Press, 1977), 181; Andy McGraw, "Ethical Friction: Ethnomusicological Perspectives on Music in the Richmond City Jail," in *Transforming Ethnomusicology, Volume II: Political, Social & Ecological Issues*, ed. Beverley Diamond and Salwa El-Shawan Castelo-Branco (Oxford: Oxford University Press, 2018), 164.

50. Harbert, "I'll Keep on Living After I Die," 74.

51. Joseph C. Mouledous, "Organizational Goals and Structural Change: A Study of the Organization of a Prison Social System," *Social Forces* 41, no. 3 (March 1963): 285.

52. See Nina C. Öhman, "Vocal Virtuosity, Value Creation, and the Transformation of Contemporary Gospel Music," in *The Oxford Handbook of Economic Ethnomusicology*, ed. Anna Morcom and Timothy D. Taylor (New York: Oxford University Press, 2020).

53. John Henry Taylor Jr., interview with author, Louisiana State Penitentiary, Angola, LA, December 16, 2008.

54. Veillon, interview.

55. Joe Beyer Russell, Michael Dyer, Calvin Lewis, Gary Jameson, Johnny Jones, John Kennedy, and Frederick Jones, interview with author, Louisiana State Penitentiary, Angola, LA, April 11, 2008.

56. Russell et al., interview.
57. The 13th Amendment, ratified in 1865, says: "Neither slavery nor involuntary servitude, except as a punishment for crime whereof the party shall have been duly convicted, shall exist within the United States, or any place subject to their jurisdiction."
58. See Larry Brewster, "The Impact of Prison Arts Programs on Inmate Attitudes and Behavior: A Quantitative Evaluation," *Justice Policy Journal* 11, no. 2 (Fall 2014); Susan Dewey, Kym Codallos, Robin Barry, Kirstin Drenkhahn, Michala Glover, Alec Muthig, Susan Lockwood Roberts, and Betty Abbott, "Higher Education in Prison: A Pilot Study of Approaches and Modes of Delivery in Eight Prison Administrations," *Journal of Correctional Education* 71, no. 1 (April 2020): 57–89; and Paul Clements, "The Rehabilitative Role of Arts Education in Prison: Accommodation or Enlightenment?" *International Journal of Art & Design Education* 23 (June 2004): 169–178.
59. Gary Frank, interview with author, Louisiana State Penitentiary, Angola, LA, November 5, 2012.
60. Jesse Lee, Jason Hacker, Brian Russel, Laird Veillon, Mickey Lanerie, Frederick Jones, Donald Thomas, and Darren Green, interview with author, Louisiana State Penitentiary, Angola, LA, April 11, 2008.
61. Trent, interview.
62. Myron Hodges, email correspondence with author, April 12, 2022.
63. Robert F. Pecorella, "Property Rights, State Police Powers, and the Takings Clause: The Evolution Toward Dysfunctional Land-Use Management," *Fordham Urban Law Journal* 44, no. 1 (April 2017): 59.
64. US Constitution, amend. IV.
65. Gavin Steingo, *Kwaito's Promise: Music and the Aesthetics of Freedom in South Africa* (Chicago: University of Chicago Press, 2016), 103, 121.
66. Craig Anthony Arnold, "The Reconstitution of Property: Property as a Web of Interests," *Harvard Environmental Law Review* 26, no. 2 (2002): 281.
67. Trent, interview.
68. Benjamin, *Illuminations*, 224.
69. Russell et al., interview.
70. Lee et al., interview.
71. Lee et al., interview.
72. Trent, interview.
73. Michael Dyer and Calvin Lewis, interview with author, Louisiana State Penitentiary, Angola, LA, November 7, 2012.
74. Lee et al., interview.
75. Cazelot, interview.
76. Trent, interview.
77. Robin Polk, interview with author, Louisiana State Penitentiary, Angola, LA, July 13, 2009.
78. Leotha Brown, interview with author, Louisiana State Penitentiary, Angola, LA, July 13, 2009.

79. Brown, interview.
80. Lee et al., interview.
81. Russell et al., interview.
82. For a longer discussion of this Western European root of prison as epiphany, see W. B. Carnochan, "The Literature of Confinement," in *The Oxford History of the Prison: The Practice of Punishment in Western Society*, ed. N. Morris and D. J. Rothman (New York: Oxford University Press, 1995), 383.
83. George Rawick, ed., *The American Slave: A Composite Autobiography*, vol. 1 (Westport, CT: Greenwood Press, 1972), 55.

References

Abrahams, Roger D. "Mr. Lomax Meets Professor Kittredge." *Journal of Folklore Research* 37, no. 2–3 (May–December 2000): 99–118.
Acts Passed at the Second Session of the Fifteenth Legislature of the State of Louisiana, Begun and Held in the City of New Orleans, December 13, 1841. New Orleans: J. C. De St. Romes, 1842.
Adams, Jessica. *Wounds of Returning: Race, Memory, and Property on the Postslavery Plantation.* Chapel Hill: University of North Carolina Press, 2007.
Adamson, Christopher R. "Punishment After Slavery: Southern State Penal Systems, 1865–1890." *Social Problems* 30, no. 5 (June 1983): 555–569.
Alexander, Michelle. *The New Jim Crow.* New York: Penguin, 2019.
Alford, C. Fred. "What Would It Matter If Everything Foucault Said About Prison Were Wrong? 'Discipline and Punish' after Twenty Years." *Theory and Society* 29, no. 1 (February 2000): 125–146.
Allen, William Francis, Charles Pickard Ware, and Lucy McKim Garrison. *Slave Songs of the United States.* New York: A. Simpson, 1867.
Anderson, Iain. *This Is Our Music: Free Jazz, the Sixties, and American Culture.* Philadelphia: University of Pennsylvania Press, 2007.
The Angolite. Angola, LA. 1953–present.
Annual Report of the Chief Engineer of the Board of Public Works, for the year ending December 31, 1860, to the Legislature of the State of Louisiana. Baton Rouge: J. M. Taylor, State Printer, 1861.
Arend, Orissa. "Black vs. Blue." *New Orleans Magazine*, October 1, 2015. https://www.myneworleans.com/black-vs-blue/.
Arnold, Craig Anthony. "The Reconstitution of Property: Property as a Web of Interests." *Harvard Environmental Law Review* 26, no. 2 (2002): 281–364.
Baade, Christina L. "Incarcerated Music: Broadcasting and the Tactics of Music Listening in Prison." In *Music and the Broadcast Experience: Performance, Production, and Audiences*, edited by Christina L. Baade and James Andrew Deaville, 310–324. New York: Oxford University Press, 2016.
Balogh, Brian. *The Associational State: American Governance in the Twentieth Century.* Philadelphia: University of Pennsylvania Press, 2015.
Baptist, Edward E. *The Half Has Never Been Told: Slavery and the Making of American Capitalism.* Boulder, CO: Basic Books, 2014.
Benjamin, Walter. *Illuminations.* New York: Schocken, 2007.
Berendt, Joachim-Ernst. *The Jazz Book: From Ragtime to Fusion and Beyond.* 7th ed. Chicago: Chicago Review Press, 2009.
Bergeron, Monica L. "Second Place Isn't Good Enough: Achieving True Reform Through Expanded Parole Eligibility." *Louisiana Law Review* 80, no. 1 (2020): 109–163.

Bergeron, Roy L., Jr. "Faith on the Farm: An Analysis of Angola Prison's Moral Rehabilitation Program Under the Establishment Clause." *Louisiana Law Review* 71, no. 4 (Summer 2011): 1221–1257.

Bergner, Daniel. *God of the Rodeo: The Search for Hope, Faith, and a Six-Second Ride in Louisiana's Angola Prison*. New York: Crown, 1998.

Berliner, Paul. *Thinking in Jazz: The Infinite Art of Improvisation*. Chicago: University of Chicago Press, 1994.

Birch, Kelly. "Slavery and the Origins of Louisiana's Prison Industry, 1803–1861." PhD diss., University of Adelaide, 2017.

Blue, Ethan. *Doing Time in the Depression: Everyday Life in Texas and California Prisons*. New York: New York University Press, 2012.

Bourdieu, Pierre. *Outline of a Theory of Practice*. Translated by Richard Nice. Cambridge: Cambridge University Press, 1977.

Bowman, Gary W., Simon Hakim, and Paul Seidenstat. *Privatizing Correctional Institutions*. New Brunswick, NJ: Transaction Publishers, 1993.

Brasseaux, Ryan A. "A Biographical Sketch: James Carrol Booker III." *Louisiana History* 39, no. 4 (Fall 1998): 480.

Braverman, Harry. *Labor and Monopoly Capital: The Degradation of Work in the Twentieth Century*. 25th anniversary ed. New York: Monthly Review Press, 1998.

Breunlin, Rachel, and Helen A. Regis. "Putting the Ninth Ward on the Map: Race, Place, and Transformation in Desire, New Orleans." *American Anthropologist* 108, no. 4 (December 2006): 744–764.

Brewster, Larry. "The Impact of Prison Arts Programs on Inmate Attitudes and Behavior: A Quantitative Evaluation." *Justice Policy Journal* 11, no. 2 (Fall 2014): 1–28.

Browne, Ray B. "Some Notes on the Southern Holler." *Journal of American Folklore* 67, no. 263 (January–March, 1954): 73–77.

Bunch, Mary J. "Outlawry and the Experience of the (Im)possible: Deconstructing Biopolitics." PhD diss., University of Western Ontario, 2010.

Burton, Velmer S., Francis T. Cullen, and Lawrence F. Travis III. "Collateral Consequences of a Felony Conviction: A National Study of State Statutes." *Federal Probation* 51, no. 3 (September 1987): 52–60.

Butler, Anne, and C. Murray Henderson. *Angola, Louisiana State Penitentiary: A Half-Century of Rage and Reform*. Lafayette: Center for Louisiana Studies, University of Southwestern Louisiana, 1990.

Butler, Melvin L. *Island Gospel: Pentecostal Music and Identity in Jamaica and the United States*. Urbana: University of Illinois Press, 2019.

Cardon, Nathan. "'Less Than Mayhem': Louisiana's Convict Lease, 1865–1901." *Louisiana History* (Fall 2017): 416–439.

Carleton, Mark T. *Politics and Punishment: The History of the Louisiana State Penal System*. Baton Rouge: Louisiana State University Press, 1971.

Carleton, Mark T. "The Politics of the Convict Lease System in Louisiana: 1868–1901." *Louisiana History* 8, no. 1 (Winter 1967): 5–25.

Carnochan, W. B. "The Literature of Confinement." In *The Oxford History of the Prison: The Practice of Punishment in Western Society*, edited by N. Morris and D. J. Rothman, 381–406. New York: Oxford University Press, 1995.

de Certeau, Michel. *The Practice of Everyday Life*. Translated by Steven F. Rendall. Berkeley: University of California Press, 2011.

Chammah, Maurice. "Prison Plantations." The Marshall Project, May 1, 2015. https://www.themarshallproject.org/2015/05/01/prison-plantations.

Chase, Robert T. "We Are Not Slaves: Rethinking the Rise of Carceral States through the Lens of the Prisoners' Rights Movement." *Journal of American History* 102, no. 1 (June 2015): 73–86.

Cheliotis, Leonidas. "Decorative Justice: Deconstructing the Relationship between the Arts and Imprisonment." *International Journal for Crime, Justice and Social Democracy* 3, no. 1 (April 2014): 16–34.

Cheliotis, Leonidas. "Our Violence and Theirs: Comparing Prison Realities." *South Atlantic Quarterly* 113, no. 3 (Summer 2014): 443–446.

Cheliotis, Leonidas, and Aleksandra Jordonoska. "The Arts of Desistance: Assessing the Role of Arts-Based Programmes in Reducing Reoffending." *Howard Journal of Crime and Justice* 55, no. 1–2 (May 2016): 25–41.

Childs, Dennis. *Slaves of the State: Black Incarceration from the Chain Gang to the Penitentiary*. Minneapolis: University of Minnesota Press, 2015.

Christianson, Scott. "Prisons: History." In *Encyclopedia of Crime and Justice* 3, edited by Joshua Dressler, 1168–1175. New York: Macmillan, 2002.

Chude-Sokei, Louis. *The Last 'Darky': Bert Williams, Black-on-Black Minstrelsy, and the African Diaspora*. Durham, NC: Duke University Press, 2006.

Churcher, Kalen M. A. "Journalism Behind Bars: The Louisiana State Penitentiary's Angolite Magazine." *Communication, Culture & Critique* 4, no. 4 (December 2011): 382–400.

Claxton, William, and Joachim-Ernst Berndt. *Jazzlife: A Journey for Jazz Across America in 1960*. Cologne, Germany: Taschen, 2013.

Clements, Paul. "The Rehabilitative Role of Arts Education in Prison: Accommodation or Enlightenment?" *International Journal of Art & Design Education* 23 (June 2004): 169–178.

Cleveland, William. *Art in Other Places: Artists at Work in America's Community and Social Institutions*. New York: Praeger, 1992.

Coates, Ta-Nehisi. "Outlaw Culture." *Atlantic*, April 13, 2012.

Cowley, John. "'Take a whiff on me': Leadbelly's Library of Congress recordings 1933–1942. An assessment." *Blues and Rhythm* 59 (March/April 1991): 16–20.

Crowther, Bruce. *Captured on Film: The Prison Movie*. London: B. T. Batsford, 1989.

Daughtry, J. Martin. *Listening to War: Sound, Music, Trauma, and Survival in Wartime Iraq*. New York: Oxford University Press, 2015.

de Tocqueville, Alexis, and Gustave de Beaumont. *On the Penitentiary System in the United States and Its Application to France, The Complete Text*. New York: Springer, 2018.

de Tocqueville, Alexis, Harvey Claflin Mansfield, and Delba Winthrop. *Democracy in America*. Chicago: University of Chicago Press, 2002.

Derbes, Brett Josef. "'Secret Horrors': Enslaved Women and Children in the Louisiana State Penitentiary, 1833–1862." *Journal of African American History* 98, no. 2 (Spring 2013): 277–290.

Dewey, Susan, Kym Codallos, Robin Barry, Kirstin Drenkhahn, Michala Glover, Alec Muthig, Susan Lockwood Roberts, and Betty Abbott. "Higher Education in Prison: A Pilot Study of Approaches and Modes of Delivery in Eight Prison Administrations." *Journal of Correctional Education* 71, no. 1 (April 2020): 57–89.

Dougan, John M. "The Mistakes of Yesterday, the Hopes of Tomorrow: Prison, Pop Music, and the Prisonaires." *American Music* 17, no. 4 (Winter 1999): 447–468.

Dougan, John M. *The Mistakes of Yesterday, the Hopes of Tomorrow: The Story of the Prisonaires*. Amherst: University of Massachusetts Press, 2012.

Doyle, Peter. *Echo and Reverb: Fabricating Space in Popular Music, 1900–1960*. Middletown, CT: Wesleyan University Press, 2005.

Du Bois, W. E. B. *The Souls of Black Folk*. New York: Dover, 1994.

DuVernay, Ava, director. *13th*. Sharman Oaks, CA: Kandoo Films, 2016. DVD.

Eisenach, Eldon J. "Bookends: Seven Stories Excised from the Lost Promise of Progressivism," *Studies in American Political Development* 10, no. 1 (Spring 1996): 168–183.

Elkins, Caroline. *Legacy of Violence: A History of the British Empire*. New York: Alfred A. Knopf, 2022.

Ellison, Ralph. *The Collected Essays of Ralph Ellison: Revised and Updated*. New York: Random House, 2011.

Ellison, Ralph. *Living with Music: Ralph Ellison's Jazz Writings*. Edited by Robert G. O'Meally. New York: Modern Library, 2003.

Engel, Carl. "Views and Reviews." *Musical Quarterly* 23, no. 3 (July 1937): 388–395.

Fellezs, Kevin. "Gender, Race, and the Ma(s)king of Joni Mitchell." In *The Cambridge Companion to the Singer-Songwriter*, edited by Katherine Williams and Justin A. Williams, 201–214. Cambridge: Cambridge University Press, 2016.

"Figures Showing What Has Been Accomplished by the Board of Control—Value of the Property." *Times Picayune* (New Orleans), April 15, 1906, 23.

Fikentscher, Kai. *"You Better Work!" Underground Dance Music in New York*. Music/Culture. Hanover, NH: University Press of New England, 2000.

Filene, Benjamin. "'Our Singing Country': John and Alan Lomax, Leadbelly, and the Construction of an American Past." *American Quarterly* 43, no. 4 (December 1991): 602–624.

Fisher-Giorlando, Marianne. "Plantation Prisons." In *Encyclopedia of Prisons & Correctional Facilities*, edited by Mary Bosworth, 702–705. Thousand Oaks, CA: SAGE Publications, 2005.

Fisher-Giorlando, Marianne. "The Walls." *64 Parishes* (Winter 2019). https://64parishes.org/the-walls.

Fisher-Giorlando, Marianne. "Women in the Walls: The Imprisonment of Women at the Baton Rouge Penitentiary, 1835–1862." In *The Wall Is Strong: Corrections in Louisiana*, 4th ed., edited by Burk Foster, Wilbert Rideau, and Douglas Dennis, 16–25. Lafayette: University of Louisiana Press, 2014.

Fisk Jubilee Singers and Theodore F. Seward. *Jubilee Songs: As Sung by the Jubilee Singers of Fisk University*. New York: Biglow & Main, 1872.

Fleetwood, Nicole. *Marking Time*. Cambridge, MA: Harvard University Press, 2020.

Follett, Richard. "Slavery and Technology in Louisiana's Sugar Bowl." In *Technology, Innovation, and Southern Industrialization: From the Antebellum Era to the Computer Age*, edited by Susanna Delfino and Michele Gillespie, 68–95. Columbia: University of Missouri Press, 2008.

Forret, Jeff. "Before Angola: Enslaved Prisoners in the Louisiana State Penitentiary." *Louisiana History* 54, no. 2 (Spring 2013): 133–171.

Fortier, Alcée. *Louisiana: comprising sketches of parishes, towns, events, institutions, and persons, arranged in cyclopedic form*. Madison, WI: Century Historical Association. 1914. https://hdl.handle.net/2027/coo1.ark:/13960/t4mk6w87b.

Foster, Burk, Wilbert Rideau, and Douglas Dennis. *The Wall Is Strong: Corrections in Louisiana*. 4th ed. Lafayette: University of Louisiana Press, 2014.
Foucault, Michel. *Discipline and Punish: The Birth of the Prison*. Translated by Alan Sheridan. New York: Vintage, 1979.
Foucault, Michel. *Power/Knowledge: Selected Interviews and Other Writings, 1972–1977*. Edited by Colin Gordon. New York: Pantheon, 1980.
Fox, Aaron A. *Real Country: Music and Language in Working-Class Culture*. Durham, NC: Duke University Press, 2004.
Franklin, H. Bruce. "Songs of an Imprisoned People." *MELUS* 6, no. 1 (1979): 6–22.
Fraser, Max. "Down in the Hole: Outlaw Country and Outlaw Culture." *Southern Cultures* 24, no. 3 (Fall 2018): 83–100.
Friedman, Lawrence M. *Crime and Punishment in American History*. New York: Basic Books, 1993.
Furlonge, Nicole Brittingham. *Race Sounds: The Art of Listening in African American Literature*. Iowa City: University of Iowa Press, 2018.
Gellert, Lawrence. *Negro Songs of Protest*. New York: American Music League, 1936.
Gillespie, Kathryn. "Placing Angola: Racialization, Anthropocentrism, and Settler Colonialism at the Louisiana State Penitentiary's Angola Rodeo." In *Colonialism and Animality: Anti-Colonial Perspectives in Critical Animal Studies*, edited by Kelly Struthers Montford and Chloë Taylor, 250–276. New York: Routledge, 2020.
Gilroy, Paul. *The Black Atlantic: Modernity and Double Consciousness*. Cambridge, MA: Harvard University Press, 1993.
Goffman, Erving. *Asylums: Essays on the Social Situation of Mental Patients and Other Inmates*. New Brunswick, NJ: Aldine Transaction, 2009.
Goffman, Erving. *Interaction Ritual: Essays on Face-to-Face Behavior*. New York: Doubleday, 1967.
Goffman, Erving. *Stigma: Notes on the Management of Spoiled Identity*. New York: Simon & Schuster, 1963.
Gonthier, David. *American Prison Film since 1930: From* The Big House *to* The Shawshank Redemption. Lewiston, NY: Edwin Mellen Press, 2006.
Gottschalk, Marie. *The Prison and the Gallows: The Politics of Mass Incarceration in America*. Cambridge: Cambridge University Press, 2006.
Gowder, Paul. *The Rule of Law in the United States: An Unfinished Project of Black Liberation*. New York: Hart Publishing, 2021.
Green, Archie. "Hillbilly Music: Source and Symbol." *Journal of American Folklore* 78, no. 309 (July–September 1965): 204–228.
Grestein, Mary R. "Germanic Warg: The Outlaw as Werwolf." In *Myth in Indo-European Antiquity*, edited by Gerald James Larson, C. Scott Littleton, and Jaan Puhvel, 131–156. Berkeley: University of California Press, 1974.
Hair, William Ivy. *The Kingfish and His Realm: The Life and Times of Huey P. Long*. Baton Rouge: Louisiana State University Press, 1997.
Haley, Sarah. *No Mercy Here: Gender, Punishment, and the Making of Jim Crow Modernity*. Chapel Hill: University of North Carolina Press, 2016.
Hallett, Michael. *The Angola Prison Seminar: Effects of Faith-Based Ministry on Identity Transformation, Desistance, and Rehabilitation*. New York: Routledge, 2017.
Handbook on the Anti-Drug Abuse Act of 1986. Washington, DC: US Dept. of Justice, Criminal Division, 1987. https://www.ojp.gov/pdffiles1/Photocopy/157817NCJRS.pdf.

Harbert, Benjamin J. "Doing Time: The Work of Music in Louisiana Prisons." PhD diss., University of California, Los Angeles. 2010.
Harbert, Benjamin J. "Ethnomusicological Vérité: Filming Musicians in Louisiana and California State Prisons." Paper presented at Society for Ethnomusicology Annual Meeting, Middletown, CT, 2008.
Harbert, Benjamin J, director. *Follow Me Down: Portraits of Louisiana Prison Musicians.* New York: Films for the Humanities & Sciences, 2012. DVD.
Harbert, Benjamin J. "Guest Editor's Introduction." Special Issue on Women's Prison Music. *American Music* 31, no. 2 (Summer 2013): 127–133.
Harbert, Benjamin J. "Only Time: Musical Means to the Personal, the Private, and the Polis at the Louisiana Correctional Institute for Women." Special Issue on Women's Prison Music. *American Music* 31, no. 2 (Summer 2013): 203–240.
Harbert, Benjamin J. "Prometheus Sings: The Mythology of Prison Music." Master's thesis, University of California, Los Angeles. 2007.
Hardt, Michael. "Affective Labor." *Boundary 2* 26, no. 2 (Summer 1999): 89–100.
Harkins, Anthony. *Hillbilly: A Cultural History of an American Icon.* New York: Oxford University Press, 2005.
Harris, Robert L. "Early Black Benevolent Societies, 1780–1830." *Massachusetts Review* 20, no. 3 (Fall 1979): 603–25.
Hartman, Saidiya V. *Scenes of Subjection: Terror, Slavery, and Self-Making in Nineteenth-Century America.* New York: Oxford University Press, 1997.
Harvey, David. *A Brief History of Neoliberalism.* Oxford: Oxford University Press, 2005.
Hicks, Michael. "The Imprisonment of Henry Cowell." *Journal of the American Musicological Society* 44, no. 1 (Spring 1991): 92–119.
Hindmarsh, D. Bruce. *The Evangelical Conversion Narrative: Spiritual Autobiography in Early Modern England.* Oxford: Oxford University Press, 2007.
Hirsch, Jerrold. "Modernity, Nostalgia, and Southern Folklore Studies: The Case of John Lomax." *Journal of American Folklore* 105, no. 416 (Spring 1992): 183–207.
Hirsch, Lily E. *Music in American Crime Prevention and Punishment.* Ann Arbor: University of Michigan Press, 2012.
Hobsbawm, Eric J. *Bandits.* New York: New Press, 2000.
Hofman, Ana. "Music (as) Labour: Professional Musicianship, Affective Labour and Gender in Socialist Yugoslavia." *Ethnomusicology Forum* 24, no. 1 (February 2015): 28–50.
Hood, Mantle. "The Challenge of 'Bi-Musicality.'" *Ethnomusicology* 4, no. 2 (May 1960): 55–59.
Ivanova, Velia. "The Musical Heritage of Incarceration: The Curation, Dissemination, and Management of the Lomax Collection Prison Songs." PhD diss., Columbia University, 2021.
Jackson, Bruce. *Inside the Wire: Photographs from Texas and Arkansas Prisons.* Chicago: University of Chicago Press, 2013.
Jackson, Bruce. *Wake Up Dead Man: Hard Labor and Southern Blues.* Athens: University of Georgia Press, 1999.
Jackson, George. *Blood in My Eye.* Baltimore: Basic Classic Press, 1990.
Jackson, Mark Allan. *Jail House Bound: John Lomax's First Southern Prison Sojourn, 1933.* Morgantown: West Virginia University Press, 2012.
Jacobs, Harriet A. *Incidents in the Life of a Slave Girl.* New York: Oxford University Press, 1988.

"Jail Sonny Thompson Orchestra on Dope Charge." *Jet* 4, no. 7. June 25, 1953, 59.
"James Black." *DRUMMERWORLD*. www.drummerworld.com/drummers/James_Black.html.
John, Dr., and Jack Rummel. *Under a Hoodoo Moon: The Life of Dr. John the Night Tripper*. New York: St. Martin's Press, 1994.
Johnson, James B., Jr. "Prison Songs—Past and Present." *Louisiana Magazine*. 1968, 12–13.
Khoury, James. "Subculture at Angola: Jazz Music, Collaboration, and Experience." Final paper (MUSC 324: Music in U.S. Prisons), Department of Performing Arts, Georgetown University, 2017.
Kitwana, Bakari. *The Hip Hop Generation: Young Blacks and the Crisis in African American Culture*. New York: Basic Civitas, 2002.
Kun, Josh. *Audiotopia: Music, Race, and America*. Berkeley: University of California Press, 2005.
Leeper, Clare D'Artois. *Louisiana Place Names: Popular, Unusual, and Forgotten Stories of Towns, Cities, Plantations, Bayous, and Even Some Cemeteries*. Baton Rouge: Louisiana State University Press, 2012.
Library of Congress. *Report of the Librarian of Congress for the Fiscal Year Ending June 30, 1934*. Washington, DC: US Government Printing Office, 1934.
Lichtenstein, Alex. *Twice the Work of Free Labor: The Political Economy of Convict Labor in the New South*. New York: Verso, 1996.
The Lifer. Edited by Wilbert Rideau, Tommy Mason, Robert Jackson, and Kenneth Plaisance. West Feliciana Parish, LA: Documents and Published Materials–Published Works, National Museum of African American History and Culture, January/February/March 1974.
Loeber, Rolf, and Dale Hay. "Key Issues in the Development of Aggression and Violence from Childhood to Early Adulthood." *Annual Review of Psychology* 48, no. 1 (February 1997): 371–410.
Lomax, Alan. *The Land Where the Blues Began*. New York: Pantheon, 1993.
Lomax, Alan, and Gage Averill. *Alan Lomax: Selected Writings, 1934–1997*. Edited by Ronald D. Cohen. New York: Routledge, 1997.
Lomax, John A. "'Sinful Songs' of the Southern Negro." *Musical Quarterly*, no. 2 (1934): 177–187.
Lomax, John A., and Alan Lomax. *American Ballads and Folk Songs* (1934: reprint). New York: Dover, 1994.
Lomax, John A., Alan Lomax, and George Herzog. *Negro Folk Songs as Sung by Lead Belly "King of the Twelve-String Guitar Players of the World," Long-Time Convict in the Penitentiaries of Texas and Louisiana*. New York: Macmillan, 1936.
Lomax, John A., Alan Lomax, Ruth Crawford Seeger, and Harold William Thompson. *Our Singing Country: A Second Volume of American Ballads and Folk Songs*. New York: Dover, 2000.
Louisiana Advisory Committee to the United States Commission on Civil Rights. "A Study of Adult Corrections in Louisiana." May 1976.
Louisiana Department of Public Safety and Corrections. "Demographic Dashboard: Population Count." December 31, 2021. https://doc.louisiana.gov/demographic-dashboard/.
Lucas, Ashley. "When I Run in My Bare Feet: Music, Writing, and Theater in a North Carolina Women's Prison." *American Music* 30, no. 2 (2013), 134–162.

Mahon, Maureen. *Right to Rock: The Black Rock Coalition and the Cultural Politics of Race.* Durham, NC: Duke University Press, 2004.

Mancini, Matthew J. "Convict Leasing." *64 Parishes.* May 27, 2011. https://64parishes.org/entry/convict-leasing.

Mancini, Matthew J. *One Dies, Get Another: Convict Leasing in the American South, 1866–1928.* Columbia: University of South Carolina Press, 1996.

Mann, Sandi, and Rebekah Cadman. "Does Being Bored Make Us More Creative?" *Creativity Research Journal* 26, no. 2 (2014): 165–173.

McGraw, Andy. "Ethical Friction: Ethnomusicological Perspectives on Music in the Richmond City Jail." In *Political, Social & Ecological Issues,* edited by Beverley Diamond and Salwa El-Shawan Castelo-Branco, 164–184. Vol. 2 of *Transforming Ethnomusicology.* Oxford: Oxford University Press. 2018.

McGraw, Andy. "Musical Sanctuary in the Richmond City Jail." *Tacet: Sound in the Arts* 4 (2016).

McLennan, Rebecca M. *The Crisis of Imprisonment: Protest, Politics, and the Making of the American Penal State, 1776–1941.* New York: Cambridge University Press, 2008.

Mendonça, Maria. "Gamelan in Prisons in England and Scotland: Narratives of Transformation and the 'Good Vibrations' of Educational Rhetoric." *Ethnomusicology* 54, no. 3 (Fall 2010): 369–394.

Menjívar, Cecilia. "Liminal Legality: Salvadoran and Guatemalan Immigrants' Lives in the United States." *American Journal of Sociology* 111, no. 4 (January 2006): 999–1037.

Meyer, Richard E. "The Outlaw: A Distinctive American Folktype." *Journal of the Folklore Institute* 17, no. 2/3 (May–December 1980): 94–124.

Micucci, Matt, and Brian Zimmerman. "Song of the Day: Cannonball Adderley Quintet, 'Work Song.'" *JAZZIZ Magazine* 25 (November 2020). www.jazziz.com/song-of-the-day-cannonball-adderley-quintet-work-song/.

Miller, Karl Hagstrom. *Segregating Sound: Inventing Folk and Pop Music in the Age of Jim Crow.* Durham, NC: Duke University Press, 2010.

Mitchell, Joshua A. "'All Those Little Spools and Lights': The Moving Image at Angola Prison." *Film History* 32, no. 2 (Summer 2020): 28–54.

The Monroe (LA) News-Star. May 22, 1953, 12.

Monson, Ingrid. *Freedom Sounds: Civil Rights Call Out to Jazz and Africa.* New York: Oxford University Press, 2007.

Morris, Norval. "The Contemporary Prison." In *The Oxford History of the Prison: The Practice of Punishment in Western Society,* edited by Norval Morris and David J. Rothman, 202–231. New York: Oxford University Press, 1995.

Mouledous, Joseph C. "Organizational Goals and Structural Change: A Study of the Organization of a Prison Social System." *Social Forces* 41, no. 3 (March 1963): 283–90.

Mouledous, Joseph C. "Pioneers in Criminology: Edward Livingston (1764–1836)." *Journal of Criminal Law and Criminology* 54, no. 3 (September 1963): 288–295.

Mouledous, Joseph C. *Sociological Perspectives on a Prison Social System.* Master's thesis, Department of Sociology, Louisiana State University, Baton Rouge, 1962.

Mullen, Patrick B. "The Dilemma of Representation in Folklore Studies: The Case of Henry Truvillion and John Lomax." *Journal of Folklore Research* 37, vol. 2-3 (May–December 2000): 155–174.

Nellis, Ashley. *No End in Sight: America's Enduring Reliance on Life Imprisonment.* The Sentencing Project, 2021. https://www.sentencingproject.org/wp-content/uploads/2021/02/No-End-in-Sight-Americas-Enduring-Reliance-on-Life-Imprisonment.pdf.

Neuman, Gerald L. "The Lost Century of American Immigration Law (1776–1875)." *Columbia Law Review* 93, no. 8 (December 1993): 1833–1901.
Neville, Art, Aaron Neville, Charles Neville, and Cyril Neville. *Brothers: An Autobiography*. Cambridge, MA: Da Capo Press, 2001.
Novak, William J. "The American Law of Association: The Legal-Political Construction of Civil Society." *Studies in American Political Development* 15 (Fall 2001): 163–188.
Novak, William J. *The People's Welfare: Law and Regulation in Nineteenth-Century America*. Chapel Hill: University of North Carolina Press, 1996.
Nunn, Erich. *Sounding the Color Line: Music and Race in the Southern Imagination*. The New Southern Studies. Athens: University of Georgia Press, 2015.
Odum, Howard W., and Guy B. Johnson. *The Negro and His Songs: A Study of Typical Negro Songs in the South*. Chapel Hill: University of North Carolina Press, 1925.
Odum, Howard W., and Guy B. Johnson. *Negro Workaday Songs*. Chapel Hill: University of North Carolina Press, 1926.
Öhman, Nina C. "Vocal Virtuosity, Value Creation, and the Transformation of Contemporary Gospel Music." In *The Oxford Handbook of Economic Ethnomusicology*, edited by Anna Morcom and Timothy D. Taylor. New York: Oxford University Press, 2020.
Oshinsky, David M. *"Worse Than Slavery": Parchman Farm and the Ordeal of Jim Crow Justice*. New York: Simon & Schuster, 1997.
Oster, Harry, to Rae Korson. LWO 5059AFS 12575–12596AFC. Harry Oster collection of Louisiana, Mississippi, and Iowa recordings, 1957–1966. American Folklife Center, 1967/003. January 5, 1957.
Oster, Harry. *Angola Prison Spirituals*. Louisiana Folklore Society LFS A-6, 1959. LP.
Oster, Harry. *Angola Prisoners' Blues*. Liner notes and recording, recorded 1952–1959 at Louisiana State Penitentiary, CD-419, Lafayette, LA, Louisiana Folklore Society LFS A-3, 1959, reissued by Arhoolie in 1996. Double LP.
Oster, Harry. *Living Country Blues*. Detroit: Folklore Associates, 1969.
Oster, Harry. *Southern Prison Blues*. Liner notes and recording, recorded 1968 at Louisiana State Penitentiary, TR 2066-AB. LP.
Patton, Tracy Owens, and Sally M. Schedlock. "Let's Go, Let's Show, Let's Rodeo: African Americans and the History of Rodeo." *Journal of African American History* 96, no. 4 (Fall 2011): 503–521.
Pecorella, Robert F. "Property Rights, State Police Powers, and the Takings Clause: The Evolution Toward Dysfunctional Land-Use Management." *Fordham Urban Law Journal* 44, no. 1 (April 2017): 59–90.
Pelot-Hobbs, Lydia. "Organizing for Freedom: The Angola Special Civics Project, 1987–1992." Master's thesis, University of New Orleans, 2011.
Perkinson, Robert. *Texas Tough: The Rise of America's Prison Empire*. New York: Metropolitan Books, 2010.
Perrault, Stephanie L., Charles E. Pearson, Carey L. Coxe, Sara A. Hahn, Thurston H. G. Hahn III, Dayna Lee, Katherine M. Roberts, and Joanne Ryan. *Archaeological Data Recovery at Angola Plantation 16WF121 and 16WF122 West Feliciana Parish, LA*. Baton Rouge: Coastal Environments, 2006.
Pierson, George Wilson. *Tocqueville in America*. Garden City, NY: Doubleday, 1996.
Porterfield, Nolan. *Last Cavalier: The Life and Times of John A. Lomax, 1867–1948*. Folklore and Society. Urbana: University of Illinois Press, 2001.

"Radio: Hoosegow Harmony." *Time*, 43, no. 6 (February 7, 1944). http://content.time.com/time/subscriber/article/0,33009,791348,00.html.

Rahaim, Matthew. *Musicking Bodies Gesture and Voice in Hindustani Music*. Middletown, CT: Wesleyan University Press, 2012.

Rathge, Adam R. "Mapping the Muggleheads: New Orleans and the Marijuana Menace, 1920–1930." Dayton, OH: University of Dayton Press, 2018.

Rawick, George, ed. *The American Slave: A Composite Autobiography*. Westport, CT: Greenwood Press, 1972.

Reed, Teresa L. *The Holy Profane: Religion in Black Popular Music*. Lexington: University Press of Kentucky, 2003.

Rego, Triana. "Male Antisocial Behavior and Psychological Development: 'Growing Up' and Its Impact on Aggressive Conduct." *Journal of Psychology and Clinical Psychiatry* 5, no. 1 (2016).

Rice, Timothy. *May It Fill Your Soul: Experiencing Bulgarian Music*. Chicago: University of Chicago Press, 1994.

Rideau, Wilbert. *In the Place of Justice: A Story of Punishment and Deliverance.*. New York: Alfred A. Knopf, 2010.

Rideau, Wilbert. "Veterans Incarcerated." *Penthouse: The International Magazine for Men* 7, no. 8. 1976, 162–166.

Rideau, Wilbert, and Billy Sinclair. "Prisoner Litigation: How It Began in Louisiana." *Louisiana Law Review* 45, no. 5 (May 1985): 1061–1076.

Riley, Herlin and Johnny Vidacovich. *New Orleans Jazz and Second Line Drumming*. Van Nuys, CA: Alfred Publishing, 2006.

Rion, Sharon Johnson. *Beyond His Time: The Maurice Sigler Story*. Lanham, MD: American Correctional Association, 2001.

Rosen, Deborah A. "Slavery, Race, and Outlawry: The Concept of the Outlaw in Nineteenth-Century Abolitionist Rhetoric." *American Journal of Legal History* 58, no. 1 (March 2018): 126–156.

Roth, Michael P. *Prisons and Prison Systems: A Global Encyclopedia*. Westport, CT: Greenwood Press, 2006.

Rothman, David J. *The Discovery of the Asylum: Social Order and Disorder in the New Republic*. Boston: Little, Brown, 1971.

Rothman, David J. "Perfecting the Prison: United States 1789–1865." In *The Oxford History of the Prison: The Practice of Punishment in Western Society*, edited by Norval Morris and David J. Rothman, 111–129. New York: Oxford University Press, 1998.

Rothman, Joshua D. *The Ledger and the Chain: How Domestic Slave Traders Shaped America*. New York: Basic Books, 2021.

Rotman, Edgardo. "The Failure of Reform: United States, 1865–1965." In *The Oxford History of the Prison: The Practice of Punishment in Western Society*, edited by Norval Morris and David J. Rothman, 151–177. New York: Oxford University Press, 1995.

Rusche, George, and Otto Kirchheimer. *Punishment and Social Structure*. New Brunswick, NJ: Transaction Publishers, 2003.

Russell, George. *George Russell's Lydian Chromatic Concept of Tonal Organization* 4th ed. Brookline, MA: Concept Publishing Company, 2001.

Russell, George. *The Lydian Chromatic Concept of Tonal Organization for Improvisation*. Cambridge, MA: Concept Publishing Company, 1964.

Russell, Maureen. "Highlights from the Ethnomusicology Archive: California-Arts-in-Corrections." *Ethnomusicology Review* (December 2015). https://ethnomusicolog

yreview.ucla.edu/content/highlights-ethnomusicology-archive-california-arts-corrections.

Sager, Rebecca. *Faith, Politics, and Power: The Politics of Faith-Based Initiatives*. New York: Oxford University Press, 2010.

Sakakeeny, Matt. *Roll with It: Brass Bands in the Streets of New Orleans*. Durham, NC: Duke University Press, 2013.

Scarpaci, J. Vincenza. "Labor for Louisiana's Sugar Cane Fields: An Experiment in Immigrant Recruitment." *Italian Americana* 7, no. 1 (Fall/Winter 1981): 19–41.

Schafer, R. Murray. *The Soundscape: Our Sonic Environment and the Tuning of the World*. New York: Simon & Schuster, 1993.

Schnur, Alfred C. "The New Penology: Fact or Fiction?" *Journal of Criminal Law & Criminology* 49, no. 4 (Fall 1959): 331–334.

Schott, Matthew J. *Louisiana Politics and the Paradoxes of Reaction and Reform 1877–1928*. Lafayette: University of Louisiana Press, 2000.

Schrift, Melissa R. "The Wildest Show in the South: The Politics and Poetics of the Angola Prison Rodeo and Inmate Arts Festival." *Southern Cultures* 14, no. 1 (Spring 2008): 22–41.

Seeger, Anthony. *Why Suyá Sing: A Musical Anthropology of an Amazonian People*. Urbana: University of Illinois Press, 2004.

Sellen, Johan Thorsten. *Slavery and the Penal System*. New York: Elsevier, 1976.

The Sentencing Project. "State-by-State Data: State Imprisonment Rate: Louisiana." US Bureau of Justice Statistics Data. 2019. https://www.sentencingproject.org/the-facts/#map.

Shaik, Fatima. *Economy Hall: The Hidden History of a Free Black Brotherhood*. New Orleans: The Historic New Orleans Collection, 2021.

Shen, Aviva, "Angola prison rodeo offers risks and rewards for Louisiana's hard-knock lifers." *The Guardian*, October 29, 2016. https://www.theguardian.com/us-news/2016/oct/29/angola-prison-rodeo-louisiana.

Simerman, John. "'The Only Way We Get Out of There Is in a Pine Box.'" *The Marshall Project*, December 14, 2021. https://www.themarshallproject.org/2021/12/17/the-only-way-we-get-out-of-there-is-in-a-pine-box.

Slobin, Mark. *Motor City Music: A Detroiter Looks Back*. New York: Oxford University Press, 2018.

Sloop, John M. *The Cultural Prison: Discourse, Prisoners, and Punishment*. Tuscaloosa: University of Alabama Press, 1996.

Slotkin, Richard. *Gunfighter Nation: The Myth of the Frontier in Twentieth-Century America*. New York: Atheneum, 1992.

Smith, Caleb. "Editor's Introduction." In *The Life and the Adventures of a Haunted Convict*, xv–lxii. New York: Random House, 2016.

Smith, Caleb. *The Prison and the American Imagination*. New Haven, CT: Yale University Press, 2009.

Smith, Clint. *How the Word Is Passed: A Reckoning with the History of Slavery Across America*. New York: Little, Brown, 2021.

Smith, Michael P. "Behind the Lines: The Black Mardi Gras Indians and the New Orleans Second Line." *Black Music Research Journal* 14, no. 1 (Spring 1994): 43–73.

Smith, Rachel A. "Segmenting an Audience into the Own, the Wise, and Normals: A Latent Class Analysis of Stigma-Related Categories." *Communication Research Reports* 29, no. 4 (October 2012): 257–265.

"Sonny Thompson Bandmen Get 10 Years for Dope." *Jet* 4, no. 9, July 9, 1953, 60.
Spencer, Jon M. *Blues and Evil*. Knoxville: University of Tennessee Press, 1993.
Stagg, Edward W., and John Lear. "America's Worst Prison." *Collier's*, November 22, 1952, 13–16.
Steingo, Gavin. *Kwaito's Promise: Music and the Aesthetics of Freedom in South Africa*. Chicago: University of Chicago Press, 2016.
Sterne, Jonathan. *The Audible Past: Cultural Origins of Sound Reproduction*. Durham, NC: Duke University Press, 2003.
Stoever, Jennifer Lynn. *The Sonic Color Line: Race and the Cultural Politics of Listening*. New York: New York University Press, 2016.
Street, John. "Rock, Pop and Politics." In *The Cambridge Companion to Pop and Rock*, edited by Simon Frith, Will Straw, and John Street, 243–255. New York: Cambridge University Press, 2000.
Strinati, Dominic. *An Introduction to Theories of Popular Culture*. New York: Routledge, 2004.
Suhor, Charles. "Don Suhor: From Dixieland to Bopsieland." *The Jazz Archivist*, 2016.
Suhor, Charles. *Jazz in New Orleans: The Postwar Years Through 1970*. Studies in Jazz, 38. Lanham, MD: Scarecrow Press, 2001.
Sullivan, Larry E. *The Prison Reform Movement: Forlorn Hope*. Boston: Twayne Publishers. 1990.
Szwed, John. *Alan Lomax: The Man Who Recorded the World*. New York: Viking Penguin, 2010.
Tallaksen, Amund R. "Junkies and Jim Crow: The Boggs Act of 1951 and the Racial Transformation of New Orleans' Heroin Market." *Journal of Urban History* 45, no. 2 (March 2019): 230–246.
Tatro, Kelley. "The Hard Work of Screaming: Physical Exertion and Affective Labor Among Mexico City's Punk Vocalists." *Ethnomusicology* 58, no. 3 (Fall 2014): 431–453.
Taubes, Gary, and Cristin Kearns Couzens. "Big Sugar's Sweet Little Lies." *Mother Jones*, October 31, 2012. www.motherjones.com/environment/2012/10/sugar-industry-lies-campaign.
Taylor, Frederick Winslow. *The Principles of Scientific Management*. New York: Harper, 1911.
Toch, Hans. *Living in Prison: The Ecology of Survival*. New York: Free Press, 1977.
The Town Talk. Alexandria, LA, October 3, 1953, 10–11.
Travis, Jeremy. "Invisible Punishment: An Instrument of Social Exclusion." In *Invisible Punishment: The Collateral Consequences of Mass Imprisonment*, edited by Marc Mauer and Meda Chesney-Lind, 15–36. New York: The New Press, 2002.
Turkington, Courtney Harper. "Louisiana's Addiction to Mass Incarceration by the Numbers." *Loyola Law Review* 63, no. 3 (2017): 557–591.
US Census Bureau. "Quick Facts: Louisiana." July 1, 2019. https://www.census.gov/quickfacts/LA.
Vandal, Gilles. "Regulating Louisiana's Rural Areas: The Functions of Parish Jails, 1840–1885." *Louisiana History* 42, no. 1 (Winter 2001): 59–92.
Vujosevic, Ranko. "Dr. Harry Oster: His Life, Career and Field Recordings." *Blues Notes, Monthly Publication of the Johnson County Blues Society*, no. 9 (August 1995): 1–9.
Whiddon, Scott. "'To Live Outside the Law, You Must Be Honest': Words, Walls, and the Rhetorical Practices of the Angolite." In *Agency in the Margins: Stories of Outsider*

Rhetoric, edited by Anne Meade Stockdell-Giesler, 165–196. Madison, NJ: Fairleigh Dickinson University Press, 2010.

White, Shane. *The Sounds of Slavery. Discovering African American History through Songs, Sermons, and Speech*. Boston: Beacon, 2005.

Wikberg, Ronald Gene. "A Graphic & Illustrative History 1879 to 1979: Life Sentences in Louisiana." Angola, LA: Louisiana State Penitentiary, n.d.

Wolfe, Charles K., and Kip Lornell. *The Life and Legend of Leadbelly*. New York: Da Capo, 1999.

Woodfox, Albert, and Leslie George. *Solitary: Unbroken by Four Decades in Solitary Confinement. My Story of Transformation and Hope*. New York: Grove Press, 2019.

Index

For the benefit of digital users, indexed terms that span two pages (e.g., 52–53) may, on occasion, appear on only one of those pages.

007 Continentals, 146–47, 149
10-6 rule, 175, 178, 181

Acklen, Adelicia, 22–23, 25
Adderley, Nat, 103–4
aesthetics of propinquity, 267
Aias, Norby, 115–16, 117
Alcoholics Anonymous, 71, 147
All-Stars, the, 80, 100–2
Allen, Oscar K., 48
"Amazing Grace" (John Newton), 199
"America's Worst Prison" (*Collier's* article), 67–68
American Ballads and Folk Songs, 47–48
American Folklore Society, 26
Angola Museum, 146, 233–34
Angola's Most Wanted Band, 266, 269
Angolite, the, 65–66, 96, 116–17, 126–27, 129, 135, 172, 175
"Another One Bites the Dust" (Queen), 245
Anthropology of Music, the, 62
Anti-Drug Abuse Act of 1986, 208–9
Arnold, Craig Anthony, 267
Arts and Crafts Festival, Angola, 207, 239
associationalism, 55–57, 62–63, 68, 148, 151–52, 168–69, 172–73, 241, 261, 264, 271–72, 277
  chartering and, 55, 57, 77–78, 118, 168, 264, 265, 266
astonishment, 16, 50, 275–76
atmospheric inversion, 32–33
audiotopia, 215–16, 218, 224
authenticity, 149, 156, 161, 212, 213, 221, 223, 256
  Lomax recordings and, 43–44, 99–100
avant-garde, 125, 129–30

Ayler, Albert, 130

B-Line, the, 75, 81, 153, 157, 166
Ballam, Adrian, 78–82, 85, 87, 89, 115–16
Balogh, Brian, 56, 63–64, 151, 168–69
band room, 104–5, 114–15, 117–18, 129–30, 138–40, 167, 202, 203–4, 208, 210, 224, 242–43, 262–72
banquets, 137, 166–67, 171–72, 173–81, 205, 211, 213, 224–25
"Barracuda" (Heart), 245
Baton Rouge Penitentiary, 20–21, 24
Beaches, 143
bebop, 81
Bell, Jerry, 202, 211–12
benevolent societies. *See* mutual aid societies
Benjamin, Walter, 268
Berendt, Joachim-Ernst, 99–100
Beyer, Russel Joe, 1–2, 263
bi-musicality, 9–11
Bible College. *See* New Orleans Baptist Theological Seminary (NOBTS)
Big House, the, 45
Big River Band, the, 216–21
Black codes, 18–19
Black Jumpers, 205–6
Black nationalism, 126, 128
Black Panther Party, the, 127–28, 131, 142, 157, 173, 176–77
Black Power Movement, the, 127–28
Black, "Buckskin" Bill, 150–52, 155
Black, James, 127–30, 134, 136, 139–41
Bland, Bobby, 112–13
"Blood In My Eye" (Tribe), 184
Blue, Ethan, 46
blues, talking, 59

Board of Control, 28–35
boll weevil, 36–37
Booker, James, 135, 136, 141
Booth, Maude Ballington, 36
Brady, Everett, 193
Bratcher, "Speedy," 87
Brooks, Cato, Jr., 175–76
Brown, Leotha, 3–4, 103–5, 112, 136, 141, 167, 181, 273–74
Browne, Ray B., 132
Buckskin Bill Show, the (WAFB television show), 150
bullies, in the field, 108
Burger, Warren, 154
Burton, Charles, 80
Buzzard Dance, 33–35
by-laws, 114, 116–17, 118, 131, 260–61, 265
Byrd, James, 216

Cain, Burl, 233, 237, 240–41, 242, 261
Camp A, 41, 59, 62, 74, 77, 83, 85, 100, 222
Camp C, 85
Camp D. *See* women's camps
Camp E, 67, 70–71, 75
Camp F, 39, 103, 141, 154–55, 201, 247, 261–62, 273
Camp H, 60, 67, 79, 230–31
Camp H, 260
Camp I, 77, 82, 164
camp system, 63–64, 69, 81–82, 88–89, 108
canaries, 276–77
carceral associationalism, 56–59, 101
Catt, Douglas, 70, 79
Cavaliers, the, 71–74, 79
Cazelot, Wilfred, 244, 271
chain gangs, 36–37, 103–4
Charles, Ray, 112–13
Charles, Roosevelt, 59, 60
Cheatham, Adelicia. *See* Acklen, Adelicia
Cheliotis, Leonidas, 8
Chevalier, Theophile, 26
Childs, Dennis, 35, 84–85, 94
Chinese laborers, 24
Church of God in Christ, 241
civil rights movement, 62, 78, 102, 130
Claxton, William, 99–100
Clinton, Bill, 220–21, 231–32

cliques, 115, 195, 268
club banquets. *See* banquets
clubs, prisoner, 57–58, 168, 170, 205–6
Cole, Isaac, 75, 80
Coleman, Ornette, 62, 126
Coltrane, John, 119–20, 130, 131–32
"Come Morning" (Grover Washington), 180
Connick, Harry, Jr., 140–41
Connick, Harry, Sr., 181
Connor, George, 176–77
constitutional rights, 262, 263–64, 266–71
    Eighth Amendment, 170–71, 188, 209, 264
    First Amendment, 263–64, 268, 269–70
    Fourteenth Amendment, 170–71, 263–64
    Fourth Amendment, 263–64, 266–67
    Thirteenth Amendment, 27
conversion stories. *See* testimony, use of
"Convict Poker" (rodeo event), 245–46
convict-leasing, 24–27
Cook, Edwin, 173, 176, 177
cotton
    early production of, 22–23
    picking, 106
count, the, 271–72
counter-public sphere, 126–27
country music, 115–16, 163, 213–15. *See also* outlaw country
Courvelle, Jerry, 108
Cowell, Henry, 46–47
Cozart, Reed, 73
Crism, 126
Crocker, Sid, 151
Crowther, Bruce, 44–45
Crummie, Oscar, 75, 80
Culligan, Michael E., 73
Culpepper Trio, the, 172

d'Iberville, Pierre Le Moyne, 15–16
Dale Carnegie Club, the, 71, 91
Daniels, Charlie, 242
Dantzler, "Hot Rod," 146–47
Daugherty, Mary Margaret, 67–68
Daughtry, Martin, 32–33
Davis, Charlie, 139–40, 146
Davis, James Houston, 98–99

de Tocqueville, Alexis, 20, 54
Deakle, Terry, 202, 216
Def Posse, 209–11, 212
deindustrialization, 166–67
Democracy in America, 54
desegregation, 141, 170, 181, 188, 192, 197–98, 201–2, 203, 205–6, 215
Desire Projects, 176–77, 206
diatonicism, 120–21, 124
"Dirt Dauber" (James Black), 134
Disco Jazz, 205–6
Dixie Blue Boys, the, 190–92
"Dixie" (Daniel Decatur Emmett), 146–47
Dolphy, Eric, 62
Dougan, John, 46
drug convictions, 53, 74, 78–79, 86, 91, 100–1, 102, 105, 107, 119, 127–28, 135, 140
drums, legal restriction of, 23
Dukes, Leroy, 74–78, 80
Duplessis, Billy, 146
Dyer, Michael, 196–97, 198, 208–12

Easterly, Rudolph, 67
education department, 71, 73–74, 82, 90, 116–17, 121, 130, 136, 139, 202, 210, 268
Edwards, Edwin, 156, 206
Eighth Amendment. *See* constitutional rights
Eisenach, Eldon, 56
Elayn Hunt Correctional Center, 7, 183–84, 216, 272
Eldridge, Charles, 86–87
Ellison, Ralph, 85, 173–74, 179
embodied knowledge, 227
"Embraceable You" (George Gershwin), 94–95
Engel, Carl, 49–50
escapes, 39
ethical distance, 32–33, 41–42
ethnomusicology, 5, 8–9, 62, 143, 235–36
evangelical organizations, 232, 239, 240–43, 252, 261–62, 270
Evans, Bleu, 191
Evans, Darryl, 178

"Fables of Faubus" (Charles Mingus), 62

facework, 158–63, 174
Facts not Rumors (WLSP show), 90
family connections, 159, 171, 182, 248
Favor, "Cadillac" Jack, 147–48, 150–51
Favor, Jack, 207
federal receivership, 187, 188
festivals. *See also* holidays: performances; holidays: plantation
 plantation, 166–67, 206–7
field holler, 48, 132–33
fields
 conditions post-prisoners' rights, 194
 decline in work, 237
 singing post-prisoners' rights, 196–201
Filene, Benjamin, 44
"Firecracker" (Mass Production), 199
First Amendment. *See* constitutional rights
floods, 36–37
folklore, early history of, 26, 41–42
Follett, Richard, 22
Follow Me Down, 7, 183–84, 234–35, 237, 259–60–
"Folsom Prison Blues" (Johnny Cash), 149
Fontaine, Napoleon "Nappy," 81, 115–16
Foucault, Michel, 119–20, 148–49
Fourteenth Amendment. *See* constitutional rights
Fourth Amendment. *See* constitutional rights
Frank, Gary, 265
Franklin & Armfield, 22
Franklin, Chris, 276
Franklin, H. Bruce, 47–48
Franklin, Isaac, 22–23
Freeman, A. J., 240
fresh fish day, 115
Full Gospel Businessmen Fellowship, 241
Fuqua, Henry L., 36–37
Furlonge, Nicole, 38

G, Kenny, 141
gal-boys, 109–10, 145–46, 167. *See also* sex trade
Georgetown University, 106, 124, 140
"Get Down" (show on WGNO), 176–77
Gilroy, Paul, 178–79
"Gloria Estefan" (Time Factor), 207

Godwin, Chauncy, 234–35
Goffman, Erving, 158–61, 162–63
Gonthier, David, 45
"Gonzo" (James Booker), 135
Good Morning—Angola Style (WAFB television show), 151, 152–53
Gospel Melodies, the, 225–31, 260–61
gospel music, 97, 112–13, 141, 143, 221–31, 242, 252–53, 257–62
Great Depression, 36–37, 38–39
Greater New Orleans Tourism and Convention Commission, 146
Green, Darren, 248
Gremillion, Jack, 152
Gresham, Peggy, 164–65
Guidry, John, 175–76
Guidry, Rohillion and Wayne, 176–77
Guste, William J., 163–64
Guts and Glory Band, the, 242–43, 244–46
"Guts and Glory" (rodeo event), 147–48

Haley, Sarah, 94
"Half Nelson" (Miles Davis), 94–95
Hall, Eddie, 175
Hall, William "Red," 254–56
Hardy, A. U., 172
Harris, Arsia "Streamline," 95–96
Harris, Basil, 146
Hartman, Saidiya, 26
Harvey, David, 243
Hayes, Kevin, 211–12, 213
Heel String Gang, the, 67–68, 82–83
Henderson, C. Murray, 145, 153–55, 157–58, 164–66, 167–69, 170–71, 172–73, 176, 181
heritage, 26, 233
Herzog, George, 44
Hester, Theo, 21
hillbilly music, 69–70
Himes, R. L. "Tighty," 39
hip-hop, 184, 208, 209–11
hobby crafts, 243–44, 253–54
Hodges, Myron, 205, 211–12, 213–15, 217, 221, 239–40, 244–45, 251–53, 266
holidays
  performances, 75, 76–77, 81–82, 86–87, 90, 137
  plantation, 35, 81–82, 113–14, 116

"Hook and Sling" (Eddie Bo), 128–29
hootenanny, 107
Hope Plantation, 24
horizontal thinking. *See* vertical thinking
Houma, 16
"How I Got Over" (Mahalia Jackson), 112–13
Howard, Bobby, 155–56, 207, 216
Howell, Ralph "Rabbit," 115–16
Human Relations Public Speaking Club, 172, 202, 212
Hunt, Elayn, 156, 176

I Am a Fugitive from a Chain Gang!, 45–46
"I Like It Like That" (Chris Kenner), 136–37
"I'll Keep On Living After I Die" (Dixie Hummingbirds), 230, 257–58
"I'll Remember April" (Gene de Paul), 120, 122–23
"I've Got a Tiger by the Tail" (Buck Owens), 138
"If My Body Could Follow My Mind" (Big River Band), 220
improvisation, 245
In the Bag (Cannonball and Nat Adderley), 128
incentive systems. *See* privileges
inflection, 188–89
  musical, 203, 204, 218–20, 226, 227–29, 231
  political change and, 193–94
Inmate Council, the, 68–69, 82, 91–93, 146
Inmate Council, Women's, 95
Inmate Lending Fund, the, 3, 68–69, 82, 86–87, 91–92, 117–18, 146, 147–48, 152, 167, 179, 206–7, 210, 218, 246, 251–53
Inmate Minister Program, 240–41
Inmate Missionary Transfer Program, 240–41
Inmate Rodeo Committee, 251
Inmate Welfare Fund, the. *See* Inmate Lending Fund, the
interstitiality, 63–64, 98–99
Ionian scale. *See* diatonicism
Ivanova, Velia, 47, 233

Jackson, Bruce, 107

INDEX 335

Jackson, George, 131, 184
Jackson, Johnny, 176–77
jam sessions, 116–17, 118
Jambeaux Band, 211–12
James, Samuel L., 25–26, 27–28, 258
Jameson, Gary, 275
Jaycees, the, 153, 164, 170
jazz
    development in 1950s Angola, 70–71
    early cinematic representations of, 45–46
    freedom and, 62, 77–78, 85, 126–28
    intellectualism, 119–20, 121–22, 125, 128, 132, 139–40, 142
    pre-1950s at Angola, 40
Jazz on the River (WLSP show), 141
Jazz Record Show (WLSP show), 117
Jazzmen Inc., the, 115–16
Jazzmen, the, 1, 248–51, 266
Jehovah's Witnesses, 241
Jew's harp, 23
Jim Crow laws, 74, 78, 89, 119, 130, 138, 140
John Dr., 119, 146
Johns, Henry, 36
Johns, Stella, 36
Johnson, Freddie, 214–15
Johnson, Jimmy, 112, 204
Johnson, Johnny, 176
Johnson, Lyndon B., 187
Johnson, Templer "West Coast," 216
Jones, Frederick, 268–69, 274
Jones, Johnny, 240, 248–49
Jones, Johnny A., 175–76
Jones, Ray, 143–44, 183, 225–27, 248, 257
Judd, Willie, 115–16, 117
"Jungle Boogie" (Kool and the Gang), 176–77

Kennedy Sisters, the, 177, 178, 179
Kennedy, Yvonne, 178
Kenner, Chris, 136–37
Kennon, Robert Floyd, Sr., 68
Kent, Penny, 97–98
Khoury, James, 101
Kind of Blue (Miles Davis), 123
Kirchheimer, Otto, 17
Kun, Josh, 215

labor
    affective, 114, 137–38, 140
    cultural, 46–47, 48–49
    racialization of, 24–25, 199
    speculative, 253
Lanerie, Mickey, 266, 270
Lateef, Yusef, 103, 128–29, 130
Le Flor, Charlie, 214
Ledbetter, Huddie "Lead Belly," 37–38, 39, 40–41, 43–44, 48–50, 273–75
Lee, Emmanuel, 183–84
Lee, Jason, 269, 270
"Let the Good Times Roll" (Louis Jordan), 94–95
Lewis, Calvin, 240, 249–50, 263, 275–76
Liberace, 135
Library of Congress, the, 47
life sentences, 181, 182
Lifer, the, 175
Lifers Association, the, 173, 175–76, 178–79
Lindsay, Michael, 167
Lindsay, Stanley, 196–97, 198–99, 202, 203, 207
listenership, 38, 126, 127–28, 129
litigation, prisoner, 187, 231–32
Little Country Band, 247–48
Livingston, Edward, 20, 21–22, 28, 68
Lomax, Alan, 39–40, 42–43, 49, 132–33
Lomax, John A., 37–38, 40–45, 47–50, 59, 113, 143–44, 221, 273, 274
Long, Huey P., 36–37, 39
"Lot of Livin' to Do, A" (Charles Strouse), 138
"Louise" (Robert Pete Williams), 61
Louisiana civil code, 19
Louisiana Correctional Institute for Women, 7, 98–99, 154, 183–84
Louisiana Prison Chapel Foundation, 240–41
Louisiana Revised Statutes 1999, 241–42, 252, 261, 270
Louisiana State University, 59, 62, 121, 135
"Love Supreme, A" (John Coltrane), 138
Lydian Chromatic Concept of Tonal Organization, the, 121–27, 128, 130–31, 132, 137, 142
Lydian scale, 123–24

MacDonald, James, 153

Maduell, Charles, 119, 146
Maggio, Ross, Jr., 164–65, 187, 191, 192–93, 195, 215–16
main prison, 87–91, 201–2
Main Prison Gospel Band, the, 257, 270
major scale. *See* diatonicism
Marsalis, Ellis, 140–41
Marshall, Robert, 216
Marsh, James, 199–201, 247
Martin, Lula Mae, 76–77
Matthews, Odea, 94
Maxey, Hoagman, 60, 100
McElroy, John "Hats and Coats," 81, 82, 84–85
McHatton, Pratt, and Company, 21
McKeithen, John J., 147, 153
McWaters, Mark, 90
Megasound, 211, 212–15, 217
Merriam, Alan, 62
metaphor, 2, 19–20, 260–61, 276
of caged bird, 276–77
Methodist Men's Club, the, 71, 147
Midler, Bette, 143–44
"Midnight Special" (Lead Belly), 273–74
Mighty Harmonizers, the, 224–25
Miller, Brent, 157
Mingus, Charles, 115–16
minstrelsy, 75, 83–85
Mississippi State Penitentiary, 42–43, 132–33
Monkey Puzzle (Ellis Marsalis Quartet), 128
Monson, Ingrid, 125
"Mood for Mex (Desire for Travel)" (Louis Surgent), 94–95
Moody Bible Institute, 240–41
Morgan, Matthew, 266
mortification, 19–20, 166
Mouledous, Joseph C., 62–64
"Mr. Big Stuff" (Jean Knight), 177
"Music Room Sounds" (*Angolite* column), 117, 119
mutual aid societies, 56, 57–58, 69, 169–70, 172

National Museum of African American History and Culture, the, 140, 234
Neal, Otis, 189–92, 193–94, 203
neoliberalism, 243

Nesbit, Fred "The Professor," 91
Neville Brothers, the, 140
Neville, Aaron, 242
Neville, Charles, 75, 76–78, 105, 106–8, 109–10, 112–13, 114–15, 116–17, 119–22, 128, 129–30, 131–32, 133–35, 136–40, 146, 157
Neville, Charmaine, 211–12
New Deal, the, 46
New Orleans, 167, 169
New Orleans Baptist Theological Seminary (NOBTS), 240–41, 252
New Orleans Chamber of Commerce, 146, 206
New Orleans musicians, 120, 128–29, 135, 136–37, 141, 249–50
New Orleans Parish Prison, 20, 24
new penology, the, 68–69, 70
new prison. *See* main prison
Nic Nacs, the, 75, 87, 91–97, 100–2, 115–16, 117–18, 121–22, 129–30, 131, 133–34, 135–38, 142, 149, 157
Notte, Don, 191–92
Novak, William, 55, 148
Nunn, Erich, 48

Oklahoma Roundup Association, 147
Oklahoma State Penitentiary, 147
Oliver, Thomas "Fuzzy," 240
Oliveux, James "Boss Dick," 147
Omnibus Crime Bill of 1984, 208–9
"On and On" (Gladys Knight & the Pips), 178
"One Monkey Don't Stop" (Jean Knight), 178
Operation Starting Line, 242
"Ornithology" (Charlie Parker), 95, 118
Oster, Harry, 59–62, 64, 94, 95, 99–101, 221
outlaw country, 150, 157–58, 160–61
outlawry
in the fields, 108–10, 111, 114, 195
history of, 18–19
music's relation to, 147–48
musical representation of, 43, 44–46, 48–49, 99–100
state power and, 18, 110
within the prison, 68, 145–46, 154, 222

Parchman Farm. *See* Mississippi State Penitentiary

parish prisons, 19
"Pass Me Not, O Gentle Savior" (Fanny Crosby), 260
Patterson, Albert, 226, 229, 258–59
pedagogy, 227–29
Pell Grants, 240–41, 242
Penitentiary
　associationalism and, 167–69, 187
　Auburn model, 20–22
　evangelism and, 241–42, 261
　history of, 19–21
　lingering influence at Angola, 27–28, 68, 88, 212, 271–72
　prisoner rhetoric and, 79, 86, 116, 183–84
　public relations and, 72–73, 159–60, 165–66
　rehabilitation mission and, 56, 64, 68, 151
　self-reflection and, 212
"Pennies from Heaven" (Arthur Johnston and Johnny Burke), 95
permissions. *See* privileges
phonograph, John A. Lomax's, 39–40, 41–42
Pinetop Quartet, the, 77
Pittman, Roland, 216
plantation bell, 23
plantations. *See* slavery, history of
Play-Boys, the, 87
Polk, Robin, 203–5, 208, 213–15, 217, 247, 257, 273
Ponce, Walter, 191–92
post–civil rights, 209, 231
post–prisoners' rights, 57, 187–88, 190, 201–2, 209, 215–16
principles, musical and political, 125–27, 131, 142
Principles of Scientific Management, the *See* scientific management
prison films, 2, 44–46
Prison Litigation Reform Act, 231–32
prison music, early definition of, 47–50
prison radio, 46–47. *See also* WLSP
prison reform, 187–88. *See also* new penology, the
Prison Reform Administration, 27–28
Prisoner Grievance Executive Committee, 141

prisoner sublime, the, 178–79, 180–81
prisoners' rights, 154, 171, 174, 175, 187, 188–89, 231–32
privacy, 184–85, 229–30, 262–64, 267, 268
privileges, 57, 264–65, 271–72
Pro-Fascinations, the, 175–76, 177, 179
Probst, John, 120–21
Prometheus, 276
Pure Heart Messengers, the, 143, 181–84, 236–37, 248, 257–59, 266

Quinn, Walter, 112

Rabelais, Dora, 155
Raising Hell (Run-DMC), 208
Ranch House, 238–39, 266
rap, 201, 208–12, 218–19, 235, 238
Reconstruction, 17, 21–22
recreation department, 77, 78, 82, 89, 179, 202, 210, 243, 254, 265, 268, 270, 271
recreation yards, 201–2
Red Hat Cell Block, the, 67, 234
rehabilitation rhetoric, 79. *See also* penitentiary
Resurrection (band), 257
Rhythm Makers, the, 75–78
Richard, Floyd, 75
Richardson, Benny Will "22," 132–33
Rideau, Wilbert, 145–46, 169–70, 179
rights, negotiated, 57, 86
Robbins, David, 209–10, 211
Roberts, Mike, 266
Robinson, Prentice, 226
rock 'n' roll, 61, 115–16
rodeo
　Angola, 149–52, 153, 181–82, 206–7, 216, 242–53, 266
　development at Angola, 146–48
　as public relations, 192–93
Rollins, Rodney, 248–50
Rubenstein, Arthur, 135
rules. *See* principles, musical and political
Rusche, Georg, 17
Russell, George, 120–21, 122–23, 142

sacred music, early accounts of, 36. *See also* gospel music
Sadler, William "Old Wooden Ear," 65–66

338 INDEX

San Quentin on the Air, 46–47
Scared Straight, 218–19, 220–21
scars, showing, 161–63, 256, 257–58, 272–73
Schaffer, R. Murray, 23
scientific management, 28–29, 285n.76
Scientists of Soul, the, 179
Second Great Awakening, 169
second-line, 128, 129, 167, 169–70, 205–6, 215, 249
segregation, 78, 138–40, 145–46
Server, Willie, 223–24
sex trade, 145–46, 167, 195–96
sexual assault, 109–10, 167, 196–97
Sharpe, Lin, 81, 96–97
Shepp, Archie, 130
Sigler, Francys, 94
Sigler, Maurice, 59, 68–69, 70–72, 77, 78, 81, 90, 95–96, 97–99
"Signifying' Monkey, the," 111
Simmons, Evette, 76–77
Sinclair v. Henderson, 170–71, 188
Sinclair, Billy, 145–46
Slattery, John, 234–35
slavery, history of, 21–24
Slave Songs of the United States, 23
slave sublime, the, 178–79
sling blade, 199–200
Slotkin, Richard, 39–40
Social, Economic, and Athletic (SEA) Club, 172
"Sociological Perspectives on a Prison Social System," 62
sociology, 69
Southern Prison Blues, 59, 61
Southern studio strategy, 191
Southern University, 128, 136
Spotville, Jewell, 181–85, 210, 225, 229–30, 257–58
"Stardust" (Hoagy Carmichael), 94–95
Stark, Samuel, 111–12, 237–38
Starlighters, 115–16
"Stay With Me" (Big River Band), 220
Steingo, Gavin, 267
Stewart, Ben "Since I Fell for You," 95
stigma, 160–61, 173, 174
Stitt, Sonny, 120
Storms, Johns, 214–15
Storyland (WAFB television show), 150

"Strange Fruit" (Billie Holiday), 138
Students of Islam, 241
Studio in the Country, 191–92
subjugated knowledge, 119–20, 126–27
sugar
  cane planting, 22
  cutting and harvesting, 23, 50–51, 107, 111–12, 113–14, 131–32, 223
  mill, 23, 36–37, 71, 166–67, 194–95
  national consumption of, 194–95
Sugar Lake, 15–16
surfaces, 144–45, 165, 183
  faith-based uses of, 261
  legal, 145
  musical, 144–45
  popular culture and, 144
  as prisoner's burden, 161
  privacy and, 185
  rodeo, 148–49
  as theorized by Ellison, 173–74, 179
surfacework, 162–63, 166, 171, 174, 180–81, 246, 256
Surgent, Louis "Fuzz," 85–87, 91–92, 96, 102, 115–16, 117
Sutton, John L., 36
Swedish laborers, 24
"Sweet Georgia Brown" (Ben Bernie and Maceo Pinkard), 94–95
Sweet, Russell, 115–16, 118, 146, 149
Szwed, John, 40

Tassin, Ida Mae, 76–77
Tate, Joe, 77
Taylor, Frederick Winslow, 28–29, 285n.76
Taylor, John Henry, Jr., 195, 222–31, 232, 258–62
"Tears of a Clown" (Smokey Robinson), 199
Teekell Report, the, 97–98
Teekell, Lloyd, 97–98
Ten-Sixers, the, 181, 225
testimony, use of, 178–79, 182–83, 230, 256, 257–58, 272–73
Texas State Penitentiary at Huntsville, 46
Thirteenth Amendment. *See* constitutional rights
Thirty Minutes Behind the Walls, 46
"This is Your Life" (Big River Band), 218–19

Thomas, Donald, 269
Thompson, Lester "Big Noise," 82–85, 91, 92–93, 114, 115–16, 117, 120
Time Factor, 202–5, 207–8, 211–12, 213
"Tone the Bell" (Eagle Gospel Singers), 113
Top Hillbillies, the, 70, 75, 79, 87
tourism, 155, 206–7, 232
traveling bands, 3, 72–74, 77, 152–53, 215–18, 230
Trent, Matthew, 266, 268, 269–70, 271, 272
trusty system, 145–46
   analysis of, 63–64
   effects of, 108–9
   end of using prisoner guards, 188, 194, 195–96
   origin of, 36–37
   uses of, 57, 267
truth-in-sentencing laws, 175, 187, 210, 232, 237
Tune Toppers, the, 87
Tunica, 15–16

Ulmar, Billy, 152
United Methodist Men Fellowship, 241
Utopia Urumba, 205, 209, 211–12

vaudeville, 70, 77
Veillon, Laird, 15, 51–52, 257, 263
Venardo, Charles, 115, 180–81
Versatile Variety, the, 208, 209–10
vertical thinking, 120, 122–24, 133. See also *Lydian Chromatic Concept of Tonal Organization, the*
Veterans Incarcerated, 191
"Véxilla Regis," 16
Vinnett, George, 176–77
Violent Crime Control and Law Enforcement Act of 1994, 220–21, 240–41
volunteerism, 165–66, 217, 251, 261

WAFB, 150, 151–52
Walker, Victor G., 98–100
Wall, Richard, 176, 179
War on Drugs, 208–9
War on Poverty, 187
Washington, Daniel, 197–98, 203, 205
WDSU-TV, 89–90

Welch, Guitar, 59, 60
Wesleyan University, 123–25
West Feliciana Parish Citizens Committee, the, 73
West, Frank "Bloody," 115–16, 117, 119
Westernaries
   under Bud Wilkerson, 154–56, 157–66
   under Russell Sweet, 149–51, 152–53
Wethersfield State Prison, 20–21
"When Will I 181–83, See You Again?" (Jewell Spotville),
Whitley, John, 216–17, 218, 220–21, 230
Wilkerson, Bud, 154–56, 157–58, 159, 160, 161–62, 163–65, 181
Wilkerson, Larry, 114, 211–12, 217, 219–20, 239–40
Williams v. Edwards, 188, 190
Williams, "Sonny Boy," 82
Williams, Andre, 250
Williams, Robert Pete, 60, 61
Willows, the. *See* women's camps
Wilson, Ebba, 218
Wiltz, Thomas "Twin," 172–73
"Wind Beneath My Wings" (Jeff Silbar and Larry Henley), 143–44, 181–82
"Wings of Another" (Big River Band), 219–20
Winslow, Les, 71–72, 73–74, 101
WLSP, 89–90, 97, 116–17, 119–20, 135, 240–41, 273
WMRY, 135
Wold, Eddie, 146
women's camp, 60–61, 75, 76–77, 80, 86–87, 93–95
Wood, Anna Lomax, 42–43
Woodfox, Albert, 106–7, 157
"Work Song" (Nat Adderley), 103–4
work songs, 223
   cinematic representation of, 45–46
   connections to Africa, 40, 133
   function, 47–48, 107, 111–14, 131–34, 200
   Harry Oster recordings of, 60–61
   improvisation and, 198
   rolling and, 199–200
WXOK, 75

Xavier Preparatory School, 135

"Yakety Sax" (Boots Randolph), 120